Deciphering the Signs of God

A Phenomenological Approach to Islam

ANNEMARIE SCHIMMEL

STATE UNIVERSITY OF NEW YORK PRESS

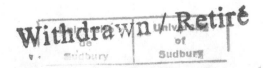

To the memory of Friedrich Heiler
(1892–1967)

First published
in U.S.A. by
State University of New York Press
Albany

For information, address State University of New York Press,
State University Plaza, Albany, NY 12246

Printed in Great Britain

Library of Congress Cataloging-in-Publication Data

Schimmel, Annemarie.
Deciphering the signs of God: a phenomenological approach to Islam / Annemarie Schimmel.
p. cm.
Includes bibliographical references (p. 258) and index.
ISBN 0-7914-1981-9. — ISBN 0-7914-1982-7 (pbk.)
1. Islam. I. Title.
BP161.2.S29 1994
297—dc20

93-42354
CIP

Contents

List of Abbreviations

AM	*Aḥādīth-i Mathnawī*, Furūzānfar
ARW	*Archiv für Religionswissenschaft*
BIFAO	*Bulletin de l'Institut Français d'Archéologie Orientale*
CIBEDO	*Christlich-islamische Begegnung Dokumentationsstelle*, Frankfurt
D	*Dīwān-i kabīr*, Rūmī
EI	*Encyclopedia of Islam*, 2nd edition, Leiden 1954–
ERE	*Encyclopedia of Religion and Ethics*, ed. Hastings, 1908–
IC	*Islamic Culture*, Hyderabad/Deccan
IRAN	*Journal of the British Institute of Persian Studies*
JA	*Journal Asiatique*
JAOS	*Journal of the American Oriental Society*
JPOS	*Journal of the Palestine Oriental Society*
JRAS	*Journal of the Royal Asiatic Society*
M	*Mathnawī-yi maʿnawī*, Rūmī, ed. Nicholson
MW	*The Moslem* (later: *Muslim*) *World*
REI	*Revue des Etudes Islamiques*
RGG	*Die Religion in Geschichte und Gegenwart*, 3rd edition
RHR	*Revue de l'Histoire des Religions*
SWJA	*Journal of the Scientific Society of South West Africa*
WI	*Die Welt des Islams*
WZKM	*Wiener Zeitschrift für die Kunde des Morgenlandes*
ZDMG	*Zeitschrift der Deutschen Morgenländischen Gesellschaft*

Preface

To deliver the Gifford Lectures is a great honour and privilege for any scholar working in the general field of 'religion', and I am deeply grateful to the Trustees of the Gifford Lectures for having invited me to speak in Edinburgh in the spring of 1992 – an experience which I thoroughly enjoyed. Yet at the same time, the lecturer, overwhelmed by the names of his or her illustrious predecessors, is troubled by the question of whether one can really do full justice to the chosen topic – in this case, a phenomenological approach to Islam. It probably seems preposterous to give a sweeping survey of different aspects of Islam, a religion which has been much studied, much misunderstood, and sometimes accused by historians of religion as being rather primitive. At the same time, however, scholarly study of Islam has in recent years attracted more and more people, spurred on by the political developments in the Muslim world and in other areas increasingly populated by Muslims. Needless to say, many of these political and sociological studies have little interest in the 'spiritual' values of Islam, instead ranging from questions of religious authority to the position of children in medieval Muslim society; from Muslim responses to Western education to the changing role of the Sufis; from the mechanics of conversion to the formation and functioning of the biosphere in the Koran; and concerning the question of human rights and their implementation in the modern world. Indeed, it was this ever-growing amount of literature which made me decide to avoid lengthy and elaborate references and to mention in the Bibliography only works actually cited in the text or the notes. I beg the reader's indulgence for this way of handling the material.

The Lectures have grown out of a lifelong occupation with the languages and values of Islam, and from innumerable discussions with Muslim friends, whether highly learned and sophisticated scholars in the Muslim lands and in the diaspora, or simple, illiterate villagers, particularly women, in Pakistan, India and Turkey. They owe much to the inspiration of my academic teachers in Islamic Studies – Richard Hartmann, Hans Heinrich Schaeder and Ernst Kühnel in Berlin, to mention only the most important ones – but even more to my collaboration with Friedrich Heiler, who opened the world of the history of religions to me. These Lectures are dedicated to his memory. Similarly, I would like to thank my students in Marburg, Ankara, Bonn and Harvard, as well as my friends and all those who have patiently listened to my lectures in Europe, North America and the Near and Middle East, and who have alerted me to new aspects of Islamic thought, art and poetry. I am very grateful to Dr Shams Anwari-Alhoseyni, Cologne, for adorning the book with his calligraphic renderings of Koranic verses. I also express my gratitude to my 'writing angel', Christa Sadozay MA, in Cologne, who typed the manuscript, and to Mr Ivor Normand MA, in Edinburgh, for his careful and meticulous copy-editing of the text.

The Swedish Lutheran bishop and Islamicist, Tor Andrae, to whom we owe some of the most sensitive works about the Prophet Muhammad as well as about early Sufism, once remarked:

> Like any movement in the realm of ideas, a religious faith has the same right to be judged according to its real and veritable intentions and not according to the way in which human weakness and meanness may have falsified and maimed its ideals.

Trying to approach Islam with this in mind, I hope that the Lectures may help to clarify some of the structures underlying life and thought in Islam. Depending on their field of interest and specialization, readers will no doubt be able to add numerous parallels and influences, both from Islamic sources and from other religions. However, when such parallels are drawn here, it is not with the intention of dwelling on the 'Reste arabischen Heidentums' again, as does Julius Wellhausen's classic of that name (1897); nor do I want to prove, or suggest, that this or that external influence has determined the development of Islam. Nobody denies that such influences exist in Islam; for no religion can grow in a vacuum, and the religious leader, founder or prophet can only ever use the language to which his listeners are – at least to a certain extent – accustomed, and whose images and symbols they understand. Without soil, air, rain and fertilization by insects, no tree – and we may well compare religion to a 'good tree' (cf. Sūra 14:24) – could ever grow strong enough to house birds or to provide shade and luscious fruit to those who come close to it (as Mawlānā Rūmī says in the story of Daqūqī in his *Mathnawī*, III 2,005ff.). But these influences are not absolute values: a religion takes into itself only those ideas, customs and tendencies which are in one way or another compatible with its innermost essence. Furthermore, as every religion has an outward and inward aspect, any sentence, proposition or legal prescription may be understood and interpreted differently by different people. Age-old similes come to mind: the water takes the colour of the glass, or else the 'white radiance of eternity', the colourless Light, becomes visible only in its reflections in ever-changing colours.

My aim is to point to the colourful reflections, Goethe's 'farbiger Abglanz'; or, in Koranic words, to try to decipher some of the signs, or *āyāt*, which through their infinite variety point to the One Truth.

Introduction[I]

And We shall show them Our signs in the horizons and in themselves.

Sūra 41:53

When I was teaching the history of religions at the Islamic Faculty of Divinity in Ankara in the 1950s, I tried to explain to my students Rudolf Otto's distinction between the *mysterium tremendum* and the *mysterium fascinans* – the Numen that reveals itself under the aspect of awe-inspiring majesty and fascinating beauty. Suddenly one of the students stood up and said proudly: 'But, Professor, we Muslims have known that for centuries. God has two aspects: His *jalāl* – majesty, power and wrath – and His *jamāl* – beauty, kindness and mercy.' Ever since then, the idea of approaching Islam from a phenomenological angle has been on my mind, all the more because I kept finding that Islam was badly (if at all) represented in the few major books in this field, as though historians of religion still needed the admonition of the eighteenth-century German thinker Reimarus:

> I am convinced that among those who accuse the Turkish religion of this or that fault, only a very few have read the Alcoran, and that also among those who indeed have read it, only a precious few have had the intention of giving the words the sound meaning of which they are capable.

For many historians of religion, Islam, a latecomer in history, is still not much more than 'a Christian heresy', as it was repeatedly called for centuries until the time of Adolf von Harnack, or else an anti-Christian, inhuman, primitive religion – ideas which one now encounters rather frequently owing to the political situation in the war-torn Middle East and the rise of fundamentalist groups. However, the problem is how to give an accurate picture of a religion that stretches from its cradle, Arabia, to the east through major parts of Asia, into central China and Indonesia and the Philippines, and to the west over Turkey and part of the Balkans to North Africa and its Atlantic borders; that appears in various parts of Black Africa and gains new converts in the traditional Christian areas such as Europe and America, partly as a result of the increasing number of immigrants from the Muslim world, partly also by conversion to this or that branch of Islam, Sufism, pseudo-Sufism, or fundamentalism alike; a religion whose sacred script is revealed in Arabic, but whose participants have composed and still continue to compose innumerable works – theological and literary, catechisms and poetry, newspapers and historical studies – in a plethora of languages among which Arabic, Persian, Turkish, Urdu and Swahili boast an inexhaustible treasure of high and popular literature, not to mention the other idioms – with Arabic still ruling supreme in the religious sphere. Nobody can follow up the ever-increasing number of publications in the various fields of

Islamic studies either, and thus the researcher feels handicapped and somewhat hopeless when trying to write about Islam, to find a structure that could do justice to this often maligned religion, and to embed it into the general history of religions.

It is certainly possible to learn about Islam by using the vertical, that is, historical method, and the study of its history is refined day by day thanks to documents that come to light from the enormous but barely tapped sources in libraries in East and West; a hitherto overlooked inscription in a mosque in Zanzibar or a Muslim poem in a south Indian idiom can open surprising insights into certain historical developments, as can a completely fresh look at the very beginnings of Islamic civilization.

One can also use cross-sections to attempt to categorize different aspects of Islam by type of religion. Here, the traditional contrast of 'prophetic' and 'mystical' religions as elaborated by Nathan Söderblom and Friedrich Heiler offers itself comfortably, with Islam apparently constituting a paradigm of a 'prophetic' religion which, however, is tempered by a strong strand of legalism on the one hand, and mysticism in its different forms on the other hand. One can also study it from a sociological viewpoint and look at the human condition; at sects and social groups; the relation between master and disciple; at trends to universality and to expansion by either mission or war. If one approaches it by applying the different concepts of the Divine, one will find an uncompromising monotheism which, however, sometimes turns into 'pantheistic' or monistic trends by overstressing the oneness of the Divine.

Again, one may ask about its attitude towards the world – whether it is world-negating, like Buddhism (an attitude that appears among the early Sufis), or world-dominating, like mainstream normative Islam. What are its psychological peculiarities; and how does the Muslim react to the encounter with the One God – is one moved predominantly by awe, fear, hope and love, or does one simply feel unshakable faith and trust?

All these approaches are valid and offer the researcher ways to understand a religion, in this case Islam, somewhat better. However, more than other branches of scholarship, the study of religion is beset with difficulties, the most important one being the necessity of formulating one's stance on the object of one's research while at the same time suspending judgment, since one is dealing with something which, after all, constitutes the most sacred area in the lives of millions of people. Can one really deal with religion – in general or in its specific forms – as if one were dealing with any other object of study, as is nowadays claimed by many historians of religion? Personally, I wonder if a completely objective study of religion is possible when one respects the sphere of the Numinous and the feeling of the otherworldly in one's approach, and realizes that one is dealing with actions, thought systems and human reactions and responses to something that lies outside purely 'scientific' research.

It is therefore difficult to remain distanced when dealing with religion, and the personal bias of the researcher cannot but be reflected in the study – a bias which, in my case, certainly leans more towards the mystical and poetical trends inside Islam than towards its legalistic aspect, which, in any case, is not the topic dealt with here (although it would be most welcome to interpret the refined Islamic legal system and its applications in a comprehensive comparative work).

In the rare cases where historians of religion have ventured to include specimens of Islamic culture into their phenomenology, the lack of linguistic skills is sadly visible, and the tendency to rely upon largely outdated translations has led to strange shifts in emphasis, such as the disproportionate use of old translations of Persian poetry in which the imagery of sacred intoxication and ecstasy abounds. These phenomena certainly have their place in Sufism, but should be viewed in relation to the ideals of mainstream Islam.

Nevertheless, I believe that the phenomenological approach is well suited to a better understanding of Islam, especially the model which Friedrich Heiler developed in his comprehensive study *Erscheinungsformen und Wesen der Religion* (Stuttgart 1961), on whose structure I have modelled this book. For he tries to enter into the heart of religion by studying first the phenomena and then deeper and deeper layers of human responses to the Divine until he reaches the innermost sacred core of each religion, the centre, the Numinous, the *deus absconditus*. Heiler always liked to refer to Friedrich von Hügel's remark that the spirit awakens when coming into contact with material things. That is, the highest spiritual experience can be triggered off by a sensual object: a flower, a fragrance, a cloud or a person. Islamic thinkers have always pondered the relation between the outward manifestations and the Essence, based on the Koranic words: 'We put Our signs into the horizons and into themselves' (Sūra 41:53). For the Muslim, everything could serve as an *āya*, a sign from God, and the Koran repeats this truth over and over again, warning those who do not believe in God's signs or who belie them. The creatures are signs; the change between day and night is a sign, as is the loving encounter of husband and wife; and miracles are signs (cf. Sūra 30:19–25): they all prove that there is a living God who is the originator of everything. These signs are not only in the 'horizons', that is, in the created universe, but also in the human souls, that is, in the human capacity to understand and admire; in love and human inquisitiveness; in whatever one may feel, think, and experience. The world is, as it were, an immense book in which those who have eyes to see and ears to hear can recognize God's signs and thus be guided by their contemplation to the Creator Himself. Sensual and spiritual levels meet through and in the signs, and by understanding and interpreting them one may be able to understand the Divine wisdom and power; one will also understand that, as the Koran proclaims repeatedly, God teaches by means of comparisons, parables and likenesses to draw the human heart beyond the external, peripheral faces of creation.

For one has to keep in mind that spiritual aspects of life can be revealed only by means of sensual ones – the wind becomes visible only though the movement of the grass, as the nineteenth-century Indo–Muslim poet Ghālib sings; the dust which we may see from far in the desert hides the rider who stirs it up; and the foam flakes on the surface of the ocean point to the unfathomable abyss. These signs are necessary, for the human heart longs to catch a glimpse of the Divine – even though God is beyond all forms and imagination – and yet one hopes to 'touch' the Numinous power in some way or another: does one not respectfully kiss the copy of the Koran in which God's word is written down?

Everything can become an *āya*, a sign, not only the verses of the Koran which are called by this very name. To be sure, it is not the ever-hidden *deus absconditus* but the *deus revelatus* who can be found through them, He, who reveals His will through His word; who has talked through the prophets; and whose guidance leads humankind on the right path to salvation. The Muslims understood that everything created praises the Creator with its own *lisān al-ḥāl*, the silent eloquence – for this is the purpose for which they were created. Thus, the entire universe could be seen, as it were, in a religious light: that is why every human act, even a seemingly profane one, is yet judged from religious viewpoints and regulated according to the divinely revealed Law.

Cultic and ritual duties too could be interpreted beyond their external importance as signs towards something higher: prayer is the loss of one's small self in communion with the Holy, or the sacrifice of one's soul before the overpowering beloved Lord; pilgrimage points to the never-ending journey of the soul towards God; fasting teaches one to live on light and praise, as do the angels; and thus each and every outward ritual form could become a sign of spiritual experience. But even those who see only the 'husk' and dutifully fulfil the external ritual will still feel themselves to have obeyed God and thus prepared themselves for the way that leads to happiness in the Hereafter, for surrender to God and/or His word is the meaning of the word *islām*.

Likewise, symbolic actions could serve to illuminate certain spiritual aspects of Islam: hence the Prophet's casting some sand and pebbles against the enemies in the battle of Badr (624), upon which Sūra 8:17 was revealed ('You did not cast when you cast ...'), which indicates that the one who has been absolutely obedient to God can act, so to speak, through God's power.

There is no doubt that previous religions have left their traces upon Islam, for every religion has adapted trends and systems from earlier strata of religious life that seemed to express its own concerns, and the colourful bushes of folk Islam with their often scurrilous flowers have grown from the same root as the straight tree of normative Islam. The tension between the two major aspects of Islam –

the normative–legalistic and the popular, mystically tinged one – forms a constant theme in Islamic cultural history. The way in which Islam has taken into its embrace variegated forms and strange elements, especially in the Indian and African contexts, is fascinating – as much as the normative traditionalists dislike these developments and regard them as contradicting the pure monotheism which is expressed and repeated thousands of time in the *shahāda*, the profession of faith, and in Sūra 112, the final word of the Koran about the God who is One, neither begetting nor begotten.

In both aspects, Islam knows the concepts of the sacred power – *baraka*, blessing power[2] – and this word will occur frequently on the following pages, for not only has the holy person *baraka*, but also the black stone of the Kaaba radiates it, and the copy of the Koran is filled with blessing power, as is the sacred Night of Might (cf. Sūra 97), in which the first revelation took place.

In order to give a form for a cross-section through different phenomena of Islam, the model used by Friedrich Heiler appeared to me most convenient and clearer than that of Gerardus van der Leeuw, admirable as his collection of material is. Heiler's book and approach has been severely criticized by some scholars; it has also been summarized in English with an undue emphasis on the Christian part of it, which resulted in a lop-sided picture that lacks the stupendous breadth of Heiler's material. To offer an idea of Heiler's model, I give overleaf the fine summary by J. J. Waardenburg (1973) in his *Classical Approaches to the Study of Religion*, vol. 1.

The model of the concentric rings may seem somewhat artificial; but, strangely enough, it was prefigured more than a millennium ago in the work of Abū'l-Ḥusayn an-Nūrī (d. 907), a mystic of Baghdad, and apparently also by his contemporary al-Ḥakīm at-Tirmidhī.[3] Based on Koranic verses, Nūrī invented a circular form which leads, as does Heiler's model, from the external encounter of the sacred to the innermost core of religion, thus showing that there is no deity but God. His fourfold circles read as follows:

The breast, *ṣadr*, is connected with *islām* (Sūra 39:22) – that is, in our model, the institutional, external element of religions.

The next circle mentions the heart, *qalb*, as the seat of *īmān*, 'faith' (Sūra 49:7): the heart is the organ through which true faith, the interiorization of a mere external acceptance of a religious form, can be achieved; it is thus the organ for the spiritual aspects of religious life.

The *fu'ād*, the inner heart, is the seat of *ma'rifa*, intuitive, 'gnostic' knowledge (Sūra 53:11); that means that, here, the divine, immediate 'knowledge from Us' (Sūra 18:65) can be realized.

Finally, one reaches the *lubb*, the innermost kernel of the heart, which is the seat of *tawḥīd* (Sūra 3:190), that is, of the experience that there is only the One who was and shall be from eternity to eternity without a companion, visible and tangible only when He reveals Himself to humankind.

All the outward manifestations, the different forms of revelations, are signs. The word about God is, in Rūmī's lovely phrase, like 'the scent of heavenly apple trees' (*M* VI 84). The externals are as necessary as the breast to enclose the mysteries of the heart, but the Essence of the Divine remains forever hidden; the human being can only seize the hem of His favour and try to find the way to Him through His signs.

The similarity between Nūrī's four circles of religious experience and Friedrich Heiler's circular structure seems to indicate to me that there is a way that is at least to a certain extent legitimate for my undertaking; for, as the early Sufis liked to recite:

> *wa fī kulli shay'in lahu shāhidun*
> *Yadullu ʿalā annahu wāḥidun*
> In everything there is a witness to Him
> that points to the fact that He is One.

Everything – from the stone to the dogmatic formula – calls out *Quaere super nos*, 'Seek beyond us!' The plurality of signs is necessary to veil the eternal One who is transcendent and yet 'closer than the neck vein' (Sūra 50:16); the plurality of signs and the Unicity of the Divine belong together. The signs show the way into His presence, where the believer may finally leave the images behind.

For 'everything on earth is perishing but His Face' (Sūra 28:88).

NOTES

1. For general surveys, see Charles J. Adams (1967), 'The history of religions and the study of Islam'; Willem Bijlefeld (1972), 'Islamic Studies within the perspective of the history of religions'; J. Jacques Waardenburg (1980), 'Islamforschung aus religionswissenschaftlicher Sicht'; idem (1978), 'Official and popular religion in Islam'; and James E. W. Royster (1972), 'The study of Muhammad. A survey of approaches from the perspective of the history and phenomenology of religion'.
2. Joseph Chelhod (1955), 'La *baraka* chez les arabes ou l'influence bienfaisante du sacré'.
3. Paul Nwyia (1970), *Exégèse coranique et langage mystique*, p. 326ff.; cf. also al-Ḥakīm at-Tirmidhī (1958), *Al-farq bayna'ṣ-ṣadr wa'l-qalb* ..., ed. N. Heer.

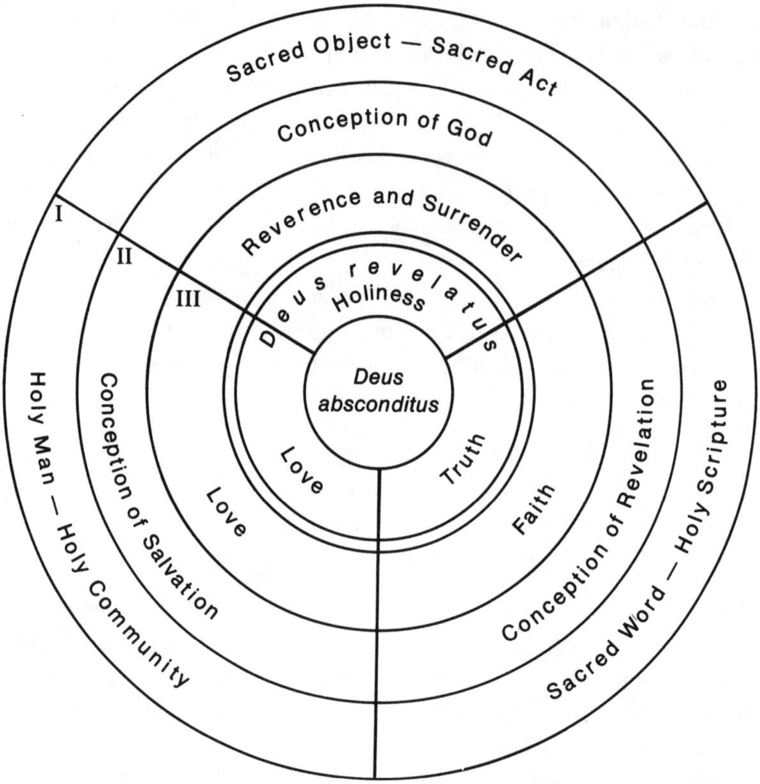

I. The *world of outer manifestations* comprises three sectors:

1) the sacred *object*, the sacred *room* in which the cult takes place, the sacred *time*, in which the most important ritual is performed, the sacred *number*, by which the sacred objects, rooms, times, words, people are measured, the sacred *act* (rite).

2) the sacred *word*: (1) the spoken word: a) the word of God, the incantation, the name of God, the oracle, the myth, the legend, the prophecy, the gospel, the doctrine; b) the word to God, prayer in adoration, penance, praise, thanksgiving, supplication, surrender; c) the sacred silence; (2) the written word: the holy scripture.

3) the holy *man* and the holy *community*. All that is within the scope of the physically observable, visible, audible, tangible. Religion is not an airy spirituality, but a physical communion with the Divine.

II. The first inner ring is the *world of religious imagination*, the thoughts, images, ideas concerning God's invisible being and visible works:

1) the conception of God (theology),

2) the conception of creation (cosmology and anthropology, including original conditions and original sin),
3) the conception of revelation: the intimation of the divine will in the proclaimed word, in history, in the soul (Christology),
4) the conception of redemption: (1) the redeemer; (2) the object of redemption; (3) the road to redemption (soteriology),
5) the fulfillment in the future or in the world to come (eschatology).

III. The second inner ring represents the *world of religious experience*, i.e. what happens deep down in the soul, as opposed to the fanciful or rational images of God, the religious values which are laid aside in the confrontation between man and sacred objects and in the performance of sacred acts: 1) reverence (towards the divine in itself, its holiness), 2) fear, 3) faith and complete trust in God, who reveals himself, works, rules, loves, and helps, 4) hope, 5) love, yearning for God, surrender to him, reciprocation of God's love. Next to these values, there are peace, joy, and the urge to share. Then there are the extraordinary religious experiences: inspiration, sudden conversion, vocation and enlightenment, vision and audition, ecstasy, cardiognosis and the various extensions of physical powers, such as automatic speaking and writing, speaking in foreign tongues and stigmatisation, and so on.

IV. The *objective world of religion*, the center of the circles, is the Divine Reality, which is understood through all external manifestations, inner notions, and experiences of the soul, in a double sense:
1) as the *Deus revelatus*, the God who has his face towards man, as absolute holiness, truth, justice, love, mercy, salvation, the personal God, experienced as 'Thou' and as a being of communion (Trinity),
2) as the *Deus ipse* or *absconditus*, the divinity, experienced as 'It', as absolute unity.

There is a correlation between the segments of the various rings: the physical forms of expression, thoughts, feelings, correspond finally to divine reality. Although that reality can never be completely expressed in human forms of expression, thoughts, and experiences, there is a certain correspondence to the divine, the *analogia entis*: the created being corresponds to the non-created divine being.

I

Sacred Aspects of Nature and Culture

Of His signs are the night and the day and the sun and the moon.
Sūra 41:37

INANIMATE NATURE[1]

From earliest times, human beings have been impressed and often overawed by the phenomena of nature which they observe from day to day in their environment. They certainly felt awe when looking at stones, which never seemed to change and which could easily be taken as signs of power and, at a later time perhaps, as representing eternal strength. In the ancient Semitic religions, stones, in particular those of unusual shape, were regarded as filled with power, *mana*, and the fascination with stones – expressed in the Old Testament by the story of Jacob and the stone of Bethel – has continued down through the ages.

Turkic peoples were equally fascinated by stones and their mysterious powers: stories about *taş bebekleri* – stones which slowly turned into children – are frequent in Turkey. Stones are used in rain-producing rituals (especially jade), and small *niyyet taşları* serve to indicate whether one's intention, *niyya*, will come true, which is the case when the stone sticks on a flat surface such as a tombstone.[2]

Syria and Palestine, the home of the ancient Semitic stone cult, still boast strangely-shaped stones which are sometimes considered to be resting places of saints. In Syria, rollstones are supposed to give some of their 'power' to a person over whose body they are rolled. To heap stones into a small hill to make a saint's tomb before it is enlarged into a true shrine seems common practice everywhere, be it in the Near East or in the Indo–Pakistani regions.[3]

Mythology speaks of a rock which forms the foundation of the cosmos; of green colour, it lies deep under the earth and is the basis of the vertical axis that goes through the universe, whose central point on earth is the Kaaba. The black stone – a meteor – in the south-eastern corner of the Kaaba in Mecca is the point to which believers turn and which they strive to kiss during the pilgrimage, for, as a mystical *ḥadīth* claims: 'The Black Stone is God's right hand'.[4] This stone, as legend tells, is pre-existent, and, while it was white in the beginning, it turned black from the hands of sinful people who touched it year after year.

However, this black stone, described in wonderful and fanciful images by pious poets, is by no means the only important stone or rock in the Muslim world. The Dome of the Rock in Jerusalem is extremely sacred because, so it is said, all the prophets before Muhammad rested there, and the Prophet of Islam met with them at the beginning of his heavenly journey to perform the ritual prayer on this very spot. The stone beneath the actual dome is blessed by Muhammad's footprint, and some traditions even claim that the rock hangs free in the air. At the end of time, Isrāfīl, the archangel, will blow the trumpet that announces resurrection from this very rock. The spiritual – besides the historical – connection between the two sacred places with stones (Mecca and Jerusalem) is evident from the poetical idea that the Kaaba comes as a bride to the Dome of the Rock.[5]

Not only in Jerusalem can one see the imprint of the Prophet's foot, *qadam rasūl.* One finds such stones in various countries, often brought home by pious pilgrims especially in India – even Emperor Akbar, otherwise rather critical of Islamic traditions, welcomed the arrival of such a stone which his wife Salīma and his aunt Gulbadan had acquired during their pilgrimage.[6] Often, majestic buildings are erected over such stones, which the faithful touch to participate in their *baraka* and then pass their hands over their body. As early as c. 1300, the reformer Ibn Taymiyya (d. 1328) fought against the custom of touching a stone with the Prophet's footprint in Damascus, something that appeared to him as pure superstition, incompatible with the faith in the One God.[7]

Shia Muslims know of stones with the impression of ʿAlī's foot. A centre of this cult is the sanctuary of Maulali (Mawlā ʿAlī) on top of a steep rock near Hyderabad/Deccan, where one can admire an immense 'footprint'.

The importance of stones is reflected in the symbolic use of the term. Rūmī compares the lover to a marble rock that reverberates with the Beloved's words and echoes them (*D* l. 17,867), but even more important is Ibn ʿArabī's idea that the Prophet is a *ḥajar baht*, a 'pure stone' on which the Divine message was imprinted, as it were – an idea that continued down through the centuries and which is prominent in the theological work of Shāh Walīullāh of Delhi (d. 1762).[8]

Stones could serve to express the aspect of Divine Wrath, as in the numerous Koranic references to the 'stoning' of disobedient peoples (Sūra 105:4 et al.). In this connection, the 'stoning of Satan' is administered during the pilgrimage by the casting of three times seven pebbles on a certain spot near Mina, and Satan is always referred to as *rajīm*, 'stoned', i.e. accursed.

Numerous other customs are connected with stones: thus, among the Persian Khāksār dervishes, it is customary to bind a rather big stone on one's stomach – the *sang-i-qanāʿat*, 'stone of contentment', which points to the suppression of hunger – for that is how the Prophet overcame his hunger.[9] A special role is ascribed to gemstones, some of which were regarded as filled with *baraka.* Early Muslim scholars had a vast knowledge of mineralogy and enlarged the inherited Greek mineralogical works by their observations. Hence, precious and semi-precious stones play a considerable role in folklore and literature.

It is said that the Prophet himself recommended the use of *ʿaqīq*, agate or carnelian,[10] a stone that was plentiful in Yemen and which therefore became connected with the whole mystical symbolism of Yemen whence the 'breath of the Merciful' reached the Prophet (*AM* no. 195). Muslims still like to wear an agate ring or locket, inscribed with prayer formulas or Divine Names (among the Shias, often with the names of the Panjtan), and later Persian and Urdu poets have compared themselves to an *ʿaqīq* bezel which contains nothing but the name of the Divine Beloved. But not only believers in general like to wear such stones; a twelve-pointed agate (symbolizing the twelve imams of the Shia) used to be worn by the members of the Bektashi order of dervishes (Hacci Bektash Stone).

From ancient times, it was believed that the ruby could avert illness – and indeed, in medical tradition, pulverized ruby was an ingredient of *mufarriḥ*, 'something that cheers you up', a kind of tranquillizer – hence its connection with the beloved's ruby lip, or with ruby-like red wine. A beautiful myth tells that ordinary pebbles, when touched by the sun, can turn into rubies after patiently waiting in the depth of the mines – an idea that came to symbolize the transformation of the human heart which, touched by the sun of grace, can mature during long periods of patience and, by 'shedding its blood' in suffering, may be transformed into a priceless jewel.

The emerald is thought to avert evil, but also to blind serpents and dragons. Its green colour – the colour of paradise – gave this stone a special place in Muslim thought. Thus, according to a saying, the *lawḥ maḥfūẓ*, the Well-preserved Tablet on which everything is written from pre-eternity, consists of emerald; it is a true *tabula smaragdina*, as it is also known from medieval gnostic imagery. Henry Corbin, then, has followed the Sufi path which, at least according to some authors like Simnānī (d. 1335), ends in the light of the emerald mountain: the highest station for the wayfarer who has passed through the blackness of mystical death.[11]

The sight of mountains has always inspired human hearts, and mountains have often been regarded as seats of deities all over the world. This was, of course, an idea impossible in Islam, all the more so because the Koran has stated that the mountains, though put in their places to keep the earth stable, are yet like clouds (Sūra 27:88) and will be, in the horrors of the Day of Judgment, 'like combed wool' (Sūra 70:9). Furthermore, Mt Sinai was shattered by the manifestation of the Lord's grandeur (Sūra 7:143), an event that means for Rūmī that it 'danced' in ecstasy (*M* I 876). Mountains are, thus, nothing but signs of God's omnipresence; they prostrate themselves before God (Sūra 22:18) along with all the other creatures, and yet the feeling that one might find more than a purely earthly experience on certain mountains is attested in the Islamic tradition as well – suffice it to think of Abū Qubays near Mecca, according to tradition the first mountain on earth, which later served as a meeting place of the saints, or of Huseyin Ghazi near Ankara, the site of the shrine of a medieval Muslim warrior saint, and similar places.

One could imagine the high mountains as a liminal area between the created universe and the spacelessness of the Divine (cf. the initial oath of Sūra 52); thus, Mt Qāf was thought of as a mountain encircling the whole earth, even though the sight of the Caucasus or, in Southern Asia, of the Himalayas has certainly contributed to, or sparked off, such ideas. In antiquity, some people tried to imitate the sacred mountains, as for example in the Babylonian Ziggurat; the Malwiyya, the spiral minaret of Samarra in Iraq, may be the result of subconscious memories of this tendency.

The earth was always experienced as a feminine power, and although the concept of 'Mother Earth' is not as outspoken in the Islamic tradition as elsewhere, the Koranic words according to which 'women are your fields ...' (Sūra 2:223) show that the connection was a natural one. Was not Adam made of dust, the soft maternal material which was then to be enlivened by the spirit?[12] That is why Iblīs, Satan, claimed superiority over him, as his own origin was fire. And thus, the dervishes might remind their listeners that all existence is dust except the Beloved – after all, man is created from dust (Sūra 22:5 et al.) and will return to dust. Dust has a purifying quality: when water for the ritual ablution is wanting, one can perform the purification with dust, *tayammum*.

The ancient myth of the *hieros gamos*, the marriage between heaven and earth which, as it were, preforms human marriage – the 'sowing of the seed' into the earth and into the females – surfaces only in some cases, especially in the verse of Rūmī, who takes his imagery from the oldest strata of myths. Although he remarks that 'the earth like the wife and the sky like the man' are no longer of interest for the true seeker (*D* l. 15,525), the lover may yet address the spiritual beloved:

> You are my heaven, I am your earth –
> You alone know what You've put into me!
> (*D* no. 3,038)

Earth and dust become sanctified by contact with powerful and beloved people, and, humble in themselves, acquire new wealth. Sa'dī's story about an amazingly fragrant piece of purifying clay, which was permeated with the scent of the beloved who had used it while bathing, points to this feeling. Thus, the dust of sacred places and of mausoleums can bring blessing: prayer beads and little tablets are formed from the mud of Ḥusayn's mausoleum in Kerbela for the use of pious Shiites. The Turkish poet Fuzuli (d. 1556) therefore claims with apparent humility:

> My poetry is not rubies or emeralds,
> my poetry is dust, but the dust of Kerbela![13]

Dust from Kerbela and Najaf, 'Alī's burial place, was deposited in some mausoleums of Shiite kings in India (thus in the Gol Gunbad in Golconda), just as some dust from Mawlānā Rūmī's tomb in Konya was brought to Iqbāl's mausoleum in Lahore because of the Indo-Muslim philosopher-poet's deep veneration for the medieval Persian mystical poet.

Many visitors to an Indo-Pakistani shrine will have been offered dried-up rose petals and dust from the sarcophagus – and, trusting in the sacred purity of this dust, they dutifully swallow it. Indeed, the dust of saints' and sayyids' tombs is the true treasure that a province can boast – when Nādir Shah of Iran came to conquer Sind in 1738, the Hindu minister of the Kalhora rulers countered his requests for an immense indemnity by offering him a small bag containing the most precious thing that Sind had to offer, that is, the dust of saints and sayyids.[14]

Much more central, however, is the role of water, for 'We have made alive everything through water' (Sūra 21:30), and, 'He has sent down water from the sky ...' (Sūra 13:17), to mention only two prominent Koranic statements with regard to water.[15] This water not only has the power of purifying people externally, but also becomes – as in other religious traditions – a fitting symbol for the purification of hearts. Water is constantly quaking and moving – that is, as Kisā'ī thinks, its act of exalting the Lord in unison with all other creatures.

There are numerous sacred springs and ponds in the Islamic world – the Zamzam near the Kaaba gushed forth, as legend has it, when Hagar, left alone with little Isma'il, was thirsty. The well is forty-two metres deep, and its water is slightly salty. Most pilgrims carry some Zamzam water home in special flasks to make the *baraka* of the spring available to friends and family; some also dip their future shrouds into the well, hoping that the water's blessing power may surround them in the grave. According to popular tales, the water of the Zamzam fills all the springs in the world during the month of Muḥarram, while in Istanbul legend has it that some Zamzam water was used to build the dome of the Hagia Sophia; otherwise it would have crumbled.

In Arabic folklore, especially in Syria and Jordan, fountains are generally thought to be feminine, although the type of watery fairies (nixies) known in European folklore seems to be absent from traditional Muslim lore. Salty springs, on the other hand, are regarded as male; that is why barren women bathe there.

Springs are often found near the shrines of saints, and it is likely that the locality of many sacred places was chosen just because of the blessing of a nearby water course or fountain. The tank near Sālār Mas'ūd's shrine in Bahraich is supposed to cure leprosy. The pond of Mangho Pir near Karachi seems to be a prime example of aetiological legends transforming a weird pre-Muslim sacred spot into a Muslim shrine, for not only is this pond close to the dwelling-place of a thirteenth-century saint, but it also houses a huge number of enormous crocodiles whose ancestor the saint, angered for some reason, produced out of a flower. The large pond at Bāyezīd Bisṭāmī's sanctuary in Chittagong (Bangladesh) is inhabited by utterly repellent white tortoises, and in the same area, in Sylhet, a well filled with fish forms an important part of the sanctuary.

Even if one concedes the necessity for a source of water for ablutions in the vicinity of a shrine-cum-mosque, in such cases ancient traditions still seem to have survived. As far as the water for purification is concerned, its quality and quantity are exactly defined by the lawyer-divines, for to enter the water means to re-enter the primordial matter, to be purified, rejuvenated, reborn after dying – hence, the ablution could become a truly spiritual experience for some Muslims, and the theme of entering the water and being like a corpse moved only by the water's flow is frequent in mystical literature. The old Indian tale of the sceptic who, submerged in water, lived through an entire human life in a single moment has also reached Islam: unbelievers who doubted the reality of Muhammad's nightly journey were instructed in a similar way. The best-known example is the tale of the Egyptian Sufi master Dashṭūṭī, who had the Sultan bend his head into a bowl of water so that he immediately lived through an entire life story.[16]

One should not shy away from water – it is, after all, its duty, indeed its pleasure, to purify the dirty, as Rūmī emphasized time and again: the water of Grace waits for the sinner. The life-bestowing quality of water led almost naturally to the concept of the Water of Life, the goal of the seekers, far away near the *majmaʿ al-baḥrayn*, the 'meeting place of the two oceans', as is understood from Sūra 18:60, 61. The Water of Life is found, like a green fountain, in the deepest gorges of the dark land, and only Khiḍr, the prophet-saint, can lead the seeker there, while even great heroes such as Alexander missed the blessed fountain and failed to achieve immortality.

The earth is supposed to rest on water, the all-surrounding ocean, but the Koran also speaks several times of the ocean on which boats travel (thus Sūra 14:32) and of its dangers for travellers (thus Sūra 17:67), who remember the Lord only during the horrors of their journey. One also finds the comparison of the world with foam-flecks (Sūra 13:17), and in another Koranic verse it is stated that the world is 'decked out fair' (Sūra 3:14). From this point, it was easy for the Sufis to see the created universe as small, pretty foam-flecks in the immense, fathomless ocean of God – mystics in all religious traditions know this image, especially those with 'pantheistic' tendencies. Are not waves and foam peripheral, surfacing for a single moment from the abyss, only to return into it? Rūmī has described this vision:

> The ocean billowed, and lo!
> Eternal wisdom appeared
> And cast a voice and cried out –

That was how it was and became –
The ocean was filled with foam
and every fleck of this foam
Produced a figure like this
and was a body like that,
And every body-shaped flock
that heard a sign from the sea,
It melted and then returned
into the ocean of souls …
(D no. 649)

The journey of the fragile boat, that is 'man', which will be shattered by the wave of the pre-eternal Covenant, appears time and again in mystical imagery. Many Sufis, especially those writing in later times, were well aware that there is only one real existence which we experience in different states of aggregate: water, ice, droplet and rain are all the same, for water, being without a form of its own, can accept and produce every form.

The image of the ocean for God (or, in poetry, for Love, which may even be an 'ocean of fire') is generally valid, but the Prophet too has been called an ocean in which the Koran constitutes the precious pearl.[17] More frequent, however, is the combination of the Prophet with the rain.

For rain was sent down to quicken the dead earth (Sūra 41:39), and it is still called *raḥmat*, 'mercy', in some areas of the Turkish and Persian world. Thus it was easy to find cross-relations between the 'rain of mercy' and him who is called in the Koran *raḥmatan li' l-ʿālamīn*, 'Mercy for the Worlds' (Sūra 21:107). Muhammad himself, as Abū Ḥafṣ ʿOmar as-Suhrawardī tells in his *ʿAwārif al-maʿārif*, was fond of the precious rain, and 'used to turn to the rain to accept blessings from it and said, "One that was still recently near his Lord"'.[18]

Was the Prophet, sent with a life-bestowing message to his compatriots, not comparable to the blessing, fertilizing rain? This thought inspired some of the finest poems in his honour, especially in the Eastern Islamic world. The Sindhi mystical poet, Shāh ʿAbdul Laṭīf (d. 1752), devoted his *Sur Sārang* to him, ingeniously blending the description of the parched land that longs for rain with the hope for the arrival of the beloved Prophet, who appears as the rain-cloud that stretches from Istanbul to Delhi and even further. A century later, Mirzā Ghālib in Delhi (d. 1869) composed a Persian *mathnavī* about 'The Pearl-carrying Cloud', i.e. the Prophet, and towards the end of the nineteenth century Muḥsin Kākōrawī (d. 1905) sang his famous Urdu ode in honour of the Prophet, skilfully blending the theme of the cloud and the 'rain of mercy' with time-honoured indigenous Indian rain poetry.[19]

But rain has yet another aspect to it. It comes from the ocean, rises, evaporating, to the sky, condenses again in the clouds and returns finally to the ocean to be united with its original source or else, as was popularly thought, to become a pearl enshrined by a pure oyster. The latter is often connected with the April rain, and to this day in parts of Turkey drops of April rain are carefully collected and preserved for healing purposes. In medieval times, artisans produced vessels, called in Turkey *nisan tasĭ*, for this precious rain, which were often beautifully decorated.

As is natural in areas where droughts are frequent and rain is a real blessing, the custom of *istisqā*, the prayer for rain, is found from the earliest days of Islam; in such cases, the community of believers went out of the town in shabby clothes to implore Divine help. Many stories of saintly people who, in some way or another (sometimes even by threatening God), were able to bring down the heavenly water reflect the important role of the *istisqā*.

One has, however, to distinguish between the blessing, fertilizing rain and the dangerous *sayl*, the torrent or flash flood. The Koran says: 'Evil is the rain of those who have been warned' (Sūra 26:173), for the Divine wrath can devastate their hearts as a rainstorm ruins the fruits in the orchards. It was the Baghdadian Sufi Abū'l-Ḥusayn an-Nūrī (d. 907) who – probably for the first time in Arabic literature – beautifully described the two kinds of spiritual rain which can descend upon the human heart's garden either to quicken it or to destroy it in the form of terrible hail (Sūra 24:43).[20]

Most obvious is the danger posed by water, of course, in the deluge which, as is said, began by an overboiling kettle in Kufa and which destroyed all sinful people, while the Ark was taken to heaven (Sūra 29:14). The term *baḥr* in the Koranic revelation can be interpreted as 'ocean' but also as a 'large river' such as the Nile; and the Nile – connected with the story of Moses – as well as the Tigris (owing to its situation as the river on which the capital Baghdad was built in the mid-eighth century) are the rivers most frequently mentioned by later authors. Does the Tigris not consist of the tears which Iraq shed after the death of the last Abbasid caliph at the hands of the Mongols in 1258? Thus asks a fourteenth-century Persian poet,[21] while Khāqānī, two centuries earlier, had interpreted the mighty river as tears of mourning for the once glorious Lakhmid kingdom of which only the ruins of Seleukia-Ktesiphon were left.[22]

However, besides this half-realistic use of the river-imagery, rivers also acquired a symbolic meaning. The Shiite theologian Kulaynī in the tenth century seems to have been the first to use the comparison of the Prophet with a mighty river. It is remarkable that Goethe, eight centuries later in Germany and, of course, unaware of this early Arabic text, symbolized Muhammad as a river which, springing from a small, fresh and refreshing fountain, steadily grows and, by carrying with him whatever comes into his way – small brooks, rivulets and rivers – brings them home to the father, the all-embracing ocean. Iqbāl

(d. 1938), the Indo–Muslim philosopher-poet, admired Goethe's intuitive understanding of the dynamics of prophethood. He translated (very freely, to be sure) the German poem into Persian. Later, he even assumed the pen name *Zindarūd*, 'Living Stream', to point to his close connection with the spirit of prophetic inspiration.[23]

Rivers can also become signs of Divine activity. One of the finest expressions of this feeling is the Sindhi poet Qāḍī Qādan's (d. 1551) verse:

> When the Indus is in spate then the canals overflow.
> Thus the love of my Beloved is too mighty for my soul.[24]

For the human heart is too narrow to contain all the blessing water of the Divine grace and love.

Rivers, so it is understood, are not only this-worldly: Paradise is described in the Koran at several points (Sūra 48:17 et al.) as 'gardens under which rivers flow'. The cooling, purifying quality of limpid water is part and parcel of eternal beatitude, and Yunus Emre (d. 1321) rightly sings that the rivers in Paradise repeat the name of God in an uninterrupted litany (see below, p. 238).

Sometimes, four paradisiacal rivers are mentioned, and the structure of many gardens, especially those surrounding a mausoleum or a kiosk, reflects with its four canals the arrangement in the hoped-for Paradise, in which rivers or fountains like *kauthar* and *salsabīl* will refresh the blessed.

Water in its different manifestations appears – with only a few exceptions, such as the deluge – as blessing power; fire, however, is generally charged with negative power. The word 'fire', used so frequently in the Koran, denotes almost without exception the Hellfire. To be sure, God can transform the burning pyre into a rose-garden, as he did for Abraham, for whom fire became 'cool and pleasant' (Sūra 21:69) when Nimrod had cast him into it; but burning is utterly painful, be it real burning in Hell or burning in the fire of separation, of unrequited love, which appears to the longing lover worse than Hellfire. And yet, this burning is necessary for the heart's purification (see below, p. 95). Perhaps some subconscious reminiscences of the Zoroastrian fire cult added to the dangerous aspect of fire in Islam – did not Iblīs boast of his fiery origin as a proof of his superiority over Adam? Later poets would sometimes claim that their hearts were burning in love more than the great fire temples of ancient Iran, while folk poets compared their hearts to the potter's kiln which does not reveal the fire that rages inside.[25]

However, despite allusions to Hell, fire also has its positive qualities. It gains its specific place by the Divine manifestation through the burning bush on Mt Sinai. This was a wholesome fire, and later poets have tended to compare the red tulip that looks indeed like a flame to the fire on the sacred mountain.

Another expression of the Divine aspect of fire is the frequently-used image of the 'iron in fire', a symbol well known in both the Christian and the Indian traditions. Rūmī explains the *anā'l-ḥaqq*, 'I am the Truth' (= I am God) of the martyr mystic al-Ḥallāj (d. 922) by comparing him to a piece of iron in the fire: the red, glowing iron calls out 'I am fire', and yet its substance is still iron, not fire (*M* II 1,347ff.). For no absolute union between man and God is possible as long as the material, bodily aspects of the creature persist.[26]

A different use of fire occurs in al-Ḥallāj's story of the moth which, slowly approaching the candle, first sees its light, then feels its heat and finally immolates itself in the flame, to assume complete identification (see below, p. 23). But is it not so – as a later poet asks – that the moth knows no difference between the candle of the Kaaba and that of the idol temple? The end of the road is, in either case, complete annihilation.

Candles are lighted in mausoleums and shrines and used during festive nights in honour of a saint. In Turkey, Muslims used to celebrate *kandīl*, 'candle', that is the nights of major feasts such as the Prophet's birthday or of his heavenly journey, and the mosques are decorated with artistically illuminated signs and inscriptions. These, formerly of live candles, have now of course been replaced by electric bulbs, and thus the modern woman who formerly might have placed a candle near a sacred place to fulfil a vow may now simply bring a bulb to the saint's shrine or the mosque.

Other fiery manifestations of power and 'signs of God' are thunderstorms, lightning (Sūra 30:24) and thunder. The Koran states (Sūra 13:13) that 'the thunder praises Him', while for Ibn 'Arabī, lightning is a manifestation of the Divine Essence. Hence, Divine 'Flashes' are symbolized from early times as 'lightnings' during which the wayfarer may proceed a little bit, while in the intervals the road is dark and it is not possible to walk – an idea derived from Sūra 2:20. Dangerous as the lightning is, it nevertheless releases the element of fire inherent (according to ancient physiology) in the straw as in other things – thus, it is similar to the fire that immolates the moth which it thereby helps to achieve release from the material world. These ideas, however, belong on the whole to a later development in Islamic thought.[27]

Much older is the role of the wind, which comes as a promise of His Mercy (Sūra 7:57) because it announces the arrival of rain. The gentle wind carried Solomon's throne (cf. Sūra 34:12), but the icy wind, *ṣarṣar*, destroyed the disobedient cities of 'Ad and Thamud (Sūra 69:6 et al.). Thus, the term *ṣarṣar* becomes a cipher for any destructive power. Many later poets in the Persianate world would boast that the scratching of their pen was like *ṣarṣar* to destroy their patron's enemies, while others, less boastful, would see the two aspects of God's activity, the manifestations of His *jamāl*, kindness and beauty, and His *jalāl*, majesty and wrath, in the two aspects of the wind which destroys the infidels and yet is a humble servant to the prophet Solomon.

One aspect of the kindly wind is the southern or eastern breeze, called *nafas ar-raḥmān*, 'the breath of the Merciful', which reached the Prophet from Yemen, carrying the fragrance of Uways al-Qaranī's piety, as formerly a breeze brought the healing scent of Yūsuf's shirt to his blind father Jacob (cf. Sūra 12:94).

'God is the light of the heavens and of the earth' (Sūra 24:35). Thus states the Koran in the Light Verse, and the Scripture emphasizes time and again that God leads people from the darkness to the light, *min aẓ-ẓulumāt ilā' n-nūr*.

Light plays a central role in virtually all religious traditions, and the concept of the light which in itself is too radiantly evident to be perceived by the weak human eyes has clear Koranic sanction.[28] In the early days of Koranic interpretation, scholars believed that Muhammad was intended as the 'niche' of which the Light Verse speaks, as the Divine light radiates through him, and again, the Koran had called him *sirāj munīr*, 'a shining lamp' (Sūra 33:46). As such, he is charged with leading people from the darkness of infidelity and error towards the light. One of the prayers transmitted from him is therefore, not surprisingly, a prayer for light:

> O God, set light in my heart and light in my tomb and light before me, and light behind me; light on my right hand and light on my left; light above me and light below me; light in my sight and light in my perception; light in my countenance and light in my flesh; light in my blood and light in my bones. Increase to me light and give me light, and appoint for me light and give me more light. Give me more light!

This prayer has been repeated by the pious for many centuries.

At a rather early stage, Muhammad himself was surrounded with light or even transformed into a luminous being: the light of prophethood was inherited through the previous prophets and shone on his father's forehead when the Prophet was begotten. In the Shia tradition, this light is continued through the imams. Small wonder, then, that Muhammad's birth was marked by luminous appearances, and later stories and poems have never failed to describe the light that radiated from Mecca to the castles of Bostra in Syria – the luminous birth and/or epiphany of the founder of a religion is a well-known theme in religious history (cf. the birth of Zoroaster, the Buddha, or Jesus). For light is the Divine sign that transforms the tenebrae of worldly life.

But not only the birth of the Prophet happened with manifestations of light; even more importantly, the night when the Koran was revealed first, the *laylat al-qadr* (Sūra 97), was regarded as filled with light. Pious Muslims still hope to be blessed with the vision of this light, which indicated the appearance of the last, all-encompassing revelation.

As for the Prophet, numerous myths grew around his luminous being: his light was the first thing that God created, and mystics have embellished the concept of the pre-eternal Muhammad as a column of light with ever more fanciful and surprising details which are reflected in mystical songs even in Bengal.[29]

The symbolism of light is widely used, yet in one case even a whole philosophy of light was developed by a Muslim thinker. This is the so-called *ḥikmat al-ishrāq*, the Philosophy of Illumination by Shihābuddīn as-Suhrawardī, who had to pay with his life for his daring theories (he was killed in 1191). According to him, 'existence is light', and this light is brought to human beings through innumerable ranges of angelic beings. Man's duty is to return from the dark well in the 'western exile' where he is imprisoned by matter to the Orient of Lights, and his future fate will be determined by the degree of illumination that he has acquired during his life.[30]

But this search, the quest for more and more light, is central not only in Suhrawardī's illuminist philosophy; rather, the Koranic statement that man should come from the tenebrae to light led certain Sufi masters to elaborate a theory of the development of the human soul so that an individual, during long ascetic preparations, may grow into a true 'man of light' whose heart is an unstained mirror to reflect the Divine light and reveal it to others. Henry Corbin has described this process lucidly in his study on *L'homme de lumière dans le soufisme iranien* (1971). The equation God = light, based on Sūra 24:35, was natural for Muslims, but it was a novel interpretation of this fact when Iqbāl applied it not to God's ubiquity but to the fact that the velocity of light is the absolute measure in our world.[31]

The central role of the concept of 'light' can also be gauged from the considerable number of religious works whose titles allude to light and luminosity, beginning from collections of *ḥadīth* such as Ṣāghānī's *Mashāriq al-anvār*, 'Rising points of the lights' or Baghawī's *Maṣābīḥ as-sunna*, 'The lamps of the sunna' to mystical works like Sarrāj's *Kitāb al-luma'*, 'Book of the Brilliant Sparks', 'Irāqī's *Lama'āt*, 'Glitterings' and Jāmī's *Lawā'iḥ*, 'Flashes' – each of them, and many more, intended to offer a small fraction of the Divine or the Prophetic light to guide their readers in the darkness of this world.

The most evident manifestation of the all-embracing and permeating light is the sun; but the sun, like the other heavenly bodies, belongs to the *āfilīn* (Sūra 6:76), 'those that set', to whom Abraham turned first until he understood that one should worship not these transient powers but rather their Creator, as Sūra 41:37 warns people 'not to fall down before the sun and the moon' but before Him whose signs they are. Islam clearly broke with any previous solar religion, and the order of the ritual prayer takes great care to have the morning prayer performed before sunrise and the evening prayer after sunset lest any connection with sun-worship be imagined (and yet their timing perfectly fits into the cosmic rhythm). The break with the solar year and its replacement by a lunar year underlines this new orientation. Nevertheless, the sun's role as a symbol for the radiance of the Divine or of the Prophet is evident. The *ḥadīth* has Muhammad say: 'I am the sun, and my companions are like stars' (*AM* no. 44) – guiding stars for those who will live after the sun has set. And in another *ḥadīth* he is credited with claiming: 'The hatred of the bats is the proof that I am the sun' – the contrast of the nightly bats, enemies of the sun and of the true faith, was often elaborated, for example in Suhrawardī Maqtūl's delightful Persian fables.[32]

The Prophet's connection with the sun becomes particularly clear in the later interpretation of the beginning of Sūra 93, 'By the morning light!', which was understood as pointing to the Prophet. It was perhaps Sanā'ī (d. 1131) who invented or at least popularized this equation in his long poetical *qaṣīda* about this Koranic chapter.[33] The 'morning light' seemed to refer to the Prophet's radiant cheek, while the Divine Oath 'By the Night!' (Sūra 92) was taken to mean the Prophet's black hair.

As a symbol of God, the sun manifests both majesty and beauty; it illuminates the world and makes fruits mature, but were it to draw closer it would destroy everything by its fire, as Rūmī says, warning his disciple to avoid the 'naked sun' (*M* I 141).

More important for Islamic life than the sun, however, is the moon, the luminary that indicates the time. Did not the Prophet's finger split the moon, as Sūra 54:1 was interpreted? And it was this miracle that induced the Indian king Shakravarti Farmāḍ to embrace Islam, as the Indo-Muslim legend proudly tells.[34]

The moon is the symbol of beauty, and to compare one's beloved to the radiant moon is the highest praise that one can bestow upon him or her. For whether it is the *badr*, the full moon, or the *hilāl*, the slim crescent – the moon conveys joy. To this day, Muslims say a little prayer or poem when they see the crescent for the first time; on this occasion, they like to look at a beautiful person or something made of gold and to utter blessings in the hope that the whole month may be beautiful. It is told that the great Indian Sufi Niẓāmuddīn Awliyā used to place his head on his mother's feet when the crescent appeared in the sky, out of reverence for both the luminary and the pious mother. Poets have composed innumerable verses on the occasion of the new moon, in particular at the end of the fasting month, and one could easily fill a lengthy article with the delightful (but sometimes also tasteless) comparisons which they have invented. Thus, for Iqbāl, the crescent serves as a model of the believer who 'scratches his food out of his own side' to grow slowly into a radiant full moon, that is, the person who does not humiliate himself by begging or asking others for help.

It was easy to find connections between the moon and the Arabic alphabet. The twenty-eight letters of the alphabet seemed to correspond to the twenty-eight days of the lunar month. And does not the Koran mention twenty-eight prophets before Muhammad by name, so that he is, as it were, the completion of the lunar cycle? Indeed, one of his names, *Ṭāhā* (Sūra 20:1), has the numerical value of fourteen, the number of the full moon.

While the moon is a symbol of human beauty, it can also be taken as a symbol of the unattainable Divine beauty which is reflected everywhere: the traditional East Asian saying about the moon that is reflected in every kind of water has also found its way into the Islamic tradition. Thus, in one of Rūmī's finest poems:

> You seek Him high in His heaven –
> He shines like the moon in a lake,
> But if you enter the water,
> up to the sky He will flee ...
> (*D* no. 900)

Some mystically-inclined Turks even found a connection between the words *Allāh*, *hilāl* 'crescent' and *lāla* 'tulip', all of which consist of the same letters *a-l-l-h* and seem therefore mysteriously interconnected.

The stars, although belonging to the *āfilin*, 'those that set', can serve as signs for mankind (Sūra 6:97); they too prostrate before the Lord – 'and the star and the tree prostrate both' (Sūra 55:6). The importance of the 'star' as a mystical sign can be understood from the beginning of Sūra 53, 'By the Star!'

The stars as guiding signs gained extreme practical importance in navigation, and inspired mathematical and astronomical works in the early centuries of Islam. The great number of astronomical terms in Western languages which are derived from the Arabic prove the leading role of Muslim astronomers. Among the stars that were particularly important were the polar star and Suhayl, Canopus, and the Pleiades, as well as Ursa Major, which often appear in literature. The Koran speaks also of shooting stars, *shihāb*, which serve to shy away the devils when they try to enter the heavenly precincts (Sūra 72:8–9).

Astronomy went along with astrology, and the properties of the zodiacal signs (as they were known from classical antiquity as well as from Oriental lore) were taken over and elaborated by Muslim scientists. Niẓāmī's (d. 1209) Persian epos *Haft Paykar*, 'The Seven Pictures' or 'Beauties', is the best example of the feeling that everything is bound in secret connections – stars and days, fragrances and colours. Those who had eyes to see could read the script of the stars in the sky, as Najmuddīn Kubrā (d. 1220/1) informs his readers, and astrological predictions were an integral part of culture. Thus arose the use of astrologically suitable names for children, a custom still practised in parts of Muslim India, for example. Indeed, it is often difficult to understand the different layers of Islamic poetry or mystical works without a certain knowledge of astrological traditions, and complicated treatises such as Muhammad Ghawth Gwaliorī's (d. 1562)

Jawāhir-i khamsa, 'The Five Jewels', point to astounding cross-relations involving almost every 'sign' in the universe. The ancient tradition of interpreting the planets – Jupiter as the great fortune, Saturn as the (Hindu) doorkeeper of the sky, Venus as the delightful musician, etc. – was used by artists at many medieval Muslim courts. There is no dearth of astrological representations on medieval vessels, especially on metal.

Astrology, as it was practised by the greatest Muslim scientists such as al-Bīrūnī (d. 1048), offered believers another proof that everything was part of cosmic harmony – provided that one could read the signs. But when it came to the sky itself, the ancient idea that this was the dwelling-place of the High God could not be maintained. The sky is clearly a symbol pointing to Divine transcendence, because God is the creator of the seven heavens and of the earth; and, as the Throne Verse (Sūra 2:255) attests, 'His Throne encompasses heavens and earth'. The heaven is, like everything else, obedient to God's orders, bending down before His Majesty. And yet, one finds complaints about the turning spheres, and Muslims seem to join, at times, the remarks of their predecessors in Iran and ancient Arabia for whom the turning wheel of the sky was connected with cruel Fate (see below, p. 32).

Light and darkness produce colours. Here, again, one enters a vast field of research. The combination of the different stars with colours, as found in Niẓāmī's poem, is not rare – as Saturn is the last of the then known planets and its colour is black, 'there is no colour beyond black'. The luminous appearances which the Sufi may encounter on his spiritual path are again different, and so are the seven colours which are observed in mystical visions in different sequences.[36] One thing, however, is clear: green is always connected with Paradise and positive, spiritual things, and those who are clad in green, the *sabzpūsh* of Persian writings, are angels or saints. This is why, in Egypt, Muslims would put green material around tombstones: it should foreshadow Paradise. Green is also the colour of the Prophet, and his descendants would wear a green turban. Thus, green may constitute, for example, in Simnānī's system, the eternal beatitude which, manifested in the emerald mountain, lies behind the black.

Dark blue is the ascetic colour, the colour of mourning. Red is connected with life, health and blood; it is the colour of the bridal veil that seems to guarantee fertility, and is used as an apotropaic colour. Red wine, as well as fire (in its positive aspects) and the red rose, all point to the Divine Glory, as it is said that the *ridā al-kibriyā*, 'the cloak of Divine Glory', is radiant red.

Yellow points to weakness, as the weak yellow straw and the pale lover lack fire and life-giving blood; in its honey-coloured hue, yellow was used for the dresses of the Jews during the Middle Ages.

A full study of the colour symbolism of the Sufi garments is still required. Red was preferred by the Badawiyya in Egypt, green by the Qādiriyya, and the

Chishtis in India donned a frock whose hue varied between cinnamon and rosy-yellowish. Whether some masters wore cloaks in the colour that corresponded to the colours that they had seen in their visionary experiences is an open question, but it seems probable.[38] But in any case, all the different colours are only reflections of the invisible Divine light which needs certain means to become visible – in the *ṣibghat Allāh* (Sūra 2:138), 'the colouring of God', the multicoloured phenomena return to their original 'one-colouredness', a term used by Sufis for the last stage of unification.

PLANTS AND ANIMALS

The Tree of Life is a concept known from ancient times, for the tree is rooted in the earth and reaches the sky, thus belonging to both spheres, as does the human being. The feeling that life power manifests itself in the growth of a tree, that leaves miraculously sprout out of bare twigs and fruits mature year after year in cyclical renewal, has impressed and astounded humanity through the ages. Hence, the tree could become a symbol of everything good and useful, and the Koran states, for this reason, that 'a good word is like a good tree' (Sūra 14:24).

Trees are often found near saints' tombs: the amazing number of trees connected with the name of ʿAbdul Qādir Gīlānī in Sind was mentioned by Richard Burton and others.[40] Visitors frequently use such trees to remind the saint of their wishes and vows by hanging rags – sometimes shaped like minute cradles – on their branches or, as for example in Gazurgah near Herat, driving a nail into the tree's trunk.

It is natural that Paradise, as an eternal garden, should boast its very special trees, such as the Tuba, whose name is developed from the greeting 'Happiness', *ṭūbā*, to those pious people who believe (Sūra 13:29); that is, the Tuba tree is the personified promise of eternal bliss that one hopes for in Paradise. Likewise, the boundaries of the created universe are marked by the Sidra tree, mentioned in Sūra 53:14 – the 'Lote tree of the farthest boundary', which defines the limit of anything imaginable; and it is at this very Sidra tree where, according to legend, even the mighty Gabriel had to stay back during the Prophet's heavenly journey while the Prophet himself was blessed with reaching the immediate Divine Presence beyond Where and How.

Thinkers and mystics could imagine the whole universe as a tree and spoke, as did Ibn ʿArabī, of the *shajarat al-kawn*, the 'tree of existence', a tree on which man is the last, most precious fruit. On the other hand, Bāyezīd Bisṭāmī, in his mystical flight, saw the 'tree of Unity', and Abū'l-Ḥusayn an-Nūrī, at about the same time, envisaged the 'tree of gnosis', *maʿrifa*.[41]

A detailed account of the 'tree of the *futuwwa*', the 'manly virtue' as embodied in later *futuwwa* sodalities, is given in a fifteenth-century Turkish work:[42] the trunk of this tree, under which the exemplary young hero lives, is 'doing good';

its branches are honesty; its leaves proper etiquette and restraint; its roots the words of the profession of faith; its fruits gnosis, *maʿrifa*, and the company of the saints; and it is watered by God's mercy.

This is reminiscent of the Sufi *shajara*, the 'family tree' that shows the disciples their spiritual ancestry, leading back to the Prophet: drawings – often of enormous size – symbolize the continuous flow of Divine guidance through the past generations, branching out into various directions.

Some thinkers embellished the image of the 'tree of the world' poetically. Probably nobody has used the image of the tree for different types of humans more frequently and extensively than the Ismaili philosopher-poet Nāṣir-i Khusraw (d. after 1072), for whom almost everything created turned into a 'tree':

> You may think, clever man, this world's a lovely tree
> Whose tasty, fragrant fruits are the intelligent …

or else:

> The body is a tree, its fruit is reason; lies and ruse
> are straw and thorns … [43]

The close connection between the tree and life, and especially spiritual life, is beautifully expressed in the *ḥadīth* according to which the person who performs the *dhikr*, the recollection of God, is like a green tree amid dry trees – a likeness which makes the Muslim reader think immediately of dry wood as fuel for Hell, as it is alluded to in the Koranic curse on Abū Lahab's wife, 'the carrier of fuel wood' (Sūra 111:5). Thus Rūmī sings in one of his quatrains:

> When the spring breeze of Love begins to blow –
> every twig that's not dry begins to move in dance!

For Love can move only the living branches, while the dried-up twigs remain unmoved and are destined to become kindling for Hellfire.

The Tree of Life, whose branches are the Divine Names,[44] is rooted in the Divine Presence; or else, the profession of faith can be seen as a tree whose outer rind, formed by the negation *lā*, is pure negativity, and whose sap flows through the *h*, the last and essential letter of *Allāh* (see Figure, p. 19) (*M* IV 3,182ff.).

In addition, not only the created universe but also God Himself can be symbolized through a tree: poets, especially in the Indo–Pakistani areas, sang of the tree 'God'. Qāḍī Qādan in Sind (d. 1551) sees the Divine Beloved as a banyan tree whose innumerable air roots seem to hide the fact that the tree in reality is only one (as the phenomena hide the Divine Unity), while Sulṭān Bāhū in the Panjab (d. 1692) sings of God as the jasmine tree that grows in his heart, watered by the constant repetition of the profession of faith until His fragrance permeates his entire being.[45]

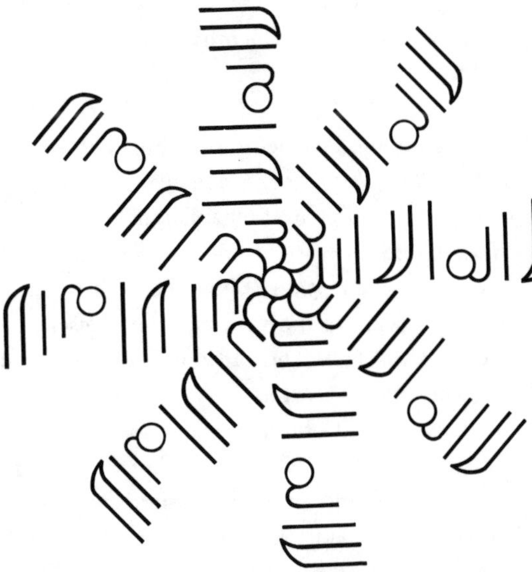

The *shahāda*, centred on the essential letter *h*, with the *lā* as the 'outer rind'.

Hence comes the idea encountered in popular traditions, for example, that to plant a tree on someone's grave not only has a practical aspect to it but is also thought to lessen the punishment in the grave and console the dead person. The *baraka* of a tree can be transferred by touching it or, in certain places, by creeping under a low-bent tree or its strangely-shaped branches; a very typical tree of this kind can be seen near a shrine in Ucch (southern Panjab).

Parts of the tree carry the same *baraka* as does the whole tree, be it its leaves or its twigs. The custom of beating people – in jest or earnest – with fresh twigs is basically an old fertility rite, which conveys some of the tree's life power. It was practised in medieval Egypt when the jester, *ʿifrīt al-maḥmal*, jokingly beat the spectators when the *maḥmal* on which the cover of the Kaaba was carried to Mecca was paraded in grand style through the streets of Cairo; similar customs can be observed during the Muḥarram processions in Hyderabad/Deccan.

The tree's blessing power is also preserved in the wreath. The custom of garlanding pilgrims returnnig from Mecca or honoured guests is a faint reflection of this feeling of the tree's *baraka*, as is the garlanding of saints' tombs; every visitor to major shrines in the subcontinent knows of the numerous little shops that sell flowers and wreaths near the entrance to the sacred places.

Not only does the tree in general bear the flow of vital power, but also specific trees or their twigs play a role in folklore and literature. Sometimes the *baraka* of such trees is ascribed to the fact that they had grown out of the *miswāk*, the toothpick of a saint which he threw away and which took root to grow into a powerful tree. A good example is the Junaydi shrine in Gulbarga/Deccan.

On a Koranic basis, it is the date palm which has a special relation with life: the Koranic account of Mary's labour (Sūra 19:23ff.) tells that the Virgin, during her birth pangs, grasped the trunk of a dried-up palm tree, which showered dates upon her as a Divine sign of the Prophet to be born. (The idea has inspired Paul Valéry's beautiful poem *La palme.*) The Arabs love date palms, and dates were and are used in several dishes prepared for religious purposes, such as the twelve dates in the *ḥalwā* prepared for feasts in the *futuwwa* sodalities.[46] Another important tradition in the *Tales of the Prophets* points to the idea that fig trees are protected and should not be burnt, as the fig tree offered its leaves to cover Adam's and Eve's shame after the Fall. And did not God swear in the Koran (Sūra 95:1) 'By the the fig and the olive'? The olive is even more prominent in the Koran, not only in the Divine Oaths but also as the mysterious tree, 'neither eastern nor western' (Sūra 24:35), whose oil shines even without being touched by fire. The cypress is called 'free' and reminds Persian and Turkish poets of their beloved's tall, slender stature, while the plane tree seems to resemble a human being – do its leaves not look like human hands which it lifts as if it were in prayer?

Such comparisons lead to the concept of the garden – the garden as a replica of Paradise, Paradise an eternal garden in which every plant and shrub sings the praise of God. The Koran had repeatedly emphasized the reality of resurrection by reminding the listeners of the constant renewal of Nature in spring, when the rains had quickened the seemingly dead earth. Therefore Persian and Turkish poetry abounds in such poems, for the fresh greenery of bushes and trees looked as if Paradise had descended on earth.[47]

Abū'l-Ḥusayn an-Nūrī in ninth-century Baghdad elaborated the comparison of the heart with a garden filled with fragrant plants, such as 'recollection of God' or 'glorification of the Lord', while a somewhat later mystic speaks of the 'garden of hearing' in which the leaves are of God pleasure and the blossoms of praise.[48] The garden of the heart, then, is blessed by the rain of grace, or, in the case of sinners, the rain of wrath destroys its poisonous plants. Likewise, one may see human beings similar to plants – some like fragrant flowers, some like grass.

Certain plants are thought to be endowed with special powers: the wild rue, *sipand*, is used against the Evil Eye (usually in fumigation), and the so-called *Peyghamber gul* in Afghanistan, a small yellow plant with little dark lines, seems to bear the marks of the Prophet's fingers. But in the Islamic tradition, as elsewhere, the rose has pride of place. The Prophet kissed the rose and placed it on his eyes, for 'the red rose is part of God's glory, *kibriyā*'.[50] On the other hand, legend claims that the rose grew out of the drops of perspiration which fell from the Prophet's body during his nightly journey – therefore it carries his sweet fragrance.

To the poets, the violet could appear as an old ascetic who, sitting in his dark blue cloak on the green prayer rug, namely the lawn, meditates modestly, his head bent on his knee, while the lily can be interpreted – owing to the shape of its petals – as *Dhū 'l-fiqār*, ʿAlī's miraculous sword, or else it praises God with ten tongues. The tulip may appear as a coquettish beau with a black heart, but in the religious tradition it reminds the spectator of bloodstained shrouds, especially those of the martyrs of Kerbela, with the black spot resembling a heart burnt by sorrows.[51] In Iqbāl's poetry, on the other hand, it symbolizes the flame of Sinai, the glorious manifestation of God's Majesty, and at the same time it can stand for the true believer who braves all the obstacles that try to hinder his unfolding into full glory.

All the flowers and leaves, however, are engaged in silent praise of God, for 'there is nothing on Earth that does not praise its Creator' (Sūra 59:24 et al.), and every leaf is a tongue to laud God, as Saʿdī (d. 1292) sings in an oft-imitated verse which, if we believe the historian Dawlatshāh, the angels sang for a whole year in the Divine presence.[52]

This feeling of the never-ending praise of the creatures is expressed most tenderly in the story of the Turkish Sufi, Sünbül Efendi (sixteenth century), who sent out his disciples to bring flowers to the convent. While all of them returned with fine bouquets, one of them, Merkez Efendi, offered the master only a little withered flower, for, he said, 'all the others were engaged in the praise of God and I did not want to disturb them; this one, however, had just finished its *dhikr*, and so I brought it'. It was he who was to become the master's successor.

Not only the plants but the animals too praise God, each in its own way. There are mythological animals such as the fish in the depth of the fathomless ocean on which is standing the bull who carries the earth; and the Persian saying *az māh ta māhī*, 'From the moon to the fish', means 'all through the universe'. However, it is difficult to explain the use of fish-shaped amulets against the Evil Eye in Egypt and the frequent occurrence of fish emblems and escutcheons in the house of the Nawwabs of Oudh. A pre-Islamic heirloom is likely in these cases. While in the Koran animals are comparatively rarely mentioned, the *Tales of the Prophets* tell how animals consoled Adam after the Fall.

There seems to be no trace of ancient totemism among the Arab Muslims, while in the Turkic tradition names like *bughra, bugha* 'steer' or *börü* 'wolf' could be understood as pointing to former totem animals of a clan. Yet, in some dervish orders, mainly in the off-centre regions of the Islamic world, one encounters what appear to be 'totemistic' relics: for example, the ʿIsawiyya in North Africa take a totem animal and behave like it during a certain festival, when a steer is ritually (but not according to Islamic ritual!) slaughtered.[53] The identification of cats and dervishes among the Heddawa beggar-dervishes seems to go back to the same roots.[54] Although these are exceptional cases, some remnants of the belief in the sacred power of certain animals still survive in Sufi traditions in general. One of them is the use of the *pūst* or *pōst*, the animal skin which constitutes the spiritual master's seat in a number of Sufi brotherhoods. When medieval dervishes such as Ḥaydarīs and Jawāliqīs clad themselves in animal skins, they must have felt a sort of identification with the animal.

One problem when dealing with the role of animals in religion is the transformation of a previously sacred animal into an unclean one, as happened for example in ancient Israel with the prohibition of pork, the boar being sacred to the Canaanites. The prohibition of pork is one of the rare food taboos that lives on in Islam. There, however, the true reason for its prohibition is unknown, and it is generally (and partly correctly) attributed to hygienic reasons. Yet, it seems that the ugliness of boars shocks the spectator perhaps even more than the valid hygienic reasons, and I distinctly remember the old Anatolian villager who, at Ankara Zoo, exclaimed at the sight of the only animal of this kind (a particularly ugly specimen, to be sure): 'Praised be the Lord, who has forbidden us to eat this horrible creature!' Besides, pigs are in general thought to be related in some way or another to Christians: in ʿAṭṭār's *Manṭiq uṭ-ṭayr*, the pious Shaykh Ṣanʿān is so beside himself with love for a Christian maiden that he even tends her swine, and in Rūmī's poetry the 'Franks' who brought pigs to the sacred city of Jerusalem occur more than once.[55] With the deeply-rooted aversion of Muslims to pork and to pigs, it comes as a true cultural shock for parents when their children, in British or American schools, have to learn nursery rhymes about 'three little piggies', illustrated by pretty drawings, or are sometimes offered innocent marzipan pigs.

The Muslims have devoted a good number of scholarly and entertaining works to zoology, for example al-Jāḥiẓ's and Damīrī's works; but on the whole the characteristics of animals were provided either by the rare allusions in the Koran or, after the eighth century, by Bidpai's fables known as *Kalīla wa Dimna*, which became widely read in the Islamic world after Ibn al-Muqaffaʿ (d. 756) had first rendered them into Arabic.

The Koran (Sūra 2:26) mentions the tiny gnat as an example of God's instructing mankind by means of likenesses. In the *Tales of the Prophets*, we learn that it was a gnat that entered Pharaoh's brains, thus causing his slow and painful death – the smallest insect is able to overcome the mightiest tyrant. The bee (Sūra 16:68) is an 'inspired' animal whose skill in building its house points to God's wisdom. In later legend, ʿAlī ibn Abī Ṭālib appears as the *amīr an-naḥl*, 'the Prince of the bees' because they helped him in a battle, and popular tradition in both medieval Turkey and Indo–Pakistan claims that honey becomes sweet only when the bees constantly hum the *ṣalawāt-i sharīfa*, the blessings over the Prophet, while gathering the otherwise tasteless sap.[56]

The ant appears in Sūra 27:18ff., a weak creature which was nevertheless honoured by Solomon, and the legend that it brought a locust's leg to the mighty king is often alluded to – 'a locust's leg' is an insignificant but well-intended gift from a poor person. The spider, on the one hand, is a creature that builds 'the weakest house' (Sūra 29:41), and yet it was a spider that helped the Prophet during his hegira: when he spent the night with Abū Bakr in a cave, the spider wove its web so deftly over the cave's entrance that the Meccans who pursued the Prophet failed to recognize his hiding-place. So legend tells.

Although not mentioned in the Koran, the moth or butterfly that immolates itself in the candle's fire was transformed into a widespread symbol of the soul that craves annihilation in the Divine Fire. It reached Western literature through Goethe's adaptation of the motif in his poem *Selige Sehnsucht.*[57]

As for the quadrupeds, the title of Sura 2, *Al-Baqara* 'The Cow', is taken from the sacrifice of a yellow cow (Sūra 2:67ff.) by Moses; but during a religious discussion at Emperor Akbar's court in 1578, a pious Hindu happily remarked that God must have really loved cows to call the largest chapter of the Koran after this animal – an innocent misunderstanding that highly amused the Muslim courtiers.[58]

The lion, everywhere the symbol of power and glory, appears in the same role in Muslim tradition, and ʿAlī ibn Abī Ṭālib, whose proper name was first Ḥaydara (or Ḥaydar), 'Lion', was praised from early days as the 'lion of God' and therefore surrounded by numerous names that point to his leonine qualities, such as *Ghaḍanfar*, 'lion', or *Asadullāh*, 'God's lion', or in Persian areas *ʿAlīshīr*, and under Turkish influence *Aslan ʿAli and ʿAli Arslan* (both *shīr* and *arslan* mean 'lion'). The true saint, it is said, is like the golden lion in the dark forest of this world, and fierce lions bow before him or serve him as obedient mounts. But perhaps the most moving role of the lion is found in Rūmi's *Fīhi mā fīhi.* People travelled from near and far to see a famous strong lion, but nobody dared to come close to him from fear; however, if anyone had stroked him, he would have been the kindest creature imaginable. What is required is absolute faith, then there is no danger any more.

In popular belief, the cat is the lion's aunt, or else she is born from his sneezing.[59] The Prophet's fondness for cats is often referred to, and whether or not the *ḥadīth* that 'Love of cats is part of faith' is genuine, it reflects the general feeling for the little feline. For the cat is a clean animal; her presence does not annul ritual prayer, and the water from which she has drunk can still be used for ablution. There are variants of the story of how Abū Hurayra's cat, which he always carried in his bag, saved the Prophet from an obnoxious snake, whereupon the Prophet petted her so that the mark of his fingers is still visible in the four dark lines on most cats' foreheads, and, because the Prophet's hand had stroked her back, cats never fall on their backs. Whether the custom that a 'Mother of cats' and later the 'Father of cats' accompanied the Egyptian *maḥmal* on the pilgrimage to Mecca is a dim survival of the ancient Egyptian cat cult is not clear.[60] Love of cats is particularly evident in Maghribi tradition, where, among the Heddawa for example, the novices are called *quēṭāṭ*, 'little tom-cats'. Ibn Mashīsh is credited with love of cats, and there is also an old Sufi shrine in Fez called *Zāwiya Bū Quṭūṭ*, 'that of the father of cats', just like *Pisili Sultan*, 'Lady with kitten', in Anatolia. Yet, despite the cat's positive evaluation in early literature, there is no dearth of stories (especially in Persian) about hypocritical cats which, while peacefully murmuring their prayers or the *dhikr*, never forget to kill the mice which they have cheated by their alleged repentance from bloodshed.

While the cat is a clean animal, the dog is regarded as unclean, and his presence spoils the ritual prayer. He appears as fierce and greedy (anyone who has encountered the street dogs in Anatolia will appreciate this remark), and thus the dog could represent the *nafs*, the lower soul 'which incites to evil' (Sūra 12:53). Sufis were seen with a black dog besides them, which was explained to the onlooker as the hungry *nafs*; but, as the dog can be trained and become a *kalb muʿallam*, an 'instructed dog', thus the lower faculties too can be turned into something useful. On the other hand, the Koran mentions the dog that faithfully kept company with the Seven Sleepers (Sūra 18:18–22), and this legendary creature, called *Qiṭmīr* in legends, became a symbol of fidelity and trustworthiness. The poets would love to be 'the dog of fidelity' at their beloved's door or, in Shia Islam, at the shrine of an imam. By unswervingly watching there, they hoped to be purified as was the dog of the Seven Sleepers, who was honoured by being mentioned in the sacred Book. The proper name *Kalb ʿAlī*, ''Alī's dog', in some Shia families expresses this wish. And when poets tell how the demented lover Majnūn used to kiss the paws of the cur that had passed through the quarter of his beloved Laylā, they mean to point out that even the lowliest creature can become a carrier of blessings by his association with the beloved.[61] The remarkable amount of positive allusions to dogs in Persian poetry (contrary to the rather negative picture of cats in the same literature) may stem from the Zoroastrian love for dogs which, in the dualistic Zoroastrian system, belonged to the good side of creation.

The camel, mentioned as sign of God's creative power in Sūra 88:17 ('Don't they look at the camel how it was created?') became in later tradition a fine symbol of the *nafs* which, restive and selfish in the beginning, could be educated (similar to the dog) to carry the seeker to his goal, the Divine Presence, dancing on the thorny roads despite its heavy burden when listening to the driver's song.

Among the negative animals represented in the Koran is the donkey, whose braying 'is the ugliest possible voice' (Sūra 31:19) and whose stupidity is understood from the remark that the ignorant who are unable to understand and appreciate the contents of the sacred scriptures are like 'the donkey that carries books' (Sūra 62:5). In legend, the donkey is said to be accursed because Iblīs managed to enter Noah's Ark by clinging to its tail. Traditionally, the donkey is connected in Islamic literature (as in classical antiquity) with dirt and sensuality and became, in mystical parlance, the representative of the material world which has to be left behind, just as Jesus's donkey remained on earth while he was uplifted to heaven.[62]

There is, however, the white mule Duldul (the name means 'large hedgehog') which the Prophet gave to ʿAlī and on which he performed many of his heroic deeds. Nowadays, Duldul's pictures can be found on the walls of shrines and on cheap prints in India and Pakistan to bring blessing to the building and to its owner.

The horse is the typical Arabic animal, created, according to a myth, from the swift southern wind, and Arabic literature abounds with praises of the beautiful creature. The beginning of Sūra 100 speaks of the 'running horses' which appear as galloping through the world towards the final goal – the Day of Judgment. But it rarely appears in truly religious contexts, although it may serve in the Sufi tradition again as a *nafs*-animal, which has to be starved and broken in order to become useful for its owner; the numerous allusions to the 'restive horse' and the miniature drawings of starved horses seem to be related to this concept.[63] In Shia circles, it is believed that a white horse will carry the Mahdi when he descends to earth at the end of time; therefore a fine steed with henna-coloured feet is led every year in the Muḥarram procession (the so-called *dhū 'l-janāḥ*) to make sure that his horse is saddled in case he should suddenly appear. It is touched by the pious for the sake of blessing.

A strange mount, smaller than a horse and larger than a mule, was Burāq (connected with *barq*, 'lightning'), that carried the Prophet during his *miʿrāj* through the heavens into the Divine Presence. It is described as having a woman's face and a peacock's tail, and was the embodiment of swiftness and beauty. Poets and painters have never tired of describing it with new colourful details. Burāq nowadays appears frequently on pictures; and, in the eastern lands of the Muslim world, especially in Pakistan, trucks and buses are decorated with its 'likeness', perhaps in the hope that its *baraka* will bring the vehicle as swiftly to its goal as the real Burāq carried the Prophet through the universe.[64]

Serpents, so important in the Christian tradition, do not play a central role in Islam. The Koran (Sūra 7:117, 20:66ff.) alludes to Moses' rod that turned into a serpent to devour the rods of Pharaoh's sorcerers. For they can appear as *nafs*-animals which are blinded by the spiritual master, who resembles an emerald.[65] Also, it was Iblīs in the shape of a small snake which, carried into Paradise owing to the peacock's negligence, induced Adam and Eve to eat from the forbidden fruit. However, the role of the snake and its greater relative, the dragon, is not as central as one would expect. Yet, both snakes and dragons (the latter appearing more frequently in the indigenous Persian tradition) are connected in popular belief with treasures which they guard in ruined places. Perhaps that connects them with the mighty serpent which, according to the *Tales of the Prophets*, surrounds the Divine Throne.

Much more important in symbolic language is the world of birds, which, like everything, adore the Lord and know their laud and worship, as the Koran states (Sūra 24:41). The soul bird, common in early and ancient societies, was well known in the Islamic world. Pre-Islamic Arabs imagined soul birds fluttering around a grave. Later, the topic of the soul bird, so fitting to symbolize the soul's flight beyond the limits of the material world, permeates mystical literature, and still today one can hear in some Turkish families the expression *Can kusu uçtu*, 'his/her soul bird has flown away', when speaking of someone's death. The tradition according to which the souls of martyrs live in the crops of green birds to the day of Resurrection belongs in this connection.[66]

Again, just as plants in general play a considerable role in Islamic beliefs and folklore and yet some special plants are singled out for their religious or magic importance, the same is the case with birds. If the rose is the supreme manifestation of Divine beauty or the symbol of the beloved's cheek, then the nightingale is the soul bird par excellence. It is not only the simple rhyme *gul-bulbul*, 'rose-nightingale', in Persian that made this bird such a favourite of poets, but the plaintive nightingale which sings most expressively when roses are in bloom could easily be interpreted as the longing soul. This idea underlies even the most worldly-looking use of this combination – unbeknown to most authors.

The falcon is a different soul bird. Its symbolic use is natural in a civilization where falconry was and still is one of the favourite pastimes. Captured by a cunning old crone, Mistress World, the falcon finally flies home to his owner; or else the hard, seemingly cruel education of the wild, worthless fledgling into a well-trained hunting bird can serve as a model for the education which the novice has to undergo. The Sufis therefore liked to combine the return to his master's fist of the tamed, obedient bird with the Koranic remark (Sūra 89:27–8) 'Return, oh you soul at peace ...', for the soul bird has undergone the transformation of the *nafs ammāra* into the *nafs muṭma'inna*. On the other hand, however, the falcon as a strong, predatory bird can also serve to symbolize the irresistible power of love or Divine grace, which grasps the human heart as a hawk carries away a pigeon.

The pigeon, or dove, is, as in the West, a symbol of loving fidelity, which is manifested by its wearing a collar of dark feathers around its neck – the 'dove's necklace'.[67] In the Persian tradition, one hears its constant cooing *kū, kū*, 'Where, where [is the beloved]?' (In India, the Papiha bird's call is interpreted similarly as *Piū kahān*, 'Where is the beloved?')

The migratory stork is a pious bird who builds his nest preferably on minarets. Is he not comparable, in his fine white attire, to pilgrims travelling once a year to Mecca? And his constant *laklak* is interpreted as the Arabic *al-mulk lak, al-ʿizz lak, al-ḥamd lak*, 'Thine is the kingdom, Thine is the glory, Thine is the praise'.

Similarly the rooster, and in particular the white rooster, is regarded as the bird who taught Adam how and when to perform the ritual prayer; thus he is sometimes seen as the muezzin to wake up the sleepers, a fact to which a *ḥadīth* points (*AM* no. 261); Rūmī even calls him by the Greek word *angelos*, 'an angel'.

The peacock, due to whose negligence the serpent, i.e. Satan, was carried into Paradise, is a strange combination of dazzling beauty and ugliness: although his radiant feathers are put as bookmarks into copies of the Koran, the ugliness of his feet and his shrieking voice have always served to warn people of selfish pride. While some authors dwell upon his positive aspects as a manifestation of the beauty of spring or Divine beauty, others claim that the bird is loved by Satan because of his assistance in bringing him into the primordial Paradise. Nevertheless, peacocks – sacred to Sarasvati in former times – are kept in many Indo–Pakistani shrines. Hundreds of them live around a small shrine in Kallakahar in the Salt Range; and in other places, peacock feathers are often used to bless the visitor.

Like the peacock, the parrot, probably unknown in early Islamic times, belongs to India and has brought from his Indian background several peculiarities: he is a wise though somewhat misogynistical teacher[69] whose words, however, are sweet like sugar. That is why, in Gulbarga, deaf or stuttering children are brought to the minute tomb of a pet parrot of the saint's family; sugar is placed on the tomb, and the child has to lick it. The parrot's green colour connects him with Paradise, and it is said that he learns to speak by means of a mirror behind which someone utters words (see below, p. 31).

In the Muslim tradition of India, one sometimes encounters the *hāns*, the swan or, rather, large gander who, according to folk tales and poems, is able to live on pearls. Diving deep, he dislikes the shallow, muddy water – like the perfect saint who avoids the dirty, brackish water of this world.

Muslim authors' interest in birds can be easily understood from the remark in Sūra 27:16 according to which Solomon was acquainted with the 'language of the birds', *Manṭiq uṭ-ṭayr*. This could easily be interpreted as the language of the souls, which only the true master understands. The topic of the soul birds had already been used in Ibn Sīnā's (d. 1037) *Risālat aṭ-ṭayr* and his poem on the soul, and Sanāʾī (d. 1131) has described and interpreted in his long *qaṣīda*, *Tasbīḥ aṭ-ṭuyūr* 'The birds' rosary', the different sounds of the birds. The most extensive elaboration of the stories of the soul birds is given in ʿAṭṭār's *Manṭiq uṭ-ṭayr*: the *hudhud*, the hoopoe, once the messenger between Solomon and the Queen of Sheba, leads them through the seven valleys in their quest for the *Sīmurgh*.[70]

However, it becomes clear from ʿAṭṭār's epic, as from other poems such as some of Nāṣir-i Khusraw's *qaṣīdas*, that by no means all birds are examples of the positive aspects of the human soul.[71] Some are connected with the hibernal world of matter, like the crow and the raven which inhabit ruins and, contrary to other birds, enjoy the winter, the time when the world seems to be dead and the life-giving water is frozen. Was it not the raven that showed Cain how to bury his slain brother Abel (Sūra 5:31)?

Mythical birds are not lacking in Muslim lands. There is the *Humā*, the shade of whose wings conveys kingdom to the one touched by it, and the *ʿAnqā*, the 'long-necked' female bird which has become a metaphor for something non-existent: *adĭ var özü yok*, 'He has a name but no reality', as the Turkish saying goes. Its Persian counterpart, the Sīmurgh, was a resourceful bird in early Persian tradition, rescuing, as the *Shāhnāma* has it, little Zāl and bringing the outcast child up with her own chicks; the colourful feather which she gave to Zāl allows its owner to perform licit magic. The Sīmurgh was, however, transformed into a symbol of the Divine by Suhrawardī the Master of Illumination (d. 1191) and by ʿAṭṭār, who invented the most ingenious pun in Persian mystical literature: the thirty birds, *sī murgh*, who have completed their pilgrimage through the seven valleys, discover that the goal of their quest, the divine Sīmurgh, is nothing but themselves, being *sī murgh*.

The Koran mentions (Sūra 5:60) the transformation of sinners into pigs and monkeys, and some medieval authors took over these ideas, beginning, it seems, with the Ikhwān aṣ-ṣafā of Basra. Ghazzālī mentions the 'animal traits' (pig = appetite, greed; dog = anger) in his *Iḥyā ʿulūm ad-dīn*,[72] and the Divine threat that greedy, dirty and sensual people will appear on Doomsday in the shape of those animals which they resembled in their behaviour is quite outspoken in the works of Sanāʾī and ʿAṭṭār, and somewhat softened in some of Rūmī's verses.

Yet, there is still another side to animals in Islamic tradition. Muslim hagiography is replete with stories that tell of the love that the 'friends of God' showed to animals, and kindness to animals is recommended through moving stories in the *ḥadīth*. Early legend tells of Sufis who were famed for their loving relations with the animals of the desert or the forest, and later miniature paintings often show the saints with tame lions (or their minor relatives, namely cats) or surrounded by gazelles which no longer shy away from them. For the one who has subdued the animal traits in his soul and has become completely obedient to God will find that everything becomes obedient to him.

Finally, the dream of eschatological peace involves the idea that 'the lion will lie down with the lamb', and Muslim authors too have described the peaceful kingdom which will appear (or has already appeared) under the rule of this or that just and worthy sovereign, or else which will be realized in the kingdom of the Beloved.[73]

MAN-MADE OBJECTS

Man-made things used as objects of worship or regarded as filled with a sacred power are often called 'fetish' (from Portuguese *feitiço*). The term can be applied to almost everything made by human hands which then occupied a special place in human life: even a sacred book which is used more or less as a cult object without remembering its spiritual content can turn into a fetish. However, to put one's trust in the power of a 'fetish' is absolutely prohibited in Islam, as such an act is incompatible with the faith in the One God who is the Creator of everything; hence, man-made objects were less important in the Islamic context than in other religions, even though certain shades of their former role may have survived and they continued to be used in symbolic language.

Yet a look at some of these objects may be interesting. Among man-made objects, weapons had a very special value in early societies, and the role of the blacksmith in ancient civilizations is well known. In the Islamic tradition proper, this 'cult' of weapons seems to be lacking; only in the Iranian epical tradition, in the *Shāhnāma*, does the blacksmith Kāvah act as hero and liberator. In the Koranic tradition, David appears as a master in making coats-of-mail (as every prophet was instructed in a practical profession). But the mystical power of arms survives in one specific historical example. That is ʿAlī's famous double-edged sword, *Dhū 'l-fiqār*, with the aid of which he performed his greatest heroic feats. Later, the name of *Dhū 'l-fiqār* was often applied to a patron's sword or to any sharp instrument (including the poet's sharp tongue!) to express the greatest possible achievement in overcoming enemies; hence, it is also used as a proper name.

Islamic arms and armour are often inscribed with religious formulas to enhance their power. Besides the Koranic verse of victory (Sūra 48:1), one frequently finds the *ḥadīth*: *lā fatā illā ʿAlī, lā sayf illā Dhū 'l-fiqār*, 'there is no true herioc young man but ʿAlī and no sword but *Dhū 'l-fiqār*'. The names of the 'rightly guided caliphs' in Sunni circles and those of the Shia imams in the Shiite world are used; in Shia environments, the invocation *Nādi ʿAliyyan*, 'Call upon ʿAlī, the manifestor of miracles ...', is quite common on weapons and on other objects.

Similar texts are also inscribed on different parts of the armour, from breastplates to leggings, from helmets to shields; but in all these cases, it is the words of the Koran or of the Prophet that endow the object with specific power. An old object of pride was the axe or double axe, the use of which is connected with certain Sufi orders such as the Hamadsha in North Africa, and in Iran, where some Sufis in former times also used a mace, a typical sign of ancient male sodalities.

When trees, and twigs as part of a tree, were widely used for religio–magic purposes, one may explain the rod or wand as an artificial twig. It enhances man's power, and is a sign of guidance. The Koranic story of Moses, whose serpent-turned-wand devoured those of Pharaoh's sorcerers (Sūra 20:66 et al.), is a typical example of the living power of the rod. Furthermore, Moses split the sea with it and caused water to gush forth from the rock. *Żarb-i Kalīm*, 'The stroke of Moses', was therefore chosen as a telling title for a collection of Iqbāl's Urdu poetry in which he harshly criticizes the modern development in the Muslim world – as though his pen might work the miracles associated with Moses' rod.

During the Friday services, the preacher in the mosque carries a wand; that points to his authority.[74] Likewise, many Sufi masters own either a long rod (or several of them) or else a high pole. Often, the upper end of the ceremonial pole is decorated with the 'hand of Fatima' to avert the Evil Eye, or else complicated caligrams made of pious invocations (verses from the Koran, the names of saintly people, etc.) crown the high pole, which is seen as a sign of leadership although its power is, again, mainly due to the use of sacred texts.

A further development of the rod seems to be the flag or banner. Some Sufi masters are known as 'he of the flag', for example the Pīr Jhāndēwārō in Sind, who wielded an authority similar to that of his cousin, the Pīr Pāgārō, 'he with the turban'. In processions, the members of the different Sufi brotherhoods marched with their colourful flags through the cities, as lively descriptions of medieval Cairo tell, and when a Mamluk sultan's pious wife was buried in 1467, her bier was covered with the red flag of the dervishes of Aḥmad al-Badawī 'for the sake of blessing'.[75]

To mark a pious person's tomb in the wilderness, people often put little colourful flags around or on top of a heap of stones. Similarly, in the *majlis* meetings of the Shia during the first ten days of Muḥarram, flags in different colours, often with precious embroidery, are placed in a corner to remind the participants of the flags which heroes like ʿAbbās, the standard-bearer of Kerbela, had carried. These flags are touched by the participants for the sake of the *baraka*. The use of blessed flags or even *ṭūghs*, poles with yak tails, was apparently well known among Sufis and Sufi-related groups such as the *futuwwa* sodalities.

The intrinsic religio–magic value of the flag appears again in connection with the blacksmith Kāvah, who unfurled his apron which thus became the famous *dirafsh-i kāviyānī*, the flag under which he helped to liberate Iran from tyranny. For this reason, the term *dirafsh-i kāviyānī* was used in later times by authors who wanted to show their compatriots the right way, even if only in the area of Persian grammar.[76]

Much more important for the general Muslim tradition, however, is the concept of the *liwā al-ḥamd*, the 'banner of praise' which Muhammad will carry on Doomsday (*AM* no. 331). The believers will gather in the field of Resurrection under this green flag to be led, thanks to his intercession, to eternal bliss. Each

Muslim dynasty had its own flags and banners, and the poets of medieval Arabia liked to compare the flowers of the garden to flags of different tribes, hence different colours.[77] The favourite comparison, which continued for many centuries in Persian and even Ottoman Turkish literature, was that of violets with the black banners of the Abbasids. And as flags serve to delineate a ruler's territory, it is not surprising that one of the Turkish terms for a certain administrative unit is *sancak*, 'flag'. Flags were embroidered with the emblems of strength, or of Islam. In later times, many of them bore the sign of the crescent or were decorated with the words of the profession of faith (now generally woven into the material), while it seems that in former times pictures of lions were quite common (as they continue to be in Iran), for the 'lion on the flag' became a standard metaphor for something lifeless and powerless.

One of the most fascinating objects in religious history is the mirror,[78] from ancient times an object sacred to the Japanese goddess Amaterasu. Mirrors were made of steel and had to be polished carefully so that they could reflect persons or objects. The Koranic saying (Sūra 83:14) 'What they were earning was overshadowing their hearts' could easily be applied to the mirror of the heart that was covered by the rust of blameworthy actions, and thus no longer capable of reflecting the Divine light. This theme was to become a favourite with the Sufis, who tried (and continue to try) to instruct the disciple in how to polish this mirror by constant recollection of God lest any dust, rust or verdigris of evil actions or thoughts be collected on it. Even to breathe on it (that is, to speak) would stain its purity. This latter comparison remains true also at a time when metal mirrors were replaced by glass mirrors.

The mirror plays an important role in traditional sagas and tales. A famous one is Alexander's mirror, which he placed on high to overcome an obnoxious serpent. As everyone who saw this monster had to die, it was concluded that if the serpent were to see its own reflection it was bound to expire as well. By this trick, the country was saved. Alexander's 'world-showing mirror', often set parallel to Jamshīd's world-showing goblet, appears in Persian literature time and again.

As the pure heart is a mirror of God, those whose hearts are perfectly purified and polished can serve as mediators for God's beauty. This is the spiritual guide's role. ʿIsā Jund Allāh of Burhanpur (d. 1621) says, with a somewhat different metaphor:

> Even though straw and woodchips can be heated by the rays of the sun, they cannot be ignited. But if one places a mirror before them and focuses the rays through it upon the straw, then it can be ignited. The Pīr's essence is like the mirror.[79]

The mirror symbol also serves to explain how the disciple learns to speak and to act: as a parrot is placed before a mirror behind which someone is talking whom the bird (thinking his mirror image to be another parrot) tries to imitate, the disciple is instructed by the words of the master, who serves as God's mirror.

A person whose heart has become a pure mirror will be able to recognize other people's wishes and thoughts as though they were his own, and the famous *ḥadīth* 'The believer is the believer's mirror' (*AM* no. 104) has served through the ages as a fine educational device: when one sees some unpleasant traits in one's neighbour, one should recognize them as one's own faults and try to eliminate them from one's own character.

However, not only the heart is a mirror of things Divine; rather, the whole universe could be considered to be a mirror of God's beauty and majesty. God, who 'was a hidden treasure and wanted to be known' (*AM* no. 70), as the Sufis' favourite extra-Koranic saying stated, created the world as a mirror to contemplate His own beauty in it. Only the ignorant prefer to admire this mirror's reverse side instead of looking at God's reflection in the seemingly 'empty' face-side (see below, p. 229).

The mirror's secret is perhaps most beautifully alluded to in a story which Mawlānā Rūmī repeated at least thrice in his work: someone wanted to bring a gift to Yūsuf, the manifestation of Absolute Beauty, but the only present that he could think of was a mirror so that the beloved could admire his own beauty in it.[80] Likewise, the lover's mirror-like heart is filled so completely with his beloved's picture that finally mirror and image can no longer be distinguished and his beloved is, in this mirror, closer to the lover than to himself: the mirror unites both.[81]

The mirror, as becomes clear from its ancient connection with Amaterasu, is a feminine object, the purest vessel of reception: thus, the story of Yūsuf and the mirror is at the same time the story of his relation with Zulaykhā, who wanted to come as close as possible to the Eternal Beauty. The loving soul, in its mirror-like quality, assumes the receptive, feminine role just as the world, created as God's mirror, appears as feminine. It was perhaps the subconscious understanding of the mystery of the mirror as a feminine receptacle that was needed to manifest the masculine creative power which made it so important not only in mystical thought but also in Islamic art, which abounds in mirror structures that reflect the central motif of an arabesque or the sacred words of a pious invocation in never-ending repetition.

Most man-made objects which play important roles in different religions appear in the Islamic tradition only at random or in a negative connotation: the wheel has no significant role unless one thinks of the poetical concept of the wheel of the sky; and the cross, the central reality and symbol in Christian theology and meditation, is used only negatively, as Islam denies the crucifixion of Christ (Sūra 4:157). Does not the cross with its four arms remind the wise of the four elements from whose bondage one tries to escape to reach essential *tawḥīd*, monotheism? And when Persian poets like to speak of the 'cross-shaped' hairstyle of the young Christian cupbearer, it is more or less a pleasant literary game.

Even more repellent to Muslims were the idols fashioned in the ancient world, whether primitive stone figures or the wonderful creations of classical antiquity. The Koran tells how Abraham broke the idols of his father Azar (cf. Sūra 6:74) to become the first true monotheist. 'To break the idols' is necessary for anyone who honestly attests that there is 'no deity save God', and for this reason Muslim modernist thought tends to call an 'idol' anything that diverts human interest from God, be it communism, capitalism or nationalism, or many man-made inventions which are taken for support instead of the One God.

And yet, the terminology of 'idols' (Arabic *ṣanam*, Persian *but*) permeates the entire corpus of Persian, Turkish and Indo-Muslim literatures, for the Beloved is very often addressed as *but*, so that a confusing oscillation between strict monotheistic religion and the literary game with the 'idols' can be observed throughout the literary history of the Persianate world. In this respect, the mystics might argue that, as God created Adam 'according to His form', one could find a way to the absolute object of love by seeing the Divine through human 'idols' – after all, 'the metaphor is the bridge towards reality'. But the constant appearance of 'idols' has caused much misunderstanding, not only among externalist theologians but also among non-Muslim readers of this kind of literature.[82]

Among the objects that could serve in antiquity as small idols was the coin, which was usually imprinted with representations of deities. In Islamic times, these were largely replaced by the words of the *shahāda*. The feeling that coins could have a 'religious' value continued in at least some areas: in the Deccan, Indian friends may fasten the *imām żāmin kā rūpia*, 'the rupee of the protecting Imam', around a departing person's arm to protect him or her during the journey, and formerly a square rupee with the names of the rightly guided caliphs was dipped in water which was then administered to a woman in labour.[83]

The aversion of the Sufis to coins (that is, to money in general, as paper money appears only in post-Mongol times) may or may not have something to do with the feeling that coins were indeed a kind of idol that could divert the seeker from the trust in the one true God and provider of nourishment.

Islam is known as an absolutely iconoclastic religion. Although the prohibition of painting, let alone stone carving, is based not upon a Koranic text but rather upon the Prophet's saying, it was a safeguard against idol-worship, as the represented object is thought to be really present in the picture.[84] It was said that the painter or sculptor would be asked on Doomsday to infuse life into his works

– a task in which he would of course miserably fail. Nevertheless, there are the wall paintings in Omayyad desert castles such as Qusayr Amra, or the pictorial decoration of Seljukid palaces, especially in Anatolia, where even statues were used; and representations of birds and quadrupeds, as well as of scenes from courtly life or illustrations of various tales, are found on many metal and ceramic objects. In the Middle Ages, book illumination was used to illustrate first scientific treatises and also, at a rather early point, the *Maqāmāt al-Ḥarīrī*, these delightful short stories in brilliant rhyme prose interspersed with punning verses.

The art of wall-painting was practised mainly in bathrooms and bath-houses. It is said that angels would not enter a room with pictures in it; and, as they were not thought to enter bathrooms in any case, pictures could be safely placed there. The historian Bayhaqī tells about the 'pleasure house' of the Ghaznawid king Masʿūd I in Herat in the early eleventh century, and it seems more than a mere accident that four centuries later Jāmī (d. 1492), in the same city of Herat, gives a detailed poetical account of the sensual paintings with which the lovesick Zulaykhā decorated her palace in the hope of seducing Yūsuf. But, however sensual they may have been, one knew that they had no soul, and the frequent idiom of the 'painted lion' or the 'painted hero Rustam' meant only utter lifelessness.

Nevertheless, the development of miniature painting continued to increase, and in modern times the problem of whether or not photography is part of the prohibited representation has resulted in many legal opinions being issued pro and con. The fascination with 'group photos' and videos in the Islamic world seems quite unexpected in the iconoclastic atmosphere of traditional Islam. Perhaps Jāmī's verse expresses the heart of the matter:

> The *sharīʿa* prohibits painting because
> it is impossible to paint your beauty![85]

The open question here is, as so often, whether the beautiful beloved is human or Divine.

In contrast to the Muslim's aversion to pictures, especially icons in sacred rooms (an attitude that influenced the heated Byzantine conflict between iconoclasts and iconodules, which lasted nearly a century, 716 to 787), Christianity was often seen as a religion of pictures; the iconostasis in the Eastern Orthodox churches with which the Muslims were most familiar made them sometimes call the world of forms and colours a *dayr*, 'monastery'.

One development in the field of iconoclasm is remarkable: in the Middle Ages, it seemed perfectly possible to show representations of the Prophet and his companions in historical works such as Rashīduddīn's *World History* or Turkish chronicles of early Islamic history. In our day, this is considered absolute anathema, so much so that in some Muslim countries even reproductions of such medieval pictures in a scholarly book can cause it to be banned.[86] In the later Middle Ages, the Prophet was shown with his face veiled, but nowadays even this seems to go too far. Angels, on the other hand, appear frequently in colourful miniatures or delicate line drawings,[87] and one may encounter pictures of a well-formed Angel Gabriel with the ram that was to be substituted for Ismāʿīl on the walls of Turkish restaurants.

One witnesses also a proliferation of pictures on paper and woven fabrics of objects filled with *baraka*, be it the Kaaba, the Prophet's mausoleum in Medina, his mount Burāq, ʿAlī's mule Duldul, or an object that was venerated from early days, the Prophet's sandal, to which a good number of medieval poets and poetesses had devoted Arabic poetry (see below, p. 183). In mosques, one finds calendars with pictures of the Holy Places, and postcards and postage stamps from Arabia show the Kaaba – but never any human being; while recent painters in Iran do not shy away from scenes from the lives of the prophets, which are depicted in an almost pseudo-Nazarean style. A speciality of Afghanistan and Pakistan are figurative paintings on trucks or on the walls of tea-houses, where large-eyed maidens alternate with warplanes and representations of Burāq or portraits of a political leader.[88]

Besides *baraka*-filled objects of metal, wood or stone, one finds woven objects, whose role in Islamic tradition is much larger than that of the previously mentioned items. Woven pieces or rug-like fabrics have served to cover sacred objects. The tradition of veiling the Kaaba with black velvet with golden embroidery, the *kiswa*, is probably the best-known example of this custom. In the Middle Ages, sovereigns might compete to send the *kiswa* (which was usually dispatched from Cairo) to Mecca, thus making a claim, as it were, to their rights over the Holy Places. The *kiswa* itself, renewed every year, is cut in small pieces which some fortunate pilgrims take home for the sake of blessing.

A similar custom is observed at saints' tombs. Visitors, usually as the result of a vow, bring covers which can also be obtained in the small stalls close to the shrine's entrance. The cover is placed on the sarcophagus and stays there for a while, and its hem is touched or kissed; often, the visitor places his or her head for the length of a *Fātiḥa* under the cover to obtain blessings. Then the cover is taken off again and either distributed as a whole or cut into small pieces for deserving visitors, serving sometimes as an additional head-cover or veil for a woman. Pious mothers will collect fragments of such tomb-covers for their daughters' trousseaus to ensure the girl's happiness.

One of the finest modern Sindhi short stories describes dramatically the role that such a cover plays in popular piety. Jamāl Abrrō's *Muñhuñ kārō*, 'With Blackened Face', tells of a poor man who stole the sumptuous cover which had been dedicated by a wealthy man in gratitude for a son's birth; the thief had hoped to procure some money by selling it to obtain some medicine for his dying child, but was beaten to death by the furious visitors.[89] A small cover is the *mindīl*, often represented in medieval art, and mentioned for example as a sign of asking for pardon.[90]

But the most important object among man-made things is the garment, headgear included. To change one's garment means to change one's personality, as everyone experiences when putting on an official dress, a uniform or a graduation cap and gown, and the priest wearing the liturgical garments acts not as a private person but as the official administrator of the sacred action.

For the garment is the human being's alter ego; thus, to burn a piece of an enemy's clothing serves as a substitute for killing him – a practice still known in East and West. The fact that garments and persons are, so to speak, interchangeable lies at the base of the Koranic saying that 'women are men's garment' and vice versa (Sūra 2:187), which indicates a most honourable position: husband and wife are each other's alter ego. Thus, Ibn Sīrīn explains that if one dreams of a woman's veil or cover, the meaning is 'her husband'.[91]

As the garment carries the owner's *baraka*, it was used to convey a king's, a prince's or a saint's power to another person: the English word 'gala' is derived from *khilʿa*, 'the honorary robe which the ruler has taken off', *khalaʿa*, 'to bestow it on someone worthy'. In early Islam, the most famous case of such an investiture (in the true sense of the word) is the Prophet's taking off his striped Yemenite cloak, the *burda*, to grant it to the poet Kaab Ibn Zuhayr as a sign of forgiveness.[92] The word *burda* was then metaphorically applied to the great poem in honour of the Prophet which the Egyptian Sufi al-Būṣīrī (d. 1296) sang after dreaming that the Prophet had cast his *burda* over him to heal him – and he was then healed. Just as the original *burda* was filled with *baraka*, thus al-Būṣīrī's 'secondary *burda*' was regarded as extremely blessed and was copied time and again, written on walls to protect the house, translated and enlarged not only in his Egyptian homeland but in all parts of Muslim world to the borders of southern India.[93] Ibn Sīrīn's interpretation fits in: to dream that one is given a garment by the Prophet means great fortune.

The Prophet's actual cloak, so it is said, was later sold to the Omayyad caliph Muʿāwiya and then reached the Abbasid caliphs. Several cloaks attributed to him are found in the Islamic world – one in Istanbul, another in Qandahar (Afghanistan) – and it was this latter *khirqa-i sharīf*, 'the noble cloak', that inspired Iqbāl to some moving Persian poems.[94]

As the Prophet's mantle contains special blessing, it used to be said that the Prophet's mantle was inherited by so-and-so, or fell on his shoulders, to describe a scholar of special standing. The Sufi custom that the master bestows a patched frock upon his disciples is the same symbol for the transmission of *baraka*, and when the disciple swears 'by the cloak of my shaykh' it is as if he were swearing by a person who – after the Prophet – is the most important in his life.

The protective value of the Prophet's cloak is also reflected in the term *ahl al-kisā* or *ahl al-ʿabā*, 'the people of the cloak', which means the closest relatives of the Prophet (Fāṭima, ʿAlī, Ḥasan and Ḥusayn), who are wrapped in his cloak and form so to speak a sacred and blessed unity.

Garments in general can be used for protective purposes: when one wraps a child in an aged person's dress, one hopes that it may grow to a ripe old age; or when the anxious mother dresses up her little boy as a girl, she wants to protect him from the Evil Eye or malicious djinns who might be more interested in a baby boy than in a girl: the dress helps to 'change its identity'. The Evil Eye or any other danger can also be averted – so Muslims hope – by means of a talismanic shirt, which ideally should be of cotton spun and woven by forty pure virgins and would be covered with Koranic inscriptions and invocations.

Islam developed a strict order of dress. The most important rule was to cover the essentials, that is, for men the area between navel and knee, and for women the body, although in this case the degree of covering varies from a normal decent dress to the full *ḥijāb* or the *burqaʿ* which covers the entire person. The question of whether a good Muslim is allowed to wear shorts, for example while rowing, caused intensive discussions among Muslim students at Harvard in the spring of 1992.

One must not forget that the strict rule for decently covering the body and the necessity of wearing a fitting garment during prayer caused major changes in border lands in the wake of Islamization. Muhammad Mujeeb (1972) has highlighted the importance of the Muslims' introducing stitched garments into India, as the loosely-knotted *lungi* and the graceful *saree* are not practical for performing the prayer rite (and the use of *shalwār qamīṣ* instead of the saree was emphasised when Islamic concepts were being increasingly stressed in Pakistan in the 1980s).[95] Much earlier, C. H. Becker spoke of the influence of the Bohora-Ismaili traders in East and Central Africa who brought with them different types of sewn dresses and at the same time propagated the religion that ordered the wearing of such clothing.[96]

The dress prescribed for the pilgrimage, *iḥrām*, shows by its very name that it is connected with the sphere of the sacred, *ḥaram*, that is, an area to which access is prohibited to those who do not follow the proper rites. The two white unsewn pieces of cloth for men and the long straight gown for women distinguish the pilgrims from the normal believer and subject them to a number of taboos.

In classical times, each stratum of society could be easily recognized by the style of dress worn (as was the case in medieval Europe as well), and it is speculated that one of the reasons for the order to the Prophet's wives to cover themselves decently (Sūra 24:31) was to distinguish them from the lower class and from servant-women. In medieval towns, the scholars' high hats with veils, *ṭaylasān*, were well known,[97] and one of the reasons that upset the adversaries of the martyr-mystic al-Ḥallāj was that he changed his attire frequently, now posing as a soldier, now as a scholar or a Sufi. Arabic, Persian and Turkish sources give many more or less detailed descriptions of fashions and fabrics, which are supported by the allusions to different garments in poetry and are illustrated in Oriental miniatures as well as in the travelogues of European merchants and visitors to the Middle East. It was therefore an immense shock for Muslims when three political leaders in the 1920s tried to force the population in their countries to exchange the time-honoured dress of men and the even more traditional dress of women for European-style clothes: Ataturk was successful in Turkey, Reza Shah Pahlavi in Iran somewhat less, and Amānullāh of Afghanistan failed.

Of special interest are customs in the Sufi orders[98] where the investiture with the *muraqqa*ʿ, the patched frock, or the *khirqa*, the woollen cloak, were central: legend claims that the dervish frock and the turban were given to the Prophet during his heavenly journey, and he handed them over to ʿAlī. A patched frock made of rags of Sufi cloaks that were torn during the whirling dance was regarded as particularly blessed owing to the 'power' of the ecstatic state of its former owner. The Sufis developed a far-reaching symbolism not only of the cloak but also of its different parts such as the hem, collar and sleeves, as is described extensively in Hujwiri's *Kashf al-Maḥjūb*. For the Mevlevis, the black coat that is thrown off when the mystical dance begins and the dervishes emerge in their white garments is seen as the material part of man, while the white garment points to the spiritual body. The Khāksār dervishes know a *kafanī*, which is the 'shroud' garment, for the dervish has to die to this world and what is in it; they also have the *lung*, a kind of apron worn under the garment and connected with the mysteries of initiation.[99]

In *futuwwa* circles, which are offsprings of the Sufi tradition, the investiture with the *futuwwa* trousers was the most important part of the initiation rite, and the term 'fastening the belt' (or the string that keeps the trousers in place) could develop into the expression 'binding the belt of servitude', or, as we would say, 'girding one's loins' for work, to perform services for the master.

The Sufis' types of headgear have different shapes and colours, as have the coats, and the headgear plays an important role; it shows the person's standing. The headgear could be the so-called *tāj*, 'crown', which is sometimes high, broadening towards the top, and sometimes round and made of a certain number of wedges: thus the twelve wedges in the Bektashi order remind the dervish of the twelve Shia imams. Another type is the high conical felt hat, *sikke*, of the Mevlevi dervishes.

Symbolically, the headgear can even be a favour from God, as Nāṣir-i Khusraw says in his *Saʿādatnāma*:

> When God grants you the cap, *kulāh*, of loftiness,
> Why do you bind your heart to someone else?

For to bless someone by placing headgear on his head means to honour him, and thus *dastārbandī*, 'turban-winding', is a highly important occasion in the dervish orders; it means the instalment of a worthy representative of the master. That the Pīr Pāgārō in Sind has received his surname from the turban, *pāgrī*, belongs here.

Turbans in different shapes and colours were also worn by non-dervishes, and their use is most prominent among scholars. To enlarge one's turban often came to mean 'to show off, to boast'. Therefore, the Indo–Persian poet Ṭālib-i Amulī (d. 1627) satirized those who neglect useful work because 'they are too busy with building up the domes of their turbans'.

One part of the dervish's outfit was the earring, at least in some brotherhoods, and the term *ḥalqa be-gūsh*, 'ring in the ear', means servitude: one is the servant of the person whose earring one wears. Such earrings could assume different shapes, and some of the itinerant dervishes in the Middle Ages as well as certain groups among the Bektashi used to wear heavy iron earrings in one or both ears.

Given the importance of garments and clothing in tradition and daily life, it would be surprising if the garment had not become a favourite metaphor. Models are given in the Koran: a *ḥadīth* speaks of the *libās al-birr*, 'the garment of kindness', and Sūra 7:26 of the *libās at-taqwā*, 'the dress of piety'. It is told in the *Tales of the Prophets* that, after the Fall, Adam's and Eve's clothes flew away and God addressed Adam: 'Let thy battle cry be My name and thy clothing what thou weavest with thy own hand' (for Adam's profession was agriculture as well as spinning and weaving), yet one felt that the garment sent down to cover their shameful parts should not be interpreted in the literal sense but also as the order and rules of the Divine Law: 'This garment', says Kāshānī, 'is the *sharīʿa* which rectifies the ugly traits in the rational soul'. Ibn ʿArabī's interpretation of a dream points to the same meaning: faith is seen as a cloak, and, among the people that appeared in that specific dream, only ʿOmar, the second caliph, has a sufficiently long cloak, that is, full faith in God.[100] Thus, when Niẓāmuddīn Awliyā of Delhi promises a disciple that he would 'cast a cloak over him to veil his sins', external and internal meaning are well interwoven. But a 'normal' dress cannot cover one's shameful acts, as Nāṣir-i Khusraw warns.

Someone who embraces Islam 'puts on the robe of honour of Islam', and during his heavenly journey the Prophet was invested with two cloaks, namely spiritual poverty, *faqr*, and trust in God. The 'robes of poverty and patience' are also mentioned by Shiblī, the Baghdadian Sufi (d. 945) who claimed to wear them on the Feast Day instead of the new garments which people usually don on festive days – in fact, to celebrate *ʿīd*, the Feast of Fast-breaking, without wearing new garments is considered a sign of utter destitution.

Given the metaphorical uses of 'garment', it is not difficult to speak of the 'robe of martyrdom', and when the Christian, according to St Paul, is 'clad in Christ', then the highest stage that a Muslim mystic may dream of is to be clad in the *libās al-ḥaqqāniyya*, the robe connected with the Divine Name *al-ḥaqq*, the Absolute Truth.

The Koran mentioned 'garments of fire' for the inhabitants of Hell (Sūra 22:19), and Satan's garment, as Kisā'ī claims, is God's wrath. The pious, on the other hand, can hope that the Lord will clothe them on the day of Resurrection with forgiveness and good actions to constitute a garment in Paradise, while the sinner is naked, deprived of the 'robe of piety'.

This image leads to another aspect of the weaving, spinning and clothing area: it was thought that one spins and weaves one's own eternal garment by one's actions and thoughts. Rūmī too admonishes his listeners to 'eat the fruit which one has planted oneself and dress in the garment which one has oneself spun' (*M* V 3,181). These images are elaborated particularly in the cotton-growing areas of the Deccan and of Pakistan.[101] The traditional folk songs which used to accompany spinning everywhere in the world were transformed into songs where spinning becomes a symbol for the uninterrupted *dhikr*, the recollection of God, and the soul that has performed this religious act dutifully will find a precious trousseau on her wedding day, that is, on Doomsday, while the lazy girl who has neglected the 'spinning' of the recollection will then be naked and disgraced. This imagery may also explain the belief of the Kurdish Ahl-i Ḥaqq, who saw metempsychosis as a wandering from one (bodily) garment to another one, always wearing – so one may think – what has been woven in the previous life.[102]

God Himself appears as the master weaver and tailor, as He is the supreme master of everything. He 'makes the night to a cloak', says Sūra 78:10, and it is He who weaves the whole history of the universe on the loom of days and nights. Furthermore, He can be approached only through the garments which He has put over his unfathomable Essence – the 70,000 veils of light and darkness hide Him as the garment hides the body and as the body hides the soul. '*Kibriyā*, "Glory" is His cloak', as a *ḥadīth qudsī* says (*AM* no. 404), and his shirt – according to the same source – is mercy with which He will clothe those who hope for it.

Without the 'garments', that is, without His manifestations of mercy and majesty, God would remain forever the *deus absconditus*, and when Meister Eckhart in Germany speaks in recurrent images of 'God in his *kleithûs*', His 'house of garments, His wardrobe', by which he means the tangible and palpable signs of His mercy, his elder contemporary in Anatolia, Mawlānā Rūmī, sings in one of his most moving poems:

O seize the hem of His favour
because from you He will flee …

(*D* no. 900)

To seize some powerful person's hem means to partake of his *baraka*, and the Muslim poet, a mouthpiece for so many other bards, knows that the mystery of God can be touched only through the signs, through the twofold woof and warp of the created universe, through phenomena which both hide and reveal Him like garments.

For the Muslim, the concept of the garment or shirt may carry still another connotation. In *Sūra Yūsuf*, the Koran speaks of the scent of Yūsuf's shirt, which healed his blind father Jacob (Sūra 12:94). The whole range of fragrance in Islamic culture would deserve a special study, beginning with the Prophet's love of fragrance, which belonged to the few things that God had endeared to him (*AM* no. 182), and including the idea of the fragrant breeze that comes from Yemen, carrying the spiritual message of love and piety. Scent reminds mankind of something long forgotten, something that cannot be seen, something precious, intangible – words are the scent of paradisiacal apple trees (*M* VI 84); the scent of the musk-deer leads the seeker to the deserts of China, that is, to the deserts of eternity.

NOTES

1. An interesting approach is H. A. R. Gibb (1962), 'The structure of religious thought in Islam', especially Part I, 'The animistic substrate'. See also William F. Albright (1955), 'Islam and the religions of the ancient Orient'; M. Ghallab (1929), *Les survivances de l'Egypte antique dans le folklore égyptien moderne.*
2. Hikmet Tanyu (1979), *Türklerde taşla ilgili inançlar.*
3. There are numerous examples in Kriss and Kriss-Heinrich (1960), *Volksglaube im Islam.*
4. Yaḥyā Bakharzī (1966), *Awrād al-aḥbāb*, vol. 2, p. 249 cites this *ḥadīth*. On Bakharzī, see also F. Meier (1957), 'Ein Knigge für Sufis'.
5. According to popular belief, the black stone will testify on Doomsday for all those who have kissed it. See H. Lazarus-Yafeh, 'The ḥadjdj', in her (1981) *Some Religious Aspects of Islam.*
6. Abdul Qādir Badaoni (1864–9), *Muntakhab at-tawārīkh*, vol. 2, p. 310; English translation (1972) vol. 2, p. 32.
7. See Muhammad Umar Memon (1976), *Ibn Taimiyya and Popular Religion.*
8. H. S. Nyberg (1919), *Kleinere Schriften des Ibn al-ʿArabī*, p. 216f.; see also J. M. S. Baljon (1986), *Religion and Thought of Shāh Walī Allāh*, p. 34 and index under *ḥajar baht.*
9. R. Gramlich (1981), *Die schiitischen Derwischorden Persiens*, vol. 3, p. 5.
10. E. Doutté (1908), *Magie et religion*, p. 84 about the *ʿaqīq*; Kriss and Kriss-Heinrich (1962), *Volksglaube im Islam*, vol. 2, p. 58f.; A. Schimmel (1992b), *A Two-colored Brocade*, ch. 11.
11. For the topic, see H. Corbin (1971), *L'homme de lumière.*
12. Suhrawardī (1978), *ʿAwārif* (trans. R. Gramlich), p. 32, tells how ʿAzrāʾil tore out the dust for Adam's creation.
13. A. Bombaci (1971), 'The place and date of birth of Fuzuli', p. 96.
14. J. Parsram (1924), *Sind and its Sufis*, p. 65.
15. See Martin Lings (1968), 'The Qur'anic symbolism of water'.
16. For the origin of this story, see H. Zimmer (1957), *Maya*, p. 50. It appears in Amīr Khusraw's *Āʾina-i Iskandarī*, quoted in Rückert (1874, ed. Pertsch),

Grammatik, Poetik und Rhetorik der Perser, p. 70; further in Jāmī (1957), *Nafaḥāt al-uns*, pp. 563–4 about some little-known saints. According to Kriss and Kriss-Heinrich (1960), *Volksglaube in Islam*, vol. 1, p. 76f., the story is told about the fifteenth-century Egyptian Sufi ad-Dashṭūṭī, probably because his anniversary is celebrated on the eve of the day of the Prophet's heavenly journey, i.e. 26–27 Rajab. It occurs also in a Sindhi folktale, 'Der Zauberer Aflatun', in A. Schimmel (1980b), *Märchen aus Pakistan*, no. 21.

17. Nāṣir-i Khusraw (1929), *Dīvān*, translated by A. Schimmel in Nāṣir-i Khusraw (1993), *Make a Shield from Wisdom*, p. 59.
18. Suhrawardī (1978), *'Awārif* (transl. R. Gramlich), p. 190.
19. A. Schimmel (1966), 'Der Regen als Symbol in der Religionsgeschichte'. For specific 'rain poems' in honour of Muhammad (Shāh 'Abdul Laṭīf, Muḥsin Kākōrawī, et al.), see Schimmel (1988), *And Muhammad is His Messenger*, p. 81ff.
20. Paul Nwyia (1970), *Exégèse coranique*, p. 330.
21. Thus Khājū-i Kirmānī, in Dawlatshāh (no date), *Tadhkirat ash-shu'arā*, p. 250.
22. Khāqānī (1959), *Dīvān*, pp. 358–60 (the *Madā'in qaṣīda*).
23. Iqbāl (1923), *Payām-i mashriq*, pp. 151–2; idem (1932), *Jāvīdnāma*, 'Sphere of Mercury', p. 66.
24. *Qāḍī Qādan jō kalām* (1978), no. 37.
25. Thus Shāh 'Abdul Laṭīf (1958), *Risālō*, 'Sur Ripa II', verses 13–15; see also A. Schimmel (1976a), *Pain and Grace*, p. 171.
26. The topos of the 'iron in fire' appears among the Sufis not only in Rūmī's *Mathnawī* (II 1,347ff.) but also among the Nūrbakhshīs and in Dārā Shikōh's discussions with Bābā Lāl Dās: see Massignon and Huart (1926), 'Les entretiens de Lahore', p. 325. For its use in the Christian tradition (Origen, Symeon the New Theologian, Richard of St Victor, Jacob Boehme), see E. Underhill (1911), *Mysticism*, p. 549ff.; also A. Schimmel (1978c), *The Triumphal Sun*, p. 464 note 181.
27. For the theme, see A. Schimmel (1978a), *A Dance of Sparks*.
28. T. Izutsu (1971b), 'The paradox of light and darkness in the Garden of Mystery of Shabastari'; see also M. Mokri (1982), *La lumière et le feu dans l'Iran ancien ... et leur démythification en Islam.*
29. The mythological elements in the concept of the Light of Muhammad go back, to a large extent, to Sahl at-Tustarī; see G. Böwering (1979), *The Mystical Vision of Existence in Classical Islam: The Qur'anic Hermeneutics of the Sufi Sahl at-Tustarī* (d. 283/896). For its reception in Bengal, for example, see Asim Roy (1983), *The Islamic Syncretistic Tradition in Bengal*; he, however, ascribes this and other phenomena to Hindu influences. A beautiful description of the Prophet's light is the proem in 'Aṭṭār (1962), *Manṭiq uṭ-ṭayr.*
30. For Suhrawardī *shaykh al-ishrāq*, see Suhrawardī (1945), *Opera metaphysica et mystica*, ed. by H. Corbin; idem (1970), *Oeuvres en Persan.*
31. Iqbāl (1930), *The Reconstruction of Religious Thought in Islam*, p. 64; for a related idea in the mystical theories of Mīr Dard, see A. Schimmel (1963a), *Gabriel's Wing*, p. 100.
32. Translated in Wheeler M. Thackston (1982), *The Mystical and Visionary Treatises of Suhrawardī.*
33. Sanā'ī (1962), *Dīvān*, p. 34ff. For the use of the sun-metaphor in Rūmī's work, see A. Schimmel (1978c), *The Triumphal Sun*, ch. II, 1, pp. 61–75.
34. Y. Friedmann (1975), 'Qiṣṣa Shakarwarti Farmāḍ'.
35. Iqbāl (1915), *Asrār-i khudī*, line 450.
36. The best survey is Fritz Meier's introduction to his (1956) edition of Najmuddīn Kubrā's *Fawā'iḥ al-jamāl*, in which the role of the colours in ecstatic experiences is analyzed in detail. Based on the statements of Kubrā and his disciples, notably Simnānī, H. Corbin (1971) discusses the theme in *L'homme de lumière*. See

also Corbin (1972), 'Réalisme et symbolisme des couleurs en cosmologie Shiite', English translation (1986) in *Temple and Contemplation.* For philological approaches, see W. Fischer (1965), *Farb- und Formbezeichnungen in der Sprache der arabischen Dichtung*; H. Gätje (1967), 'Zur Farbenlehre in der muslimischen Philosophie'; Toufic Fahd (1974), 'Génèse et causes des couleurs d'après l'Agriculture Nabatéenne'.

37. For the combination of yellow, autumn and Jewish garments, see Mas'ūd ibn Sa'd-i Salmān (1960), *Dīvān*, p. 471, and Khāqānī (1959), *Dīvān*, pp. 133, 428.
38. Bakharzī (1966), *Awrād al-aḥbāb*, vol. 2, discusses this problem, especially on p. 34ff.; he thinks that the dervish's cloak should reflect the person's state of mind. See also Fazlur Rahman (1966), *Islam*, p. 160.
39. For an extensive treatment of vegetable and animal symbols, see A. Schimmel (1992b), *A Two-colored Brocade*, chs 11–14, and idem (1978c), *The Triumphal Sun*, chs II, 3 and 4, pp. 75–123. For practical aspects, see G.-H. Bousquet (1949), 'Des animaux et de leur traitement selon le Judaïsme, le Christianisme et l'Islam'.
40. About trees for 'Abdul Qādir, see R. Burton (1851), *Sindh*, p. 177; W. Blackman (1925), 'Sacred trees in modern Egypt'; and numerous references in Kriss and Kriss-Heinrich (1960), *Volksglaube im Islam*, vol. 1. For the artistic aspect, see Gönül Öney (1968), 'Das Lebensbaum-Motiv in der seldschukischen Kunst in Anatolien'.
41. Al-Ghazzālī (1872), *Iḥyā' 'ulūm ad-dīn*, Book IV, p. 282, sees Love as the 'good tree' mentioned in Sūra 14:24. For further mystical interpretations, see A. Jeffery (1979), *Ibn al-'Arabi's* shajarat al-kawn. A fine example of the 'Muhammadan Tree', whose leaves are covered with the ninety-nine noble names of the Prophet, is a Turkish miniature in the Berlin Staatsbibliothek, used as the cover for A. Schimmel (1988), *And Muhammad is His Messenger.*
42. F. Taeschner (1979), *Zünfte und Bruderschaften in Islam*, p. 364.
43. Nāṣir-i Khusraw (1929), *Dīvān*, in idem (1993) tr. A. Schimmel, *Make a Shield from Wisdom*, p. 71ff.
44. S. Murata (1992b), *The Tao of Islam*, p. 103: Ṣadruddin Qūnāvī speaks of the tree, rooted in the Divine Existence, whose branches are the Divine Names.
45. *Qāḍī Qādan jō kalām* (1978), no. 56; Sultan Bahoo (1967), *Abyāt*, no. 1; cf. also Mas'ūd Bakk's *ghazal* in Ikrām (1953), *Armaghān-i Pāk*, p. 150.
46. Taeschner (1979), *Zünfte*, p. 528.
47. Schimmel (1976c), 'The Celestial Garden in Islam'.
48. Sam'ānī, *Rawḥ al-arwāḥ*, quoted in Murata (1992b), *The Tao of Islam*, p. 71.
49. Nāṣir-i Khusraw (1929), *Dīvān*, pp. 472–3, dramatically describes how the garden of the world (or of religion) is slowly destroyed by a pig that first posed as a sheep.
50. Rūzbihān Baqlī (1966), *Sharḥ-i shaṭḥiyāt*, § 265.
51. Irène Mélikoff (1967), 'La fleur de la souffrance. Recherches sur le sens symbolique de *lâla* dans la poésie mystique turco-iranienne'. Professor Karl Jettmar mentions (Akademie-Journal 1, 1992, p. 28) that, during the Bronze Age, people in northern Afghanistan used to celebrate a tulip festival; in the same area, a tulip festival connected with 'Alī ibn Abī Ṭālib was celebrated until recently.
52. Dawlatshāh (no date), *Tadhkirat ash-shu'arā*, p. 224.
53. U. Topper (1991), *Sufis und Heilige im Maghreb*, p. 167.
54. R. Brunel (1955), *Le monachisme errant dans l'Islam: Sidi Heddi et les Heddawa.*
55. Pigs in connection with the Resurrection appear in Rūmī, *Mathnawī* II, 1,413; in connection with Jerusalem in *Dīvān-i kabīr*, lines 3,882, 7,227, 12,883. Khāqānī (1959), *Dīvān*, *qaṣīda* no. 1, also uses this motif, and combines such pigs with the elephants which were used to besiege Mecca in 570.

56. See Schimmel (1988), *And Muhammad is His Messenger*, pp. 102–3; the Sindhi ballad in N. A. Baloch (ed.) (1960), *Munāqiba*, pp. 196–8; *Yunus Emre Divanī* (1943), p. 542, no. CLXXV. About ʿAli's connection with the bees, see R. Paret (1930), *Die legendäre Maghazi-Literatur*, p. 196ff.
57. Al-Ḥallāj (1913), *Kitāb aṭ-ṭawāsīn*, ed. L. Massignon: '*Ṭāsīn al-fahm*'. For the transformation of Ḥallāj's story into Goethe's poem 'Selige Sehnsucht' in the *West–Östlicher Divan* see H. H. Schaeder (1942), 'Die persische Vorlage für Goethes "Selige Sehnsucht"'.
58. Related by Badaoni (1864–9), *Muntakhab at-tawārīkh*, vol. 2, p. 221 (English translation (1972), vol. 2, p. 215).
59. A. Schimmel (1985), *Die orientalische Katze*.
60. E. M. Lane (1836), *Manners and Customs*, p. 434.
61. J. Nurbakhsh (1989), *Dogs. From a Sufi Point of View*.
62. Rūmī's language becomes extremely coarse when he juxtaposes Jesus, the spiritual part of man, and the donkey, the material part. See Schimmel (1978c), *The Triumphal Sun*, index s.v. 'donkey'.
63. Schimmel (1972), 'Nur ein störrisches Pferd ...'. For Khāqānī, 'religion' is 'a steed of Arab birth', which should not be disgraced by putting a saddle of Greek philosophy on its back. Interestingly, Iqbāl used this verse in his last political letter a few weeks before he died (1948, *Speeches and Statements*, p. 169).
64. See R. A. Bravmann (1983), *African Islam*, ch. V on the use of the Burāq motif among African Muslims.
65. For the serpent as a *nafs*-symbol, see Schimmel (1975a), *Mystical Dimensions of Islam*, p. 113.
66. I. Goldziher (1903), 'Der Seelenvogel im islamischen Volksglauben'.
67. Hence the title of Ibn Ḥazm's famous book on courtly love, *Ṭawq al-ḥamāma* (1914 etc.), 'The Dove's Necklace', which has been translated into numerous Western languages.
68. A *ḥadīth* says: 'Don't curse the rooster, for he wakes you up for prayer' (*AM* no. 261). See also F. Meier (1977), 'Niẓāmī und die Mythologie des Hahnes'.
69. A typical example is Ziā'uddīn Nakhshabī's *Ṭuṭīnāma*: see Muhammad S. Simsar (1978), *The Cleveland Museum of Art's* Ṭūṭīnāme*: Tales of a Parrot.*
70. ʿAṭṭār's *Manṭiq ut-ṭayr* (1962) is rightly the best-known example of the 'soul birds'; see also Carl W. Ernst (1992b), 'The symbolism of birds and flight in the writings of Rūzbihān Baqlī'.
71. Nāṣir-i Khusraw expresses the view that the raven wears black, the colour of the Abbasids, who treacherously deprived Fāṭima's children of the caliphate; *Dīvān* in (1993) tr. Schimmel, *Make a Shield from Wisdom*, pp. 18, 66, 67.
72. See S. Murata (1992b), *The Tao of Islam*, p. 258 about Ghazzālī's views, p. 278 in a general context. The Persian poet Anvarī (d. after 1190) expressed the canine qualities of the lower soul in a fine *ghazal*: see A. Schimmel and Stuart Cary Welch (1983), *A Pocket Book for Akbar: Anvarī's* Dīvān, p. 61.
73. The most famous representation of the 'peaceful kingdom' is the Mughal miniature of Emperor Jahāngīr and Shah ʿAbbās of Iran standing on a lion and a lamb respectively (a picture which also points to the fact that Jahāngīr was a descendant of Bābur, 'Tiger', while Shāh ʿAbbās belonged to the Turcomans of the White Sheep, Aqqoyunlu. See, for example, S. C. Welch (1979a), *Imperial Mughal Painting*, p. 121. An example of an early poetical expression of this wonderful time is ʿAbdul Wāsiʿ-i Jabalī's poem, in Dawlatshāh (no date), *Tadhkirat ash-shuʿarā*, p. 84.
74. For the preacher's rod, see C. H. Becker (1924), *Islamstudien*, vol. 1, p. 451f.
75. Sultan Khushqadam's wife was buried under the red flag of Badawī dervishes

in 1467; see Ibn Taghrībirdī (1928), *An-nujūm az-zāhira fī ta'rīkh Miṣr wa'l-Qāhira*, vol. 7, p. 809.

76. Ghālib called the second edition of his book *Qāṭi'-i Burhān*, 'Dirafsh-i kāviyānī' (Delhi 1865); in this work, he harshly criticized the Persian lexicographical work *Burhān-i qāṭi'*. S. Ghālib (1969a), *Kulliyāt-i fārsī* (17 vols).
77. G. Schoeler (1974), *Arabische Naturdichtung ... von den Anfängen bis aṣ-Ṣanaubarī*, gives a number of examples of this comparison.
78. For a general overview, see A. E. Crawley (1908), 'Mirror', in *ERE*, vol. 8; T. Burckhardt (1974), 'The symbolism of the Mirror'.
79. Rashīd Burhānpūrī (1957), *Burhānpūr kē Sindhī Auliyā*, transl. in A. Schimmel (1986), *Liebe zu dem Einen*, pp. 95–6.
80. Thus in *Mathnawī* I, 3,200ff.; *Dīvān*, lines 15,880 and 17,950, as well as in *Fīhi mā fīhi*, ch. 59.
81. The classic work on mirror symbolism is Aḥmad Ghazzālī (1942), *Sawāniḥ*, available in several translations. J. C. Bürgel (1988), *The Feather of Simurgh*, deals with 'The Magic Mirror' in ch. 6. The idea of the heart as a pure mirror for the Divine Beloved is alluded to in Bāyazīd Bisṭāmī's remark that he was the blacksmith of himself until he had made his self into a pure mirror ('Aṭṭār (1905), *Tadhkirat al-awliyā*, vol. 1, p. 139). One may also see under the aspect of the 'mirror' the famous story of the contest between the Greek and the Chinese painters which, via Niẓāmī's *Iskandarnāma*, received its perfect form in Rūmī's *Mathnawī*, I, 3,467ff.: the Greek artists polished the marble wall so perfectly that it reflected the colourful paintings produced by the Chinese in ever greater beauty.
82. Bakharzī (1966), *Awrād al-aḥbāb*, vol. 2, p. 246 explains the use of *but* as 'The gnostics call '*but*' everything your heart wants to see and possess, positive and negative alike'. The whole question of 'idols' and 'idol worship' forms an important part of H. Ritter (1955), *Das Meer der Seele*.
83. Jafar Sharif (1921), *Islam in India*, p. 21.
84. For the whole subject, see Sir Thomas Arnold (1928), *Painting in Islam*; also M. Ipşiroğlu (1971), *Das Bild im Islam. Ein Verbot und seine Folgen.*
85. Jāmī (1962), *Dīvān-i kāmil*, p. 265, no. 345.
86. This happened, for example, in Pakistan, to Emel Esin's (1963) work *Mecca the Blessed, Medina the Radiant*, an account of the pilgrimage written by a deeply religious Turkish Muslim lady who, to the dismay of the 'fundamentalists', published some fourteenth- and fifteenth-century Turkish miniatures on which the Prophet is represented with an unveiled face.
87. Every work on Islamic manuscripts contains angel pictures, beginning with the pictures of the archangels in medieval and post-medieval manuscripts of Qazwīnī's *'Ajā'ib al-makhlūqāt*. For an amazing proliferation of angel representations, see Ebba Koch (1983), 'Jahangir and the angels'.
88. Among the Sufis, especially in Turkey, representation, often by means of caligrams, is not unknown: see M. Aksel (1967), *Türklerde Dini Resimler*, and Fred de Jong (1989), *The Iconography of Bektashiism*. In recent decades, truck-painting has developed into a whole new branch of art; see Jürgen Grothues (1990), *Automobile Kunst in Pakistan.*
89. Translated into German by A. Schimmel, 'Geschwärzten Gesichts', in Rolf Italiaander (ed.) (1972), *Aus der Palmweimschenke.*
90. For the *mindīl* or *mandīl*, see F. Rosenthal (1971), *Four Essays on Art and Literature in Islam*, ch. IV.
91. H. Klopfer (1989), *Das Traumbuch des Ibn Sīrīn*, p. 84. Sanā'ī (1950), *Ḥadīqat al-ḥaqīqat*, pp. 122–3, gives different interpretations of garments and colours that one sees in one's dreams.

92. R. Paret (1928), 'Die Legende von der Verleihung des Prophetenmantels (*burda*) an Ka'b ibn Zuhair'.
93. The classic edition is Būṣīrī (1860), *Die Burda*, ed. and transl. by C. A. Ralfs. About the poem and its use, see A. Schimmel (1988), *And Muhammad is His Messenger*, pp. 180–7.
94. Iqbāl (1933), *Musāfir*, p. 29ff.
95. M. Mujeeb (1972), *Islamic Influences on Indian Society*, p. 11.
96. C. H. Becker (1932), *Islamstudien*, vol. 1, p. 379.
97. J. van Ess (1979), *Der* Ṭaylasān *des Ibn Ḥarb*, deals with poems written about this headgear.
98. A number of articles try to explain the meaning of the Sufi frock with rather fanciful interpretations, thus S. Mahdihasan (1960), 'The garb of the Sufi and its significance', and Muhammad Reza Shafii Kadkani (1989), 'Anmerkungen zum Flickenrock der Sufis'. Every handbook on Sufism in Arabic and Persian deals with this topic more or less extensively: see, for example, the chapter in Hujwīrī (1911) *Kashf al-maḥjūb*, pp. 45–57.
99. R. Gramlich (1981), *Die schiitischen Derwischorden*, vol. 3, pp. 4, 5, 84, 86.
100. S. Murata (1992), *The Tao of Islam*, p. 149: 'religion as a shirt'.
101. For the topic of spinning songs, see R. Eaton (1978), *Sufis of Bijapur, 1300–1700*, pp. 155–64. A fine example of a mystical spinning song in Sindhi is Shāh 'Abdul Laṭīf (1958), *Risālō*, 'Sur Kapā'itī'.
102. R. Gramlich (1976), *Die schiitischen Derwischorden*, vol. 2, p. 53, speaks of the *libās-i adamiyat*, 'the garment of humanity', as one of the stages through which the spirit has to pass; such ideas may have led the Kurdish Ahl-i Ḥaqq to the belief that the soul dons 1,001 corporeal habits and then no longer appears in human guise. See H. R. Norris (1992), 'The Ḥurūfī legacy of Faḍlullah of Astarabad', p. 94.

II

Sacred Space and Time

ان في خلق السموات والارض واختلاف الليل والنهار لايات لاولي الالباب

See, in the creation of the heavens and the earth and the alternation of day and night there are signs for those with insight.

Sūra 3:190

SACRED SPACE

'The Muslim lives in a space defined by the sound of the Koran.' Thus writes S. H. Nasr to point to the situation of the Muslim believer.[1] He is certainly right, and yet Islamic tradition has known and still knows, as do all religions, a good number of places which are or seem to be endowed with special blessing power and which then serve in literature as symbols of the human experience of 'coming home'.

Thinking of places with such sacred power, one can begin with the cave. Humankind has been fascinated by caves for millennia, as prehistory and history prove, and Islam continued in this respect, though from a somewhat different vantage point. Is not the cave singled out by the very name of Sūra 18, *al-Kahf*, 'The Cave', a Sūra in which – along with other stories – the Seven Sleepers, the *aṣḥāb al-kahf*, are mentioned at some length? The seven pious youths 'and the eighth with them was their dog' (Sūra 18:22) have turned in popular Islam into protective spirits whose names, and especially that of their dog Qiṭmīr, written on amulets, carry *baraka* with them.[2]

In the historical context, it is well known that the Prophet Muhammad received his initial revelation in a cave on Mt Hira where he used to retire for meditation. It was in the solitude of this place that he was blessed with the first auditions which forced him to go into the world and preach what he had learned: the constant change between the *khalwa*, the lonely place of meditation in the dark cave, undisturbed in his concentration upon God, and the *jilwa*, the need and duty to promulgate the Divine word that he had heard, was to remain the model for the Muslims – a spiritual movement of whose necessity Iqbāl reminds the believers of our time.

Yet, there is a second cave in the Prophet's biography: the cave where he found shelter during his hegira from Mecca to Medina. And again, after re-emerging from the mysteriously protected place where he, as Sufi tradition has it, introduced his friend Abū Bakr into the mysteries of the silent *dhikr*, his life as a political leader in Medina began: once more, he undertook the way out of the *khalwa* of meditation into the *jilwa* of preaching and acting.

The Prophet's example of retiring into the cave was imitated by a number of mystics who lived for long periods in caves. The extremely narrow cave in which Sharafuddīn Manērī of Bihar (d. 1381) spent several decades of his life is only one of the numerous examples of this pious custom; Muhammad Ghawth Gwaliorī (d. 1562) also belongs to the Sufis who, year after year, performed their meditation in a cave, to emerge in the end filled with overwhelming spiritual energy. The experience of the *arbaʿīn, chilla, khalwat,* forty days' meditation in a narrow, dark room or a subterranean place, belongs here as well. The intimacy of the experience of God's proximity in such a *khalwa* could lead the pious to address Him in prayer as 'Oh Cave of them that seek refuge!'[3]

The cave is difficult to reach for men and animals, and is hence safe. But when one lives on the plains, the sacred space has to be separated from the profane environment by an enclosure (one remembers here that the Latin term *sanctus* is derived from *sancīre*, 'to limit, enclose', and hence 'make sacred'), and so the cult takes place in a spot removed from the ordinary space, which keeps away not only animals but also, as was thought, demons. Lonely prayer places in Sind and Balochistan are surrounded by simple thorn hedges (as are some shrines in the desert),[4] and it is probably not too far-fetched to think that the border of the prayer rug also serves as a kind of enclosure which marks the praying person's inviolable 'sanctuary' – even though the whole world can serve as a prayer place.

More important is the house, the man-made dwelling-place which serves both for protection and as a sanctuary: in Sind and Balochistan, the house of the *wadērō*, the big landlord, could serve as a shelter for women accused of immorality or other transgressions.[5] However, the concept of 'house' has a much wider range: the 'House of Islam', *dār al-islām,* is the area which, as Walter Braune says aptly, is built on five pillars and in which the believers live in safety, while the *dār al-ḥarb*, 'the abode of war', is the world outside the ideal home of the believers.[6] To enlarge this 'house' is incumbent upon the community, so that finally the whole world may become a 'House of Islam'.

And not only that. In religious language, the house is one of the most frequently-used metaphors for the human heart – a house that has to be cleansed by constantly using the 'broom of *lā*', that is, the beginning of the profession of faith, *lā ilāha illā Allāh,* 'There is no deity but God'. Only when the house is clean and no dust of profane thought has remained can the *dulcis hospis animae,* the 'sweet guest of the soul', enter and dwell in it. The Baghdadian Sufi an-Nūrī (d. 907) used this metaphor,[7] and Mawlānā Rūmī sang in one of his most famous stories in the *Mathnawī* (M I 3,056–63):

> A man knocked at the door of his beloved.
> 'Who are you, trusted one?' thus asked the friend.
> He answered: 'I!' The friend said: 'Go away –
> Here is no place for people raw and crude!'
> What, then, could cook the raw and rescue him
> But separation's fire and exile's flame?
> The poor man went to travel a whole year
> And burnt in separation from his friend.

And he matured, was cooked and burnt, returned
And carefully approached the friend's abode.
He walked around it now in cautious fear,
Lest from his lips unfitting words appear.
The friend called out: 'Who is there at my door?'
The answer: 'You – you dear are at the door!'
He said: 'Come in, now that you are all I –
There is no room in this house for two 'I's!'

In order to enter the precincts of the house, one has to cross the threshold, the liminal place par excellence that cuts off the sacred from the profane. It is therefore a rule that one must not step on the threshold: as the bride in Muslim India is carried over it into her new home, the devotee is warned not to step on the threshold of the master's house or the shrine. To enhance the religio–magic power of the threshold, one may sacrifice a sheep over it or at least sprinkle some blood on it.[8]

While Muslims carefully avoid touching the threshold with their feet, which are sullied by the dust of the profane world, one often sees men and women at shrines devoutly kissing the step that will lead them into the sacred presence of the saint. 'One should rub one's face on the threshold like a broom', says a Turkish handbook of religious etiquette.[9] The threshold's sanctity is also attested by dream exegesis: threshold and door mean, in the dream, women, i.e. the sacred, *ḥarīm*, part of the house.[10]

Since the door or gate allows the visitor to enter the private, 'sacred' sphere, gates of mosques and shrines are often huge and impressively decorated. Alternatively, shrines may have an extremely low door which forces the entering person to bow down humbly; again, there are narrow doors through which the visitor squeezes himself in the hope of obtaining blessings. A typical example is the *bihishtī darwāẓa*, the 'paradisiacal door' in Farīduddīn Ganj-i shakar's shrine in Pakpattan, where, during the anniversary of his death, thousands of pilgrims strive to enter into the saint's presence in order to secure entrance to Paradise.

The door opens into the sacred space, and the Muslim knows that 'God is the Opener of the doors', *mufattiḥ al-abwāb*, as He is called in a favourite invocation, for it is He who can open the doors of His mercy or generosity, not forgetting the gates of Paradise.[11] In later Sufism, the seven principal Divine Names are even called *hadana*, 'doorkeepers'. Metaphorically, the concept of the door or gate is important by its use in the well-known *ḥadīth* deeply loved especially in Shia tradition, in which the Prophet states: 'I am the city of wisdom and ʿAlī is its gate' (*AM* no. 90), that is, only through ʿAlī's mediation can one understand the Prophet's true teaching. As the gate, *bāb*, can be the person through whom the believer may be led into the Divine presence, it is logical that the spiritual guide could also be considered, or consider himself, to be The Gate, the *Bāb*. This claim was voiced most prominently by Mirzā Muḥammad ʿAlī of Tabriz, which led to the emergence of a new religious movement, Babism, in early nineteenth-century Iran.

After entering the house, one finds the high seat, *ṣadr*, or the throne, *sarīr*, both of which possess special *baraka*; and anyone who has seen an old Pakistani woman throning on her bed and ruling the large household knows that this is more than simply an elevated place: the seat carries authority with it. But those lowest in rank, or most modest, will sit in the 'place of the sandals', that is, where the shoes are left close to the entrance.

In the Arabic tradition, the hearth plays no major role, while among the Turks the fireplace, *ocak*, as is typical of peoples from northern climates, was the veritable centre of the house, and the term *ocak* is used in modern Turkey to denote the true centre of the community.

The Muslim house boasts carpets and rugs, pile-woven or flat-woven, and the rug can be as important as the high seat, the place for the master of the house. The title *sajjāda nishīn* or *pōst nishīn* for the person who 'sits on the mat' of a Sufi master, i.e. his true successor, conveys an impression of the rug's importance. The numerous flying carpets in Oriental folk tales seem to translate the subconscious feeling that the carpet is something very special.

There is also a place with negative power in or close to the house: the privy, which is regarded as a dwelling-place of unclean and dangerous spirits and is therefore avoided by angels. The bath itself, however, sometimes decorated with paintings plays an important role in connection with the strict rules of ritual purity.[12]

Larger and higher than the normal house is the citadel or fortress, ideally built in a circular shape. If the heart can be imagined as a house for the Divine Beloved, it can also be seen as a fortress with several ramparts – again one of Nūrī's images, which prefigures St Teresa's Interior Castle.[13] For the Sufis, the *shahāda* became the stronghold and citadel in which they felt safe from the temptations of the world, as though the rampart and moats of sacred words helped them to survive in the inner chamber, which could be compared to the *h*, the last letter of the word *Allāh*.[14] Is not God a fortress, *ḥiṣn*, and a stronghold, *ḥirz*?[15] The word *ḥirz* is also used as a name of one type of protective prayers and litanies, while the term *taḥṣīn*, literally 'to make into a fortress', can be used for the religio–magic circumambulation of villages or groups of people to protect themselves against enemies.

The sacred space par excellence in Islam seems to be the mosque, and many visitors – Rudolf Otto, S. H. Nasr, Martin Lings, Frithjof Schuon and others – have emphasized the 'feeling of the Numinous', the experience of otherworldliness when standing in one of the great mosques in North Africa or

Turkey.[16] These buildings were, as they felt, perfect expressions of the emptiness which is waiting to be filled with Divine blessing, that is the experience of the human being, poor (*faqīr*) as he or she is, in the presence of the All-Rich, *al-ghaniy*.

However, the mosque was first no more than a house, a building in which instruction and legal business were conducted as well: it was and is not – unlike the church – a consecrated building. Its name, *masjid*, is derived from *sajada*, 'to prostrate', meaning 'place of prostration'. A mosque for larger groups, where believers could gather on Friday for the midday prayer with following sermon, is called *jāmiʿ*, 'the collecting one'. In the early Middle Ages, up to around AD 900, only one *jāmiʿ* was found in each city; the *minbar*, the pulpit from which the preacher gives his short sermon, was the distinctive mark of a city, as was the minaret. In later times, when mosques proliferated, a certain distance was still kept between the major mosques, or a new *jāmiʿ* was built only when the first one, too small for the growing number of the faithful, could not possibly be enlarged.

To build a mosque is a highly meritorious act, and a tradition which is frequently quoted in India (especially in Bengal) states: 'Who builds a mosque for God, be it as small as the nest of a *qaṭā* bird, for him God will build a house in Paradise'.[17] The paradisiacal recompense can also be granted to someone else: when the Ottoman Sultan Mehmet the Conqueror (1449–81) erected a mosque in the recently conquered city of Istanbul in remembrance of his father, the intention was the same as offering prayers for the well-being of the deceased monarch's soul.[18] Popular piety therefore claims that a mosque is like a boat of salvation or, even more fancifully, that it will be transformed into a white camel to carry its founder on Doomsday across the *ṣirāṭ*-bridge.[19]

The increasing feeling of the sanctity of the mosque is understood from the custom of using its precincts for *istikhāra*, that is, performing two prayer cycles and then sleeping in the mosque in the hope of being guided by a dream. And Turkish calligraphers would collect the soot produced by the oil lamps in, for example, the Süleymaniye mosque in Istanbul to use it as an ingredient of their ink which, they felt, would thus carry some of the mosque's *baraka* with it.

The shapes of mosques vary according to the architectural styles of the different countries, and from simple mud mosques in Africa to pagoda-like structures in China almost every form is found. Mosques in Gujarat, with their narrow rows of highly decorated pillars, resemble Hindu temples, and for the Western observer the Turkish mosque with its central dome and the elegant needle-like minarets seems to be the paragon of the concept of 'mosque', although large mosques with wide prayer halls or endless rows of naves belong to a much earlier, classical period (Samarra, Cordoba).

But whatever the outward shape, every mosque has a *miḥrāb*, a niche pointing to the direction of Mecca, which could be shaped, again, according to the material available and to the artistic taste of the builder. Often, words from Sūra 3:37 are written around the *miḥrāb*: 'Whenever Zakariya entered the *miḥrāb* ...', for the term is used for the place where the young Mary dwelt and was mysteriously nourished by the Lord. What appear to be the most unusual and impressive *miḥrābs* in the world of Islam are located in the Indian subcontinent: the *miḥrāb* of the Great Mosque in Bijapur/Deccan, built in 1635 and measuring six to seven metres across, is completely decorated in a highly sophisticated style with à-jour inscriptions, half-relief, and colourful niches in gold and red. The Faisal Mosque in Islamabad, completed some 350 years later, boasts as its *miḥrāb* the likeness of an opened copy of the Koran in white marble, inscribed in 'medieval' Kufi calligraphy with verses from Sūra 55, *Ar-Raḥmān*, 'The Merciful'.

While the *miḥrāb* is common to *masjid* and *jāmiʿs*, the *jāmiʿ* alone contains an elevated pulpit for the Friday sermon, usually three steps high; larger odd numbers of steps can be found in vast buildings. This *minbar*, again, can consist of the most diverse materials; the artistically carved wooden *minbars* of medieval Egypt and Anatolia are worthy of mention. The preacher, who stands on the *minbar*, briefly sits down between the two parts of his address in memory of the Prophet's sitting on the first *minbar*, a simple platform.[20]

One may find a few huge candlestands, and the floor is usually covered with prayer rugs. A stand for the Koran and sometimes boxes in thirty parts for the thirty *juz'* of the Koran belong to the necessary items in the mosque; a clock that shows the times of prayer is a more recent addition. The walls are plain, for too much colour or decoration might distract the praying person's eye and mind. They are covered with tiles (as in Iran and Turkey) or with white marble; if there is any decoration, then it is only calligraphy, whether Koranic verses or the name of God in enormous letters, or sometimes also the names of the four rightly guided caliphs (as in the Aya Sofya in Istanbul).

The minaret, again connected only with the *jāmiʿ*, and built in diverse shapes according to local traditions, was sometimes conceived of as a tower of victory, the visible sign of Islam's presence in a newly conquered area: the Qutub Minar in Delhi from the early thirteenth century is a good example of this type of minaret. For those who loved esoteric meaning, it was not difficult to connect it, owing to its shape, with the letter *alif* that is always taken to symbolize the *Aḥad*, the One God. And was not the building of a mosque in a newly acquired territory, as it were, a new 'brick' in the extension of the House of Islam?

In some mosques, a special corner is reserved for women; in others (often in Turkey), women are expected to pray on the balcony-like gallery. In state capitals, one may find a *maqṣūra*, a special enclosure for the rulers.

Another sacred place of major importance is the burial place of a saintly person. The Prophet himself, according to one tradition, prohibited visits to tombs, while according to another he suggested turning to 'the people of the graves' when facing difficulties.[21] Visits to tombs and cemeteries became a common practice and offered rare opportunities for an outing to many women. The Prophet's warning against frequenting the tombs was reinforced in the nineteenth century by the Wahhabis in Central Arabia, who did not even honour the sanctity of the Prophet's own mausoleum.

Among the places with special *baraka* are, understandably, the tombs of the martyrs of faith such as Kerbela, Najaf and Mashhad. Kerbela, where the Prophet's grandson Ḥusayn ibn 'Alī fell in fighting against the Omayyad forces in 680, is in the Shia world coterminous with 'utter tragedy', and its name was explained as a combination of *karb* and *balā*, 'grief and affliction'. The earth of Kerbela, with its strong *baraka*, is still 'exported' to other countries (see above, p. 5). When Muḥarram is celebrated in Shia cities, especially in India, a place called 'Kerbela' is chosen close to a tank or a river; there the *tābūts*, replicas of Ḥusayn's sarcophagus, are submerged at the end of the ritual. To make people partake in the *baraka* of the sacred places, one can even call children after them: Najaf or Nazaf Khan, and Madīnakhan, appear in the Indian subcontinent.

A mausoleum often develops from a simple heap of stones, and even a great Sufi like Gēsūdarāz (d. 1422) tells, tongue in cheek, the story of the travellers whose dog died on the road and was buried. They marked the faithful creature's tomb, and when they returned to the same place after some years, they found that a flourishing town had developed around the 'saint's' burial place.[22] Even more obscene anecdotes about the growth of a pilgrimage centre are not uncommon in Muslim literature.

The tombs of saints are highly venerated.[23] People will throng at the tomb's doors or windows to make vows; they hang rags on nearby trees or on the window grill, or post petitions on the wall hoping for the saint's intercession, and as the saint's *baraka* increases after he has left this world, people want to be buried near to him: that is how the enormous cemeteries in the Islamic world came into existence. The cemetery of Makli Hill near Thatta in Sind is credited with the presence of 125,000 saints; the Qarāfa in Cairo allows a survey of hundreds of years of Muslim cultural history in Egypt, and, during a walk through the hilly cemetery of Khuldābād, 'Abode of Eternity' near Daulatabad in the northern Deccan, one gains a comprehensive survey of the entire history of the Deccan from the fourteenth to the nineteenth centuries, for poets, emperors, scholars and politicians rest peacefully in this lovely place.[24]

Rulers erected their mausoleums usually during their lifetime and surrounded their future burial site with charitable foundations to ensure benefits for their souls. When the last Mamluk sultan Qanṣauh al-Ghawrī's dead body was never found on the battlefield of Marj Dabiq in August 1516, the historian Ibn Iyās attributed this strange event to the fact that the ruler had illegally appropriated the marble of someone else's mausoleum and used it to embellish his own mausoleum 'and God did not allow him to be buried in it, and therein is a sign for those who have eyes to see'.[25] Often, the mausoleums of rulers were surrounded by vast gardens, sometimes divided by canals so as to resemble the gardens of Paradise 'under which rivers flow' and to give the deceased, as it were, a foretaste of heavenly bliss.

In cases when a famous person's burial place is unknown, or when Muslims want to gain some of his *baraka* in their own village or town, they erect a *maqām*, a memorial. In the Fertile Crescent, one finds a number of *maqāms* in places where ʿAlī's camel allegedly stopped.[26] But more prominent are the *maqāms* of saints, for example, places devoted to the memory of Bāyezīd Bisṭāmī, who died in 874 in northern Iran but is venerated in Zousfana in the High Atlas as well as in Chittagong in Bangladesh (and probably in other places as well). The Turkish bard Yunus Emre (d. 1321) has *maqāms* in at least seven Anatolian towns, and the city of Mazar-i Sharif in Afghanistan grew around an alleged tomb of ʿAlī. The most recent example of a '*maqām*' is that of Muḥammad Iqbāl (buried in Lahore) in the garden near Mawlānā Rūmī's mausoleum in Konya, erected by the Turks, to underline the spiritual connection between the two religious poets.

Often, the actual mausoleum of a saintly person is connected with the *dargāh*, the seat of the mystical guide who continues the saint's work. To stay for a few days at a *dargāh*, as a waiter or servant, can make the visitor a special recipient of Divine grace, and many people avail themselves as much of the living *baraka* of the 'master of the prayer rug' or his assistants as of the healing power of a tank or well close to the shrine. The shrine serves as a sanctuary, and people may swear innocence before it; some regular visitors may even be able to 'see' the saint.[27]

The master who resides in the *dargāh* has a spiritual territory, *wilāyat*, and it was customary that he would assign to his *khalīfa*, substitute or vicegerent, a certain area over which his influence would extent; the borders of the spiritual territories of two *khalīfas*, or, more complicated, of *khalīfas* of two different masters were strictly defined and had by no means to be transgressed. The protecting power of the saint was thought to work only inside his territory.[28]

Shrines and *dargāhs* were and still are usually open to non-Muslims; in some of them, women are not admitted inside (similarly, men are excluded from women saints' shrines). As humans have apparently always prayed at the same places, there is a certain continuity in the use of such places, as if a special *baraka* were inherent in this or that spot. That is well known in the Jewish–Christian–Muslim sequence in Near Eastern sanctuaries, and holds true in many cases also for Indian Muslim and formerly Hindu places of worship. Therefore, the borders between religions often seem blurred in the *dargāhs* and shrines – certainly one of the valid reasons for the aversion of traditionalist orthodox Muslims to saint-worship. It has been rightly stated for India that 'While the mosque distinguishes and separates Muslims and Hindu, the *dargāh* tends to bring them together'.[29]

Other sacred places in the Islamic world are, for example, the Ismaili *Jamaatkhana*, to which the outsider is only rarely given access even at times outside the service; the *dā'ira* of the Indian Mahdawis, which is mainly devoted to *dhikr* rather than to ritual prayer; or the *imāmbārah* of the Twelver Shia, where the implements of the Muḥarram processions are kept and which the Shia rulers, especially in Lucknow, Hyderabad/Deccan and Bengal, built in the hope of heavenly reward. There are, further, the different types of Sufi convents such as the *ribāṭ*, whose name conveys the idea of fortification and fighting at the frontier but becomes in the Maghrib a true dervish centre founded by a shaykh and frequented by his followers. The *taqiya*, in Turkish *tekke*, contrasts with the large *khānqāh* (the *Khānqāh Siryāqūs* near medieval Cairo is a glorious example of such an institution)[30] and the *dargāh*, a term mainly used in India, and the solitary master would perhaps dwell in a *zāwiya*, 'corner', a term which, again in the Maghrib, is used to mean rather a hospice for Sufis. The use of names for these institutions varied in different times and different countries, but one thing is common to all Sufi institutions: none of them is a 'consecrated' building. For the pious, they assumed a sacred quality owing to the master's and the dervishes' presence.

When the Muslim speaks of the 'two sacred places' (*al-ḥaramān*; accusative and genitive *al-ḥaramayn*), he means Mecca and Medina. The word *ḥaram*, from the same root as *ḥarām*, 'prohibited', designates the place where anything profane is excluded, as the *ḥarīm*, the place reserved for women, is accessible only for the *maḥram*, a male member of the family who is related to the inmates. To enter the heart of the sanctuary, in this case the precincts of the Kaaba in Mecca, one is required to put on the *iḥrām*, the garment that obliges the pilgrim to observe a number of taboos such as avoidance of sex, of cutting one's hair or of paring one's nails. This is valid not only during the season of the *ḥajj* in the last lunar month but also during the 'smaller pilgrimage', the *ʿumra*, which can be performed at any time.

In the sacred precincts, no animal may be hunted or killed, and Iqbāl alludes to this prohibition by admonishing his co-religionists to return spiritually to Mecca and gather in the protective shade in the Kaaba because 'no gazelle', that is, no living being must be hunted there while they, oblivious to their spiritual centre, have become an easy prey for the non-Muslim hunters – and non-Muslims are excluded from the sacred place, Mecca.[31]

The name of Mecca is connected, in general thought, with a great assembly-place, and one can encounter, in the West, expressions like 'the Mecca of gamblers' or 'of racing cars'. For this reason, Muslims now prefer to spell the city's name as *Makkah* to distinguish it from these strange and appalling definitions.

The city of Mecca, Muhammad's home town, is situated between two ranges of hills and formerly housed an ancient Arabian sanctuary. The Koran (Sūra 42:7) calls the place *umm al-qurā*, 'the mother of the cities' (hence the name of its university), and numerous legends have grown around this place from where, as Muslims believe, the creation of the Earth began. Thus, as the praying Muslim turns to Mecca whence the Earth was expanded, he turns spiritually to the centre of truth, the source of all spirituality. Mecca's unique role is emphasized in a proverb in which its inhabitants proudly claim that a person who sleeps at Mecca is equal to someone worshipping God in another place.[32]

The central sanctuary, the Kaaba, blesses the city with its presence: it appears as an omphalos, the navel of the earth,[33] and is, as pious people believe, situated exactly opposite the heavenly Kaaba in the seventh heaven. During the deluge, the Meccan Kaaba was taken into heaven, where Noah's Ark surrounded it seven times. As for the heavenly Kaaba, it is constantly circumambulated by angels whose movements the pilgrim should remember while performing the *ṭawāf*, 'circumambulation' around the earthly Kaaba. But sometimes, as legend tells, the Kaaba itself comes to turn around visiting saints such as the great Sufi woman Rābiʿa (d. 801), or wanders to a Sufi in faraway lands.[34] The Koran (Sūra 2:125ff.) speaks of Abraham's building or restoring the Kaaba; and, when the Prophet reconquered Mecca in 630, he cleaned the building of all the idols, whose number is given as 360, which may point to an old astral cult connected with the sanctuary (the moon god Hubal is well known from pre-Islamic times).

The Kaaba is an almost cubic stone building measuring 12 m^2 and 15 m high; it is usually covered with the black *kiswa*, and many poets have compared this black veiled structure with a longed-for bride whom one wants to reach and kiss.[35] Thus, comparisons of the kissing of the black stone in the Kaaba's south-eastern corner with kissing the black beauty spot or the lips of the beloved are common in Persian poetry.

As Mecca and the Kaaba are, for the pious, certainly the most sacred place on Earth to which the living and the dead turn, one should not spit or stretch out one's legs in the direction of the Kaaba, nor perform bodily needs in its direction. After death, the believer should be buried lying on his right side with his face turned towards the Kaaba.

As every Muslim has to direct his or her position towards the Kaaba during the five daily prayers (Sūra 2:144), it became important for Muslim mathematicians and astronomers to enable believers to find the right direction, *qibla*, when travelling by land or sea; lately, they have even discussed the problem of how to determine the *qibla* while travelling in a spaceship. Mathematical and geographical research developed refined methods of finding the correct direction; in later times, small compasses facilitated this.[36] But it was not always easy to determine the exact position of the prayer niche, *miḥrāb*, in a mosque, especially when the mosque was built in an already crowded quarter and one had to adjust the structure of the building with one face following the alignment of the street while the other showed the direction towards Mecca. There were different ways of achieving the correct result, so that one may even find slightly varying directions in one and the same city.[37] Legends, mainly from India, tell how a saint's prayer could correct the position of the *miḥrāb* when an architect had miscalculated it. That was a useful miracle, for the Muslims are indeed called the *ahl al-qibla*, 'those that turn towards the *qibla*', and warnings are issued about talking against the *ahl al-qibla*, for they are all united by turning to the same centre of prayer-life.

Poets loved to compare the beautifully arched eyebrows of their beloved to a *miḥrāb* – was not Adam, the first human being, a *qibla* before whom the angels prostrated and through whom one could find the way to the Divine beauty?[38] It is therefore not surprising that the Persian line

> *Mā qibla rāst kardīm bi-simṭ-i kajkulāhī*
> We have directed our prayer direction towards the one sporting his cap awry

became commonplace in later Persian and Persianate poetry.[39]

For the mystically minded poets knew that the Kaaba in Mecca, central as it is, is still a mere sign – *the ka'ba-i gil*, 'Kaaba of clay', is often juxtaposed with the *ka'ba-i dil*, 'the Kaaba of the heart' – and everyone has his or her own *qibla*, the place of worship to which one turns intentionally or unintentionally. For *qibla* became a general term for the place on which one concentrated one's attention: when a calligrapher is called with the honorific title *qiblat al-kuttāb*, it means that he is the person to whom everyone in the writing profession turns in admiration. Rūmī describes, towards the end of his life, the different *qiblas* to whom humans turn instead of looking towards Mecca, the central direction of worship:

> The Kaaba for the spirits
> and Gabriel: the Sidra-tree,
> The *qibla* of the glutton,
> that is the table-cloth.
> The *qibla* for the gnostic:
> the light of union with God,
> The *qibla* of the reason,
> philosophizing: vain thought!
> The *qibla* of the ascetic:
> the beneficent God,
> The *qibla* of the greedy:
> a purse that's filled with gold.
> The *qibla* of those who look at

true meaning, is patience fine,
The *qibla* of those who worship
the form: an image of stone.
The *qibla* of those esoterics
is He, the Lord of Grace,
The *qibla* of these exoterists
is but a woman's face ...
(*M* VI 1,896f.)

Despite such psychologically insightful verses, Mecca was and remained the veritable centre of Islamic piety. Moreover, it is not only the place to which to turn in prayer and which to visit during the pilgrimage; it has also inspired innumerable people in their religious achievement. The great medieval theologian, al-Juwaynī (d. 1085), was honoured by the title *imām al-ḥaramayn* because of his prolonged exile in the sacred places. Pilgrims, particularly scholars who stayed for months, even for years in Mecca, were inspired to compose their most important works there. Zamakhsharī (d. 1144), with the honorific title *Jār Allāh*, 'God's neighbour', as result of his prolonged sojourn in Mecca, wrote his comprehensive commentary on the Koran in this place, and at the beginning of the following century Ibn ʿArabī received the initial but comprehensive inspiration for his voluminous *Futūḥāt al-makkiyya*, 'The Meccan Openings', while circumambulating the Kaaba.[40] Again, centuries later, the Indian reformer Shāh Walīullāh (d. 1762) wrote his *Fuyūz al-ḥaramayn*, 'The Effusions of Grace from the Two Sacred Places' under the impression of his sojourn in the sacred cities.

The stay in Mecca had certainly an 'Arabicizing' influence on pilgrims from foreign countries, and numerous reform movements in North and West Africa, Bengal and Central Asia were sparked off when Muslim leaders came to Mecca, where they found what seemed to them true Islam but which often contrasted with the 'Islam' in their homeland, which now appeared to them utterly polluted by the pernicious influences of popular customs and pre-Islamic practices. They then felt compelled to reform Islam at home as a result of their stay in Mecca.

Another noteworthy aspect of Mecca's central position was the understanding that he who rules over Mecca and Medina is the rightful caliph – hence the claim of the Ottomans who conquered Mamluk Egypt and the areas under its dominion, including the Hijaz, in 1516–17 and thus became the overlords of the *ḥaramayn*. But the mystics often voiced the opinion that 'Mecca is of this world, faith is not of this world', and that God can be found everywhere and that His presence is not restricted to the Kaaba.

The role of the second sacred place, Medina, was increasingly emphasized in the later Middle Ages. After all, it was the city where the Prophet was buried, and with the growing glorification of the Prophet and the deepening of mystical love for him and trust in him, Medina gained in status.

The role of Medina in the history of Islam cannot be overstated. The Prophet's hegira in 622 to this town, that only after some time was to become a *Muslim*, 'home', forms the beginning of the Muslim calendar, for now the Prophet's revelations had to be put into practice and create political and juridical foundations for the fast-growing community of believers. Besides this practical side of the hegira, medieval mystics have seen it as a subtle hint to the fact that one has to leave one's home to find superior glory; and for a modernist like Iqbāl, the hegira shows that one should not cling to narrow, earthbound, nationalist concepts.[41] The Muslims who migrated from India to the newly-created Pakistan in the wake of the partition in 1947 called themselves *muhājir*, 'one who has participated in the hegira' from 'infidel Hindustan' to the new home where they hoped to practise their faith without difficulties, and modern North American Muslims may find consolation in the thought that they, like the companions of the Prophet, have left their former home and found a new place in not-yet-Muslim America.

For most pilgrims, it is their dream to visit the Prophet's tomb, the *rawḍa*, in Medina in connection with the pilgrimage, and the Saudi authorities, despite their aversion to 'tomb-worship', allow these visits.[42] Pictures of the *Rawḍa*, as of the Kaaba, decorate many houses; printed on calendars, woven into rugs, painted on walls, they convey the blessing of the Prophet's spiritual presence. The sanctity of Medina is understood from the medieval belief that the plague never touches this city.

Poetry in honour of Medina seems to develop from the late thirteenth century, the first major representative of this genre being Ibn Daqīq al-ʿĪd (d. 1302).[43] The greater the distance between the poet's country and Medina, the more emotional he waxes:

> More beautiful than all the flowers are the flowers of Medina …

and, as Jāmī thinks, the angels make their rosaries from the kernels of Medina's dates.[44] It makes hardly any difference whether the poet in Anatolia around 1300 sings:

> If my Lord would kindly grant it,
> I would go there, weeping, weeping,
> and Muhammad in Medina
> I would see there, weeping, weeping,

or whether he lives in eighteenth-century Sind, like ʿAbdur Ra'ūf Bhattī, whose unassuming poem has the refrain:

> In the luminous Medina, could I be there, always there ... [45]

For Medina is *al-madīna al-munawwara*, the luminous city, and the pious imagine that there is a column of light over the *Rawḍa*, as the modern Sudanese writer, al-Fayṭūrī, states:

> Over the Prophet's bones, every speck of dust is a pillar of light.[46]

In Indo–Pakistan, poetical anthologies with the title *Madīna kā ṣadaqa*, 'Pious alms for Medina', are available in cheap prints, and Iqbāl wrote, close to the end of his life:

> Old as I am, I'm going to Medina
> to sing my song there, full of love and joy,
> just like a bird who in the desert night
> spreads out his wings when thinking of his nest.[47]

Besides the *ḥaramayn*, the city of Jerusalem is surrounded with special sanctity, for it was not only the place on whose rock, as mentioned earlier (p. 2), all the previous prophets had rested, but also, more importantly, the first *qibla* of the Muslims.[48] Only after the hegira was the prayer direction changed to Mecca (Sūra 2:144). Connected also with the Prophet's heavenly journey and with mythological tales about the events on Doomsday, when Isrāfīl will blow the trumpet from there, Jerusalem holds pride of place in the hearts of the Muslims, and many early ascetics spent some time there.[49]

The orientation to the Kaaba is certainly central for the Muslim, but it is not only the direction in prayer that plays a great role in his life and thought. One has to remember the importance given to the right side as well. The term 'right', *yamīn*, belongs to a root with connotations of felicity and happiness; the right side *is* the 'right', prosperous side. One eats with the right hand (or rather with its first three fingers), while the left hand is unclean, being used for purification after defilement. One should enter a room with the right foot first, and sleep if possible on the right side to ensure happy and good dreams. On the Day of Judgment, the Book of Actions will be given in the sinners' left hands, and they are the 'people of the left' (Sūra 56:41). When Ibn ʿAbbās states that Paradise is to the right side of the Throne and Hell to its left, then popular belief has it that during ritual prayer the Prophet and Gabriel are standing at the praying person's right side while Hell is waiting at his/her left.[50] The importance of the right side is attested not only in surnames like *Dhū 'l-yamīnayn*, 'someone with two right hands' for an ambidextrous and successful individual, but also in the idea that 'God has two right hands'.[51] Thus, the orientation towards the right is a time-honoured and generally accepted fact. Yet there are other spatial peculiarities as well.

The Koran emphasizes that East and West belong to God (Sūra 2:115) and that true piety does not consist of turning to the East or West (Sūra 2:177); it mentions also the wondrous olive tree that is 'neither from the East nor from the West' (Sūra 24:35). Yet, as the right side was thought to be connected with positive values, it seems that an 'orientation' in the true sense of the word, that is 'turning to the East', was well known to Muslim thinkers from early days despite the different directions in which the *qibla* had to be faced in the expanding empire. The worn-out juxtaposition of the material West and the spiritual East is not a modern invention: Suhrawardī the Master of Illumination spoke of the *ghurbat al-gharbiyya*, the 'western exile' where the soul is pining and whence she should return to the luminous East. Persian poets sometimes confront Qandahar in the East and Qairouwan in the West, combing the latter name with *qīr*, 'tar', because the dark West makes them think of pitch-black misery. Similarly, the Dakhni Urdu poet Wajhī (d. after 1610) located, in his story *Sab ras*, King Intellect in the West and King Love in the East, while Sindhi folk poets like to speak of the 'journey eastwards' of the spiritual seeker although both their traditional goals of pilgrimage, Mecca and the ancient Hindu cave of Hinglaj, are situated west of Sind. One wonders whether the language called *Pūrabī*, 'eastern', in which God addressed the Delhi mystic Niẓāmuddīn Awliyā, was indeed the Purabi dialect of Hindwi or whether it points to a 'spiritual language' in which he heard the Divine Beloved speak.

The 'Orient of lights', the place where the light rises, appears sometimes also as Yemen, which in Suhrawardī's work represents the true home of spirituality because the 'country on the right hand' was the home of Uways al-Qaranī, who embraced Islam without ever meeting the Prophet and concerning whose spirituality the Prophet said, as legend tells: 'I feel the breath of the Merciful coming from Yemen'. *Ḥikma yamaniyya*, 'Yemenite wisdom', and *ḥikma yūnāniyya*, 'Greek philosophy', contrast, as do intuitive gnosis and intellectual approach, as do East and West.[52]

Not only this 'Morgenlandfahrt' of the medieval Muslim thinkers is fascinating, but also the way in which some of them transformed a geographical concept into its opposite. India, which in most cases is the land of 'black infidelity', became in a certain current of Persian poetry the home of the soul. 'The elephant saw India in his dream'; that means that the soul was reminded of its primordial home whence it had been carried away to live – again – in Western exile. And the steppes of Asia, where the musk-deer lives and moonlike beauties dwell, could become at times a landscape of the soul – where the soul, guided by the scent of the musk-deer, finds its eternal home.[53]

Again, the concept of the *quṭb*, the Pole or Axis, the central figure in the hierarchy of the saints, points to the importance of the upward orientation, as Henry Corbin has lucidly shown: the polar star, thought to be located opposite the Kaaba, is the guiding light for the traveller.[54]

On a different level, one meets the concept of sacred space in attempts of medieval Sufis – especially in the tradition of Ibn ʿArabī – to map the spiritual world and describe the strata of Divine manifestations through which the inaccessible Divine Essence reveals Itself. One usually speaks in descending sequence of *ʿālam al-lāhūt*, 'the world of divinity', *ʿālam al-jabarūt*, 'the world of power', *ʿālam al-malakūt*, 'the realm of the Kingdom', and *ʿālam an-nāsūt*, 'the realm of human beings'. In certain cases, the highest level beyond the *ʿālam al-lāhūt* is thought to be the *ʿālam al-hāhūt*, the 'Divine Ipseity' as symbolized in the final *h* of the word *Allāh*. Very frequently, the *ʿālam al-mithāl*, 'the realm of imagination', *mundus imaginalis*, is placed between the world of the heavenly Kingdom and that of humanity, where it constitutes so to speak a reservoir of possibilities which await realization and can be called down by the spiritual ambition of the saint.

One also sees attempts to chart the Otherworld, for the Koranic mention of various stages in Paradise, such as *ʿilliyūn* (Sūra 83:18, 19), *jannat ʿadan* (Sūra 15:45 et al.) and the like, invited searching souls to develop an increasingly complicated celestial geography. Again, the main contribution in this field is owed to Ibn ʿArabī and his followers. And as late as 1960, a Turkish thinker produced a lengthy study about the geography of Hell.

The importance of sacred space and place is reflected in the emphasis which Islam plays on the concept of the road, a theme that can be called central in Islamic thought.[55] Does not the Muslim pray with the words of the Koran: *ihdinā 'ṣ-ṣirāṭa 'l-mustaqīm*, 'Guide us on the straight path!' (Sūra 1:6)? This petition from the *Fātiḥa*, repeated millions of times every day around the world, has lent the title 'Islam, the straight Path' to more than one study on Islamic piety (and one may add that titles of books that contain Arabic terms like *nahj* or *minhāj*, both meaning 'path, right way', are often used for religious works).

God guides, and He can let people go astray in the desert (*aḍalla*), but the straight path is manifested – so one can say – in the *sharīʿa*, a term usually (and rightly) translated as 'religious law'. Its basic meaning is, however, 'the road that leads to a water course or fountain', that is, the only road on which the traveller can reach the water that is needed to survive; for in the desert, it is incumbent on everyone to follow the well-established path lest one perish in the wilderness – and the *sharīʿa* offers this guidance.

The concept of *ṭarīqa*, 'path', which expresses the mystical path in general and has become the normal term for Sufi fraternities, belongs to the same cluster of images, with the understanding that the narrow path, *ṭarīqa*, branches out from the highway. There can be no *ṭarīqa* without the *sharīʿa*.[56]

In this connection, one may also think of the frequent use of the word *sabīl*, 'way', in expressions like 'to do something', 'to fight', or 'to give alms' *fī sabīl Allāh*, 'in the way of God', that is, in the right direction, guided by the knowledge that one's action is God-pleasing and will result in positive values. The feeling that the establishment of fountains and the like is particularly useful *fī sabīl Allāh* is the reason why fountains near mosques and in the streets are often simply called *sabīl*, literally 'way'. Finally, the term for the legal school which Muslims adhere to, and according to whose rules Muslims judge and are judged, is *madhhab*, 'way on which one walks', a term often used in modern parlance for 'religious persuasion'.

But the 'way' is also very real: the pilgrimage to Mecca, *ḥajj*, is one of the five pillars of Islam. Legend tells that Gabriel taught the rites of the *ḥajj* to Adam and Eve,[57] and the decisive ritual was set by the Prophet's last pilgrimage shortly before he passed away. The pilgrimage has served numerous writers as a symbol of the soul's journey towards the longed-for goal, 'the city of God at the other end of the road' (John Masefield).[58] One's entire life could be seen as a movement through the *maqāmāt*, the stations on the journey, or the stations of the heart, in the hope of reaching the faraway Beloved. The pilgrims' progress is regulated on the normal level by the *sharī'a* and, for the Sufis, by the *ṭarīqa*; it is a dangerous undertaking whose external and internal difficulties and hardships are often described. The long journeys through deserts or beyond the sea made the *ḥajj* in former times a very heavy duty; many pilgrims died from fatigue, illness, Bedouin attacks and shipwreck; and yet, as Indonesian pilgrims state, these long, strenuous journeys served much better as a preparation for the final experience of 'reaching the goal' than the modern brief, rather comfortable air travels.[59] And as the pilgrimage to Mecca is fraught with dangers and hardships, thus the inner pilgrimage requires uninterrupted wakefulness. It is a journey through the spaces of the soul which the *sālik*, the wayfarer, traverses, day after day, year after year, for, as Ibn 'Aṭā Allāh says:

> Were there not the spaces of the soul, there would be no journey from man to God.

The mystics have always asked, as did Mawlānā Rūmī:

> Oh, you who've gone on pilgrimage – where are you? Where, o where?
> Here, here is the Beloved – O come now, come, o come!
> Your friend, he is your neighbour; he is next to your wall –
> You, erring in the desert – what air of love is this?
>
> (*D* no. 648)

In this process, the actual landscapes are transformed into landscapes of the soul: when in the old Sindhi story of Sassui Punhun the lovesick young woman runs through the deserts and steep rocks, braving all kinds of dangers, the poet makes us understand that this is a perfect symbol of the difficulties that the soul has to overcome on her path to God.[60]

The topos of the journey and the path predate Islamic times: the central part of the ancient Arabic *qaṣīda* describes most eloquently the poet-hero's journey on his strong camel or his swift horse through the desert, and the theme of such a journey was taken over by later poets. Thus Ibn al-Fāriḍ's (d. 1235) major poem, the *Tā'iyya*, is officially called *Naẓm as-sulūk*, 'The Order of the Progressing Journey'. Slightly later, Rūmī sang of the necessity of travelling in a poem whose first line he took over from Anvarī (d. around 1190):

> Oh, if a tree could wander and move with foot and wings!
> It would not suffer the axe-blows and not the pain of saws!
> (*D* no. 1,142)

Painful though the separation from home may be, it is necessary for one's development: the raindrop leaves the ocean to return as a pearl; the Prophet left Mecca to become a ruler in Medina and return victoriously.

It is the Prophet's experience not only in the hegira but even more in his nightly journey, *isrā'*, *miʿrāj*, that offered the Muslims a superb model for the spiritual journey. The brief allusion in Sūra 17:1 was elaborated and enlarged in the course of the centuries and lovingly embellished; the Persian painters in the fifteenth and sixteenth centuries represented the wondrous event in glorious pictures, often with moving details, and almost every later Persian or Turkish epic contains a poetical description of the Prophet's *miʿrāj*. The last epic in the long list of works inspired by the account of the *miʿrāj* is Iqbāl's *Jāvīdnāma* (1932), which combines the different traditional strands of the motif and weaves them into a colourful fabric of modern Islamic thought. The assumption that the *kitāb al-miʿrāj*, Arabic tales about the Prophet's nightly journey through Heaven and Hell, has influenced Dante's *Divine Comedy* to a certain extent seems to be well established thanks to Enrico Cerulli's research.[61]

The soul's journey usually traverses seven stations; the eighth may be the 'heavenly earth of Hurqalyā'. Henry Corbin has pointed out how the concept of the *quṭb*, the mystical 'axis' or 'pole', is closely connected with the theme of the upward journey, for it is the point of orientation for the soul on its ascent from the Western exile.

The ascent through the seven valleys, well known in Christianity, is most beautifully symbolized in ʿAṭṭār's Persian epic *Manṭiq uṭ-ṭayr*, which sings of the journey of the thirty soul birds towards the *Sīmurgh* at the end of the world. Like many other thinkers, ʿAṭṭār too found that the arrival at what looked like the end of the road is only a mere beginning, for 'when the journey to God ends, the journey in God begins'.

> There are two journeys, one to God and one in God, for God is infinite and eternal. And how could there be an end for the journey of the soul that has reached His presence?[62]

But we are faced with a dilemma. God is always described as *lā-makān*, 'there where no place is', or as being in *nā-kujā-ābād*, 'Where there is no Where'; and yet the Koran describes Him as the One who 'is upright on the Throne' (Sūra 7:54, 13:2 et al.) and states that His Throne 'embraces the whole universe' (Sūra 2:255). His Throne is beyond Heaven and Earth and what is in them, and yet He, who is closer to mankind than the jugular vein (Sūra 50:16), dwells in the innermost sanctuary of the human heart.

The experience of the journey to God and into His depths is expressed in a *ḥadīth*: the Prophet, speaking of his own *miʿrāj*, admonished his companions: 'Do not prefer me to Yūnus ibn Mattā because my journey is into the height and his journey is into the depths'. For there are two ways to reach the Divine: the journey upwards to Mt Qāf and beyond, and the journey into the ocean of one's soul. The same ʿAṭṭār who so eloquently describes the birds' journey to Mt Qāf in his *Manṭiq uṭ-ṭayr* has devoted another work, the *Muṣībatnāma*, to the journey that leads the seeker through the forty stations of seclusion into the ocean of his soul.[63]

Both ways are legitimate – the one into the heights of Divine glory where the Divine light permeates everything and becomes invisible owing to its radiance, and the way into the dark abyss where all words fail and the soul loses itself in sheer ecstasy, drowned in the fathomless ocean of God.

Both ways also seem correct when one thinks of the concept of orientation in Islam: the correct direction to the *qibla*, indicated by the Kaaba in Mecca, is binding for everyone, and yet the Muslim also knows that 'Whithersoever ye turn, there is the Face of God' (Sūra 2:115).

SACRED TIME[64]

At the end of the road, the carpet of time and space is rolled up. But before this point and this moment is reached, we observe the same apparent paradox that we encountered concerning God's 'place' and 'placelessness' when dealing with time and timelessness in Islamic thought.

Time measures our lives, and each religion has its own sacred times: times in which the mystery that was there at the beginning is re-enacted; festivities which are taken out of the normal flow of daily life and thus carry humans into a different dimension; sacred seasons; and sacred days and hours.

For the Muslim, the history of salvation (*Heilsgeschichte*) begins with Muhammad, as his essence is the first thing created by God and, as mystics would claim, thus precedes the 'first man' Adam. His appearance in time after the long ages in which earlier prophets taught God's commands constitutes the climax of human history; in him, the fullness of time is reached. This conviction helps to explain the Muslim's constant longing for the Prophet's time, for no other time could have been or could ever become so blessed as the years that he, bearer of the Divine Word, was acting on Earth. For this reason, all 'reform movements' are bound to reorient themselves back to the Prophet's time.

People have looked for an explanation why Muhammad appeared just around the turn of the sixth to the seventh century AD, and Ibn ʿArabī found out that the Prophet entered history in the sign of Libra, which means that he inaugurated a new age in the sign of justice, that is, he struck the balance between the legalism of Moses and the mildness of Jesus.[65]

Historically speaking, Muslim time-consciousness begins with the hegira which, as already mentioned, means the practical realization of the contents of the revelation. Furthermore, an important new beginning was made as a purely lunar year was introduced, which entailed a complete break with old Semitic fertility cults connected with the solar year and its seasons. To be sure, the solar year continued to be used for financial purposes such as taxation, as the yield of the crops was dependent upon the seasons and could not be harmonized with the lunar calendar, in which, contrary to earlier systems, no intercalation was permitted.

The month begins when the crescent moon is sighted by two reliable, honest witnesses. Although the appearance of the first slim crescent can be mathematically determined in advance, the prescription of actually observing the moon still remains valid. The crescent was thus able to become the favourite symbol of Islamic culture.[68]

Nevertheless, some rites are still celebrated according to the solar calendar. The best-known one is *Nawrūz*, the Persian New Year at the vernal equinox, which was and still is central in the Persianate world but which was accepted, to a certain degree, also by the Arabs. Some feasts of local saints again follow the solar calendar, for example that of Aḥmad al-Badawī in Tanta, Egypt, whose dates are connected with fertility, which means, in Egypt, with the rising of the Nile.

Other popular measures of time may have been in use in various parts of the Islamic world; thus, Christiaan Snouck Hurgronje mentions for the late nineteenth century a Hadramauti solar year which consisted of twenty-eight parts with thirteen days each; the twenty-eight parts corresponded one by one to the station in which the moon rises.[67] These lunar mansions were, as he states, well known among the people. Indeed, the importance given to the lunar mansions is a fascinating aspect of Muslim culture, and numerous popular sayings and superstitions express the widespread acquaintance with these concepts, which are echoed in high literature. Thus, one should avoid bloodletting when the moon is in Libra, and 'moon in Scorpio' is the worst possible, most disastrous combination, as both Muslim writers and European observers tell.[68] The poetical genre of *bārahmāsa*, 'Twelve Months' poems', in the Indo–Pakistani vernaculars shows a curious shifting from Indian to Muslim and recently even to Western months.[69]

Feasts carry a special power with them, and therefore humans behave differently on festive days, beginning with the custom of sporting new garments. One may perform supererogative acts of piety, distribute alms, or share food and sweets. That is particularly true for the two great feasts in the Muslim world which are based on Koranic sanction: one is the *ʿīd ul-fiṭr* at the end of Ramadan (Turkish *şeker bayramĭ*, 'sugar feast'), the other one the *ʿīd an-nahr* or *ʿīd al-aḍḥā* (Turkish *qurban bayramĭ*), when the sacrificial animal is slaughtered during the *ḥajj* on the tenth day of the last lunar month.[70]

Ramadan is the most sacred time of the year, for during this month the first revelation of the Koran took place. The gates of Hell are closed, the gates of Paradise open. The *laylat al-qadr*, the Night of Might (Sūra 97), is 'better than a thousand months'; it is thought to be one of the last odd nights of the month, probably the twenty-seventh. Many pious people therefore spend the last ten or so days of the month in seclusion or in the mosque, and even those who do not fast generally may try to fast at least on the first and during the last ten days for the sake of blessing. The *laylat al-qadr* is thought to be filled with light, a light that appears to a few blessed people who excel by their devotion.[71]

Although a fasting day, *ʿāshūrā*, was institutionalized at an early stage in Mecca,[72] now a whole month is devoted to fasting (Sūra 2:185), a hard discipline which requires strong intention and is particularly difficult when it happens to fall in the hot season, for the fasting Muslim is not allowed a single sip of water (if possible, one even avoids swallowing one's saliva) between dawn, when one can discern between a black and a white thread, and the completion of sunset. Nor are food, smoking, sex, perfume or injections permitted during daytime; exemptions are possible for weak, travelling or fighting people and menstruating and pregnant women; but either the lost days have to be made up for, or other penitences such as feeding a certain number of poor are required, following exact regulations. It seems that the fasting along with the community, and the festive fast-breaking, *ifṭār*, along with others, make the discipline for all its difficulties more joyful than an outsider can judge. Ramadan is a problem for northern countries, when summer days stretch for more than twenty hours and where many believers miss the wider communal support that they would enjoy in a Muslim country. According to some *fatwās*, the Muslim in such faraway northern areas (and that would be valid for southern areas as well, e.g. Muslims in southern Chile) could break the fast at the time when it is broken in the next Muslim country; that would be Turkey or North Africa for Europeans. It was also claimed that because fasting is not required during war, and hard labour in factories or agriculture is a 'war against poverty', these workers should be exempt from this religious duty; but this suggestion by President Bourguiba of Tunisia was not favourably met with.

After breaking the fast with an odd number of dates and some water, the pious Muslim will perform the evening prayer, then eat, then perform another set of prayers, the so-called *tarāwīḥ*, which comprise usually twenty, sometimes twenty-three *rak'ah* (cycles). The nights used to be formerly devoted to amusements and joyful entertainment; before the night is over, one may eat a light meal (*saḥūr* or *saḥrī*), and then formulate the intention for another day of fasting. The *'īd ul-fiṭr* is celebrated with great joy, but differences in sighting the moon may cause the feast to be celebrated with a day's difference in the same country or in faraway areas, although the sighting of the moon in Mecca is now broadcast all over the Muslim world.

The *laylat al-qadr* is filled with light because the world was illuminated by the revelation of God's Word, but the *laylat al-mīlād*, the birth of the Prophet, is equally luminous, as popular and mystical piety have it, quite in harmony with the general phenomenon that the 'birth of the saviour' in the history of religions is surrounded by light.[73] The exact date of the Prophet's birth is unknown; the twelfth day of Rabi' al-awwal, the third lunar month, is actually the date of his death, and in some areas, such as in Pakistan's North-West Frontier, it is still remembered as such (*bārah wafāt*) without displaying the joyful aspects of the birthday. Celebrations of the birthday are known first from Fatimid times, for the Fatimids (969–1171), claiming descent from the Prophet's daughter Fāṭima, had a dynastic interest in celebrating at least in courtly circles their ancestor's birthday. Around 1200, the celebrations were already widespread and elaborate, as can be understood from Ibn Khallikān's account of the *mawlid*, 'birthday' in Arbela (Irbil) in 1207. Praise-songs were composed on this occasion, and the use of candles and illuminations became popular – a custom to which the traditionalists objected because of its similarity to Christian festivities. Lately, however, the imaginative poems in honour of the Prophet's birth, as they are known from Turkey to East Africa and India from the fourteenth century onwards, were discarded in many countries because their romanticism seemed incompatible with a modern sober mind, and instead of the great 'Welcome' which all of Nature sings to the new-born Prophet (as expressed in Süleyman Çelebi's Turkish *mevlûd*), the Prophet's ethical and political achievements are emphasized. But in Cairo, Muslims continue to celebrate the day with great joy, and the sugar-dolls, called 'bride of the *mawlid*', are still sold and enchant children.

The two *'īd* are firmly rooted in Koranic tradition, and the celebration of the Prophet's birthday was a corollary of the increasing veneration which was felt for the 'best of mankind', who brought the final revelation. Another feast has no Koranic roots and yet is connected with the Prophet who, according to some *ḥadīth*, emphasized its importance. It was apparently celebrated in the early Middle Ages, for it is mentioned in Sanā'ī's (d. 1131) Persian poetry. This is the *laylat al-barā'a* (*shab-i barāt* in Persian), the night of the full moon of the eighth lunar month, Shaʿbān. Special sweets are made and, as usual for such nights, firecrackers and fireworks are used. Additional prayers are recommended, for example 100 *rakʿa* with ten recitations of Sūra 112 in each *rakʿa*; for this night is something like a New Year's Eve: God destines – so many people believe – mankind's fate for the next twelve months, and, according to a delightful belief, the angels put on file the notes which they have written about each human's action during the last twelve months. In Lebanon, the middle of Shaʿbān was celebrated as the *mawlūd*, the birthday, of all those saints whose actual memorial days were unknown, while among the Shia it is regarded as Imam al-Mahdī's birthday.[74] Sanā'ī not only mentions the *shab-i barāt* as a special sign of grace for the Prophet but also singles out the 'white nights', that is, the nights of the full moon in general; the first three days of the four sacred months – Muḥarram, Rajab, Ramaḍān and Dhu 'l-ḥijja – were also surrounded by a special sanctity; fasting was recommended at these times.[75]

In the Shia community, more sacred days are known, such as ʿAlī's birthday (13 Rajab) and the Day of Ghadīr Khum (18 Dhu 'l-ḥijja), when the Prophet invested ʿAlī as his successor. Most important, however, is the month of Muḥarram, especially its first ten days. Processions begin, people go to the *majlis*, which are meetings (separated for men and women, of course) with standards, flags and votive offerings placed in a corner, and the story of Ḥusayn's suffering in Kerbela is recited in poetry and prose with increasing intensity day by day. Pious Shiites follow the sufferings of the imam, the death of the small children, the wailing of the women and the final martyrdom of Ḥusayn and his family and friends with ever-heightened empathy, almost like the Christians who live through the mysteries of the Holy Week.[76]

In the processions on 10 Muḥarram, *tābūts* are carried, replicas of the sarcophagus of Ḥusayn. These are very high structures (5–6 m) made of wood or paper, veritable works of art in whose preparation the pious compete from the beginning of Muḥarram. A white horse is also led in the procession in case the Mahdi should suddenly appear (see above, p. 25). Everyone wants to participate in these processions and the general atmosphere of mourning. S. H. Manto's Urdu short story *Kālī Shalwār*, 'The black shalwar', tells of a prostitute's desire for the black trousers worn during Muḥarram (for Muslims avoid wearing colourful garments, jewellery and make-up); in Ahmadabad in Gujarat, the prostitutes have a special day for taking part in the celebration, during which they abstain completely from their usual activities. For Muslims know that weeping for Ḥusayn is necessary for one's salvation – even though the idea is not theologically founded.

The Muḥarram processions with flagellation and even fire-walking have turned in some areas into something akin to a carnival: in Hyderabad/Deccan, one finds buffoons dancing with the procession, and little boys may serve –

usually owing to their parent's vow – as *Ḥusayn kā majnūn*, 'Ḥusayn's madman'; fumigation with fragrant woods is also practised.[77] As in other popular festivities, such as anniversaries of a saint's death, *'urs*, the limits of normal behaviour can disappear, the borders between different classes and groups of people can be lifted, and everyone is carried away in the waves of enthusiasm, if not frenzy, that tear apart the sober rhythm of normal life.

Special food is connected with Muḥarram: on 'Ashūrā Day, the actual death of Ḥusayn, Muslims prepare a dish called *'āshūrā*, which consists of grains, raisins and numerous other ingredients to remind the pious of the last meal which the poor members of the Prophet's family prepared from the few edibles that they could scratch together. To send a bowl of *'āshūrā* to one's neighbours was customary in Turkey and the countries east of it; now, *'āshūrā* appears as a delicious everyday dessert on the menu of many Turkish restaurants.

Poets loved to sing of the tragedy of Kerbela, and the genre of *marthiya*, threnody, had its highest development at the Shia courts of India, especially Lucknow; it ranges from simple lullabies for the dying six-month-old baby 'Alī Aṣghar (thus in Golconda in the seventeenth century) to the famous *marthiyas* of Anīs (d. 1874) and Dabīr (d. 1875). The latter two excelled in long poems of the type *musaddas*, six-lined stanzas, which enabled them to describe the gruesome details most accurately at epical length. To this day, a good recitation of an Urdu *marthiya* moves the participants in a *majlis* to tears, and such recitations attract thousands of Indo-Pakistanis, for example in London.

In Iran, poets have also devoted poetry to the event of Kerbela. Most impressive among their ballads is Qā'ānī's elegy in the rhetorical form of 'question and answer', which begins with the lines:

> What's raining? – Blood! – Who? – The eye. – How? – Day and night!
> – Why? – From grief! – What grief? – The grief of the monarch of Kerbela ...[78]

This form points to the tendency in Iran to dramatize the event of Kerbela. There, the art of *ta'ziya*, a kind of passion play, occupies a prominent place.[79] In these plays, the sufferings of Imam Ḥusayn and his family are placed at the centre of the entire universal history, to become an integral part of salvation history. Not historical truth but the metahistorical importance of Ḥusayn's suffering is at the base of this *ta'ziya*, in which the most incongruous protagonists are brought together to become aware of Ḥusayn's sacrifice; Adam, Mawlānā Rūmī, the martyr-mystic al-Ḥallāj and many others are woven into the fascinating fabric of these plays which centre around an event that took place at a well-defined moment in history yet seems to belong to a different dimension of time.[80] The poets, especially the folk poets, have therefore been accused of mentioning how Ḥasan, 'Alī's elder son, entered the battlefield along with his brother Ḥusayn, although in reality he had died (probably poisoned) some eleven years earlier; but, for the poets, both appear as 'princes' or 'bridegrooms' of Kerbela.

While Muḥarram is generally observed in the Shia community, another tendency among some Indian Shiites was not only to commemorate Kerbela but also to celebrate all the death anniversaries as well as birthdays of the twelve imams with dramatic performances: eye-witnesses at the court of Lucknow in the 1830s describe such uninterrupted festivities and tell with amazement that the king's favourite elephant was trained to mourn Imam Ḥusayn during Muḥarram with long-drawn-out trumpetings: *Wāh Ḥusaynaa, wāāh Ḥusaynaa, Wāh Ḥusaayyin* ...[81]

Much more in the general line of festive days are the celebrations of saints' anniversaries, called *'urs*, 'wedding', because the saint's soul has reached the Divine Beloved's presence. Tens and even hundreds of thousands of pilgrims arrive from various parts of the country or, as in the case of Mu'īnuddīn Chishtī (d. 1236) in Ajmer, even in special trains from Pakistan which, for the occasion, are allowed to cross the otherwise closed border. Common prayer, the singing of hymns and, last but not least, the participation in the common meals which are distributed weld them into one great family (the *'urs* at Ajmer has lately been described in detail).[82] The religious events can go together with less religious aspects; the shrine of Lāl Shahbāz Qalandar in Sehwan, Sind, still bears traces in the cult of its long-forgotten past as a Shiva sanctuary, and the *'urs* of Sālār Mas'ūd in Bahraich reminds the visitor not only of the spiritual marriage of the young hero's soul with God but also of his nuptials with his bride, Zahra Bībī.[83] Many people regard a visit on the anniversary of 'their' special saint as almost equal to a pilgrimage to Mecca.[84] (To visit Mawlānā Rūmī's mausoleum in Konya seven times equals one *ḥajj* – so they claim in Konya.) Muslims like to visit mausoleums and cemeteries on Fridays before the noon prayer, and in general the gates are always open to welcome visitors. The days of the *'urs* of each saint are carefully printed in small calendars in India and Pakistan, although for the traditionalist the celebration of saints' anniversaries is nothing short of paganism, and the legalistically-minded *'ulamā* tried time and again to curtail these customs.

For the pious Muslim, almost every month has special characteristics. While in Muḥarram Muslims think of the martyrdom of Ḥusayn and avoid wedding feasts (even among Sunnis), the second month, Ṣafar, is considered unlucky because the Prophet's terminal illness began on its last Wednesday, and he supposedly said that he would bless the one who gave him news that Ṣafar was over.

In Rabī' al-awwal, the Prophet's anniversary is celebrated, while the next month, Rabī' ath-thānī, is devoted – at least for Sufi-minded Muslims – to the memory of ʿAbdul Qādir Gīlānī (d. 1166), the founder of the Qadiriyya *ṭarīqa*; hence in Indo–Pakistan it is simply called *gyārhiñ* or *yārhiñ*, 'the eleventh', because ʿAbdul Qādir's anniversary falls on the eleventh of the month.

Rajab, the seventh lunar month, is connected with the Prophet's heavenly journey, *miʿrāj*, which took place, according to tradition, on the twenty-seventh. The so-called *raghā'ib* nights at its beginning are especially blessed. This month is preferable for the smaller pilgrimage, the *ʿumra*, which, however, is permitted at any time except during the days of the *ḥajj*.

Shaʿbān is the month of the *laylat al-barā'a*: and some pious people have claimed that the letters of its very name point to five noble qualities of the Prophet: *sh*: *sharaf*, dignity, honour; *ʿayn*: *ʿuluw*, eminence; *b*: *birr*, goodness; *alif*: *ulfat*, friendship, affection; *n*: *nūr*, light. It is also related that he used to fast in Shaʿbān as a preparation for Ramaḍān. The following Ramaḍān, as the fasting moon, and finally the last month, Dhū 'l-ḥijja, as the time of pilgrimage, are considered blessed everywhere.

In this connection, it is revealing to have a look at a list of days during which the Muslim sipahis in India (especially in the Deccan) were given home leave by the British in the nineteenth century: during the Muḥarram festivities, on the last Wednesday of Ṣafar, on the Prophet's death anniversary (i.e. 12 Rabīʿal-awwal), on ʿAbdul Qādir's *ʿurs*, and on the *ʿurs* of Zinda Shāh Madār, as well as on the memorial day of Mawlā ʿAlī and of Gēsūdarāz, the great Chishti saint of Gulbarga (d. 1422). Lists from other parts of British India may have included other saints' days.

But not only 'sacred' days which are taken out of the normal flow of time by dint of their blessing power are observed; rather, each day has its peculiarities because it is connected with planetary influences, angels, colours and scents, as one can understand from Niẓāmī's Persian epic *Haft Paykar*. If any sober critic feels compelled to accuse Niẓāmī of poetical exaggeration, he should turn to the works of famous Muslim scholars such as the traditionist and theologian Jalāluddīn as-Suyūṭī (d. 1505) in Cairo and the leading *ḥadīth* scholar in seventeenth-century India, ʿAbdul Ḥaqq Muḥaddith Dihlawī (d. 1645), for both of them – like many others before and after them – have composed books about the properties of the days of the week. As God created Adam on Friday from the clay that the angel ʿAzra'il collected by force from the earth, Friday is the best day of the week. Hud and Abraham, so it is said, were born on a Friday (the latter incidentally on 10 Muḥarram!), and Gabriel gave Solomon his miraculous ring on Friday, as Kisā'ī tells. Thus, the central position of the day on which the congregation is supposed to gather at noon in the mosque is duly singled out, although in classical times Friday, in contrast to the Sabbath and Sunday, was not considered a full holiday. Only comparatively recently have some Muslim states declared it the weekly holiday, while Sunday is a working day in Pakistan and Saudi Arabia, for example. On Friday, so Muslims believe, there is an hour during which God answers all prayers – but the exact moment is unknown to mortals.[85]

Monday is the day of the Prophet's birth as well as of his triumphal entrance into Mecca in 630 – hence it is a most auspicious day, while Tuesday is considered unlucky, for God created all unpleasant things on Tuesday. Thursday is a good day for travelling, for military undertakings and also for fasting[86] (as a preparation for Friday, for the day begins at its eve: *jumʿa rāt*, 'Friday night', corresponds to the night between Thursday and Friday).

The scholars detected auspicious days for shaving, for measuring and for putting on new clothes; in short, one might organize one's whole life in accordance with the aspects of certain days. It is well known that the Mughal emperor Humāyūn (1530–56) fastidiously clung to the rules of the auspicious and inauspicious days and hours and would allow people to visit him in this or that capacity or for specific kinds of work only according to the right hour of the right day.[87]

Most blessed are, in any case, the early morning hours (the Koran urges Muslims in Sūra 11:114 to pray at the ends of the day and at night). Therefore the merchant will sell the first item at a special price to partake in this blessing; the first customer's arrival will positively determine the whole day.

The hours themselves were fixed in accordance with the prayer times, whose greatest possible extension was exactly to be measured by the length of the shadow cast by the praying person. Now, modern clocks facilitate the exact determination of the time, which, in any case, is marked by the *mu'adhdhin*'s call from the minaret. The Westerner who may be used to calling the time between approximately 3 and 6 p.m. 'afternoon' will have to learn that, for the Turks, 'afternoon', marks rather the hours between noon prayer and mid-afternoon prayer, *ʿaṣr*.

When speaking about time-consciousness in Islam, one tends to regard time as linear, which is typical of 'prophetic religions': time begins with creation, the Yesterday, *dūsh*, of Persian poets, and leads to the Day of Judgment, the Tomorrow of the Koran (cf. Sūra 54:26). But this linear time changes in a certain way into a cyclical movement, that is, 'the journey of God's servants from the place of beginning to the place of return', as Sanā'ī and Najmuddīn Dāyā Rāzī called their books concerning human beings' progress.[88] Mystics would see it as a journey from *ʿadam*, 'not-being', into the second *ʿadam*, the unfathomable Divine Essence. Later Sufis have spoken of the arc of descent from the Divine origin to the manifestation of humanity and back in the arc of ascent into the Divine homeland, under whatever image (rose-garden, ocean, reed-bed) it may have been symbolized.

A complete development of cyclical time, however, has been offered by the

Ismailis, to whose system Henry Corbin has devoted a number of studies – the seven cycles of prophets and their *nāṭiqs*, 'speakers', represent the cyclical movement in universal history.[89]

Yet, in our lives, we experience linear time. However, the believers were well aware that just as the road towards God ends in *lā-makān*, 'there where no place is', thus there is a deep difference between the time we usually know and live in and the Divine time. This is expressed in the Prophet's word: 'I have a time with God, *li maʿa Allāh waqt* (AM no. 100) – a time to which not even Gabriel, who is pure spirit, has access. The *waqt*, the 'cutting sword', as it was defined by the Sufis, is the *nunc aeternum*, the time beyond time in which there is neither before nor hereafter. The experience of the *waqt* (which roughly corresponds to the medieval German mystical term 'das Nu') is central in Sufi writing because it changes the seeker's consciousness radically. Persian thinkers have spoken, in a fine interpretation of Sūra 41:53, of the *zamān āfāqī* and *zamān anfusī*, based on the signs in the horizons, *āfāq*, and in the souls, *anfus*, which serve to point to God's activities. The *āfāqī* time, connected with the 'horizons', our created world, is the level which we experience in daily life and in which we act; but once the *waqt* takes the seeker out of himself, he experiences the *anfusī* time, the spiritual time, the moment when normal discernment has no meaning any more. It is this timelessness out of which the mystics spoke their paradoxes, for the distinction between generations and ages exists no longer – thus al-Ḥallāj can sing, as did many others:

> My mother has borne her father,
> and my daughters are my sisters,[90]

and Fāṭima is called *umm abīhā*, 'her father's mother'. This Divine Now is the still point that contains in itself all movement.

Perhaps the most ingenious attempt to symbolize the two levels of time was made by Iqbāl who saw linear, created time as it comes into existence with the very moment of creation as a *zunnār*, an infidel's girdle which has to be torn so that one may reach the eternal Now in God in a rare moment of ecstasy. He quotes Goethe's lines:

> Wenn im Unendlichen dasselbe
> sich ewig wiederholend fließt,
> Das tausendfältige Gewölbe
> sich kräftig ineinanderschließt,
> strömt Lebenslust aus allen Dingen,
> dem größten wie dem kleinsten Stern,
> und alles Drängen, alles Ringen
> ist ew'ge Ruh in Gott dem Herrn.[91]

One may find in literature allusions to *dahr*, the time, which had been regarded by both pre-Islamic Arabs and Iranians as the power ruling the universe. It is a power through which everything is determined, a blind fate. Yet, a *ḥadīth qudsī* makes God say: 'Don't curse *dahr*, for I am the *dahr*'; that is, if one understands it correctly, then even the seemingly cruel time is still subjugated to God. In later time, *dahr* was taken as coterminous not only with impersonal fate but even more with the material world – the *Dahriyya* become, in Islamic polemics, the materialists, godless and hence sinful.

Yet, Time as a power that 'weaves a garment for the invisible divinity from the two-coloured thread on the loom of days and nights' can be encountered among the poets and thinkers, and Iqbāl, who so ingeniously called people to tear the girdle of created linear time, yet sings of Time's activities in more than one poem. But Nāṣir-i Khusraw remarks, in a verse that sounds astounding in the general Islamic context:

> The Canvas of His Art is Time and Place –
> Hence Time is infinite, and boundless Space,[92]

while one generally accepts the movement from eternity without beginning, *azal*, to eternity without end, *abad*, as finite; for even time will end, as everything is perishable, and only the Divine Now will remain.

SACRED NUMBERS[93]

Space and time are measured in numbers, and Islam, like all religions, emphasizes the importance of certain numbers, in many cases following Pythagorean ideas, thus in the emphasis laid on odd numbers. The Pythagorean preference for odd numbers (which are regarded as masculine while even numbers are feminine and fraught with negative connotations) is reflected in the saying *Inna Allāha 'witr yuḥibbu 'l-witr*, 'Verily God is an odd number [i.e. One] and loves odd numbers'. For this reason, many acts are performed in odd numbers such as three or seven times: the Prophet, so it is said, broke his fast with an odd number of dates; and Snouck Hurgronje tells that in his time in Arabia the visitor was offered one cup of tea after the other, but if he should drink four cups he must have a fifth one lest the number be even.[94]

It was easy, as can be clearly seen from the above-mentioned saying, to connect the odd number with the central dogma of Islam, namely that God is One (although, properly speaking, One is not a real number). The problem of honestly attesting God's absolute unity and Oneness, however, posed grave problems to mystical thinkers, for the very act of pronouncing the profession of God's Unity presupposes the existence of a speaking subject. Hence, according to mystical thought, only God can attest His Unity; only He, as Kharrāz (d. around 896) stated, 'has the right to say "*I*"'.

But creation requires the existence of duality, of the Creator and the creation; and, as space and serial time come into existence only with the act of creation, God reveals Himself in the contrasting pair of *jalāl* and *jamāl*, majesty and beauty, in the change of day and night, in breathing in and breathing out, in the heartbeat and in the positive and negative poles that make the electric current flow. Is not the Divine creative word *kun* (written in Arabic *kn*) like a two-coloured rope that hides the Divine Unity, as Rūmī asks (see below, p. 226)?

For those who understood the signs, it seemed revealing that the Koran (as does the Torah) begins with the letter *b*, that is, with the formula *bismi'llahi* ..., and the numerical value of *b* as 2 points to the duality inherent in everything created, while the first letter of the alphabet, *alif* with its numerical value 1, is the cipher for the One and Unique God.

Islam has fought fiercely against the Trinitarian concept of the deity, the apparent 'tri-deism' in Christianity. However, Trinitarian thinking is deeply rooted in human beings, as we live in a three-dimensional world. It is therefore not surprising that one encounters a considerable number of concepts which are grouped in three, let alone the many customs and rites which have to be performed thrice, such as knocking at the door, or repeating certain questions or polite formulas; for the Prophet used to repeat his words thrice (*AM* no. 192).

The life of piety itself is divided, according to the *ḥadīth*, into three phases: *islām*, the external, legal, practical aspect; *īmān*, the interiorized faith; and *iḥsān*, 'doing good', that is, acting in the knowledge that God is always watching, so that every act has to be performed as beautifully, *ḥasan*, as possible. The Koran offered the Muslim the three stages of the *nafs*, the self, beginning with the *nafs ammāra bi 's-sū*, the 'soul inciting to evil' (Sūra 12:53), then the higher stage, *nafs lawwāma*, 'the blaming soul', which can be taken as corresponding to our conscience, but sometimes even to consciousness (Sūra 75:2), and finally the *nafs muṭma 'inna*, the 'soul at peace', the stage from which it will be called back, satisfied and satisfying, to its Lord (Sūra 89: 27, 28).

The way to God was seen as *sharī'a*, the Highway of the Law, *ṭarīqa*, the narrow path of the mystic, which leads in its end to *ḥaqīqa*, 'Divine Truth', or to *ma'rifa*, 'intuitive gnosis'. Each step on the path could be divided, again, into three degrees: the rules for the normal believer, the elite, and the elite of the elite. And as Three is the overarching principle, the first number by which a geometric figure, the triangle, can be constructed, contrasts and tensions are solved through the introduction of a third element: lover and beloved are united in Love, and in the last stage of recollection, *dhikr*, the one who recollects is united with the recollected object in the very act of *dhikr*.

One finds – outside Sunni orthodoxy – theological trinities. In Shia Islam, God, Muhammad and 'Alī are named together; in the tripartite Shia call to prayer, though not based on official texts, one adds to the general formula of the *shahāda* the words *'Alī walī Allāh*, "'Alī is the friend of God'. The Ismailis know the groups of Muhammad, 'Alī and the Imam. In other sectarian groups, similar formations of three (sometimes amazing ones!) are found, for example when the name of Salmān al-Fārisī is added to that of Muhammad and 'Alī.

From ancient times, Four was the number of the orderly universe, of the square, a number by which chaos is formed into something tangible: the four directions and the four elements are the best-known examples of this ordering power of Four.[95] In the spiritual sphere, there are four *awtād*, 'pillars', of the hierarchy of saints, as there are also four archangels. Kisā'ī even speaks of four castes of learned djinns.[96] The 'four books', Torah, Psalms, Gospel and Koran, are as well known as the 'four *takbīr*', that is, the fourfold *Allāhu akbar* pronounced in the funeral rite. That there are 'four rightly guided caliphs' as the first successors of the Prophet may be an accident, but one wonders whether it was just by chance that only four legal schools, *madhhab*, crystallized out of a large number of schools that existed in earlier times. Up to four legitimate wives are permitted, and four witnesses are required to testify in a case of adultery.

The structuring of cities or buildings according to the cosmological model of the square or the cross exists in Islam as well: the city of Hyderabad/Deccan, with its centre, the Chār Minār, the fourfold minaret, is one of the finest examples of this ordering principle. The ordering power of four is clear from a number of sayings in the *Nahj al-balāgha*, a work attributed to 'Alī, such as:

> Faith rests upon four pillars: patience, certitude, justice and striving; and patience rests upon four pillars: longing, kindness, asceticism and watchfulness ... [and so on].

The same structure is repeated in the description of infidelity, or in sayings like:

> There is no wealth but intellect; no poverty but ignorance; no heritage but good behaviour; no helper but good counsel.[97]

A particularly interesting number in Islam is Five, connected from time immemorial with the goddess Ishtar or her later counterpart Venus, and central in Manichean cosmology. Fivefold structures do not occur in crystalline forms, but occur in many vegetable forms, and thus Five is connected with the five senses.

In Islam, five is the numerical value of the letter *h*, the last and essential letter of the word *Allāh*, but it occurs on a more practical level in faith and ritual: there are five so-called pillars of Islam (profession of faith, ritual prayer, alms tax, fasting in Ramaḍān, and pilgrimage to Mecca), as well as five daily ritual prayers. In the initiation rites of the *futuwwa* sodalities, the apron is folded five times to remind the neophyte of five basics: the ritual prayer; the *ahl al-'abā* (i.e. the five members of Muhammad's household which are under his cloak and who are often called *Panjtan*, 'five people', namely Muḥammad, Fāṭima, ʿAlī, Ḥasan and Ḥusayn); the five *ūlū 'l-ʿazm*, the lawgiving prophets Noah, Abraham, Moses, Jesus and Muḥammad; the five pillars of faith; and the five parts of the creed: 'I believe in God, His angels, His books, His messengers, in resurrection and in God's decree'; not forgetting the five 'presences', *ḥaḍrāt*, of the Divine in Ibn ʿArabī's theosophy. At the initiation of a Khāksār dervish, five *ghusl* (complete baths) of the candidate are required, and the newcomer has to bring five gifts and is reminded of his fivefold duties.[98]

Pentads reign supreme in practical life and belief, but can also be encountered in several philosophical systems developed by early Muslim philosophers, as well as by the Ismailis.

God created the world in six days (Sūra 25:60 et al.), and in metaphorical language this world is often described as a cube in the midst of whose six sides the poor human being is fettered by the four elements and the five senses. The Koranic remark that God 'revealed to the bee' (Sūra 16:68) can perhaps be taken as pointing to the hexagonal shape of the beehive, which is a fitting symbol for the created world. The hexagram, an old magic sign, also plays a role in Islamic magic literature, as does the six-pointed star, which combines the macrocosmic and microcosmic triangle.

In most religious traditions, Seven is particularly important. The sevenfold circumambulations of the Kaaba and the seven stonings of Satan near Mina (repeated thrice) are central rites in Islam. Seven was sacred both to Semites (from the days of Babylonian astronomical reckoning, to which we owe the concept of the seven spheres) and to Iranians, and Islamic lore and psychology have taken over many ideas from both sources and added to them.[99]

The seven steps, or seven valleys, on the mystical path are common to mystical traditions in most parts of the world, but it is a typical Persian custom to have *haft sīn* on the Nawruz table; these are seven objects (food, flowers or the like) whose names begin with an *s*.

But while this is restricted to Iranian areas, many aspects of the sacred seven are commonly observed; the Koran has a sevenfold meaning, and there are seven canonical ways to recite it, not forgetting that a *rakʿa*, a cycle in prayer, consists of seven parts. There are in esoteric Islam seven 'angels ecstatic with love', which are explained as the theophanic forms of the Divine Names, and there are seven major prophets. The highly complicated speculations about the heptadic cycles of prophets and 'speakers', *nāṭiq*, the role of the seventh imam and its philosophical implications in Ismaili Shia Islam, have been discussed several times by Henry Corbin.[100] The Ismaili emphasis on Seven is beautifully symbolized in the heptagonal fountain in the Ismaili Centre in London. For Seven is in numerological interpretation an ideal combination of the spiritual Three and the material Four and thus points to the perfect way through life.

But while there are seven steps required to lead the wayfarer to his goal, and there are seven gates of Hell (Sūra 15:44), Eight has been, in the history of religions, the number of completion and eternity, of eternal bliss. Is not the Divine Throne carried by eight angels (Sūra 69:17)? There have been attempts to explain the octagonal fountains in the centre of a mosque's courtyard as recalling the heavenly Throne. Paradise has eight gates, one more than Hell, for God's mercy is greater than His wrath (cf. *AM* no. 64). The eightfold path (comparable to the eight blessings in the Sermon on the Mount or the eight teachings of the Buddha) has a counterpart in the eight advices in the 'Path of Junayd', the eight rules of the Naqshbandi Sufis, and the eight words of wisdom which the Khāksār novice receives at his initiation.

Hasht bihisht, 'Eight Paradises', is a Persian epic by Amīr Khusraw which tries to emulate Niẓāmī's *Haft Paykar*, 'Seven Beauties', and gardens, especially those surrounding a mausoleum, are often laid out in an eightfold shape reminiscent of Paradise, while books with titles like *Gulistān*, 'Rose Garden', or *Bahāristān*, 'Spring Garden', consist of eight chapters each, recalling the ideal garden's shape.

Nine, the glorified sacred Three, is prominent among Turks and peoples under their influence; the concept of nine spheres appears in Muslim astronomy, hence Persian literary works with the title *Nuh Sipihr*, 'Nine Spheres'. Among Turkish dynasties, nine remained important in etiquette and official life, so much so that in Mughal India the custom of bringing ninefold gifts to a high-ranking person transformed the word *toquz*, 'nine', into a term for 'present, gift'.

Ten has been, from the days of the Pythagoreans, the number of perfection and completeness, and the Arabs and Muslims used the decimal system. Perfection was reached by the *'ashara al-mubashshara*, the ten companions of the Prophet who were promised Paradise, and famous Sufi masters surrounded themselves, as legend has it, with ten favourite disciples. That Sultan Süleyman the Magnificent, the tenth Ottoman ruler, was born at the beginning of the tenth century of the hegira and had ten sons, induced Turkish historians to attribute all kinds of decades to him: for example, he conquered ten countries. Military units, incidentally, were also arranged in tens and multiples of ten (as in ancient Rome). For the Shia, on the other hand, ten is usually reminiscent of 10 Muḥarram, the day of Ḥusayn's martyrdom, and *Dehnāmas*, 'books of Ten', were composed to be read during the first ten days of Muḥarram.

Twelve, the number of the zodiacal signs, appears most prominently in the twelve imams of the Shia, between whom and the signs of the zodiac mysterious relations were established. Ibn 'Arabī also speaks of twelve categories of angels mentioned in the Koran.

The importance of Fourteen is understood from its being a lunar number, and a beautiful boy of fourteen was often compared to the full moon in radiant beauty, while the Fourteen Innocents in Shia Islam are perhaps connected with ancient groups of fourteen protecting spirits, angels or saints. Fourteen, as the number of the full moon, has more peculiarities: there are twenty-eight lunar mansions as well as letters of the Arabic alphabet; fourteen of these have diacritical marks and are, in esoterism, connected with *mulk*, the created worlds, while the other fourteen are plain and are related to the *malakūt,* the realm of angels and powers; again, fourteen of them are called *ḥurūf shamsiyya* (they assimilate with the *l* of the Arabic article *al-*) and fourteen are *qamariyya*, 'moon letters'. The correspondence between the twenty-eight lunar mansions and the twenty-eight letters induced the great medieval historian and astronomer al-Bīrūnī to claim that the 'word of God' (as revealed in the letters) and 'work of God' as shown in the lunar mansions are intrinsically intertwined.

Seventeen, rather unimportant elsewhere, plays a significant role in Islam: the number of all the *rak'as* to be prayed during one day is seventeen, and, in the ninth century, Jābir ibn Ḥayyān developed a highly interesting system built on the Seventeen.[101] In Turkish Muslim tradition, it is connected with the number of heroes and battles but also the number of the patrons of artisans' guilds, while Eighteen is loved by the Mevlevis on account of the eighteen introductory verses of Rūmī's *Mathnawi.* The concept of the 18,000 worlds was known from a rather early time.

Nineteen is the numerical value of the word *wāḥid*, 'One', and therefore highly appreciated; it is the sacred number of the Bahais. But also it plays a role in general Islam, not only because of the nineteen henchmen of Hell (Sūra 74:30), but also because many interpreters connected it with the number of letters in the *basmalah* (others, however, counted only eighteen letters in this formula). And in Shia speculation it occupied a prominent place as it is the sum of the twelve zodiacal signs and the seven planets, which correspond to the seven prophets and twelve imams.[102] But when a Muslim, a few years ago, tried to prove with the help of a computer that the entire structure of the Koran relied upon Nineteen his work was met with great mistrust, even hatred.

Among the larger numbers, Forty is exceptionally important. Not only is it the numerical value of the letter *m*, a letter specifically connected with the prophet Muhammad and in particular with his 'heavenly name' Aḥmad: as *Aḥmad* is distinguished from *Aḥad*, 'One', only by the *m*, human beings have to reach God by means of forty steps.

The general meaning of Forty in Middle Eastern traditions is preparation and purification, an often painful preparation for a rite of passage: the forty years during which the Children of Israel erred through the desert symbolize, as it were, the numerous other ascetic feats that humankind has to undertake, and Moses' forty-day fast (Sūra 7:142) prefigures the forty days of seclusion *(arba'īn, chilla)* that the Sufi has to practise to achieve mature spirituality.

In everyday life, forty days are required for purification after childbirth or a case of death to get rid of the taboo connected with these states. Many major events are measured in forties: the deluge lasted forty days; Idrīs, Hūd and Ṣāliḥ were called to act as prophets at the age of forty, and so was the Prophet Muhammad; for forty is the age of full maturity, as is borne out not only by legends and proverbs but by historical fact as well. At the end of time, so Muslims believe, the Mahdi will appear after forty caliphs have ruled, and will reign for forty years.

Forty saints – the *Kïrklar* of Turkish piety – are an important group in the mystical hierarchy, and it is claimed that the *ahl aṣ-ṣuffa*, the pious poor 'of the veranda' in Muhammad's house in Medina and prototypes of later Sufis, consisted of forty people; to commemorate them, the rope around the Khāksār dervishes' headgear consists of forty threads twisted together.[103]

Forty could also be used as a general round number; that is why 'Ali Baba had to deal with forty thieves, and the gnat that entered Nimrod's brains brought about his death after forty days. Fairytales abound in forties: someone gives birth to forty daughters at once; feasts always last forty days and forty nights; the hero is victorious in forty battles; and the student may vow to recite forty times Sūra *Yāsīn* provided he passes his examinations. There is no end to partly beautiful, partly amusing uses of Forty in Arabic, Persian and especially Turkish folklore and literature. After all, to drink a cup of coffee with someone creates, according to Turkish belief, a relationship that will last for forty years!

Among the higher numbers, seventy-two and seventy-three are worthy of mention; seventy-two is the number of diversified plurality (like the seventy-two disciples of Jesus, or of Kungfutse). In Islam it appears as the number of Muslim sects, one of which will be saved.

There are ninety-nine Divine Names. Parallel to them, there were also established the ninety-nine 'noble names' of the Prophet, and the prayer beads point by their division into thirty-three or ninety-nine to these Divine Names or remind the pious of the necessity of repeating formulas of praise and petitions ninety-nine times or a multiple of that number. And everyone is aware of the role of 1,001, the 'infinite' number of the tales of '1,001 Nights'.

As was the case in other cultures, Muslim writers liked to arrange their works in meaningful numbers of chapters or verses: as books dealing with Paradise or its earthly replica, the garden, were preferably arranged in eight chapters, Ghazzālī's *Iḥyā' 'ulūm ad-dīn*, 'The Revivification of the Sciences of Religion', that is, of Theology proper, is divided into forty chapters in four parts to lead the reader slowly from the basic teachings necessary for a truly God-pleasing life to mystically deepened aspects of life such as love, longing, trust in God, etc. While the central chapter is devoted to the Prophet Muhammad, the last one deals with death, when the soul meets its Lord. That is the end of the fortyfold path through human life. ʿAṭṭār's *Muṣībatnāma*, again, describes poetically the forty days of the *chilla* with the soul's final submersion in the ocean of the soul. And when the Indo-Muslim poet Ghālib (d. 1869) composed a *naʿt*, a eulogy for the Prophet, in 101 verses, he sings that his real intention was to write 100,000 verses; 101 is, then, at least a step toward this goal; for each rhyme shall resound a thousand times ...

NOTES

1. S. H. Nasr (ed.) (1987), *Islamic Spirituality*, vol. 1, p. 4. A general survey is Jamie Scott and Paul Simpson-Housley (eds) (1991), *Sacred Places and Profane Spaces. Essays in the Geographies of Judaism, Christianity, and Islam.* A fine introduction is Attilio Petruccioli (1985), *Dār al-Islam, Architetture del territoria nei paesi islamici.*
2. H. Basset (1920), *Le culte des grottes au Maroc.* For the *aṣḥāb al-kahf*, see S. Seligmann (1914), 'Das Siebenschläfer-Amulett'.
3. C. E. Padwick (1960), *Muslim Devotions*, p. 22.
4. M. G. Konieczny (1976), 'Unbeachtete muslimische Kultstätten in Pakistan'.
5. For a different approach, see Juan E. Campo (1991), *The Other Side of Paradise. Explorations into the Religious Meanings of Domestic Space in Islam.*
6. W. Braune (1960), *Der islamische Orient zwischen Vergangenheit und Zukunft*, p. 81. See also J. C. Bürgel (1991), *Allmacht und Mächtigkeit*, p. 23.
7. P. Nwyia (1970), *Exégèse coranique*, p. 320ff.
8. F. Taeschner (1979), *Zünfte*, p. 532.
9. Ibid., p. 574.
10. H. Klopfer (1989), *Das Traumbuch des Ibn Sīrīn*, p. 71.
11. C. E. Padwick (1960), *Muslim Devotions*, p. 215ff., ch. 13b.
12. See H. Grotzfeld (1970), *Das Bad im arabisch-islamischen Mittelalter.*
13. P. Nwyia (1970), *Exégèse coranique*, p. 332ff.
14. A. Schimmel (1983), 'The Sufis and the *shahāda*', p. 107.
15. C. E. Padwick (1960), *Muslim Devotions*, p. 22.
16. Rudolf Otto (1932), *Das Gefühl des Überweltlichen*, p. 258f.
17. J. Horovitz (1905–10), 'A list of published Mohammedan inscriptions of India', p. 15.
18. Christel Kessler (1984), 'Mecca-oriented urban architecture in Mamluk Cairo; The Madrasa Mausoleum of Sultan Shaʿbān II'.
19. M. Horten (1917b) *Die religiöse Gedankenwelt des Volkes im heutigen Islam*, p. 332f.
20. C. H. Becker (1924), 'Die Kanzel im Kultus des alten Islam'. The Sufis loved the legend of the *ḥannāna*, the palm trunk on which the Prophet used to lean while preaching; when the first *minbar* was erected, the deserted piece of wood cried and sighed because it missed the Prophet's touch.
21. F. Taeschner (1979), *Zünfte*, p. 533.
22. Gēsūdarāz (1937), *Jawāmiʿ al-kilam*, note of 16 Dhū'l-qaʿda 802 / 21 July 1400; transl. in Schimmel (1986), *Liebe zu dem Einen*, p. 87.
23. For the development of saint-worship and its paraphernalia, I. Goldziher (1890), *Muhammedanische Studien*, vol. 2, pp. 275–378 is still the classical source. The literature about saints and sacred places in Islam has increased immensely in recent years, with studies ranging from psychological approaches to exact lists of income and expenses in a Sufi convent. E. Dermenghem (1924), *Le culte des saints dans l'Islam maghrébin*, is still valuable; a very fine collection of articles is Christian W. Troll (ed.) (1989), *Muslim Shrines in India.*
24. L. Massignon (1958), 'La Cité des Morts au Caire: Qarāfa. Darb al-aḥmar'; A. Schimmel (1982c) *Makli Hill*; Carl W. Ernst (1992a), *Eternal Garden. Mysticism, History, and Politics at a South Asian Sufi Center.*

25. Ibn Iyās (1935), *Badā'i' az-zuhūr fī waqā'i' ad-duhūr*, vol. 5, p. 82.
26. Kriss and Kriss-Heinrich (1962), *Volksglaube im Islam*, vol. 2, p. 33.
27. Iqtidar Husain Siddiqui (1989a), 'The early Chishti dargāhs', especially p. 13.
28. Simon Digby (1990) writes; 'The territorial *wilāyat* of the Sufi shaykh was considered as having a direct influence on the political and material destiny of the realm over which it was exercised'. In 'The Sufi Shaykh and the Sultan: a conflict of claims to authority in medieval India'.
29. P. Jackson (1989), 'Perceptions of the *dargāhs* of Patna', p. 11.
30. J. A. Williams (1984), 'The Khānqāh of Siryāqūṣ: A Mamluk royal religious Foundation'.
31. Iqbāl (1915), *Asrār-i khudī*, line 502.
32. C. Snouck Hurgronje (1925), *Verspreide Geschriften*, vol. 5, p. 44.
33. For the theme of *omphalos*, see W. H. Roscher (1913), 'Omphalos'; idem (1915), 'Neue Omphalos-Studien'.
34. For the mystical interpretation of the Kaaba, see F. Meier (1944), 'Das Mysterium der Kaaba: Symbol und Wirklichkeit in der islamischen Mystik'; H. Corbin (1965), 'La configuration du Temple de la Ka'ba comme secret de la vie spirituelle' (English translation in Corbin (1986), *Temple and Contemplation*).
35. A. L. F. A. Beelaert (1988–9), 'The Ka'ba as a woman – a topos in classical Persian literature'. For a study of present-day imagery and actions among the pilgrims to Mecca, see William C. Young (1993), 'The Ka'ba, gender, and the rites of pilgrimage', in which the imagery of the Ka'ba as woman or bride is described by a social anthropologist.
36. David A. King (1986), 'The sacred direction in Islam. A study of the interaction of religion and science in the Middle Ages'.
37. Christel Kessler (1984), 'Mecca-oriented urban architecture', deals with this theme.
38. C. E. Padwick (1960), *Muslim Devotions*, p. 59.
39. Ḥasan Dihlawī, in Ikrām (1953), *Armaghān-i Pāk*, p. 135. But the term occurs some 200 years earlier in 'Aṭṭār (1960 ed.), *Dīvān-i qaṣā'id wa ghazaliyāt*, p. 26.
40. Compare the description in Claude Addas (1988), *Ibn 'Arabī: La quête du Soufre Rouge*.
41. Iqbāl (1961), *Stray Reflections*, no. 19, takes 'the fact that the Prophet prospered and died in a place not his birthplace' as an indication of the unnecessary clinging to one's native soil.
42. A particularly fine account is Emel Esin (1963), *Mecca the Blessed, Medina the Radiant*. Descriptions of Europeans who secretly participated in the pilgrimage (such as Richard Burton) or stayed in Mecca for a long time (such as Christiaan Snouck Hurgronje) are now increasingly complemented by travelogues and autobiographies of European and American converts to Islam.
43. For poetry in honour of Medina, see A. Schimmel (1988), *And Muhammad is His Messenger*, pp. 189–94.
44. Jāmī (1962), *Dīvān-i kāmil*, pp. 88–9, no. 61.
45. *Yunus Emre Divanı*, p. 567, no. CXXXIX; for Bhatti, see N. A. Baloch (ed.) (1961), *Maulūda*, p. 23, no. 54.
46. Published in *'Āshiq min Ifrīqiyya*; German translation in A. Schimmel (1975b), *Zeitgenössische arabische Lyrik*, p. 95. For the idea that the Prophet's tomb radiates light, see also E. W. Lane (1978 ed.), *Manners and Customs*, p. 236.
47. Iqbāl (1938), *Armaghān-i Ḥijāz*, p. 29.
48. According to popular sayings, one prayer in Jerusalem is better than 25,000 prayers elsewhere, one in Medina is 50,000 times better, and one in Mecca is 100,000 times better.
49. H. Lazarus-Yafeh (1981), 'The sanctity of Jerusalem in Islam'; L. Massignon

(1964), 'L'oratoire de Marie à l'Aqça, vu sous le voile de deuil de Fatima' speaks of the importance of Jerusalem as 'the *qibla* of Muhammad's heart' and refers too to the belief that the Kaaba will be transported to Jerusalem at the end of time.

50. Kisā'ī (1977), *The Tales of the Prophets* (translated by Wheeler M. Thackston), p. 18.
51. S. Murata (1992b), *The Tao of Islam*, ch. 3.
52. H. Corbin (1971), *L'homme de lumière*, deals with this problem.
53. For a theme from Siraiki literature, see C. Shackle (1978), 'The pilgrimage and the extension of sacred geography in the poetry of Khwāja Ghulām Farīd'.
54. This theme is elaborated in H. Corbin (1971), *L'homme de lumière.*
55. G. Fohrer (1939), *Der Heilige Weg*; K. Goldammer (1940), 'Wege aufwärts und Wege abwärts'; Hady Roger Idris (1974), 'De la notion arabo–musulmane de voie salvatrice'; Frederick M. Denny (1984), 'The problem of salvation in the Quran: key terms and concepts'.
56. A good example is E. Kohlberg (1979), '*Manāhij al-ʿārifīn*. A treatise on Sufism by Abū ʿAbd al-Raḥmān al-Sulamī', where it is stated: 'Sufism has a starting point, an end, and stages in between'.
57. Kisā'ī (1977), *The Tales of the Prophets*, p. 66. He derives the name of the hill of Marwa from *mar'a*, 'woman', as it was Eve's place, and that of ʿArafat from *taʿārafā*, 'the two [Adam and Eve] recognized each other' when they met on this spot after the Fall and their repentance. The name of the hillock Ṣafā is sometimes derived from Adam's nickname, *Ṣafī Allāh.*
58. E. Underhill (1961), *Mysticism* p. 132, beautifully sums up the predilection for the idea of pilgrimage: 'Through all these metaphors of pilgrimage to a goal runs the definite idea that the travelling self in undertaking the journey is fulfilling a destiny, a law of transcendental life'.
59. For the actual *ḥajj*, see C. Snouck Hurgronje (1888), *Het Mekkaansche Feest*; M. Gaudefroy-Demombynes (1923), *Le pélerinage à la Mecque*; J. Jomier (1953), *Le maḥmal et la caravane égyptienne des pélerins de la Mecque en XIV–XX siècles*; D. E. Long (1979), *The Hajj today: A Survey of the Contemporary Mecca Pilgrimage*; H. Lazarus-Yafeh (1981), 'Modern attitudes to the Hadjdj' in *Some Religious Aspects of Islam.* See also Juan E. Campo (1987), 'Shrines and talismans – domestic Islam in the pilgrimage paintings of Egypt'.
60. Shāh ʿAbdul Laṭīf (1958), *Risālō*, especially in the cycle about *Sassui Punhun*; cf. A. Schimmel (1976a), *Pain and Grace*, part 2.
61. For the ascension, see Schimmel (1988), *And Muhammad is His Messenger*, ch. 9, and bibliography there; some of the most important studies are W. Bousset (1901), 'Die Himmelsreise der Seele'; G. Widengren (1950), *The Ascension to Heaven and the Heavenly Book*; Marie-Rose Séguy (1972), *The Miraculous Journey of Mahomet* (based on a fifteenth-century Chagatay miniature manuscript in the Bibliothèque Nationale); R. Ettinghausen (1957), 'Persian ascension miniatures of the fourteenth century'. The most famous ascension miniature – a genre that proliferated in the fifteenth and even more so in the sixteenth century – is that by Sulṭān Muhammad in the *British Museum Niẓāmī*, which is available on postcards from the British Museum. See also S. C. Welch (1979b), *Wonders of the Age*, no. 63.
62. Sulṭān Walad (1936), *Valadnāma*, pp. 238, 356.
63. ʿAṭṭār (1959), *Muṣībatnāma*, French translation by Isabelle de Gastines (1981), *Le livre de l'épreuve.*
64. For some interpretations of time in Islam, see L. Massignon (1952), 'Le temps dans la pensée islamique'; Lennart E. Goodman (1992), 'Time in Islam'; H. Corbin (1983), *Cyclical Time and Ismaili Gnosis.*

65. H. S. Nyberg (1919), *Kleinere Schriften des Ibn al-ʿArabī*, p. 113.
66. See *EI* s.v. *hilāl.* To point with the finger at the new moon was common, hence the expression 'I became so famous that people pointed at me as though I were the new moon'.
67. C. Snouck Hurgronje (1925), *Verspreide Geschriften*, vol. 5, p. 70. These lunar mansions are often explained with popular interpretations; thus *sunbula*, 'Virgo' is thought to mean *samm u balā*, 'poison and affliction', because it falls in the hottest time of the year.
68. Thus Mrs Meer Hassan Ali (1984), *Observations on the Mussulmauns of India*, vol. 1, p. 294; at about the same time, the poet Ghālib in Delhi used the expression 'moon in Scorpio' to explain his misfortune (1969a, *Kulliyāt-i fārsī*, vol. 4, p. 213).
69. C. Vaudeville (1965), *Barahmasa, Les chansons des doux mois dans les littératures indo-aryennes.* This genre is very popular in the regional languages of Pakistan such as Sindhi and Panjabi, where it is sometimes used to point to the course of the Islamic year in romantic images, beginning with mourning in Muḥarram, until the longing 'bridal soul' finds her goal either at the Kaaba or at the Prophet's *rawḍa* in Medina in the last month of the Muslim year.
70. G. E. von Grunebaum (1958), *Muhammedan Festivals.*
71. S. D. Goitein (1966), 'Ramaḍān, the Muslim month of fasting', in *Studies*, pp. 90–110. Klaus Lech (1979) devoted an extensive study to the institution of fasting: *Geschichte des islamischen Kultus 1, 1: Das Ramaḍān-Fasten.*
72. For *ʿāshūrā* as a fasting day, see S. Basheer (1991), 'ʿAshūrā. An early Muslim fast'. According to Bukhārī (*ṣawm* 69), *ʿāshūrā* was celebrated because on this day Moses and his folk were released from Pharaoh's servitude.
73. E. Mittwoch (1926), 'Muhammads Geburts- und Todestag'. Süleyman Çelebi's *mevlûd* was often printed in Turkey in Arabic and, after 1928, in Roman letters; a good English translation is that by Lyman McCallum (1943), *The Mevlidi Sherif.* For modern *mawlid*, see P. Shinar (1977), 'Traditional and Reformist *maulid* celebrations in the Maghrib'. For the whole topic, see A. Schimmel (1988), *And Muhammad is His Messenger*, ch. 8.
74. According to tradition, mid-Shaʿbān also marks Muhammad's victorious return from Medina to Mecca in 630. In Indonesia, Shaʿbān is used to commemorate the saints and to look after the graves.
75. Sanāʾī (1950), *Ḥadīqat al-ḥaqīqa*, ch. 3, p. 209. See also Suhrawardī (1978), *ʿAwārif* (transl. Gramlich), p. 292.
76. A fine study is M. Ayoub (1978), *Redemptive Suffering in Islam.* See also Irène Mélikoff (1966), 'Le drame de Kerbela dans la littérature epique turque'.
77. Jafar Sharif (1921), *Islam in India*, pp. 160ff. A picture of an eighteenth-century representation of this 'carnival' is in A. Schimmel (1982b), *Islam in India and Pakistan* (Iconography of Religion), plate XXXVIIa.
78. E. G. Browne (1924), *A Literary History of Persia*, vol. 4, pp. 177–8.
79. Peter J. Chelkowski (ed.), (1979) *Taʿziye (Ritual and Drama in Iran).* A considerable number of *taʿziye*-texts have recently been published in both the West and Iran.
80. A typical example is the *taʿziya* play edited by A. G. Rawan Farhadi (1954), 'Le *majlis* de al-Ḥallāj, de Shams-i Tabrezi, et du Molla de Roum'.
81. Described by Mrs Meer Hassan Ali (1973 ed.), *Observations*, p. 88, as well as in Aḥmad ibn Muḥammad ash-Shīrwānī (1821), *Al-manāqib al-ḥaydariyya.*
82. P. M. Currie (1989), *The Shrine and Cult of Muin al-Din Chishti of Ajmer.*
83. See Tahir Mahmood (1989), 'The *dargāh* of Sayyid Sālār Masʿūd Ghāzī in Bahraich; legend, tradition, and reality'; Iqtidar Husain Siddiqui (1989b), 'A note on the *dargāh* of Sālār Masʿūd in Bahraich in the light of standard historical sources'; Kerrin Gräfin Schwerin (1976), 'Heiligenverehrung im indischen Islam'.

84. Nowadays, one can advertise invitations to an *'urs* in the hope of accumulating some *baraka.* An example from *Morning News,* Karachi, 20 November 1978: 'Urs mubarak of Hazrat Abdulah Shah Ghazi (Rehmatullah elaih) will be celebrated at Clifton Karachi (Hawa Bundar) from November 22 to 24th 1978. Reputed qawwal Ghulam Farid Sabri and other leading qawwals will participate. All are cordially invited to attend in large numbers and be blessed. *Space donated by Rusi S. Patel.* [author's italics]
85. S. D. Goitein (1960), 'Beholding God on Friday', deals with the possibility that the blessed in Paradise may see God on Fridays; some other peculiarities of Friday are also mentioned.
86. According to Tirmidhī (*ṣawm* 44), human actions are presented to God on Mondays and Thursdays.
87. Jafar Sharif (1921), *Islam in India,* p. 280.
88. Najmuddīn Dāyā Rāzī (1893), *Mirṣād al-'ibād min al-mabda' ilā'l-ma'ād,* transl. by Hamid Algar (1982), *The Path of God's Bondsmen from the Beginning to the Return;* Sanā'i (1969), 'Sayr al-'ibād', in *Mathnavīhā;* cf. J. C. Bürgel (1983), 'Sanā'ī's Jenseitsreise der Gottesknechte als *poesia docta*'.
89. H. Corbin (1983), *Cyclical Time and Ismaili Gnosis.*
90. al-Ḥallāj (1931), 'Dīvān', *qaṣida* no. X.
91. For Iqbāl's concept of time and his use of the *zunnār* motif (especially in the *Jāvīdnāma,* 1932), see A. Schimmel (1963a), *Gabriel's Wing,* p. 295ff.
92. Nāṣir-i Khusraw, translated by E. G. Browne (1921), in *A Literary History of Persia,* vol. 2, p. 234.
93. For a general introduction, see A. Schimmel (1993), *The Mystery of Numbers.*
94. C. Snouck Hurgronje (1925), *Verspreide Geschriften,* vol. 5, p. 33.
95. Henry Corbin (1986), 'The science of the balance', in *Temple and Contemplation,* ch. 2, deals with the 'conjugal imagery' of Sūra 4:35 by juxtaposing the four elements.
96. Kisā'ī (1977), *The Tales of the Prophets,* p. 307.
97. *Nahj al-balāgha* (1963) nos 30, 31, 38, 47, 54. One may also think of the four levels of Divine manifestations, i.e. *lāhūt, malakūt, jabarūt* and *nāsūt;* cf. the paper by Jamal Elias, 'The four faces of God ...', read at the American Oriental Society meeting in Cambridge, MA, in March 1992.
98. F. Taeschner (1979), *Zünfte,* p. 474; R. Gramlich (1981), *Die schiitischen Derwischorden,* vol. 3, p. 77.
99. U. Hartmann-Schmitz (1989), *Die Zahl Sieben im sunnitischen Islam.*
100. H. Corbin (1983), *Cyclical Time and Ismaili Gnosis,* p. 75.
101. Irène Mélikoff (1962), 'Nombres symboliques dans la littérature epico–religieuse des Turcs d'Anatolie'; Taeschner (1979), *Zünfte,* p. 44.
102. F. Rosenthal (1959), 'Nineteen'.
103. Gramlich (1981), *Die schiitischen Derwischorden,* vol. 3, p. 6.
104. A. Schimmel (1979b), 'Ghālib's *qaṣīda* in honour of the Prophet'.

III

Sacred Action

وَمِنْ آيَاتِهِ خَلْقُ السَّمَاوَاتِ وَالْأَرْضِ وَاخْتِلَافُ أَلْسِنَتِكُمْ وَأَلْوَانِكُمْ

And of His signs is the creation of the heavens and the earth and the
difference of your tongues and your colours.

Sūra 30:22

Life consists of numerous actions, many of which are deeply rooted in religious feeling or experience, or are explained by aetiology, as repetition of once sacred events. For actions are thought to gain weight by repetition.

The custom, *sunna*, of the ancestors was one of the yardsticks of social life in pre-Islamic Arabic society. After the advent of Islam, the *sunna* of the founding fathers of the religion regimented all aspects of life. Whatever contradicts or does not conform with the *sunna* as set as a model by the Prophet is abhorred because it is probably misleading, hence dangerous; thus *bid'a*, 'innovation', could often be simply classified as mere heresy. The *imitatio Muhammadi*, as Armand Abel said correctly, consists of the imitation of the Prophet's actions, not, as in the *imitatio Christi*, of participating in the role model's suffering.

The Koranic revelation itself had emphasized right conduct and salutary action, and to cling to the *sunna* of the Prophet and the ancient leaders of the community, the *salaf*, became increasingly important the further in time one was from the first generations who still had a living experience before their eyes. However, the understandable tendency to sanctify the Prophet's example could lead to a fossilization by strictly adhering to given models without realizing the spirit expressed through these models. But while the imitation of the Prophet is termed *ittibā'*, or *iqtidā*, both of which mean 'to act in conformity with …' rather than blindly 'imitating' and therefore possess a salutary quality, the simple *taqlīd*, imitation of legal decisions made centuries ago under different social and cultural circumstances, could be dangerous for the growth of a healthy community. Iqbāl blames those who blindly follow the once-and-forever determined decisions:

> If there were anything good in imitation,
> the Prophet would have taken the ancestors' path.[2]

In the framework of inherited values and traditions, classified by theologians and (in part even more strictly) by Sufi leaders, one can discover a tripartition, similar to that in other religions though not as clearly and outspokenly delineated as, for example, in Christianity or Buddhism. It is the organization of material and spiritual life into the *via purgativa*, *via illuminativa* and *via unitiva*, each of which is again divided into steps and various aspects.

VIA PURGATIVA

The *via purgativa* comprises the different ways of purifying oneself in one's attempt to get in touch with the sacred, the Divine, the Numinous. These include apotropaic rites, such as noise to shy away dangerous powers. That involves, for instance, the use of drums during eclipses to frighten the demons, or, as in parts of Muslim India, gunshots when a son is born in order to distract possible envious djinns from hurting the baby.[3] Muslims also use firecrackers (as in the Western tradition) during important and especially liminal times, such as the night of mid-Shaʿbān when the fates are thought to be fixed for the coming year, or in royal weddings, as can be seen in miniatures from Mughal India.

Fumigation is particularly popular: wild rue, *sipand,* is burnt against the Evil Eye,[4] as is storax, *tütsü.* In former times, Muslims fumigated with the precious *ʿūd,* aloes-wood, still used today on rare occasions (thus in Hyderabad/Deccan during the celebrations of the Prophet's birthday or in Muḥarram *majlises*). Certain kinds of scent were also considered to be repellent to evil spirits and evil influences. The custom of pouring a fragrant lotion over the guest's hands after a meal might originally have had such a protective value.

The idea that scent is an expression of the bearer's character is common in various parts of the world, and the 'odour of sanctity' is also known in the Islamic tradition. A story told by both ʿAṭṭār and Rūmī (*M* IV 257–305) points to the role of scent as revealing a person's predilection: a tanner came to the perfumers' bazaar and, shocked by the wonderful fragrance, fainted; he revived only after his brother rubbed some dog excrement under his nose – for the sweet fragrance did not agree with him; he was used only to the stench of the tannery. Thus, evil spirits whose being is permeated with 'stinking' characteristics shun the fragrance of incense or fragrant lotions.[5]

The belief in the Evil Eye,[6] which probably belongs among the most ancient concepts in human history, is based, among the Muslims, on Sūra 68:51ff., *wa in yakādu,* 'and they nearly had made You glide by means of their eyes'; that is, ill-intentioned enemies directed their eyes upon the Prophet whom God saved from their meanness. And Bukhārī (*aṭ-ṭibb* 66) states: 'The Evil Eye is a reality, *ḥaqq*'. Based on Koranic statements, the words *wa in yakādu* are often written on amulets against the Evil Eye. Generally, blue beads, frequently in the shape of eyes, are thought to protect people and objects, and the recitation of the last two Sūra, *al-muʿawwidhatān,* has a strong protective value. The words *aʿūdhu bi-'llāh,* 'I seek refuge with God', act, as it were, as a general protection against evil.

A simple form of averting evil or sending off unpleasant visitors (humans or djinns) is to sprinkle some salt on the floor[7] or, as in Turkey, secretly to put some salt in the shoes of a visitor whom one does not want to come again. Salt, however, has a twofold aspect: it preserves food and is highly appreciated as a sign of loyalty, similar to the Western 'eating bread and salt together'.

One can ward off evil by drawing a circle around the object which one wants to protect; walking around a sick person (usually three or seven times) with the intention of taking his or her illness upon oneself is a well-known custom, which was performed, for example, by the first Mughal emperor, Bābur, who thus took over his son Humāyūn's illness; the heir apparent was indeed healed, while the emperor died shortly afterwards.

Tying knots and loosening them again was a way of binding powers. Therefore, Sūra 113 teaches the believer to seek refuge with God 'from the women who blow into magic knots'. In some societies, such as Morocco, tattooing is also used to ward off evil.

There are also power-loaded gestures to shy away evil. To this day, a Muslim can be deeply shocked when shown the palm of the right hand with the fingers slightly apart, for this is connected with the Arabic curse *khams fī 'aynak*, 'five [i.e. the five fingers] into your eye'; that is, it means to blind the aggressor. The belief in the efficacy of the open hand is expressed in one of the best-loved amulets in the Islamic world, the so-called 'Hand of Fāṭima', a little hand worn as an elegant silver or golden piece of jewellery or else represented in red paint, even drawn with blood on a wall to protect a house. Often, it forms the upper part of Sufi poles or staffs.[8] This hand is also connected, especially among Shiites, with the *Panjtan*, the 'five holy persons' (see above, p. 79) from the Prophet's family, and their names. Also, the name of 'Ali or those of all the twelve imams are sometimes engraved in a metal 'Hand of Fāṭima'.

If the gesture of showing the open hand to someone is more than just shying away a prospective adversary but involves a strong curse, another way of cursing is connected with the prayer rite: while one opens the hands heavenwards in petitional prayer to receive as it were the Divine Grace, one can turn them downwards to express a curse. An extensive study of gestures in the Islamic world is still required.

A widely-used apotropaic matter is henna, which serves on the one hand to dye white hair and beards, giving the red colour of youthful energy. At weddings, especially in Indo–Pakistan, the bride's hands and feet are painted with artistic designs in the henna (*mēhndī*) ceremony, and the young women and girls attending the festive night happily throw henna at each other to avert evil influences. For the same apotropaic reasons, henna is also used in the Zar ceremonies in Egypt to keep away the evil spirits and djinns.[9] Among Indian Muslims, yellow turmeric can have the same function of protection of the bride, and betel, chewed by so many Indians and Pakistanis, is supposed to contain some *baraka* (one can even swear on betel).[10]

But one has not only to use protective means to keep away evil influences; rather, one has also to eliminate negative aspects and taboo matter before approaching the sacred precincts. Here, again, various rites are used to get rid of the evil, the sin, the taboo – whatever may cling to one's body or soul. There is nothing comparable to the scapegoat in Islamic lore, but the custom, known both in the Indian subcontinent and in Egypt, of sending off little rafts or boats of straw into a river is thought to carry off evil. Often, this is done in the name of Khiḍr, and the tiny vehicle is loaded with some lights or blessed foodstuffs over which the *Fātiḥa* has been recited. This sending-off of evil is usually done at weddings and on festive days. One may even look from the viewpoint of elimination at a well-known historical event: when the ashes of the martyr-mystic al-Ḥallāj were cast into the Tigris after his execution, it was probably not only the external act of getting rid of him, but subconsciously it may also have been hoped that the 'evil' influences of the man which might continue to disturb the community should be carried off by the water.

A widely-known rite for eliminating evil is the confession of sins. This custom is unknown in normative Islam, for there is no mediator between God and man to whom one could confess one's sins and be absolved. However, in Sufi and *futuwwa* circles, a brother who had committed a sin had to confess it either to his master or in front of the brethren, assuming a special 'penitent's position' (i.e. keeping his left ear in his right hand and vice versa, with the first toes of each foot touching each other, the left one on the right one).[11]

One could also try to get rid of any evil that might cling to one's body or soul by taking off one's clothing, especially the belt or the shoes. Moses was ordered 'to take off his sandals' (Sūra 20:12) because, in the sacred area which he was called to enter, nothing defiled by ordinary daily life is admitted. The expression *khalʿ an-naʿlayn*, 'the casting-off of the two sandals', became a favourite term among the Sufis. One thinks immediately of Ibn Qaṣy's (d. 1151) book by this very title, but the use is much wider: the seeker would like to cast off not only the material shoes but everything worldly, even the two worlds, in order to enter the Most Sacred Presence of the Lord.

The Turkish expression *duada baş açmak*, 'to bare one's head in petition', is reminiscent of the custom that formerly a sinner wore a shroud and approached the one whose forgiveness he implored barefooted and bareheaded.[12] Thus, to take off one's shoes when entering a house and, even more, a mosque is not so much a question of external purity lest the street's dust sully the floor and the rugs but basically a religious act, as the house is in its own way, a sacred place whose special character one has to respect and to honour (see above, p. 49). The finest Islamic example of casting off one's everyday clothes when entering a place filled with special *baraka* is the donning of the *iḥrām*, the pilgrims' dress which enables a person to enter the sacred room around the Kaaba. In pre-Islamic times, the circumambulation of the Kaaba was probably performed naked, as sacred nudity is well known in ancient religious traditions. Islam, however, strictly prohibits nudity, and only a few more or less demented dervishes have gone around stark naked, such as Sarmad, the ecstatic poet of Judaeo–Persian background, who befriended the Mughal heir apparent Dārā Shikōh (d. 1659) and was executed two years after his master in Delhi. As contrary as nudity is to strict Islamic prescriptions, it is nevertheless used as a metaphor in mystical language, and authors like Bahā-i Walad (d. 1231) and his son, Jalāluddīn Rūmī, as well as Nāṣir Muḥammad ʿAndalīb and Sirāj Awrangābādī in eighteenth-century India (to mention only a few), used this term to point to the moment when the everyday world and its objects have, as it were, been discarded and only God and the soul are left in a union attained by the absolute 'denudation' of the soul.

A different way of eliminating evil powers is exactly the contrary of taking off one's clothing; namely, covering. As human hair is regarded in most traditions as filled with power (cf. the story of Samson in the Old Testament), women are urged to cover their hair. But this rule is also valid for men, for one must not enter a sacred place with the head uncovered. A pious Muslim should essentially always have his head covered by whatever it be – cap, fez, turban – with a small, light prayer cap underneath. When a prayer cap is wanting and one has to greet a religious leader or any worthy man, or enter his house, one may simply use a handkerchief to avoid offending him.

The problem of what to cover and how to interpret the Koranic statement about the attractive parts which women should veil (Sūra 24:31) has never been solved completely. But even the modern Muslim woman, dressed in Western style, will cover her head when listening to the Koran, even if only with a hastily-grabbed newspaper when she suddenly hears a recitation of the Koran on the radio.

Purification

After the evil influences have been averted and previous sins or taboo matter cast out, purification proper can begin before one draws near the Numinous power, the sacred space.

One way of purification is to sweep a place, especially a shrine; and while pilgrims from India and Pakistan could (and perhaps still can) be observed sweeping quietly and gently ʿAbdul Qādir Gīlānī's shrine in Baghdad, modern Turks have found an easier way to purify the shrine of Ankara's protective saint, Hacci Bayram: one simply vows a broom, which is offered to the keeper of the mausoleum when one's wish has been fulfilled.

The Chagatay minister at the court of Herat, Mīr ʿAlī Shīr Navā'ī (d. 1501), called himself the 'sweeper of ʿAnṣārī's shrine' to express his veneration for the Sufi master ʿAbdullāh-i Anṣārī (d. 1089),[13] a remark which should not be taken at face value, as little as the hyperbolic expression found in literature that one 'sweeps this or that threshold with one's eyelashes' (and washes it perhaps with one's tears). But some credulous authors seem to believe that this was actually done.

Sacred buildings were and still are washed at special times: to wash the Kaaba's interior is the Saudi kings' prerogative, and many shrines are washed at the annual celebration of the *'urs*. Often, the water is scented with sandalwood or other substances to enhance its purifying power. In Gulbarga, the sandalwood used for such a purification is carried around the city in a festive procession led by the *sajjādanishīn* of the shrine.

But much more important than these customs is the constant admonition that one has to be ritually clean to touch or recite the Koran, for 'only the purified touch it', as Sūra 56:79 states.[14] This is taken very seriously: no-one in a state of impurity (thus, for example, menstruating women) may perform the ritual prayer in which Koranic verses are recited. Particularly meticulous believers would not even mention the name of God unless they were in a ritually pure state. Among them was the Mughal emperor Humāyūn, who would avoid calling people by their names such as 'Abdullāh or 'Abdur Raḥmān lest the sacred name that forms the second part of the name be desecrated. Similar expressions of veneration are also known when it comes to the Prophet's name: 'Urfī (d. 1591) claims in his grand Persian poem in honour of the Prophet:

> If I should wash my mouth a hundred times with rosewater and musk,
> it would still not be clean enough to mention your noble name.[15]

Purification means, in a certain way, a new beginning on a loftier spiritual level.

The Prophet's biography (based on Sūra 94:1) tells how the angels opened young Muhammad's breast to take out a small black spot from his heart and wash it with odoriferous fluids: this is a very convenient way of pointing to his spiritual purification before he was called to act as God's messenger.[16]

Purification can be achieved by different means. One, not very frequent in the Islamic world, is by fire. It survives in some areas where, as for example in Balochistan, a true ordeal is enacted in the case of a woman accused of adultery, who has to walk barefoot over burning charcoals. Fire-walking is also practised among some Indian Shiites during the Muḥarram procession: a young Muslim friend from Hyderabad/Deccan joyfully described to me this experience, by which he felt purified and elated. Purification through fire is spiritualized in the image of the crucible in which the base matter of the soul suffers to turn finally into gold – one would have to refer here to the entire, and very wide, alchemical vocabulary of medieval Islam whose centre is, indeed, purification by fire. A branch of this purification – comparable to European midsummer night customs – is jumping through fire at Nawruz, the celebration of the vernal equinox, as is sometimes done in Iran; but there is no obvious 'Islamic' aspect to this tradition.

Purification, however, is a central Islamic tradition, based essentially on the Divine order to the Prophet: 'And your garments, purify them.' (Sūra 74:4). To be in the water is, as was seen above (pp. 7–8), to be quickened after death, and the use of water before prayer or the recitation of the Koran (and in fact before any important action) is not only a bodily but also a spiritual regeneration.

Modernists claim that the emphasis on proper ablution proves that Islam is the religion of hygiene, but the true meaning is much deeper. To get rid of external dirt is one thing, to purify oneself before religious acts is another; as Niẓāmuddīn Awliyā of Delhi remarked: 'The believer may be dirty, but never ritually unclean'.[17] For this reason, ablution is still to be performed after a 'normal' bath or shower. It is recommended, according to a *ḥadīth*, also in times of anger and wrath, because wrath comes from the fire-born devil, and fire can be extinguished by water (*AM* no. 243).

Ablution is a sacred action, and for each of its parts – taking the water in one's hand, washing one's face, one's arms, one's feet etc – special prayers are prescribed which point to the role of this or that limb in the religious sphere. A look at the examples in widely-used religious manuals such as Abū Ḥafṣ ʿOmar as-Suhrawardī's (d. 1234) *ʿAwārif al-maʿārif* helps one to understand the deeper meaning of purification.[18] Ablution after minor defilements, *wuḍū'*, is required after sleep and after anything solid, liquid or gaseous has left the lower part of the body. Some legal schools require it after two people of opposite sex, who are not related, shake hands or touch each other's skin. After major pollutions such as sex, emission of semen, menstruation or parturition, a full bath, *ghusl*, is required during which no part of the body, including the hair, may remain dry. The ablution has to be performed in running water (or by pouring water over one's body), and the volume of the water places, ponds or tanks, as found near mosques, is exactly defined.

Mystics could be induced into ecstasy during the first moment that water was poured over their hands, and one reads of saintly people who would perform *ghusl* – even without previous major pollution – in the icy waters of Central Asian rivers. Often, such acts were done not only for the sake of ritual purification but also with the intention of educating one's obstinate *nafs*, the lower sensual faculties, the 'flesh'. *Ghusl* should be performed before putting on the *iḥrām*, and a good number of people like to perform it before the Friday noon prayer. For ritual purity is recommended for every important act; thus one should not sleep with one's spouse in a state of impurity, nor should the mother suckle her baby without previous ablution.

Ablution has been taken as a metaphor into literary language, and poets and mystics alike have called on their readers to wash not merely their bodies, their shirts and their turbans but rather their souls. Nāṣir-i Khusraw says:

> One has to wash off rebellion from the soul with (the water of) knowledge and obedience.

He even speaks of the 'soap of religion' or 'soap of intellect' which is needed to purify the human mind.[19]

But like all rituals, purification too could be overstressed, and it seems that particularly law-abiding people were obsessed with what can almost be called 'idolatry of water'. Shabistarī thus writes:

> Although the mullah takes sixty kilogrammes of water to make
> his ablution for prayer,
> his head seems hollower than a calabash in Koranic meditation.[20]

Similarly, the Buddha had made some deprecative remarks about those who concentrate almost exclusively upon ritual cleanliness, for, if water enhanced one's piety, then fishes and frogs would be the most religious creatures on Earth. In 'Aṭṭār's *Manṭiq uṭ-ṭayr*, then, the duck refuses to partake in the quest for the Sīmurgh because she is constantly in the state of ritual purity (sitting on the 'prayer rug of water') and does not want to spoil this state.

The scarcity of water in Arabia led to the possibility of replacing water by sand in cases of dire need (*tayammum*).

One of the prerequisites of ritual purity in Islam is the absence of blood: not even the smallest bloodstain must be found on one's clothing during prayer. The Christian concept of 'being washed in the blood of the lamb' would be utterly repellent to Muslims. And yet, in the history of Sufism one finds that the martyr-mystic al-Ḥallāj claimed that he had performed his ablution with his own blood; that is, after his hands and feet had been amputated, he wiped the bleeding hand-stumps over his face. This expression was taken over by later poets for whom this meant the lover's absolute purification through martyrdom. For the body of the martyr, who is killed 'in the way of God', that is, in religious war (and on a number of other occasions), is not washed before burial; the blood of the martyr is sacred.

Metaphorically speaking, one can 'perform the ablution with one's tears', which flow so profusely that they can serve, as it were, as purifying water streams. Some Sufis even thought that their remorseful weeping served 'to wash the faces of the paradisiacal houris'.[21]

Not only during one's lifetime is ablution required before important actions, but also when the Muslim is laid to his or her last rest, the dead body is washed, preferably with warm water (except for martyrs). It is repeatedly related that pious calligraphers who had spent most of their lives in copying the words of the Koran or *ḥadīth* would carefully collect the pieces of wood that fell down when they sharpened their reed pens, and these innumerable minute scraps would be used to heat the water of their last *ghusl* because the *baraka* of the pens with which they had written the sacred words might facilitate their way into the next world and inspire them to answer correctly the questions of the interrogating angels in the grave.[22]

As ablution can be spoiled by any bodily impurity, so Muslims feel that one's ritual purity (which is more than the bodily) can also be spoiled by looking at or listening to things prohibited; when a Turkish woman friend of mine saw a couple kissing each other intensely in a crowded street in Ankara, she cried out: '*abdestim bozulacak*' – 'my ritual purity is going to be spoiled!'[23]

Not only by water or, rarely, fire can one become purified, but also by abstinence, whether from sleep, from food or from sex.

Giving up sleep to perform the nightly supererogative prayers, *tahajjud*, which are recommended in the Koran (Sūra 17:79), is a custom practised by pious Muslims who enjoy the deep spiritual peace of the nightly conversation with their Lord. Mystically-minded people will use the time between 2 and 4 a.m. to meditate and perform their *dhikr*. In the Ismaili community, the very early morning hours serve for the daily gathering of the believers in quiet meditation.

Asceticism as such, however, is basically un-Islamic. The aversion of many traditionalist Muslims to exaggerated forms of asceticism is one of the reasons for the tensions between the normative orthodox circles and Sufis. Iqbāl had once stated that asceticism is incompatible with Islam, for 'the Koran is brimful with life'.[24] There is no diabolization of the 'flesh'; and, as there exists no priestly caste whose members have to administer the sacrament and therefore have to abstain from sex, celibacy has never been accepted as the norm. Rather, the fulfilment of religious obligations requires that one must not mortify the body because it enables the human being to perform the ritual duties. Thus the Muslim can pray before eating: 'My intention is to eat this food to strengthen my body so that I can fulfil God's commands'.[25]

Yet, both in mainstream Islam and in Sufism, various kinds of abstinence were and are practised. The intentional avoidance of food is, basically, a means to gather greater 'power' or *baraka* by giving up a less important source of power, but the fasting month is not observed for reasons of penitence, nor for atonement, nor for 'gaining power', but simply because it is God's decree, hence a duty[26] – a duty, to be sure, that involved other, spiritual benefits.[27] The Sufis, considering fasting to be 'the food of angels', often overstressed it both in the form described for Ramaḍān and additional fast days and in the intake of minimal quantities of food, for 'hunger is God's food by which he feeds only the elite' (*AM* no. 460). Hagiographical literature contains examples of the reduction of food-consumption that sound almost frightening, and yet it is quite possible that the remarkable longevity of a considerable number of medieval Sufis is a result of their utterly abstinent life, which led to an increasing spiritualization. To make fasting more difficult, some Sufis practised *ṣawm dāʾūdī*, that is, eating for one day normally and fasting on the next day lest the body get used to one of the two forms. In the medieval Maghrib (and perhaps elsewhere too), Sufis knew the *ṣawm al-wiṣāl*, a forty-day fast which was supposed to lead to the unitive experience.[27]

During Ramaḍān, the Muslim should not only abstain from food during daytime but also avoid evil thoughts and actions, wrath and anger, trying to follow the old adage *takhallaqū bi-akhlāq Allāh,* 'qualify yourselves with the qualities of God', that is, exchange one's lowly characteristics for better ones until one attains complete equanimity.

Modern interpretations of the fasting in Ramaḍān state that it is a good training in self-control but also a practical way to prove one's solidarity with the hungry in the world. But there has been and still is criticism of the institution of a fasting month, which seems not suited to a modern industrialized society as it makes people unable to work enough during daytime. A typical case is President Bourguiba of Tunisia's attempt to declare work as *jihād,* a 'holy war' against hunger and poverty, claiming that as the rules of fasting are lifted in war times the same should be done for modern hard-working people (see above, p. 68).

Abstinence from sex has never been required in Islam. Although the virginity of the unmarried girl is strictly protected, nevertheless celibacy was never encouraged. On the contrary, marriage is the *sunna,* the sacred custom of the Prophet's community, and numerous stories tell how the Prophet appeared to a celibate ascetic in a dream, urging him to get married in order to become a real follower of his *sunna.* Most Sufis blessed by such a dream accepted his order, even though they might consider married life a foretaste of Hell. There were some Sufis who had no interest in marriage; but the majority were certainly not ascetics – 'Abdul Qādir Gīlānī, the epitome of the Qadiriyya *ṭarīqa,* had forty-nine children.

The positive attitude toward marriage as recommended by the Prophet was probably facilitated by the fact that Islam does not know the concept of an original sin that is inherited from generation to generation through the very act of procreation.

Abstinence is a kind of sacrifice: one abstains from a pleasure and gives up a custom in the hope of obtaining in exchange something more valuable. Characteristic of sacrifice is giving up something particularly dear to please or appease the Divine powers (an idea underlying the ancient sacrifice of the first-born son).

The replacement of human sacrifice by animal sacrifice is at the centre of the story of Abraham's willingness to offer his son (Isaac, according to the Old Testament; Ismā'īl, according to the Muslims). The Muslim remembers this beginning of a new era without human sacrifice every year at the *'īd ul-aḍḥā* on 10 Dhu 'l-hijja during the pilgrimage to Mecca when a lamb, a ram or the like is slaughtered. Modern critics as well as ordinary Muslims have often asked why the enormous waste of animals at the pilgrimage site in Mecca was necessary and why every Muslim family at home should slaughter an animal. Would it not be more logical, in our time, to give the price for the animal to the poor instead of distributing the meat and the hides? But the lawyer-divines insist on the slaughtering which is not in the Koran but is *sunna* because only thus the real intention, the remembrance of the substitution of an animal for a human sacrifice, is re-enacted by the believers.[29] The sacrificed lamb or ram – so some people believe – will reappear on Doomsday to carry its owner across the *ṣirāṭ*-bridge into Paradise.

The sacrifice of blameless young animals (two for a boy, one for a girl) during the *ʿaqīqa*, the first haircut of a seven-day-old baby, is part and parcel of domestic rituals, and the sacrifice of a sheep is also customary before a Muslim builds a house or constructs any major building, as one may sacrifice animals at saints' shrines; the blood is sometimes smeared on the threshold to increase its *baraka*. Among some Sufi orders, the novice is likened to the sacrificial ram of Abraham: he offers himself completely to the master.

The highest form of sacrifice is that of one's own life, as practised for example by the martyrs of faith. One thinks also of the *fidāʾīs* in medieval Islamic history whose appearance is initially connected with the Ismaili groups centred in Alamut (Iran) and northern Syria (the so-called Assassins). However, the disciples of a Sufi shaykh could also willingly perform self-sacrifice at the master's order: a modern example is the Ḥurr, the hard core of dervishes around the Pīr Pāgārō in Sind, who were particularly active from the mid-nineteenth century to the Second World War.[30]

Self-sacrifice lives on in spiritualized form in mystical tradition: the story of the lover whose beloved tells him that his very existence is the greatest sin, whereupon he immediately dies 'with a smile like a rose' (*D* no. 2,943), is found in different variants in classical Sufi literature. Furthermore, al-Ḥallāj's song 'Kill me, O my trustworthy friends' served poets such as Rūmī for pointing to the constant growth and upward movement of the creature, which, by 'dying before dying' in a series of self-sacrifices, slowly 'dies from mineral to become a plant' (*M* III 3,901) until it returns to the Divine Essence.

Instead of substituting an animal for human sacrifice, one can also perform a *pars pro toto* sacrifice; that is, one offers a small part of one's body. The typical form, as it survives in Islam, is the sacrifice of hair,[31] beginning with the first haircut of the newborn baby. Both sexes have to shave their pubic hair. The hair is cut before the pilgrimage to Mecca (but is not touched during the *ḥajj* rites). In former times, a disciple who wanted to enter a certain Sufi order such as the Chishtiyya had all his hair shaved, and to this day dervishes devoted to the tradition of the Turkestani saint Aḥmad Yesewi (d. 1166) shave their heads, while the medieval *qalandars* and a number of *bē-sharʿ* dervishes (that is, those who consider themselves as standing outside the religious prescriptions) used to shave not only the head but every trace of hair, including the eyebrows.

An even more important *pars pro toto* sacrifice is circumcision, something which originally was probably done to increase the boy's sexual power. The

Koran does not mention circumcision, but it was apparently taken for granted, as legend tells that the Prophet was born circumcised. The Turkish name of circumcision, *sünnet*, shows that it is done according to the Prophet's *sunna*, while the Arabic term *ṭahāra* points to the 'purification' aspect; the Urdu expression *musulmānī* shows that it is by circumcision that the boy becomes a full member of the Muslim community. The act is usually performed when the boy is seven or eight years old, so that he is fully aware of its importance, and the pride of now being a true Muslim – as Turkish boys told us with beaming faces – outweighs the moments of pain during the operation. Otherwise, to distract the boys, the adults often organized music, shadow plays and the like, and had a number of boys circumcised together to divert them. The circumcision of the sons of a ruler or grandee were usually celebrated with parades and entertainment.

The question of whether or not the prayer of an uncircumcised man is valid was answered differently. A number of theologians consider it permitted, which is important especially when it comes to adult converts to Islam.

Female circumcision is practised based on a *ḥadīth* which speaks of the 'touching of the two circumcised parts', which requires *ghusl*. It is probably more widespread than is thought, but is never done as a 'public feast'.[32]

The complete sacrifice of one's sexual power by castration was never an issue in Islam. Eunuchs, usually imported from Africa and Europe, were kept for practical reasons, such as guarding the women's quarters. They could also serve in the army and reach high ranks in the military hierarchy; but no religious aim was connected with castration.[33] Nor did Islam know the custom of sacred prostitution, which played a considerable role in some other, earlier religious traditions.[34]

Simpler types of substitute offerings are common: among them are the flowers and sweets which are often brought to a saint's tomb and then distributed to the poor as well as to the visitors; and before setting out for a journey, Indian Muslims might offer to their neighbours and friends special sweets over which the *Fātiḥa* was recited in the name of a particular saint in the hope of securing a speedy journey.

Such distribution of foodstuffs leads to another kind of 'sacrifice' which is central in Islam, namely alms-giving. The prescribed alms tax, which constitutes one of the five pillars of Islam, is called *zakāt*, a term which is, typically, derived from the root *z-k-y*, 'to purify'; and to give it is a true act of purification. However, not only the prescribed alms tax but also alms in general, *ṣadaqāt*, is important in Islamic piety. Not only material gifts in cash and kind can be 'sacrificed', but also ethical behaviour and prayer: one offers oneself completely to God in the hope of receiving His mercy. The finest expression of the sacrificial character of ritual prayer, in which the lower self is slaughtered like a lamb, is found in the story of the Sufi leader Daqūqī in Rūmī's *Mathnawī* (*M* III 2,140ff.).

While alms are an exactly organized, legally prescribed action, the gift is a free act of the individual, and yet it can also be seen as a kind of sacrifice. For to give means to part with something that is dear to oneself, to distribute as it were a small part of one's being. Gifts bind people together and thus help in shaping and institutionalizing a community. A person with whom one has shared 'bread and salt', as Westerners would say, is supposed to remain loyal, hence the Persian term *namak ḥarām*, 'whose salt is prohibited', for a disloyal person.

One must not forget, however, that the recipient of the gift is under a certain obligation towards the giver. Just as by offering a lamb one hopes to attract Divine grace, the giver – even if secretly or unwittingly – hopes for a reciprocation. The Persian expression *bār-i minnat*, 'the burden of owed gratitude', expressed this feeling on the part of the recipient very well. By giving generously, one's power is strengthened, and therefore one loves to give lavishly; anyone who is blessed with Muslim friends knows the largesse of their generosity and often near-despairs under the burden of gratitude. To give in order to receive underlies (for example) the Panjabi custom of *vartan banji*, the exchange of gifts in ever-increasing, exactly measured quantities, especially at weddings.[35]

VIA ILLUMINATIVA

A certain borderline between the profane, which is excluded by the act of purification, and the ritual state, is the *niyya*, 'intention'. Every religious act must begin with the formulation of the *niyya*, and the famous saying '*Al-aʿmāl bi'n-niyyāt*', 'Works are judged according to the intentions', does not mean, in the first place, that it is the *spiritual* intention, as most readers would interpret it, but rather that it is the formulated intent to 'perform a prayer with three cycles' or to 'perform the fasting for the day'. Thus, when I asked a Turkish friend during Ramaḍān whether she was fasting, she simply answered '*niyyetliyim*', 'I have formulated the *niyya*', that is, 'I certainly am fasting'.

The customs mentioned hitherto belong to the preliminary rites which prepare men and women for the approach to the Numinous. For even in a religion in which Divine transcendence is as central as in Islam, human beings still crave an approximation to the object of their veneration or love (hence the development of saint-worship), and for this reason some Sufis sought the theophany, *tajallī*, of the Lord whom 'the looks can never reach' (Sūra 6:103) by gazing at a beautiful youth, *shāhid*, a witness to this invisible Divine beauty.

In certain religions, plays were invented to make a sacred event visible in the here and now. In Islam, this happened only in the *taʿziya* plays among the Shiites, in which the drama of Kerbela is re-enacted and the spectators are as it were participating in this event as though they were really present. This however is, again, a custom incompatible with normative Sunni Islam.

Yet, there are always new attempts to become unified, or at least to come close to the object of devotion or the power that is hidden in it. The simplest way is to touch the sacred object or the saintly person, *tabarrukan*, for blessing's sake. The believer clings to the helper's skirt, and when Mawlānā Rūmī sings:

O seize the hem of His kindness,

he expresses this feeling in an old symbol. The believer touches sacred objects such as stones, tombs or the threshold and, most importantly, the copy of the Koran in which God's word is contained, or else is softly touched by the saint's or the venerable elder's hand which he may put on the believer's head, or perhaps by some peacock feathers that carry his *baraka*. The ritualized clasping of hands at the beginning of the Mevlevi *samāʿ* belongs here.

A typical case of transferring the *baraka* is the *bayʿa*, the oath of allegiance given to a Sufi master. The novice takes the master's hand (often in a specially prescribed form of movement), and this act guarantees that the current of blessing that goes back to the Prophet reaches him through the proper channel. If a woman takes the *bayʿa*, the shaykh may touch her hand or find some other way to transfer the *baraka*; he may stretch out a rod which she grasps, or make her touch his sleeve, or perhaps place his hand in a bowl with water, lest a direct contact, prohibited by the *sharīʿa*, should happen.

A special kind of transfer of power is the custom called in Urdu *balā'ēn lēnā*, 'to take away afflictions': one passes one's hands over an ailing or suffering person, circles them over the head and then takes them onto one's own body; thus the evil is taken away and blessing power substituted.

An even stronger way to avail oneself of blessing power is kissing. Touching or kissing the feet or knees of elders, of important people or of the mystical leader is common practice, as is the kissing of the threshold at a saint's shrine. The best-known ritual of this kind is the pilgrims' attempt to kiss the black stone of the Kaaba to partake in its blessing power. The same is true for the practice of kissing the copy of the Koran, filled with the *baraka* of God's word – and when poets compare their beloved's beautiful face to a pure, flawless Koran copy, the idea that the Koran should be kissed may have played a role in this imagery.[36]

The kiss between two people is, as was known in classical antiquity, an exchange of souls; the soul, which is often thought to be contained in the breath, comes to one's lips when one expires, and can be restored by the life-giving breath of the beloved. That is why Jesus, whose breath could quicken the dead (Sūra 3:44ff., 5:110ff.), became in poetical language the prototype of the beloved who quickens the near-dead lover with his or her kiss. Mystics like Bahā-i Walad extended the topic of the spiritual kiss to contact with God: 'Go into God's bosom, and God takes you to His breast and kisses you and displays Himself so that you may not run away from Him but put your whole heart upon Him day and night'.[37]

As both breath and saliva are fraught with blessing power, the custom of breathing upon someone after reciting a prayer (*damīdan, üflemek*) is common in the Muslim world. One can also breathe certain religious formulas or invocations over water in a bowl, which thus becomes endowed with healing power. In Shia circles, the invocation *Nādi ʿAliyyan* ... is frequently used for this purpose, and among the Ismailis the *āb-i shifā* is 'healing water' over which the Imam has breathed to fill it with *baraka* to bless the believers.

Such attempts at establishing a closer connection with the sacred power and its representative were and still are practised among Muslims; but certain practices are restricted to only a segment of the believers, and are disliked by others. One of these is the sacred dance, which belongs originally to the rites of circumambulation by which one either 'sains' an object or tries to participate in its power. Orthodox Muslims are still as averse to dance as a religious experience as were the early Christians – so much so that Origen (d. 254) would claim: 'Where there is dance there is the devil'.[38]

Dance, especially the whirling dance, goes together with ecstasy, that state in which the seeker seems to be leaving the earthly centre of gravity to enter into another spiritual centre's attracting power, as though he were joining the angelic hosts or the blessed souls.

Ecstasy could thus be induced by whirling dance, which was practised as early as the ninth century among the Sufis in Baghdad, some of whom would abandon themselves to the rapture caused by music, their 'hearing', *samāʿ*.[39] Such spontaneous dance is known among a number of mystical fraternities (and has almost become a hallmark of Sufi movements in the West – as much as critical early Sufis disliked it). *Samāʿ* was institutionalized only in the Mevleviyya, the order that goes back to Mawlānā Rūmī and which was organized in its actual form by his son and second successor, Sulṭān Walad (d. 1312). Rūmī had sung most of his poetry while listening to music and whirling around his axis, and to him the whole universe appeared as caught in a dance around the central sun, under whose influence the disparate atoms are mysteriously bound into a harmonious whole. Thus, to enter the whirling means to come into contact with the eternal source of all movement – so much so, that Rūmī saw even the very act of creation as a dance in which Not-Being leapt forward into Existence (*D* no. 1,832) when it heard the sweet melody of the Divine question *Alastu bi-rabbikum*?, 'Am I not your Lord?' (Sūra 7:172); and this dance which permeates all of nature revives even the dead in their graves, for:

> Those who know the secret power
> of the whirling, live in God –
> Love is slaying and reviving
> them – they know it. Allāh Hu!

The mystic might feel the bliss of unification when he had lost himself completely in the circling movement, and thus dance can be seen as 'a ladder to heaven' that leads to the true goal, to unification. But, as this goal contradicts the sober approach of normative theologians, who never ceased to emphasize God's Total Otherness and who saw the only way to draw closer to Him in obedience to His commands and revealed law, their aversion to music and dance is understandable.[40]

VIA UNITIVA

In ancient strata of religion, sexual union was conceived as a symbol for spiritual union, and even the Upanishads, abstract as their teaching may sound in many places, describe the highest bliss as comparable to being embraced by a beloved wife. But as the normative theologians disliked the ecstatic dance as a means to 'union', they also objected to a terminology in which 'love' was the central concept.[41] Nomos-oriented as they were, they sensed the danger of eros-oriented forms of religion which might weaken the structure of the House of Islam. They could interpret 'love' merely as 'love of obedience' but not as an independent way and goal for Muslims, and expressions like 'union' with the One who is far beyond description and whom neither eyes could reach nor hands touch seemed an absurdity, indeed impiety, to them. The theological discussions about the terminology of 'Love' continued for a long time in the ninth and tenth centuries, long before the thought of a human being as target of one's love appeared in Sufism – a love which, to be sure, was never to be fulfilled but remained (or at least was supposed to remain) chaste and spiritual. The mystics then became aware that 'the metaphor is the bridge to Reality' and that love of a beautiful human being was, as they say, *'ishq majāzī*, 'metaphorical love', which would lead to *'ishq ḥaqīqī*, 'the true love' of the only One who was worthy of love.

From this viewpoint, the frank use of expressions like 'naked union' in Rūmī's poetry can be understood, and his father Bahā-i Walad, who encourages the soul to cast itself into God's bosom without reluctance, compares the intimacy between God and the soul with an explicit reference to the play between husband and wife in which even the most private parts do not remain hidden.[42] Six centuries later, the Sufi master Nāṣir Muḥammad 'Andalīb in Delhi uses similar words, comparing the soul's union with the Divine Beloved to the experience of the virgin whose hymen is pierced by her husband so that she, accustomed to his gentleness, becomes aware of his power and strength.[43] The overwhelming shock of the last ecstatic experience is thus symbolized. It seems also (according to an authentic report by someone who underwent the forty days' seclusion and spent most of the time in *dhikr*) that this results in a strong 'sensual' and even sexual feeling – a fact which perhaps also accounts for the tendency to describe the final union in sexual imagery.

Although the seekers tried to reach the state of blessed union in this life, the true *'urs*, the 'wedding' of the soul, is reached in death when the soul is finally reunited with God.

The Koranic descriptions of Paradise, with the large-eyed heavenly virgins, the houris, can be interpreted as a hint of the highest bliss of spiritual union which cannot be expressed in other terms, just as one explains the joy of sexual union to a child by comparing it with sugar (*M* III 1,406).

An interesting aspect of this imagery is the concept of the woman soul, which is encountered most outspokenly in the Indian subcontinent.[44] The Indian type of *virāhini*, the longing bride or young wife, was taken over into popular and at times also high literatures of the Muslims in Sindhi, Panjabi and other indigenous languages. Such a choice of images would have been difficult, had not a predisposition existed to compare the soul with a woman. After all, the Arabic word for 'soul', *nafs*, is feminine, and the romantic stories of young women, braving all difficulties on the path that leads them through deserts and mountains or into the depth of the Indus, form excellent symbols of the soul's wandering in the mystical path where she has to overcome the most terrible obstacles to be united, through death, with her pre-eternal bridegroom. The predilection of Sufi writers for the topic of Yūsuf and Zulaykhā (Sūra 12:23ff.) seems to point to the same experience; the love-intoxicated woman who tries to reach Absolute Beauty, and is chastised and – as later legend has it – repents and is finally united with her erstwhile beloved, may have served the mystics as a prefiguration of their own longing. This becomes particularly clear in Rūmī's use of the Zulaykhā theme, through which he seems to express his deepest feelings.[45] Many utterances of mystical love become indeed much more meaningful if one recognizes the seeker as the female part who craves for union and longs to be filled with Divine grace. The Beloved, the Lord and eternal King, is the truly acting power, while the mystic is the recipient of His grace: God is, as mystical folk poetry often says, *as-Sattār*, the 'One Who Covers' the lonely woman. That in popular Indo–Pakistani poetry the Prophet appears sometimes as the soul's bridegroom, just as the Imam is the longed-for beloved in Ismaili *gināns*, is part of this imagery.

These ideas were symbolized by dervishes who donned women's garments to show that they were the Lord's modest handmaidens, and it also underlies, to a certain extent, Rūmī's parable, in *Fīhi mā fīhi*, of the birth of Jesus in the human being when the soul, like Mary, is pregnant with the Holy Spirit.[46] Interestingly, the bond between master and disciple is called among Khāksār dervishes *izdiwāj-i rūḥānī*, 'spiritual marriage', a marriage that shall lead to the 'engendering of love'.[47]

The Sufis' love of and admiration for a beautiful young boy, ideally of fourteen years of age, has been expressed in thousands of lines of poetry and is thus an integral part of the tradition. They love to quote the apocryphal *ḥadīth*: 'I saw my Lord in the most beautiful form' (and, as is often added, 'with his cap awry'). This admiration of a young, 'moonlike' beloved, a *shāhid*, 'witness' to Divine beauty, arose in part from the strict seclusion of women in Muslim society, but could lead also to pederasty, as even early sources state with anger and chagrin. As pederasty was condemned in the Koran (cf. Sūra 27:55f.), the very imagery was disliked by many of the pious, who tried to interpret such allusions as pertaining to women (neither Persian nor Turkish has a grammatical gender). The problem of how then to translate correctly the young beloved with 'a sprouting green facial down and moustache' is discussed time and again.[48]

Sexual union is not the only way to allude to one's union with the Numinous power. One can eat or drink the matter that carries blessing and sanctity; one can 'eat power'. When the Muslim boy in southern India at the *Bismillāh* ceremony (which takes place when he has reached the age of four years, four months and four days) has to lick the words 'In the name of God ...' from the slate on which they are written with some blessed stuff such as sandalwood paste, he takes in their power, as does the ailing person who drinks water from a bowl that is inscribed with Koranic verses and formulas of blessing.

The pilgrim who visits saints' shrines and participates in eating the food that carries, as it were, the saint's *baraka* is another example of 'eating the sacred',[49] and the huge cauldron from which everyone, caste or rank notwithstanding, receives some blessed food has certainly played a role in expanding the realm of Islam in areas where food taboos were strict (as is the case in Hindu India). Scraping out the enormous cauldron in Muʿīnuddīn Chishtī's shrine in Ajmer is one of the most important rituals during the *ʿurs*, and people try to scrape some morsels from it without caring whether they burn their fingers.[50]

Communal meals were and are customary at the initiation ceremonies in Sufi brotherhoods and in the *futuwwa*, and in certain orders very elaborate communal meals are held once in a while; then one usually takes home some of the food for one's family to give them their share of the blessings. The power that can be ascribed to such food, and here in particular to sweets, is understood from Ibn Baṭṭūta's travelogue, when he tells that Rūmī's whole inspiration was caused by a piece of blessed *ḥalwa*.[51] The astounding number of allusions to food in Rūmī's poetry makes this amusing story sound almost correct – and Konya is still famed for its *ḥalwa*!

Even though the 'sacramental' idea of partaking of sacred food may be largely forgotten, the language has still, as so often, preserved the underlying feeling: the Sufi 'tastes' or experiences the 'taste' of spiritual bliss (*dhauq*). And may one not be allowed to see in the wondrous fruits which the blessed will eat in Paradise a hint of the Numinous character of 'spiritual' blessed food? To reach a higher stage by 'being eaten' underlies Rūmī's story of the chickpeas (*M* III 4,158ff.).

Although the practices and the symbolism just mentioned are certainly important, much more widespread even than food imagery is the symbolism of drinking. It is indeed a strange paradox that, in a religion that prohibits intoxicants, this particular image became the favourite of pious writers. The Koran first ordered: 'Don't approach prayer when you are drunk!' (Sūra 4:43), because intoxication hinders the person from performing the rites correctly; in a later stage of the revelation, wine was completely prohibited (Sūra 5:90); only in Paradise will the believers enjoy *sharāban ṭāhūran*, 'a pure wine' or 'drink' (Sūra 76:21).

However, the theme of sacred intoxication (*Den helige rusen*, as Nathan Söderblom's well-known study is called)[52] was an excellent symbol for the spiritual state which German mystics would call *Gottesfülle*, 'being filled with God'. Intoxication involves a loss of personal identity; the soul is completely filled with spiritual power, and the boundaries of legal prescriptions are no longer observed.

Ibn al-Fāriḍ's (d. 1235) great *Khamriyya*, the Wine-Ode, describes the wine of Love which the souls drank before the grapes were created and by which they are guided and refreshed; it makes the deaf hear and the ailing healed.[53] It is this wine that is mentioned even in a *ḥadīth*, according to which God gives to His friends a wine by which they become intoxicated and finally reach union (*AM* no. 571). It also fills Sufi poetry in manifold variants: 'the *Manṣūrī* wine, not the *angūrī* wine', as Rūmī says, is the wine by which the martyr-mystic 'Manṣūr' al-Ḥallāj was so intoxicated that he joyfully sacrificed his life in the hope of reaching union with his Beloved, while the grape wine, *angūrī*, is connected with the Christians (*D* no. 81) and, to a certain extent, the Zoroastrians. Rūmī also called his friends not to come to his grave without being intoxicated, for the wheat that will grow out of his grave's dust will be drunk; the dough made of it will be equally intoxicated; and the baker who works on it will sing ecstatic hymns – so much is he permeated by the wine of Divine Love. This imagery, praising wine and intoxication, continued through the centuries, and even Ayatollah Khomeini's small collection of Persian verse bears the surprising title *Sabū-yi 'ishq*, 'The Pitcher of Love'.[54]

Two types of Sufis are often juxtaposed: the sober and the intoxicated. The former are those who fulfil all obligations of the law and the path and are in complete self-control, while the intoxicated prefer the state of ecstasy and often utter words that would be dangerous in a state of sobriety. The borders, however, are not always clearly delineated. Sobriety, again, is of two kinds: the first sobriety is the human being's normal state and can lead, for a moment to an intoxication, a rapture in which the mystic seems to experience the absolute Unity; but when he returns from there, restored to his senses, in his 'second sobriety' he sees the whole universe differently – not as one with God but entirely permeated by Divine light.

The symbol of intoxication seems most fitting for the ecstatic state when the wine of Love fills one's whole being and causes infinite happiness – which may, however, be followed by long periods of spiritual dryness.

It is interesting that the imagery of wine and drunkenness is also used to symbolize the Primordial Covenant, *mīthāq,* in which God asked His creatures: 'Am I not your Lord?' (Sūra 7:172). Everyone from the future generations whom God drew from the loins of the children of Adam in pre-eternity had to testify that God is the Lord, lest they deny this when asked on Doomsday. The Sufis saw this moment in poetical imagery as a spiritual banquet in which the wine of Love was distributed to humanity so that everyone received the share which he or she will have in this life. Here, the imagery of wine is used not for the final goal of the mystic's unification with God and his being filled with Him, but rather as the starting point of the flow of Divine grace at the beginning of time. And thus it is written around the dome of Ge–sūdarāz's mausoleum in Gulbarga:

> They, intoxicated from Love's goblet,
> Senseless from the wine of 'Am I not?'
> Strive at times for piety and prayer,
> Worship idols now, and now drink wine ...[55]

The lovers of God are beyond beginningless eternity and endless eternity, there where no place is, all submerged in the Divine Beloved.

NOTES

1. A recent attempt to interpret various aspects of Islam is M. E. Combs-Schilling (1989), *Sacred Performances. Islam, Sexuality, and Sacrifice.*
2. Iqbāl (1923), *Payām-i mashriq*, p. 264 (last poem).
3. Jafar Sharif (1921), *Islam in India*, p. 23.
4. *The Wild Rue* has lent its name to Bess A. Donaldson's very useful (1938) study of Persian customs and superstitions. One may also remember that several mystical works have titles alluding to fragrance, such as Najmuddīn Kubrā's *Fawā'iḥ al-jamāl,* the 'fragrant breeze of beauty', or Khwāja Khurd's notes called simply *Fawa'iḥ.* A translation of Rūmī's *Mathnawī* is called *Pirahan-i Yūsufi,* 'Yusuf's shirt', to convey the idea that it brings the healing fragrance of the original to the reader whose spiritually blind eyes will be opened just as the fragrance of Yusuf's shirt healed his blind father.
5. For the theme, see E. Lohmeyer (1919), 'Vom göttlichen Wohlgeruch'. The odour of sanctity is well known in Christianity, and the Muslim should pray, following the *ḥadīth* (*AM* no. 383): 'Oh my God, quicken me with the fragrance of Paradise'. In Rūmī's poetry, following the example of Shams-i Tabrīzī, concepts like scent, fragrance and odour play an extremely important role. Rūmī's story of the tanner is inspired by ʿAṭṭār's *Asrārnāma* (see H. Ritter (1955), *Das Meer der Seele,* p. 92), where the hero is a sweeper, cleaning the latrines. The connection of fragrance and the 'scent of acquaintance' with the Prophet's love of perfume is important, and one even finds that the *mawlid* singers in Egypt sometimes sing a 'perfumed', *taʿṭīr, mawlid*: 'Send down, O Lord, perfumed blessings and peace on his tomb!' (information from Dr Kamal Abdul Malik, Toronto). I hope to deal with the whole complex of 'scent' in my forthcoming book *Yusuf's Fragrant Shirt* (New York, Columba University Press).

6. S. Seligmann (1910), *Der böse Blick*; R. Köbert (1948), 'Zur Lehre des *tafsīr* über den bösen Blick'; Hiltrud Sheikh-Dilthey (1990), 'Der böse Blick'; Jan Rypka (1964), 'Der böse Blick bei Niẓāmī'.
7. E. W. Lane (1978 ed.), *Manners and Customs*, p. 227.
8. An excellent example of this movement is the title page of Roland and Sabrina Michaud (1991), *Dervishes du Hind et du Sind.*
9. For the Zār, see Kriss and Kriss-Heinrich (1962), *Volksglaube im Islam*, vol. 2, ch. 3.
10. Jafar Sharif (1921), *Islam in India*, p. 62.
11. R. Gramlich (1981), *Die schiitischen Derwischorden*, vol. 3, p. 26ff.
12. I. Goldziher (1915b), 'Die Entblössung des Hauptes'. See also A. Gölpĭnarlĭ (1977), *Tasavvuftan dilimize geçen terimler*, pp. 46–7.
13. M. Subtelny (forthcoming), 'The cult of ʿAbdullāh Anṣārī under the Timurids'.
14. G. H. Bousquet (1950), 'La pureté rituelle en Islam'. See also the unattributed article 'What the Shiahs teach their children'; in general: I. Goldziher (1910), 'Wasser als dämonenabwehrendes Mittel'.
15. 'Urfi (d. 1591), quoted in Sājid Ṣiddīqui and Walī ʿAṣī (1962), *Armaghān-i naʿt*, p. 49.
16. H. Birkeland (1955), *The Legend of the Opening of Muhammad's Breast.*
17. The difference between 'worldly' dirt and ritual uncleanliness underlies the story that a Sufi's maidservant in ninth-century Baghdad exclaimed: 'O Lord – how dirty are Your friends!' (Jāmī (1957), *Nafaḥāt al-uns*, p. 621) – and yet a Sufi would never neglect his ritual purity.
18. Suhrawardī (1978), *ʿAwārif* (transl. R. Gramlich), p. 243f.
19. Nāṣir-i Khusraw (1929), *Dīvān*, pp. 38, 421, 507, 588, and in (1993) tr. Schimmel, *Make a Shield from Wisdom*, p. 36. Bakharzī (1966), too, speaks in the *Awrād al-aḥbāb*, vol. 2, p. 311, of 'the soap of repentance'.
20. Quoted in L. Lewisohn (ed.) (1992), *The Legacy of Mediaeval Persian Sufism*, p. 23.
21. Richard Gramlich (1992), 'Abū Sulaymān ad-Dārānī', p. 42.
22. See A. Schimmel (1984), *Calligraphy and Islamic Culture*, p. 180 note 167.
23. According to Kharijite opinion, evil talk and slander require an ablution.
24. Muhammad Iqbāl (1917), 'Islam and Mysticism', *The New Era*, 28 July 1917.
25. F. Taeschner (1979), *Zünfte*, p. 516.
26. H. Wagtendonk (1968), *Fasting in the Koran.*
27. A *ḥadīth* mentioned by Bukhārī (*ṣawm* 2, 9) claims that 'the bad breath of one who fasts is sweeter to God than the fragrance of musk'.
28. Oral communication from Professor Vincent Cornell, Duke University, Durham, NC, USA.
29. See H. Lazarus-Yafeh (1981), *Some Religious Aspects of Islam*, p. 20: according to the well-known theologian M. Shalṭūṭ, money cannot be substituted for a sacrifice because the slaughtering of the animal 'is a statute given by God'.
30. H. T. Lambrick (1972), *The Terrorist*, gives an excellent introduction into the life and thought of the Ḥurr, based on personal papers and records of the trials which he, as a British official, conducted.
31. I. Goldziher (1886), 'Le sacrifice de la chevelure des Arabes'.
32. Female circumcision is rather common in Egypt, but is also practised in some Panjabi tribes (see Jafar Sharif (1921), *Islam in India*, p. 50) and among the Daudi Bohoras.
33. D. Ayalon (1979), 'On the Eunuchs in Islam'.
34. A reflection of Hindu practices is probably the former custom of 'marrying' a girl to the shrine of Lāl Shahbāz Qalandar in Sehwan (Sind), an old Shiva sanctuary. In Sind, girls from noble families are sometimes 'married' to the Koran and remain virgins, respected by their families and friends. See R. Burton (1851), *Sindh*, p. 211.

35. For *vartan banjī* and many more customs in rural Indo–Pakistan, see the useful book by Zekiye Eglar (1960), *A Punjabi Village in Pakistan*. The still-prevailing custom of celebrating a wedding as grandly as possible, even if that means incurring heavy debts, reflects the – perhaps subconscious – hope of acquiring more power by spending whatever one can afford (and often can*not* afford ...).
36. See *ERE* s.v. Kiss; *RGG* (3rd ed.) s.v. Kuss.
37. Bahā-i Walad (1957), *Ma'ārif*, vol. 4, p. 28.
38. For a general introduction, see W. O. G. Oesterley (1923), *The Sacred Dance*; G. van der Leeuw (1930), *In den Himel ist eenen dans*; F. Meier (1954), 'Der Derwischtanz'; M. Molé (1963) 'La Danse extatique en Islam'.
39. For the use of dance and music in Rūmī's work, see A. Schimmel (1978c), *The Triumphal Sun*, and idem (1982a), *I am Wind, You are Fire*; in general: J. During (1989), *Musique et mystique dans les traditions d'Iran*.
40. Ibn Ḥanbal mentions even a *ḥadīth*: 'I was sent to eradicate musical instruments'.
41. W. Schubart (1941), *Religion and Eros*; A. Schimmel (1979a), 'Eros – heavenly and not-so-heavenly – in Sufism'.
42. Compare the chapter 'Hieroi gamoi' in F. Meier (1990a), *Bahā-i Walad* (ch. 23).
43. 'Andalīb (1891), *Nāla-i 'Andalīb*, vol. 1, p. 832. The motif of wounding the female by means of an arrow permeates literature and art from classical antiquity. A fine way of pointing to the purely symbolic aspects of 'bridal mysticism' is Rūmī's verse that 'No ablution is required after the union of spirits' (*D* no. 2207).
44. The theme of the woman soul as it occurs in the regional languages of Indo–Pakistani Islam has been taken up several times by Ali S. Asani (1991, et al.).
45. See A. Schimmel (1992c), 'Yusof in Mawlānā Rūmī's poetry'.
46. *Fihi mā fihi*, end of ch. 5.
47. R. Gramlich (1981), *Die schiitischen Derwischorden*, vol. 3, p. 101.
48. See the remark of Joseph von Hammer (1812–13) in his German translation of *Der Diwan des ... Hafis*, Introduction, p. vii.
49. For the role of *dēg* and *langar*, cauldron and open kitchen, among the dervishes, see R. Gramlich (1981), *Die schiitischen Derwischorden*, vol. 3, p. 49f.
50. See the description in P. M. Currie (1989), *The Shrine and Cult of Muin al-Din Chishti of Ajmer*, and the article by Syed Liaqat Hussain Moini (1989), 'Rituals and customary practices at the Dargāh of Ajmer'.
51. Ibn Baṭṭūṭa, *Riḥla*, translated by H. A. R. Gibb, *The Travels of Ibn Baṭṭūṭa*, vol. 2, 1962. For Rūmī's use of 'kitchen imagery', see A. Schimmel (1978c), *The Triumphal Sun*, ch. II.
52. N. Söderblom (1915), *Ur religionens historia*.
53. A translation of the *Khamriyya* is E. Dermenghem (1931), *L'écloge dun vin – poème mystique d'Omar ibn al-Faridh*.
54. Published in Teheran (200,000 copies) on the occasion of the fortieth day after Ayatollah Khomeini's death in 1989. Bakharzī (1966, *Awrād al-aḥbāb*, vol. 3, p. 240ff.), as well as virtually all Sufi theoreticians – up to Dr J. Nurbakhsh (1988) in his *Sufi Symbolism* – explain the frequent use of terms like 'wine' (*sharāb*, *mudām*) as 'wine of Love', and 'that is the "pure wine", *ash-sharāb aṭ-ṭāhūr*'.
55. Gēsūdarāz, in Ikrām (ed.) (1953), *Armaghān-i Pāk*, p. 151.

IV

The Word and the Script

وَمِنْ آيَاتِهِ يُرِيكُمُ الْبَرْقَ خَوْفًا وَطَمَعًا وَيُنَزِّلُ مِنَ
السَّمَاءِ مَاءً فَيُحْيِي بِهِ الْأَرْضَ بَعْدَ مَوْتِهَا كتبه شمس انورى

And of His signs: He shows you the lightning, for fear and hope, and that He sends down from the sky water and revives by it the earth after it was dead.

Sūra 30:24

THE WORD – ABOUT GOD, AND FROM GOD

The Primordial Covenant shows very clearly that the Divine word precedes the human word: after hearing the Divine address 'Am I not your Lord?', the future human beings answered with 'Yes, we give witness to it' (Sūra 7:172).[1]

The word, as it comes from God and reveals Him and His will, is central in Islam. But generally speaking, the sacred word is taken out of ordinary daily life and its confused noise by means of a special kind of recitation which underlines its sacred character.

There are primordial sounds, Numinous 'Urlaute' like the Indian *om*, and nobody who has heard the long-drawn-out call *Huuu* (literally 'He') at the end of a dervish ceremony such as the Mevlevi *samā*ʿ can forget this sound, whose vibrations move body and mind equally. Listening to such sounds, one understands why 'sound' could be regarded as Creative Power, and it becomes perfectly clear why musical therapy with sacred, *baraka*-loaded sounds was well known in Islamic culture and is still practised among certain Sufi groups.

Given this importance of the proper sound patterns, and as their corollary, proper recitation, it would be astonishing if special reciting styles were not applied to the Koran, which should be 'embellished' by human voices.[2] For sound patterns and meaning in the Koran are closely intertwined, one of the reasons that account for the prohibition of a 'translation' of the Koran into other languages, as then the inimitable sounds and the true spirit would be lost. The arts of Koranic recitation, *tilāwat*, *tajwīd* or *tartīl*, that is, deliberate cadences, and *tardīd*, rhythmical repetitions, are highly developed, and nowadays competitions of Koran reciters from all over the world are convened every year. But even in the normal recitation without the psalmodizing technique, a number of rules have to be observed in order to display the Divine word's full beauty.

By applying certain musical and rhetorical rules to religious texts, a very special atmosphere is created. This can be observed in popular religious songs all over the Islamic world: the Turkish *ilâhi* or *nefes* are characterized by repetitive formulas such as the form of four-lined stanzas, the fourth line of which is repeated either in full or at least in its rhyme-scheme. In Indo-Pakistani *qawwali* sessions, the alternating voices of the leader and the small choir slowly submerge the listener in an undulating sea of sound until he or she is transported to another sphere far away from daily life. As repetition serves to give form to the intangible, in languages such as Sindhi and Panjabi the theme is given by an initial line which is then repeated after every one or two lines by the chorus. This includes the repetition of the congregation's *Amīn* after the master, or leader, has uttered a lengthy chain of small prayers.

Parallelismus membrorum is a literary form well known in the ancient Oriental and then Christian tradition, and is found in a style reminiscent of that of the Psalms in the great prayers transmitted from religious leaders of early and medieval Islam. In Jazūlī's (d. 1495) *Dalā'il al-khayrāt*, a very widely-used religious text in which blessings are called down upon the Prophet, who is described in ever-changing and yet similar, often rhyming, invocations, the blessing *ṣallā 'llāh ʿalayhi wa sallam*, 'God bless him and give him peace', is repeated hundreds of times, very much like the hundredfold 'Be greeted' in Christian litanies. Furthermore, the constant repetition of this sacred formula is thought to bring the Prophet close to the reciting believers: 'the Prophet *is* with his community when they recite the blessings over him many times', says a prominent mystical leader of the early nineteenth century. Thus, such a session in which the *ṣalāwāt sharīfa* are recited hundreds of times can lead to what can be called a 'sacramental' experience.

Melodious songs in honour of saints follow a similar pattern, thus the invocation of the Chishti saint Gēsūdarāz with its constantly repeated *salām*:

As-salāmu ʿalayka yā Gēsūdarāz,
as-salāmu ʿalayka mērē Bandanawāz ...

Whole litanies exist in which the names of mystics are enumerated, as the powerful invocations in Rūzbihān Baqlī's *Sharḥ-i shaṭḥiyāt* show;[3] the same is true for the invocations of Shia imams.

The tendency to highlight the core idea by repetition can be observed in high poetry as well. There, the *radīf*, the repeated rhyme word or phrase, seems as it were to circumambulate the Lord, whom the author uses all rhetorical devices to praise, in particular the juxtaposition of two contrasting aspects of God, such as His mercy and His wrath, His guidance and His 'ruse', or His capacity to grant life and to take life. Eulogies of the Prophet, or, in Shia poetry, of ʿAlī, are structured according to the same principle. A fine example is the great hymn in honour of the Prophet by Nāṣir-i Khusraw, in which the name *Muḥammad* forms the recurrent rhyme no less than forty-three times. Constant repetitions of exclamations like 'My soul!' or of questions like *kū kū?*, 'Where, O where?', of invocations that are almost an epiclesis – 'Come, Come!' or 'Hither, Hither!' – especially in the emotionally highly-charged verse of Rūmī, are excellent examples of repetitive structures in the rhyme.[4] Long chains of anaphors can serve the same purpose; suffice it to read the chain of exclamations *Zahī zahī* 'How beautiful! How beautiful!' in the introductory praise of God in ʿAṭṭār's *Ilāhīnāma*. By the use of both anaphors and repeated rhymes, the poet tries to approach the Divine from all possible new angles to give at least a faint idea of His greatness.

Such poems should be recited with high voice to enjoy them fully; but besides the loud recitation and even shouting aloud, one may also find a recitation of sacred words with low voice, or in silence. That can be done lest the outsider understand the secrets expressed by the reciter, or to give the listener an opportunity to pray in the spirit, as in the silent recitation of the *Fātiḥa* at the end of prayers, or in meetings. The murmuring of the Zoroastrian priests, *zamzama*, was well known among the Persians, and sometimes poets compare the twittering and chirping of the birds to this practice (for they praise the Lord in their secret language, which only Solomon could properly understand). The question of whether the *dhikr*, the recollection of God, should be performed with loud voice (and even in a kind of screaming, as in the so-called *dhikr-i arra*, 'sawing *dhikr*', of some Central Asian Sufis) or should rather be done quietly caused major discussions and tensions in medieval Sufi circles.

The word – the language in itself, as Muslims felt – was something special: the word is a messenger from God, as Nāṣir-i Khusraw stated.[5] From early times, people have known sacred and secret languages. Hunters and fishermen had their own idioms, as have some merchants, or thieves still today, and each group jealously concealed its intentions under the cover of metaphors lest the power of the 'real' word be broken.[6] The same is true in higher religions whose scriptures are revealed in a specific language which then tended to become sacralized. Prime examples of sacred languages are Sanskrit and Arabic, as much as Arabic was the common language at the time the Koran was revealed and is still one of the most widespread languages in the world. Yet, the language of the Koran is something different; its proper and religiously valid recitation is possible only in Arabic because that is how God revealed His will; therefore ritual prayer must be performed only in the language of the Koran. The attempts of Ataturk in Turkey to have the call to prayer recited in Turkish caused much grievance in the Muslim community, and most traditionally-minded Turks rejoiced when the Arabic call to prayer was reintroduced after the elections of 1950. Arabic is filled with *baraka*, and there is even a *ḥadīth* that 'Knowledge of Arabic is part of one's religion'.[7] The *iʿjāz al-qurʾān*, the inimitability of the sacred Book, was the incontrovertible proof of its Divine character as well as the proof of Muhammad's prophethood. For as the Arabs were so fond of their powerful language, Muhammad's miracle had to be connected with language, as Jāḥiẓ argued, while Moses performed 'magic' miracles in consonance with the Egyptians' trust in magic, and Jesus was the healer in a culture where healing was highly appreciated.[8]

The feeling of Arabic being '*the* language' par excellence could lead to certain problems, for the question arose as to whether or not a non-Muslim Arab should be permitted to teach Arabic, or whether a non-Muslim should learn and teach it at all. A shade of this feeling that the non-Muslim cannot teach Arabic properly as he or she is excluded, as it were, from fully appreciating its sacred mysteries can be observed even today despite the great number of Arabic-speaking Copts and Syrian and Lebanese Christians, many of whom are first-class scholars of Arabic.

But when the language of the Koran could and should not be translated owing to its sanctity, how was one to inform people about its contents as Islam continued to spread into areas outside Arabia? Commentaries and interlinear translations, however insufficient, were one means, and the role of Muslims of non-Arab background in the development of Koranic sciences, not to mention philology, history and natural sciences, is immense.

Another way, which is important when one has to deal not with the elite but with the masses, was to develop the different languages which the Muslims encountered during the expansion of their rule. As in Europe St Francis and Jacopone da Todi stand at the beginning of Italian, and German nuns and mystics, in particular Meister Eckhart (d. 1328) and Mechthild of Magdeburg (d. 1283), used their mother tongue to speak of religious subjects to the general public instead of using the church's Latin, so mystical preachers in the medieval and post-medieval Islamic world contributed largely to the development of various tongues.[9] When early Sufis in Baghdad and Egypt filled Arabic with emotion and transformed it into a language of loving experience, the same happened later on a much larger scale in the areas beyond the Arab world. Aḥmad Yesewī in Turkestan (d. 1166) composed sayings about religious wisdom in his Turkish mother tongue, while 150 years later the Anatolian bard Yunus Emre was – as far as can be ascertained – one of the first poets (and certainly the most successful) to sing moving religious songs in Anatolian Turkish, thus opening a whole literary tradition which has remained alive to this day. From this vantage point, Bosnian and Albanian versions of religious Muslim literature also developed.

Even stronger is the Sufi influence on languages in the Indo–Pakistani subcontinent, where mystical leaders like Mollā Da'ūd, the writer of *Lōr Chanda* in Awadh (d. 1370), and Muḥammad Ṣaghīr (author of an early version of *Yūsuf Jalīkhā*) in Bengal, utilized their humble mother tongues to sing of Divine Love in images which even the simplest villager or the housewife could understand, while others at least praised the sweetness of the indigenous idiom without using it for their own poetry. The short verses which often induced mystics into ecstasy were uttered neither in the Persian of the intellectuals nor in the Arabic of theologians and jurists but mainly in the regional languages such as Hindwi or Sindhi. In Pashto, Pīr-i Rawshan (d. 1575) expressed the conviction that God understands every language, provided it is the language of the heart; and his own work is the first classic in his mother tongue. For, as Rūmī had told much earlier, God prefers the seemingly stupid babbling of the loving shepherd to theological high-falutin … (*M* II 1,720ff.).

The activities of wandering preachers and Sufis probably also account for the spread of Islamic themes not only into Muslim majority areas such as Kashmir and Gujarat and their respective languages but also into Tamil, Telugu and Malayalam, not forgetting (somewhat later) Malay and Indonesian. C. H. Becker once stated that the use of Swahili and Hausa as lingua francas for large parts of Africa amounted to an Islamization owing to the great amount of Arabic phrases contained in these languages, through which, then, the knowledge of Islamic culture reached African peoples.[10] One may assume that a similar development took place in India and in Central Asia.

The goal of the Muslim preachers, Sufis and religious bards was to familiarize people with the central concepts of Islam by translating them into the different languages – except, of course, for the basic formulas of the creed and the Sūras required for the correct performance of prayer, which had to be in Arabic.

If it is the 'language of the heart' that matters, then another way of transmitting the content of the revelation, though much rarer, is glossolalia, or speaking in tongues. For when the heart truly speaks, the words that gush forth can often be understood even by those who are not acquainted with the actual language of the speaker. Thus, Mawlānā Rūmī relates that he talked to a group of Greeks who, without understanding his Persian sermon, were nevertheless deeply moved by it. More cases of such heart-to-heart speaking can probably be found in Islamic hagiography.

The mystics were often blessed with what one might call automatic speaking or singing: an inspiration, derived from *ʿilm ladunī* (Sūra 18:65), the wisdom that is 'with God', overcame them and made them speak or sing, often without their being aware of the content. Ibn al-Fāriḍ's Arabic poems are a case of such an inspiration, although they look like the result of extremely sophisticated rhetorical polishing. Rūmī's lyrical and didactic work is the best example of such an experience: when he frequently compares himself to a reed flute which sings only when the lips of his beloved touch it, he has expressed well the secret of inspiration.

The genre of *wāridāt*, 'arriving things', appears still in literature, and some of the *wāridāt* that have come to Turkish mystics in our time are good examples of what must have happened during the Middle Ages. Ismail Emre, called Yeni Yunus Emre because he wrote in a style similar to that of the historical Yunus Emre, was an illiterate blacksmith from Adana, and I myself observed several times the 'birth', *doğuş*, of some of his simple mystical poems which one of his companions noted down while he was singing.[11]

But how can humans understand the Divine words at all? How does one draw nearer to the meaning of revelation? The Prophet, as Muslims felt, *is* a word from God, who had placed His word into the souls of all prophets, incarnated it in Jesus[12] and finally inlibrated it in the Koran, whose promulgation he entrusted to Muhammad.

The Divine revelation, which radiates through the prophets, is called *waḥy*, while the inspiration which poets, thinkers and human beings in general experience is *ilhām* – a distinction that must always be kept in mind.

Muslims knew that true revelation is always fraught with mystery: one can never fully understand and comprehend it; and, clear as its wording and sense may appear, they always need new interpretations, for when the Word is indeed of Divine origin, humankind can never completely discover all the possible meanings which it contains. A revelation that is *fully* understood would not be a true revelation of the unfathomable Divine being.[13] That is another reason why a 'translation' of the Koran is regarded as impossible: neither its miraculous linguistic beauty nor all the shades of its meaning can be reproduced in a version in another language.

One approach to drawing closer to the mystery of revelation is the attempt to give God, who is its originator, a name. As God calls Himself *Allāh* in the Koran, His 'personal' name is known; and, in precious copies of the Koran, one may find this name written in gold, or heightened by some other calligraphic means.

It is the so-called 'prophetic' religion that tends to address God with a name, for He has to be 'nameable' (as Kenneth Cragg puts it) so that He can be known and obeyed.[14] This name can be a sacred cipher, like the Hebrew YHWH, but even then it helps to constitute an I–Thou relation, enabling the creature to call upon the Creator. Mystical religion, on the other hand, tends to hide the Divine name, as Prince Dārā Shikōh (probably based on, or at least inspired by, an identical saying in the Upanishads) sings at the beginning of his poetry:

> *Be-nām-i ānki ū nāmī nadārad …*
> In the name of Him who has no name,
> Who lifts His head at whichever name you call …

Besides, mystics, like all lovers, were very well aware that one condition of love is *not* to reveal the beloved's name:[15]

> Sometimes I call you 'Cypress', sometimes 'Moon'
> And sometimes 'Musk-deer fallen in the snare' …
> Now, tell me, friend, which one do you prefer?
> For out of jealousy, I'll hide your name!
> ('Aynul Quḍāt Hamadhānī)

Even though the Muslims knew the Ninety-nine most beautiful Names of God, the *asmā'al-ḥusnā* (Sūra 7:180), they also knew that the greatest Name of God must never be revealed to the uninitiated, as someone who knows it would be able to perform heavy incantations and magic, for the name has a strong power:

Someone who pronounces His name,
his bones don't decay in the grave,

as Mawlānā Rūmī sings (*D* no. 3,107).

While the demented person in ʿAṭṭār's *Muṣībatnāma* claims that His Greatest Name must be 'bread', since everyone cries out this word during a famine, for some people the Greatest Name consists of 'the perfection of humanity', *kamāl-i insāniyya.*[16]

In many respects, the name resembles the garment: it is identical with the named one and yet distinct from him. That is why God revealed the names of all things to Adam so that he might have power over them (Sūra 2:31), just as someone who owns a piece of someone's garment can perform magic with it.

But according to another interpretation of the Koranic verse about 'teaching the names', God revealed to Adam His own names; for, as Rūmī explains:

He taught Adam the names out of jealousy;
He wove the veils of the particulars around the all-embracing entity.
(*D* l. 2,423)

That is, the beautiful Names of God faintly point to Him and His ninety-nine (i.e. innumerable) qualities, while they do not reveal His Essence.

The role of the *asmāʾ al-ḥusnā* in Muslim piety was and still is very important. The thousandfold repetition of one or several names in the *dhikr* is one of the central duties of the Sufi, for whom – as for the loving Zulaykhā in Rūmī's *Mathnawī* – the Beloved's name becomes food and clothing. It shows the master's wisdom in choosing for his disciple the right name to repeat (similar to the Hazir Imam, i.e. the Aga Khan, who gives the Ismaili a secret 'word', *shabad*). For the selection of the Name depends upon the station in which the wayfarer finds himself; names which may be wholesome and strengthening for one person may be dangerous for another. The properties of the Divine Names as they are used in many-thousandfold repetition have been pointed to in important works from the later Middle Ages onwards, one of the finest being Ibn ʿAṭā Allāh's *Miftāḥ al-falāḥ*, 'The Key to Well-being'. There is no lack of poetical versions of the Names and their special powers, and recently Sufi masters have published several collections with explanations as well as fine calligraphies of the Names.

The Divine Names were also important because they contained and pointed to ethical qualities. Ghazzālī urged his readers to dwell upon the ethical aspects of the Names: when reciting *al-Baṣīr,* 'The Seeing', one should become aware that God sees everything that one does; the name *al-Ḥakīm* speaks of His all-embracing wisdom, and so on. Mawlānā Rūmī follows his argumentation in this respect, and (contrary to many of his contemporaries) does not dwell upon the *dhikr* of the Names as, for himself, the constant repetition of the name of his mystical friend Shamsuddīn was enough to induce ecstasy.[17]

In the theosophy of Ibn ʿArabī and his followers, creation is seen as a result of the 'primordial sadness of the Names' which wanted to be manifested; and everything and everybody is ruled, *marbūb*, by a certain Divine Name, acts according to it and reaches his goal by means of it, for Divine activity is, as it were, channelled through the Names to the things named.[18]

The active role of the Divine Names can be discovered in another, less mystical aspect of life; that is, calling children *ʿabd*, 'slave of', followed by any of the ninety-nine Names.[19] The name ʿAbdur Raḥmān, so Muslims feel, connects the boy with the quality of *ar-raḥmān*, the 'All-Merciful', and believers hope that an *amat al-karīm*, 'handmaiden of the Generous', might display the characteristics of generosity in her life. Many proper names have therefore as their second part one of the 'Names of Kindness'; and when an American baseball player, at his conversion to Islam, took the name ʿAbdul Jabbār, 'Slave of the Overpowering', the intention was clear: he hoped to overcome his opponents. Similarly, when a family whose children have died in infancy names the new-born boy ʿAbdul Bāqī or ʿAbdud Dā'im, 'Slave of the Everlasting' or 'Slave of the Ever-Remaining', they certainly hope that the Divine Name may keep the child alive, for a strong bond exists between the Name and the named one.

That is also true when it comes to the Prophet's name.

> *Adīn güzel sensin güzel Muhammad*
> Your name is beautiful, you are beautiful, Muhammad,[20]

sings the medieval Turkish bard; and, six centuries later, Iqbāl in Lahore calls out:

> Light the world, so long in darkness,
> with Muhammad's radiant name![21]

The Prophet's name has been used for boys from the earliest times of Islamic history, for the *ḥadīth* promises that everyone who bears this blessed name would enter Paradise. Yet, Muslims were also afraid lest this name be polluted by frequent use or in inappropriate connections; hence, they tended to pronounce it with different vocalization. Best-known is Mehmet in Turkish, but one also finds Muh, Mihammad, Mahmadou etc. in the western Islamic lands. Often, Muhammad's other names such as Muṣṭafā, 'The Chosen', Aḥmad, 'Most Praised' (which is his heavenly name), or his Koranic names Ṭāhā (Sūra 20), Yāsīn (Sūra 36), Muzzammil (Sūra 73) etc. are used for the sake of blessing.[22]

The names of the prophets mentioned in the Koran, and of the Prophet's companions, especially the ten 'who were promised Paradise' and the fighters in the battle of Badr (624), are frequently used; especially in amulets, the names of his cousin and son-in-law ʿAlī and his two grandsons Ḥasan and Ḥusayn occur innumerable times in both Sunni and Shia families. The same is true for the

Prophet's first wife, Khadīja, his daughter Fāṭima and, less prominently, his daughters Umm Kulthūm, Ruqaiya and Zaynab. Shiites will never use the names of the first three caliphs, considered usurpers, nor that of Muhammad's youngest wife, ʿA'isha.

Names that show a relation with the Prophet or a saint – perhaps the one thanks to whose prayer the child is born – are frequent, especially in the eastern part of the Muslim world, such as Nabī bakhsh, 'Gift of the Prophet', or Ghauth bakhsh, 'Gift of the Help' (i.e. ʿAbdul Qādir Gīlānī), while opprobrious names are used – mostly in the lower classes – to avert the Evil Eye or djinns whom the parents hope might not care to hurt an Egyptian boy called Zibālah 'garbage' or else would take a Panjabi boy by the name of Bulākī as a girl, for *bulākī* is a woman's nose-ring.

The convert is given a new name, often corresponding to his or her previous name. When a Wilfred embraces Islam, the syllable *will* can be connected with *Murād*, 'will, wish', and many a Frieda or Friedrich is now called Farīda or Farīduddīn. When someone embarks on the Sufi path, the master may select a fitting name.

The custom of assuming religious throne-names as a sign of a politico–religious programme begins with the Abbasids, who chose names like ar-Rashīd, 'The rightly-guided one', or al-Mutawakkil, 'the one who trusts in God'. The Fatimids boasted names like al-Mustanṣir, 'the one supported with victory by God', etc.

Names combined with *ad-dīn*, 'religion', appear first in official surnames in the tenth century in the central and eastern Islamic areas; from the eleventh century onwards, they percolated down into general nomenclature, and the numerous Shamsuddīn, 'Sun of religion' (as well as other luminaries such as *qamar*, 'moon', *badr*, 'full moon', *najm* 'star' and so on), and *ʿaḍud*, 'support', continued down through the centuries. The further a country is from the Arab heartlands, the more fanciful religious names appear, and thus one finds Mehraj (= *miʿrāj*) addīn, 'Ascension of Religion', or Mustafīz- urraḥmān, 'favoured by God's effusion', in the Indian subcontinent.

There are also astrological names which depend upon the zodiacal sign, the day and the hour of the child's birth, and a given name can later be changed into an astrological one if the first one is thought unfitting, even 'too heavy', and dangerous for the person.

Often, names were selected by opening the Koran at random and taking the first word on which one's eye fell, even though it might not make any sense. The figure of Mirza *A-lam nashraḥ*, 'Did We not open ...?' (beginning of Sūra 94) is a famous example from India, and *Uzlifat*, '[when Paradise] is brought near' (Sūra 81:13), is found in Turkey. One could also extend the first letter of the Koranic page into a new name, or combine the first word with *ad-dīn*.

This custom of opening the sacred Book leads to the central problem faced by a pious person: how to find God's will and understand His working? How to learn something about one's own future in the vast plan of God's order?

To resort to oracles, usually with arrows, was common practice in ancient Arabia and therefore ruled out by Islam. But the wise word attributed to 'Alī, *tafa''al bi 'l-khayr tanalhu*, 'find something good in the oracle and you will get it' – that is, one should interpret oracles and signs in a positive sense – shows an important attitude to life.

The Koran offered itself as the infallible source for divination. Just as one could find proper names by merely opening the Book, thus religious and political events could be discovered in its words, and the cabalistic arts of *jafr* and *wifq*, counting and changing letters, was a widely-used means of finding out the future. The numerical value of the letters and the possibility of changing the sequence of the letters in a three-radical root offered specialists infinite ways of finding what they were looking for.

Secondary sources for prognostication in the Persianate world included Rūmī's *Mathnawī* and the *Dīvān* of Ḥāfiẓ. This latter oracle is still widely used among Persians. Muslims also tried to discover remarks about the future in the mysterious words of earlier sages such as the seven martyrs of Sind who, while dying in the fourteenth century, allegedly uttered some verses which were interpreted for centuries afterwards in the hope of understanding or foretelling events in the country.

A special way of learning about the future, and in particular of finding a Divinely-inspired answer to a question that bothers one, is *istikhāra*, that is, performing two units of prayer and then going to sleep, if possible in a mosque; the dreams of that night should be interpreted as pointing to the solution of one's problems.

For dreams are an important part of Muslim life.[23] A dream, it is said, consists of one forty-sixth of prophethood; a woman's dream, however, is supposedly only half as true as a man's. The idea underlying this important role of dreams relies upon the Koran (Sūra 39:42 and 6:60), where it is said that the spirits in their sleep are taken back by God into His presence. Thus they have been in immediate contact with the source of all wisdom. The fact that Yūsuf appears as the interpreter of dreams in Sūra 12 has certainly enhanced the high regard for dreams.

What one sees in one's dream – so Muslims believe – is real; it has only to be interpreted properly. The dream-book of Ibn Sīrīn (d. 728) has formed a guideline for interpretations for many centuries. Mystical leaders, then, would interpret their disciples' dreams according to their deep psychological insight.

It is often told how friends appear in dreams after their death to inform the sleeper about their post-mortem state and to give the reasons why God has forgiven them. A dead calligrapher may verify the saying that 'he who writes the *basmala* beautifully will enter Paradise', and the eccentric Sufi Shiblī (d. 945) told his friend that it was not all his meritorious acts, his fasting and prayer that saved him but the fact that he cared for a kitten that was shivering on an icy winter day. The same Shiblī is credited with a vision of God in his dream: he asked Him why He had allowed His devotee, al-Ḥallāj, to be executed so cruelly, and God's answer was: 'Whom My love kills, I'll be his blood money' (*AM* no. 407).

Of greatest importance is the Prophet's appearance in dreams.[24] Such a dream is always true, as Satan cannot assume the Prophet's form. The Prophet may appear to remind a celibate Sufi that marriage is his *sunna*; or he approves of mystical works written by the dreamer; he may show the dreamer his future grave or boast of the presence of a certain scholar, for example Ghazzālī, among his community.[25]

Political ideas could also be promulgated where a reformer (or a rebel) claimed to have received dream instructions from the Prophet.[26]

I have seen many examples of the great role which dreams play in Muslim life: what appears in a dream *must* come true in one way or another, and when my faithful help Fāṭima in Ankara told me that she had seen me in her dream, presenting her with a dress, there was no way out; I had to give it to her.

A *ḥadīth* states that 'people are asleep and when they die they awake' (*AM* no. 222). This saying, along with its parallel that 'the world is like the dream of a sleeper', was loved by the Sufis, who eagerly awaited the true interpretation of their dreams, that is, of their life in the world, in the morning light of eternity where the truth will become manifested.

In the hope of reading the future as it is foreseen in God's universal plan, some Muslims turned to astrology because the script of the stars might tell of positive and negative currents in personal and communal life. In some areas, an astrological reckoning of names and elements was therefore performed before arranging a marriage. But, all the different human attempts to predict the future notwithstanding, the central source of knowledge is the word through which God reveals His holy will in the Koran.

The prophet is forced to speak; he cannot resist the Divine power that makes him feel like an instrument without a will of his own. The first revelation that came over Muhammad is typical of the prophet's initial experience: he was ordered: *iqra'*, 'Read!' or 'Recite!' (Sūra 96:1), to which he answered: 'I cannot read' or 'I do not know how to recite'. The deep shock after this experience, which his faithful wife Khadīja understood well enough to console him, as well as several other instances, prove that his case fits exactly in the general pattern of a prophet's initiation.

This is also true for the contents of his preaching: the revelations spoke of God's absoluteness – there is no deity save Him – and ordered repentance and pure worship, and gave ethical maxims about the treatment of the poor, the widows and orphans – again typical of the 'prophetic' pattern of experience. The prophet always comes as a warner (*nadhīr*, Sūra 33:45 et al.) to his people; he is at the same time the one who announces glad tidings (*bashīr*, Sūra 2:119), that is, the promise of salvation for those who accept the Divine word and follow the now revealed order of life; finally, the prophet brings with him a message about the future (often a terrible future if people do not repent), which culminates in the description of retribution for human actions in either Paradise or Hell. All these themes are fully developed in Muhammad's preaching (see also below, p. 237). Yet, some of these points needed a wider elaboration.

Human beings have always tried to understand the world, its creation and its why and how, and an expression of this search for more than sheer historical knowledge is the myth, which contains – or rather is thought to contain – answers to such questions. Myth speaks of typical events, something that happened at a certain time; of an event that can be recalled to memory, often by ritual acts; vice versa, ritual acts are explained by aetiological myths.

Islam is in its essence a religion with but little mythological material; but the interpreters of the Koran and the tradition could not help enlarging the mythological germs found in the revelation, while mystical thinkers and poets often delved deep into the ocean of ancient mythological traditions to reinterpret them for themselves.

There are, of course, no theogonic myths in Islam, for there was no need to explain how a deity, or deities, came into existence: 'God was, and He still is as He was', as the famous tradition says.

Much more common are cosmogonic myths that tell how and why creation came into existence. The clear and simple statement that God needs only say *kun*, 'Be!' to something, and it becomes (Sūra 2:117 et al.), as well as the remarks that He created the world in six days (Sūra 25:60), were elaborated in various and often fanciful ways. Perhaps the most fascinating one is Ibn 'Arabī's grand vision of creation by means of the Divine Names that longed for manifestation. Widespread stories such as the creation of the Muhammadan Light, the primordial luminous substance of the Prophet out of which everything appeared, belong here. And did not God address him: *lawlāka ma khalaqtu 'l-aflāka*, 'But for your sake I would not have created the spheres!' (AM no. 546)? Orthodox Islam would barely agree with such mythological embellishments of the Prophet's creation, yet they occupy an important place in literature and Sufi poetry.

Anthropological myths are not lacking either: the creation of Adam and Eve, the details of Adam's first transgression and his Fall were repeated with various details in the *Qiṣaṣ al-anbiyā* and alluded to in literature up to Iqbāl's daring interpretation of the 'Fall' as a necessary precondition for man's development into a true human being.

Cultic myths are frequent: for example, how the Kaaba was built and what place it occupied in the oldest history of mankind. Shiite tradition imagined that the site of Ḥusayn's martyrdom, Kerbela, was predestined for this event millennia before the actual tragedy, so that prophets and sages of yore were already aware of its central role in the sacred history of mankind.

Islam knows no saviour figures, yet the ideas that grew around Muhammad as the intercessor on Doomsday and around ʿAlī and Ḥusayn in Shia piety, furthermore the role of Fāṭima as a kind of *mater dolorosa* whose intercession will save those who weep for Ḥusayn – all these are formally quite close to soteriological myths.

Aetiological myths have been created to explain the origins of the prescribed rites, and as the pilgrimage to Mecca is projected back to the time when Adam and Eve, after being expelled from Paradise, found each other again on Arafat near Mecca, thus forms of prayer and fasting are likewise traced back to earlier strata of human history; for as all the prophets before Muhammad brought essentially the same message, it was natural that they too had performed similar rites.

Particularly rich is the genre of eschatological myths, for the Koran dwells intensely and extensively upon the Last Judgment and the fate in the Hereafter. Thus, commentators and fanciful poets alike found a fertile ground from which they could elaborate the details of the eschatological instrumentarium (the Books, the Scales, the Bridge) and spin out delightful stories of paradisiacal bliss or horrifying descriptions of the tortures of the damned. A special addition was the introduction of the Mahdi, the rightly-guided leader from the Prophet's family, who will arrive before the end of the world; he, or Jesus, whose second coming is also connected with the last decades of the world, will finally overcome the *dajjāl* to reign for a short while to bring peace before Resurrection is announced. As long as such myths were not supported by exact data in the Koranic revelation, they were usually spiritualized by the philosophers and the mystics.

Mythological motifs connected with the Prophet, such as his heavenly journey (*isrā', miʿrāj*), which was developed out of Sūra 17:1, were understood by mystics as prefiguring the soul's flight into the Divine Presence. Did not the Prophet himself compare his feeling during ritual prayer to his experience during the *miʿrāj*, when he was standing in God's immediate presence? The colourful descriptions of the *miʿrāj* have inspired poets to see their own way as a kind of replica of his lofty experience with the difference, however, that the Prophet's *miʿrāj* took place in the body while the mystic's or poet's heavenly journey can be only made in the spirit. Artists never tired of creating pictures of the *miʿrāj* some of which are of truly dazzling beauty (see above, p. 85 note 62).

While many pious souls and imaginative people extended and expanded the realms of mythological tales over the centuries, there is also a tendency to demythologize the Koranic data and even more the popular stories connected with the Prophet. This tendency is not new, but has increased lately. Modernists would criticise the *mawlūd* poetry which told how all of Nature welcomed the new-born prophet who had been sent 'as a mercy for the worlds' (Sūra 21:107), with birds and beasts participating in the praise. Was it not nonsensical, even dangerous, to teach children such stories instead of emphasizing the rational character of the Prophet's message, and his ethical qualities as he, a veritable human being, came to lead the community to better social and cultural standards? During the relevant discussions in Egypt in the early 1930s, it was, typically, the well-known author Ṭāhā Ḥusayn who defended the 'mythological' elements in these songs, for as an artist he was able to grasp their deeper meaning. For rationalists do not understand the symbolic character of myth and strive to explain away whatever seems to be contrary to 'normal' common sense, trying, at best, to purify the kerygma from the mythological accretions, while dogmatists, on the other hand, require absolute faith in the external words or statements by which layers of deeper meaning are covered.

While myths dwell upon an event in a certain time, *in illud tempore*, saga, legend and fairytales handle temporal relationships very freely and, to produce the hoped-for effect, often connect historical persons who have no relations with each other but are woven ingeniously, or carelessly, together.

The saga is part of Arabic, Persian, Turkish and Indo–Muslim literature, but rarely has a truly religious content. Beginning with the *ayyām al-ʿarab*, the Arabs liked to tell of the heroic feats of people, and the names of ʿAntara, Shanfara and Ta'abbaṭa Sharran, the pre-Islamic warrior poets (and often outcast-heroes), are known to this day. The saga assumes a more Islamic character in the tales concerning Ḥamza, the Prophet's uncle, whose adventures were told and retold especially in Persian, and were illustrated in grand style under the Mughal emperor Akbar. The adventures of Tamīm ad-Dārī, another historical figure from the Prophet's environment in Medina, were likewise spun out with highly picturesque details, and this traveller's return forms a dramatic story of a type well known in folklore. Such stories were apparently quite attractive for new converts to Islam, for the *Ḥamza-nāma* and even more the story of Tamīm ad-Dārī became integrated in Southern Indian literature and were retold even in Tamil. A comparable saga deals with Muḥammad ibn al-Ḥanafiyya (d. 700), a son of ʿAlī from a wife other than Fāṭima, which has long been famous even in the Malayan archipelago.[27]

The comparatively scant saga material from Arabia was supplemented by sagas from Iran, and Firdawsi's (d. 1020) *Shāhnāma*, the 'Book of the Kings' in which the ancient history of Persian kings and heroes is told, offered Muslim authors of the Persianate world much narrative material and remained an inexhaustible source for new elaborations of certain themes. The *Iskandarnāma*, based on the Pseudo-Kallisthenes, was successfully integrated into the narrative tradition of the Muslim peoples, while sagas alive among the Turks, as well as Indian themes, influenced the general Muslim literature only to a small degree.

The word 'Orient' will make most people think of the *Arabian Nights*, the 'Tales of the 1,001 Nights', which appeared to the Europeans as the most typical expression of the Oriental world and have inspired, since their first translation into French by A. Galland (d. 1715), numerous poets, musicians and painters, while in the Islamic world these popular fairytales were never considered to be real 'literature'; their glittering charm was not attractive to educated Muslims (in part owing to their non-classical language).

On the other hand, animal fables of Indian origin, from the *Pançatantra* and *Hitopadeşa*, were regarded as useful models of human behaviour. After these stories had been translated under the title *Kalīla wa Dimna* into Arabic by Ibn al-Muqaffaʿ (d. 756), they were illustrated; several Persian translations were made later. They became known in Europe at a rather early point in history, and form a source for many later fables up to Lafontaine. Similarly, the Indian *Ṭūṭīnāma*, 'The Book of the Parrot', was widely read in the Indian, Persian and Turkish areas after its first Persian version by Nakhshabī (d. 1350), and it reached Europe by different routes. The growth of tales among people who can skilfully weave religious and political criticism into their narratives can still be observed in some areas and sheds light on classical narrative techniques.[28]

However, one would hesitate to call most of the works just enumerated 'Islamic' in the strictly religious sense of the word. The situation is quite different when one comes to another widespread literary genre, that is, legends.[29]

Legends were told about the early wars and fights of the Prophet and his companions, but even more about the pious, saintly people in the Muslim world. Richard Gramlich's comprehensive work about *Die Wunder der Freunde Gottes* ('The Miracles of God's Friends') is the best study of the phenomenon. Legends tell of the *karāmāt*, the charismata, of saints, from food miracles (important in a culture where hospitality is so highly valued) to thought-reading, from helping an aged couple to get a child to healing all kinds of ailments. They make the listener or reader aware that the entire cosmos participates in the saints' lives because they, being absolutely obedient to God, are obeyed, in turn, by everything.

Legends of Muslim saints generally resemble legends in other religious traditions, but it is important to remember that many of them deal with dogmatic miracles by which infidels or hypocrites are drawn into the true faith: when ʿAbdul Qādir Gīlānī as a baby refused to drink his mother's milk during daytime in Ramaḍān, or when a saintly person could walk unhurt through a pyre to prove to his Zoroastrian counterpart that fire can burn only with God's permission; or when a Sufi's cat discovers a 'materialist' posing as a pious Muslim, the success of such miracles is clear. And those who do not fulfil their vows, desecrate sacred places or incur the saint's wrath by some flippant remark will certainly be exposed to terrible punishments.

The same legend is often told about different people, whether in Morocco, Turkey or Sind. A good example is the story of the saint who wanted to settle in a certain place but was refused by the scholars. When they showed him a bowl brim-full with milk to point out that there was no room, he silently replied by placing a rose petal on top of the milk – and was, of course, gladly admitted. Another common theme is the saint's illiteracy: many of those who are known as prolific writers appear in legends as illiterate (following the example of the *ummī*, 'unlettered' Prophet) and acquainted only with the letter *alif*, the first letter of the Arabic alphabet and cipher for the One God.

The Shia developed a specific religious literature such as the *Maqātil Ḥusayn*, stories about the martyrdom of Ḥusayn and his family; the *Dehnāma*, or *Deh Majlis*, 'Books of Ten', are recited during the first ten days of Muḥarram. *Rawzakhwānī*, the recitation of the martyrologia in highly-charged style, is likewise part of the Muḥarram celebrations. Works like *Rawz at ash-shuhadā*, 'The Garden of the Martyrs', enjoyed great popularity, and in later times the literary genre of the *marthiya*, lengthy Urdu poems about the tragedy of Kerbela, became increasingly important and described the martyrs' suffering with ever more heart-rending details. In Bengal, this kind of literature, which may be called a subspecies of legend, is called *jārīnāme*, from *zār*, 'lament'.

Ages-old wisdom is condensed in proverbs, which play (or rather played) an important role; in former times, with a greater number of illiterate people (especially women) around, one could listen to an amazing variety of words of wisdom or inherited proverbs from simple villagers in Turkey, Sind and other areas.[30]

The same can be said for the treasure of poetical quotations with which even the least 'educated' people were acquainted. Anyone who has heard how Persian villagers quote verses of Ḥāfiẓ, or how Turkish or Pakistani officials have hundreds of fitting poetical quotations ready, will agree that love of poetry is (and now one probably has to say *was*) a hallmark of traditional Muslim culture, as much as the Prophet warned of poetry which was often understood as dealing primarily with the frivolous aspects of life such as free love and drinking (cf. Sūra 26:226ff.).

Sagas, fairytales, legends and poetry are part of the tradition in which educated and less educated people participate; but veritable religious instruction is of a different kind. *Ad-dīn naṣīḥa* (AM no. 282), 'religion consists of good advice'. The noblest science after the study of the Koran, namely the study of *ḥadīth*, offers a good example of the technique of teaching; for, in all branches of science, art and religion, the maintenance of the *isnād* is central. That is the spiritual chain from the present teacher or student back to the founder of the specific science or art (who is, ideally, the Prophet himself, or ʿAlī); and, just as scholars of *ḥadīth* had to know the *isnād* of a tradition to lead it step-by-step back to its origin, thus musicians, calligraphers and in particular Sufis would always place themselves in the chain of transmission that guarantees the correctness of their own performance, as it is blessed by the spiritual current that flows from generation to generation. The reliability, 'soundness' as the technical term is, of a *ḥadīth* is warranted by the uninterrupted chain of transmitters (men and women) whose biographies and personal circumstances have been rigorously examined so that the chain is unbroken and flawless. The oral transmission of *ḥadīth*, and other sciences, is important even though notes may have been used and even though the 'sound', *ṣaḥīḥ* (that is, doubtlessly authentic) *ḥadīth* were later collected in books. The most famous among these are the *Ṣaḥīḥayn*, the 'two sound ones', by Bukhārī (d. 870) and Muslim (d. 875). Yet, the 'hearing' of *ḥadīth* was considered essential, and scholars would wander through the world of Islam in quest of *ḥadīth* not only to find, perhaps, new material or an *isnād* unknown to them, but also to meet a famous scholar whose presence was a blessing in itself. Many manuscripts of Islamic sciences bear notes in the margin or at the end which show which scholar 'heard', *samāʿ*, this text from the author and the author's disciples and successors.

Oral instruction was the rule not only in the teaching of *ḥadīth* but also in other sciences and arts, and this applies even more to the esoteric teaching in mystical circles or the interpretation of philosophy. This could take the form of person-to-person teaching, and not in vain is *ṣuḥbat*, the 'being together' between master and disciple, required; for only by proximity to the guiding master could one hope to understand the true secret, and only through intense concentration upon the master, *tawajjuh*, could one expect to receive a share of his spiritual power and knowledge. For this reason, the Sufis and the sages in general insisted upon oral transmission of classical texts, for 'reading the white between the lines of the written text'[31] was as important as reading the actual letters; a true introduction into deeper and deeper levels of a seemingly simple text could only be achieved by listening to the master's words, by observing his speech and his silent actions.

When one keeps in mind this viewpoint, one understands why Shāh Walīullāh of Delhi remarked that 'the books of Sufism are elixir for the elite but poison for the normal believer'. That is, the uninitiated reader will most probably be caught in the external sense of the words and the symbols (such as wine, love, union), which he will take at face value and then go astray, while the initiated understand at least some of the meaning hidden beneath the letters. Iqbāl's aversion to Sufi poetry stems from the same experience, and when one looks at the history of translations of sacred texts in the West, from the Koran to mystical Persian verse, one understands easily that a good knowledge of the 'white between the lines' is necessary lest one distort the meaning. Therefore it is not easy for a late-born reader to relish the collections of *malfūẓāt*, 'sayings', of medieval masters,[32] or to understand the full meaning of their letters to their disciples.[33]

The teacher taught not only the seeking individual but also whole groups of students in the general tradition. This happened in the *madrasa*, the theological college where sciences such as *ḥadīth*, exegesis and law, as well as the auxiliary fields like Arabic grammar and literature, were taught. The *madrasas* served in the Middle Ages to counteract Shiite influences and were often supported by the government as institutions to maintain mainstream Sunni orthodoxy. The fact that the students very often used classical works on the central subjects in abbreviated form, *mukhtaṣar*, and depended on scholia more than on original texts, led to a deterioration of scholarship in the course of time.

The mystical master generally gathered his disciples at certain hours of the day to teach them. A widespread legendary aspect of the instruction of a group of disciples is that, in the end, each of those present claims that the master talked exclusively to him and solved exactly his problems.

The mystical teacher's method consists, among other ways, of the use of paradoxes – he tries 'to catch an elephant by a hair', for the mystical experience, being beyond time and space, can be expressed only in words that defy the limits of timebound logic. That is true for a good number of apophthegmata of early Sufis, as they are handed down in the classical handbooks of Sufism such as Sarrāj's *Kitāb al-luma'*, Kalābādhī's *Kitāb at-ta'arruf* and numerous others.

Many of these sayings may yield more meaning when they are taken as expressions of a supra-intellectual experience and not analyzed according to our normal grammatical and logical understanding. The whole problem of the *shaṭḥiyāt*, the theophatic locutions or, as Henry Corbin calls them in the sense in which the Protestant spirituals had used the term, 'paradoxa', belongs here.[34] The mystic, whose mind resembles a canal into which suddenly an overwhelming amount of water is poured, says things that are not licit in a normal state of mind. Yet, similar to the Zen *ko'an*, some such wilful paradoxes can also lead the disciple to a loftier level of understanding.

The famous *tekerleme* of the Turkish medieval poet Yunus Emre is a good example of mystical instruction by means of paradoxes:

Çĭktĭm erik dalĭna ...
I climbed upon the plum tree
to pluck grapes there –
The master of the garden screamed:

'Why do you take my walnut?'

This is interpreted by a later Turkish master, Niyazi Misri, as pertaining to the *sharīʿa* (plum), *ṭarīqa* (grape) and *ḥaqīqa* (nut): the attempt to attain reality or truth is often likened to the hard work that is needed to break a nut before one can enjoy the sweet, wholesome kernel. The poet himself closes his poem with the lines:

Yunus said a word which does
not resemble other words:
For he hides the face of Truth
from the eyes of hypocrites.

One sometimes wonders whether the oxymorons and paradoxical images used by the Sufis derive from a common root that lies beneath all mystical experience. The line in Yunus's *tekerleme*:

The fish climbed on the poplar tree

has its exact parallel in Indo-Muslim poetry; and as the Moroccan story tells that a cow had eaten a presumptuous Sufi's lion, an Egyptian poet of the nineteenth century claims, inter alia, that 'the lion is devoured by a jenny ass'.[35]

The world of timelessness, where all contrasts are obliterated and the weakest creature equals the strongest one, inspires many a mystical teacher. For this reason, riddles and conundrums were also part of teaching. It seems not unlikely that the Hindi riddles, *pahēliyāñ*, ascribed to Amīr Khusraw (d. 1325) may have been a genuine contribution of his to mystical teaching, as he was a disciple of the Chishti master Niẓāmuddīn Awliyā.

While the mystical teacher tried to introduce his disciples to ever-deeper new layers of reality by means of unusual literary forms, the *taʿlīm*, the theoretical dictation of religious texts by the Shia imam, is of a different character; it is a highly sophisticated introduction into the mysteries of the faith, and has an absolute validity for those who are exposed to it.

Besides the various types of teaching, scholarly or mystical, the sermon occupies an important place in Muslim religious life.[36] The sermon, *khuṭba*, during the noon prayer on Friday in the great mosque was established in early times, and so were the *khuṭbas* at the two feasts. The Prophet himself used to preach; rulers or governors followed his example and the *khuṭba* became a literary genre in itself, sometimes of extreme brevity, sometimes delivered in a brilliant style in which the strength and density of the Arabic phrases is admirable; sometimes it became highly elaborate. The Abbasid caliphs did not preach themselves, while the Fatimids did at times. The *khuṭba* was never a lengthy homily but was to concentrate on eschatological themes; but in more recent times it can go on for a long time, depending on the talents of the preacher (*khaṭīb*), who might comment intelligently upon current issues. In its second half, the prayer for the ruler was said so that it was also a highly political affair: to be mentioned in the Friday sermon meant being acknowledged as the true ruler of the country.

The official *khuṭba* is interrupted by a very brief pause between its first and second part during which the preacher sits down (so that 'shorter than the preacher's sitting' came to mean 'just a moment'). To attend the Friday prayers (which consist of only two *rak'a* instead of the normal four at noon) and the *khuṭba* is a duty for the community.

There were also other preachers, the *quṣṣāṣ*, popular speakers who attracted the masses by their fanciful interpretations of Koranic data and surpassed all limits in their detailed descriptions of future life. Although – or perhaps because – their fantastic stories coloured popular piety to a considerable extent, they were sharply criticized and rejected by sober theologians. Ibn al-Jawzī (d. 1200), certainly a spokesman of many other serious believers, does not hesitate to call them liars; he even goes so far as to call a well-known mystical preacher 'one of God's marvels in lying ...'.[37]

In times of crisis, speakers delivered sermons that reminded Muslims of their duty to repent; these are called *maw'iẓa*, a term often used for the Koran itself, which warns and educates people (cf. Sūra 2:66 et al.). One of the early Sufis, Yaḥya ibn Mu'ādh (d. 871), is known by the nickname *al-wā'iẓ*, the 'preacher calling to repentance'. As all his biographers emphasize that he mainly preached about hope, one can suppose that on the whole the theme of fear was prevalent in such sermons. Even women could act as preachers, for example one Maymūna al-wā'iẓa (d. 1002) in Baghdad.[38]

Teachers as well as preachers availed themselves of all kinds of literary forms, in particular of parables to make their speeches more impressive; suffice it to mention Rūmī's use of the parable of the moon that is reflected in every kind of water, be it the ocean or a small pond.

Allegorical stories offered vast possibilities for preachers and teachers to bring the central truth closer to their listeners under the guise of memorable tales: one glance at the poetical works of Sanā'ī, 'Aṭṭār and Rūmī shows their talent of catching the attention of their audiences by a seemingly inexhaustible treasure of allegories. 'Aṭṭār is certainly the greatest master of this art, while Rūmī is often carried away by the flow of inspiration and returns to the original story only after long digressions.[39] The delightful allegories of Suhrawardī the Master of Illumination are jewels of medieval Persian prose.

Beside, and correctly speaking above, all these literary forms through which the Muslims tried to approach the Divine mystery and the world in one way or another stands the clear-cut dogma, first of all the profession of faith, the *shahāda*, *lā ilāha illā 'Llāh Muḥammad rasūl Allah.* To pronounce it means to make a decision, and that is shown by lifting the right index finger. The *shahāda* is the verbal heart of Islam. The graphic form of its first part with its ten vertical strokes offers infinite possibilities for the calligrapher; the twenty-four letters of the full profession of faith – 'There is no deity save God, Muhammad is God's messenger' – seem to point, for the believers, to the twenty-four hours of the day, while the fact that none of the letters bears any diacritical marks proves its luminous character, and its seven words atone for the transgressions of the seven limbs and close the seven gates of Hell. The *shahāda*, the fortress into which the believer enters to be protected from every evil, formed a convenient topic for never-ending meditations.[40]

A longer form of the profession, a true creed, was developed out of Koranic statements, especially Sūra 4:136. Thus the believer says: *amantu bi 'llāhi* ..., 'I believe in God and His books and His angels and His messengers and the last Day, and that what happened to you could never have failed you'. There is a typical placement of the books, as the true words of God, before the prophets, who are only the instruments through whom the revelation is brought to the world.[41]

This creed, which was formulated in the eighth century, aptly sums up the basic facts in which it is the Muslim's duty to believe. Calligraphers, especially in Turkey, liked to write these words in the form of a boat, the connecting particles *wa*, 'and', forming the rows. This is called *amantu gemisi*, 'the boat of *amantu*, "I believe"', and is supposed to be filled with *baraka*, carrying as it were the believer and the artist to the shores of Paradise.

In order to instruct the community in the contents of the revelation, one needed *ʿilm*, 'knowledge', which was administered by the *ʿulamā*, the caretakers of religious instruction and learning. The Prophetic saying, that 'seeking *ʿilm* is a religious duty' (*AM* no. 676), and its more famous form, 'Seek knowledge even in China', triggered off much investigation into various aspects of knowledge, but one should not forget that the real meaning of *ʿilm* was religious knowledge, a knowledge meant not for 'practical life' but for the world to come. A *ḥadīth* has the Prophet say: 'I ask refuge by God from an *ʿilm* that has no use', that is, a knowledge which may enable its owner to find a good job in modern society but does not help him to fulfil his religious duties which, as the believer hopes, will lead him to a peaceful and happy death and a blessed life in Paradise. The content of *ʿilm* is to know how to utilize each moment of life in the service of God, and how to do everything, even though it may look a profane action, in conformance with the Divine law. This interpretation of *ʿilm* has cut off some of the most pious segments of the Muslim community from contact with the developing world, and one reads with sadness that in the 1850s a southern Indian Muslim benefactor of his co-religionists, who had founded a college in Madras in which not only traditional sciences were taught but also English and other 'modern sciences', was forced by the *ʿulamā* to close down this 'worldly' institution.[42] This may be an exceptional case, but it shows the difficulties which many Muslims from traditional families have to overcome when trying to live in modern Western societies.

Besides *ʿilm*, the great power that serves to prepare the believer for a happy life in the Hereafter, Muslims also know *ʿirfān*, a term often translated as 'gnosis'. But one has to beware not to understand 'gnosis' in the sense of the historical gnostic trends in the Hellenistic–Christian tradition. Rather, *ʿirfān* is the inspired, mystico–philosophical wisdom which permeates later Sufi and 'theosophical' writing, especially in Iran.

But everything is dominated by the moral law which is expressed, for the Muslim, in the *sharīʿa*. To obey the law means to obey God, who, as some scholars say, has revealed not Himself but rather His law, which is then interpreted by the *ʿulamā* or, in the Shia tradition, by the imams and their representatives, the *mujtahids*. That is why the *ʿulamā*, who are able to interpret God's will, are so important for the maintenance of the House of Islam: they stand for the right approach to everything in life, even though progressive Muslims attribute the decline of Islam to 'self-styled *ʿulamā*', as for example the Malaysian Prime Minister said at the inauguration of the International Institute of Islamic Thought and Civilization in Kuala Lumpur on 4 October 1991.

THE WORD TO GOD[43]

> I have prayed so much that I myself turned into prayer –
> everyone who sees me requests a prayer from me.
>
> (*D* no. 903)

Thus says Mawlāna Rūmī in a verse which is perhaps his most beautiful self-portrait and, at the same time, the ideal portrait of a God-loving human soul.

The word has the power of realization: coming from God in its beginning (as does everything), it is the source of all activity, but the human answer to it has strong power as well. Ancient peoples (and to a certain extent modern man as well) knew the magic power of the word, which can be realized in the effects of blessing and curse, of greeting and command: to speak the word can heal or hurt.

That is why the formula of greeting is so important. The Koran orders the believers to greet each other with the formula of peace, and the Prophet urged them to answer with an even more beautiful formula. Therefore the Muslim greets you with *as-salāmu ʿalaykum*, 'peace be upon you', to which you should answer: *as-salāmu ʿalaykum wa raḥmatu 'Llāhi wa barakātuhu*, 'And upon you be peace and God's blessings and mercy'.

The Arabic language uses the same word for blessing and cursing: *daʿā*, 'to call', is done *li* 'for' someone, that is, to bless the other person, or *ʿalà* 'against', which means to call down a curse. Blessing means to turn over good fortune by means of the word, and the blessings upon the Prophet, the *taṣliya* or *ṣalawāt sharīfa* (or in the Persian–Indian areas *durūd sharīf*), 'sets in motion heavenly forces', as Constance Padwick writes. The religious singer in Egypt even knows a *taʿṭīra*, 'perfumed' blessing for the Prophet: he asks the Lord to send down 'perfumed blessings and peace' on his tomb. The *taṣliya* was thought to strengthen a petition's value or to lead to forgiveness of sins; it could be used in oaths, and also to silence people: in every case, its power becomes evident.[44]

To appreciate the efficacy of formulas like *raḥimahu Allāh*, 'may God have mercy upon him', or *ghafara 'Llāh ʿalayhā*, 'May God forgive her', one has to keep in mind that in Arabic the past tense does not only express a completed action but can also be used as an optative. That is, when one pronounces the words of blessing or curse, the intention is, as it were, already fulfilled. The same holds true for the participial form: *al-marḥūm* is the 'one upon mercy is shown' but at the same time, and perhaps in a more realistic sense, the one for whom one hopes and prays that God will show him mercy.

Islamic languages are replete with formulas for wishing well or averting evil: *bāraka Allāhu fīk*, 'may God bless you', is as general a wish as *Allah razī olsun*, 'may God be satisfied with you', as the pious Turk says to thank someone, upon which one is supposed to say *hepimizden*, 'with all of us'. The Muslim blesses the hands that have prepared a delicious meal or produced a fine piece of embroidery: *elinize sağlik*, 'health to your hands' in Turkish, *dast-i shumā dard nakunad* in Persian, 'May your hands not see pain ...'. Among traditional Turks, one could conduct an entire conversation with these blessing formulas until the honoured visitor leaves and one thanks him for his coming by saying *Ayağīnīza sağlīk*, 'May your feet (which have brought you to us) be healthy!'

Important as these beautiful wishes are, the curse, on the other hand, can be as efficacious as (and perhaps even more so than) the blessing, especially when uttered by a powerful person.[45] It is contagious, and Muslims avoid contact with an accursed or afflicted person. To avoid its evil influences, Muslims again use numerous formulas such as, in Turkish, *Allah göstermesin*, 'May God not show it' (i.e. the illness or disaster with which someone else has been smitten), or, in Persian, *khudā na-khwāsta*, 'God not willing'. When mentioning some mishap or disaster, Persians used to say *haft kūh* or *haft qur'ān dar miyān* – 'may seven mountains' or 'seven Korans be between it (and us)'.

As Muslims are careful not to mention evil or opprobrious things, they also try to circumvent the taboo connected with death. Where the Arab says or writes, for example, *tuwuffiya*, 'he was consumed' (in the mercy of God), the Persian writer may say *intiqāl kard*, 'He was moved' (to another place). It would be a fascinating study to collect the different expressions in Islamic languages that are used to speak of a person's death. In classical literatures, such expressions are often worded according to the deceased person's rank, character and interests. One of the most interesting and moving forms, which I encountered in Turkey, was *sizlere ömür*, 'may you live!' instead of saying 'he passed away' (which of course is also an ellipsis). Thus one says: 'Osman Bey *sizlere ömür oldu*, has become – may you live on', that is 'he died'.

Blessings and curses work on others, while the oath is a kind of curse that has repercussions on the speaker: when one breaks the oath or solemn promise, one will be punished.[46] Therefore, one takes an oath by the object or person dearest to one's heart: 'By the head of my father!'; 'By the Prophet!'; 'By the beard of the Prophet!'; 'By the Koran!' In Sufi circles, one may find formulas like 'By the cloak of my shaykh', and a member of the former *futuwwa* sodalities might swear 'By the *futuwwa* trousers!'[47] The most frequently-used – and therefore somewhat worn-out – formula is *Wallāhi*, 'By God', which is often strengthened in threefold repetition: *Wallāhi, billāhi, tallāhi*. Superficial and irresponsible swearing was, it seems, common among the Arabs, for one finds a *ḥadīth* which looks at first sight somewhat mysterious: *ittaqū 'l-wāwāt*, 'beware of the *W*'s', that is, the swearing particle *wa* used in such formulas. It would then mean: 'Do not take an oath easily'. Another *ḥadīth* states: 'He who swears a lot goes to Hell' (*AM* no. 669).

Part of the oath is the vow.[48] One can vow anything – 'a candle my body's length' or the recitation of forty times *Sūra Yāsīn* – for the vow is a kind of contract with the one in whose power one trusts. It is therefore often done in the presence of an important person endowed with *baraka*, or preferably before a saint's shrine, or else at a sacred time, for instance in Muḥarram. One can vow, for example, that a child born by the blessings of the saint will be called after him – hence the numerous names like *Ghauth bakhsh*, 'Gift of the Help', namely 'Abdul Qādir Gīlānī. The most prominent example is Akbar's son, later the emperor Jahāngīr, whose proper name was Salīm after the pious Salīm of Sikri, whose prayer had worked to give the emperor an heir. One can also vow to 'sell' the child to the saint's shrine: in Turkey, such children bear the name *Satïlmïş*, 'sold'. It is possible to vow the celebration of a *mawlid* or to feed so-and-so many people, or to prepare a special meal, as in the Turkish *Zakarya sofrasï* to which forty people are invited and where forty kinds of food are prepared. From the vow to sweep the saint's shrine (or at least to bring a new broom) to the offering of a new cover for the sarcophagus, everything can be turned into a votive gift (although I have never seen counterparts of the silver hands and feet which one may find in Catholic churches). The numerous places such as trees or window grills, on which little rags are hanging to remind the saint of the 'contract' established by the vow, prove how common these customs are, as much as orthodox circles may object to such superstitions which betray people's craving for some power mediating between man and God, and thus, as it were, contradict Islam's pure monotheism.

The belief in demonic powers led to conjurations and exorcism, which are particularly elaborate in the *Ẓār* ritual practised mainly among Egyptian women.[49] Similar practices are also found in parts of Muslim India, and probably elsewhere. It is the magic word that serves along with complicated actions to drive out the spirit that has taken possession of the woman.

Before beginning the 'verbal sacrifice', i.e. the prayer, it is necessary to invite God by means of an epiclesis. Islamic prayer has no actual epiclesis unless one were to call the beginning of the prayer rite, the attestation *Allāhu akbar*, 'God is greater (than everything)' such, for it brings once more to mind the overarching power of God in whose presence the praying person now stands.

It is a somewhat different case in mystical writing. Rūmī's verses, with their repeated invocations such as:

biyā biyā dildār-i man dildār-i man

Come, oh come, my Beloved, my Beloved!

serve as an invocation and invitation to the mystical Beloved. In connection with Rūmī, in whose poetry and the later Mevlevi ritual the reed flute plays a central role, one may remember that in ancient Anatolia the flute-player had a sacred function: his tunes accompanied the spoken epiclesis, and thus the person who plays the flute is indeed the one 'who calls the deity'.[50] Rūmī's use of the symbol of the reed flute at the very beginning of the *Mathnawī* may have been born from a subconscious memory of these traditions, for he, too, wanted to call – call back, that is – the mystical Beloved.

Prayer is the heart of religion: *lex orandi lex credendi*, as the saying goes. Prayer is, as mentioned, a sacrifice, the sacrifice of the word, as Rūmī says:

When they pronounced *takbīr*, they went away
from our world, just like a sacrifice:
the meaning of *takbīr*, my friend, is this:
'O God, we have become Thy sacrifice!'

(*M* III 2,140ff.)

As a sacrifice, a sacred action, it has to begin with purification, whether with water, as in the ritual ablution, or purification by repentance. The human being who calls to the Powerful, Rich Lord sees himself or herself in the invocations as a poor, lowly sinner, and such epithets – *al-faqīr al-ḥaqīr al-mudhnib* – are frequent in religious poetry; the Sindhi bard ʿAbdur Ra'ūf Bhattī in the eighteenth century assumed the pen name *al-ʿāṣī*, 'the rebel', for his prayer poems.

The official confession of sins, central in Christianity, has no room in Islam as a preparation for prayer. It is practised, however, in some Sufi orders among the brethren and in the presence of the master, who gives the penitent a special formula and may or may not impose a punishment upon the sinner. But the contritional outcry of the penitent, mentioned in the Koran (e.g. Sūra 27:44; 28:16) is repeated time and again: *Yā rabbī ẓalamtu nafsī*, 'O Lord, I have wronged myself!' Even more important, if one may say so, is the formula of *istighfār*, 'I ask God for forgiveness', which can be given to a person as a *dhikr* at the first stages of the mystical path. One of my Pakistani friends, a major in the army, constantly murmured the *istighfār* while walking, driving or riding in order to clean his soul, for if repeated 3,000 or 5,000 times a day, it is supposed to purify the heart.

Some of the most moving Islamic prayers are inspired by the hope of forgiveness. The seeker's heart is hovering between fear and hope – fear of God's justice but hope for His mercy, fear of the One who is not hurt by human sins and hope for Him who can easily forgive the miserable creature's mistake. The short dialectic prayers of Yaḥyā ibn Mu'ādh (d. 871) are the most beautiful and tender examples of this feeling, which finds its perfect expression in his prayer: 'Forgive me, for I belong to Thee'.

Ritual prayer is announced by the call to prayer, *adhān*, which serves to remind the Muslim that he or she is now entering the realm of sacred time; it leads him or her into a sacred presence, similar to the enclosure that protects the spatial sanctuary from defilement. Proper attire is required: for men, the area between navel and knee, for women the whole body except face and feet has to be covered, as has the head; the dress should be beautiful (Sūra 7:31).

After the purification with water, the actual prayer rite begins with the words *Allāhu akbar*, the so-called *takbīrat al-iḥrām* which seals off the sacred time (just as the donning of the *iḥrām* seals up the sacred space). For now one finds oneself in the presence of the All-Holy King and is even more overawed than one would be in the presence of a worldly ruler. There are very many descriptions of what a Muslim experiences when entering the prayer rite: it could be seen as sacrificing one's whole being to the Lord, or it could inspire the feeling of already participating in the Resurrection, standing between Paradise and Hell; and those whose thoughts perhaps wander to worldly things instead of completely concentrating upon the prayer are severely admonished, for 'there is no ritual prayer without the presence of the heart' (*AM* no. 109).

One can perform the ritual prayer (*ṣalāt*, Persian/Turkish *namāz*) on any clean spot, but it is preferable to use the prayer rug (and pious travellers would have a small rug with them; even wooden slates of the size of 60 to 120 cm are used in some places).

The five daily prayers are not mentioned in the Koran, but must have been practised in the Prophet's day. Their number is connected in legend with Muhammad's heavenly journey: God imposed a heavy duty of prayers upon the

Muslims, which was reduced after much pleading to five. The Koran speaks of the prayers at the ends of the day and in the afternoons (Sūra 11:114) and recommends nightly prayer, *tahajjud*, which is still performed by pious people but which never became a duty.

When someone's *ṣalāt* is finished, one wishes him or her *taqabbala Allāh*, 'may God accept it', because it does not consist of a petition which should be answered but is rather a sacrifice which has to be accepted. Each *ṣalāt* consists of two, three or four unities or cycles, *rakʿa*, which comprise bodily movements such as standing, genuflexion and prostration, as well as the recitations of several Sūras of the Koran. The five daily prayers together comprise seventeen *rakʿa*. The recitations of the Sūras and formula – always in Arabic – have to be absolutely correct, yet Muslim hagiography knows of saints who, being foreign or illiterate, could not articulate the Arabic prayers correctly and were therefore despised by people, although their proximity to God was greater than anyone could perceive.[51]

It is left to the individual to recite longer or shorter pieces from the Koran during the *ṣalāt*, and most people will prefer the short Sūras which are the first that one learns by heart, but once in a while one hears of people, especially among the Sufis, who recite the whole Koran in one or two *rakʿa*. This, of course, requires an extension of the prayer which is not recommended for the rank and file, for 'The best prayer is the briefest one', as the Prophet said.

One can perform one's prayer in the quiet atmosphere of one's home, in the middle of maddening traffic noise or in the loneliness of the desert or the forest; yet the community prayer is even more esteemed, because Islam is a religion in which the individual is generally conceived of as an integral part of the community, the *umma*.[52] The equality of the believers in the mosque, where there is no ranking of rich and poor (some pious people would even avoid praying in the first rows in order not to look ostentatious), induced Iqbāl to make an important remark about the social function of the congregational prayer:

> The spirit of all true prayer is social. Even the hermit abandons the society of men in the hope of finding, in a solitary abode, the fellowship of God … It is a psychological truth that association multiplies the normal man's power of perception, deepens his emotion, and dynamizes his will to a degree unknown to him in the privacy of his individuality …
>
> … Yet we cannot ignore the important consideration that the posture of the body is a real factor in determining the attitude of the mind. The choice of one particular direction in Islamic worship is meant to secure the unity of feeling in the congregation, and its form in general creates and fosters the sense of social equality, as it tends to destroy the feeling

> of rank or race superiority in the worshippers. What a tremendous spiritual revolution will take place, practically in no time, if the proud aristocratic Brahmin of South India is daily made to stand shoulder to shoulder with the untouchable! ...[53]

Ritual prayer is an important pillar of the House of Islam, and tradition says: 'Between faith and unbelief lies the giving up of the ritual prayer'. A person about whom one says *lā ṣalāt lah*, 'He has no ritual prayer', or in Persian and Turkish, he is *bē namāz*, 'prayerless', is someone who does not really belong to the community.

The *ṣalāt* has been compared to a stream of water that purifies the believer five times a day, but even without this poetical interpretation one can see that it (ideally) educates people to cleanliness and punctuality.

As Iqbāl briefly mentioned, the body's position in prayer is important, for, as Abū Ḥafṣ 'Omar as-Suhrawardī says, 'One has to pray with all limbs'.[54] The prostration means to give away everything, to empty oneself completely from worldly concerns; genuflexion means to turn away from oneself, and standing is the honoured position of the human being. That is, one expresses one's humility and one's feeling of being one of the people who are 'honoured by God' (Sūra 17:70) by being human. One can interpret the upright position as expression of the spiritual aspects of the human being and the prostration as expression of the earthly part in us, while genuflexion is a bridge between the two. Others have seen in the movements of ritual prayer the human being's participation in the vegetal, the animal and the human spheres. One can also understand prostration as the attitude of the person who, wonder-struck, bends his or her back before God – just as the sky is bent in worship. It is the attitude of closest proximity, as the Koran ordered the Prophet: *usjud wa 'qtarab*, 'Fall down and draw near!' (Sūra 96:19). Therefore, the dark mark on one's forehead, caused by regular prayer, came to be regarded as the sign of the true believer.

The variety of positions is important, as it means that humans can participate in the different levels of creation while the angels, it is said, occupy only one position of the prayer rite throughout eternity. And when the praying person lifts his or her hands, the spiritual current flows into them to fill body and soul.

Some pious souls found that the movement of the *ṣalāt* are performed in the names of Adam ادم or Muhammad محمد when written in Arabic characters – an interpretation that shows that prayer is the central function of humans. Muslims have also explained its three movements as pertaining to youth, maturity and old age.

The word *ṣalāt* was connected, though grammatically incorrectly, with *waṣala*, 'to reach, to attain', as the praying person hopes to reach God's presence or, in the case of ecstatic Sufis, to be united with Him. Abū Ḥafṣ 'Omar as-

Suhrawardī, on the other hand, combines the word with *ṣalā*, to be burnt: he who prays is corrected and purified by the fire of contemplation, so that Hellfire cannot touch him.

The number of *rakʿa* for each prayer is prescribed, but one can add certain extra *rakʿas* or extend one's prayer by additional recitation: the *farāʾiḍ*, the absolutely binding duties, can be followed by the *nawāfil*, supererogatory prayers. An effective prayer must have at least two *rakʿa*. That is the kind of prayer which should be offered, ideally, on every occasion: before leaving the house; when entering the mosque; when going to bed; during an eclipse; or when putting on a new dress. On such an occasion, one may pray:

> Oh God, to Thee be praise who hast clothed me with this. I ask Thee for the good of it and for the good for which it was created, and I take refuge with Thee from the evil of it and the evil for which it was created.[55]

The wording of this prayer is typical of many others: one always asks for God's protection from any evil that may be connected with that object which one deals with. Special rites are practised in the communal prayer for rain.

For the Prophet, ritual prayer was a repetition of his experience during the *miʿrāj* which brought him into God's immediate presence. And when he craved this experience, he would call Bilāl, his Ethiopian muezzin: 'Oh Bilāl, quicken us with the call to prayer!' (*AM* no. 48). The time of timelessness in prayer made him say *lī maʿa Allāh waqt*, 'I have a time with God in which neither a God-sent prophet nor an angel brought near has room …' (*AM* no. 100). It is this ecstatic experience which some souls were granted while bowing down in their ritual prayer.

Once more, the most eloquent spokesman of this experience is Rūmī, who sings in a poem with breathless rhythms, quick as a heartbeat:

> At the time of evening prayer
> ev'ryone spreads cloth and candles
> But I dream of my beloved,
> see, lamenting, grieved, his phantom.
> My ablution is with tears, see,
> Thus my prayer will be fiery,
> And I burn the mosquè's doorway
> when my call to prayer hits it …
> Is the prayer of the drunken,
> tell me! is this prayer valid?
> For he does not know the timing
> and is not aware of places.

Did I pray perhaps two cycles?
Or is this perhaps the eighth one?
And which Sūra did I utter?
For I have no tongue to speak it.
At God's door – how could I knock now
For I have no hand nor heart now?
You have carried heart and hand, God!
Grant me safety, God, forgive me …
(D no. 2,831)

Prayer, properly speaking, begins with praise. For in praise one turns away from oneself and directs one's heart towards Him to whom all praise belongs. Will not the Muslim exclaim, even when admiring a man-made object, *Subḥān Allāh*, 'Praise be God', instead of admiring the artist first? For he knows that God is the real source of human art, and that one has to praise Him first and only in the second place the instrument through which He works. Out of praise of God, then, grows ethical behaviour because one attempts to reach a place among those who approach Him as it behoves.

The *Fātiḥa* is used among Muslims as much as, if not more than, the Lord's Prayer in Christianity, and for this reason '*Fātiḥa*' often becomes a general term for a religious rite, a celebration and a meeting in which numerous prayers can be recited; but the *Fātiḥa*, often repeated silently by those present, is the true centre.[56]

It is for this reason that the *Fātiḥa*, the first Sūra of the Koran, begins with the words, *al-ḥamdu lillāh*, 'Praise be to God', and by praying so, humankind joins the ranks of those whose proper destination is praise of God. Minerals, plants and animals praise Him with the *lisān ul-ḥāl*, 'the tongue of their state', that is, by their very existence. To be sure, not many have described this praise in such amazing detail as did Bahā-i Walad, who tells how he heard all the food in his stomach praise the Creator:

> I had eaten much. I saw in my stomach all water and bread. God inspired me: 'All this water and bread and fruits have tongues and praise Me with voices and supplications. That means human beings and animals and fairies are all nourishments which have turned into voices of supplication and praise for Me …'.[57]

His son, Jalāluddīn Rūmī, then translated into human language the prayer of the fruit trees in the orchard which utter, as it were, by means of their naked branches and later by dint of the plentiful fruits the same petition as do humans when they speak the words of the *Fātiḥa*:

'We worship Thee!' – that is the garden's prayer
in winter time.

'We ask for help!' – that's what it utters
in time of spring.
'We worship Thee', that means: I come imploring,
imploring Thee:
Don't leave me in this sadness, Lord, and open
the door of joy!
'We ask Thee, Lord, for help' – that is, the fullness
of ripe, sweet fruits
Breaks now my branches and my twigs – protect me!
My Lord, My God!
(*D* no. 2,046)

The hymnic prayers of the Egyptian Sufi Dhū'n-Nūn in the ninth century are among the first attempts of Muslim thinkers to make the material reality transparent for the laud that is on everything's tongue, even in 'tonguelessness'.

The laud expressed at the very beginning of the *Fātiḥa* was translated into poetry by the great masters of Islamic literature mainly in the genre of poems usually called *tawḥīd*, 'acknowledgement of God's Unity'. This laud was expressed in the choicest words that they could think of: they praise God's unfathomable wisdom and tell of the wonders which He created in the universe; they also ponder the reasons why God has created things so differently: why is the Negro black and the Turk white? Why are humans to bear heavy burdens of obedience while the ferocious wolf is not asked to account for his bloodshed? Why is there suffering, and why does the Earth now appear in lovely green and now in wintry white? But the poets always end with the praise as they began with it – the wisdom of the Creator is too great to be doubted. In everything, there is a *ḥikma*, a wisdom; and therefore when the Muslim is afflicted with a disaster or faces some sad events, loss of friends or illness, and is asked how he fares, he or she will most probably answer: *al-ḥamdu li 'llāhi ʿalà kulli ḥāl*, 'Praised be God in every state [or: for everything]'.

The great hymnic poems, be they *qaṣīdas* with monorhyme or double-rhymed poems at the beginning of major Persian, Turkish or Urdu epics, have a psalmlike quality in their majestic sounds: suffice it to think of the poems of the Pathan poet Rahman Baba (d. after 1707), of the loving songs of Indian *qawwāls*, or of Turkish *ilâhis* with their repeated lines *al-ḥamdu lillāh* or the like.

Such poems often begin with the description of God's greatness in the third person and then turn to the personal address 'Thou', again in consonance with the pattern of the *Fātiḥa*, which starts with praise and then turns to the personal God: 'Thee we worship, and Thee we ask for help', as though one were drawing closer and closer to the goal of worship. The poet will be careful to address God with appropriate Divine names: when he writes the introduction to a love epic, he will choose names that reveal His attributes of beauty, while in a heroic story the attributes of majesty are to be used. Large sections of religious poetry can indeed be seen, so to speak, as elaborations of the Prophet's saying *lā uḥṣī ʿalayka thanāʾan*, 'I cannot count the praise due to Thee!'

Ritual prayer has a preferred place in Muslim piety not only because it is one of the five pillars of religion but also because the praying person uses the verses of the Koran, which means that he or she addresses God with His own words: this close relationship between the reciting person and the Divine recipient of the prayer creates a very special bond.

At the end of the ritual prayer, after pronouncing the greetings to angels and humans, one can utter personal prayers, petitionary prayers, *duʿā* or *munājāt*, intimate conversations. Such prayers can be spoken, of course, at any time, but they are considered more effective after the ritual prayer when one is still in the state of bodily and spiritual purity.

The content of these petitionary prayers is as variegated as are the needs of human beings. One can pray for any worldly good, for health, for relief from worries, for success, for children, or when seeing the new moon, and so on and so forth. But besides these practical human wishes, there are prayers for ethical values, like the prayer 'Dress me in the garment of piety!' The Prophet's prayer *ya rabbī zidnī ʿilman*, 'O Lord, increase me in knowledge', inspired people as well, and the sinner's hope for forgiveness, the longing for Paradise, is expressed as much as the fear of Hell, although ideally both should be transcended by the loving trust in God's eternal will and wisdom.

And yet, one finds rebellious outcries against God: Hellmut Ritter gives excellent examples from ʿAṭṭār's epics, outcries which the poet puts often in the mouth of mentally deranged people, but which one can also observe, at times, when listening to a 'village saint' in Anatolia.[58] In addition, some of Iqbāl's poetical prayers express a strong resentment to God's actions and underline man's will to organize life on Earth according to his own will.

One prayer that is always answered is that for others, and not only the family and the friends are included but also all those whom God has created, even one's enemies, for they may have served to divert the praying person from his or her previous evil ways, thus leading him or her back to God and helping to acquire a happier and more blessed state, as Rūmī tells in one of the stories in the *Mathnawī* (*M* IV 56f.). Many manuscripts from Islamic lands have a short prayer formula at the end or ask the reader to include the author and/or the copyist in his prayers. Likewise, tombstones often bear the words *al-fātiḥa*, or, in Turkey, *ruhuna fatiha*, that is, one should recite a *Fātiḥa* for the deceased person's spiritual welfare because prayers as well as the recitation of the Koran can help to improve dead people's state in their lonely grave.

According to tradition, free prayer should be spoken in plain words and without rhetorical embellishment; but in later times, the Arabs' love of high-flowing, rhyming sentences is evident. Thus, many such prayers are masterpieces of Arabic and – at a later stage – Persian or Turkish high-soaring prose.[59] Suffice it to mention the prayers ascribed to Imam Zayn al-ʿĀbidīn in *aṣ-Ṣaḥīfa as-Sajjādiyya*, which is available now in an excellent English version. Ghazzālī's *Iḥyā ʿulūm ad-dīn* contains a vast treasure of prayers which are inherited from the Prophet, his companions and his family, and from certain pious and saintly members of the community in the early centuries of Islam; such a prayer, *duʿā ma'thūr*, is thought to be particularly effective (similar to classical prayer formulas in Christian prayer books). In the Persianate world, ʿAbdullāh-i Anṣārī's (d. 1089) *Munājāt* are the first example of short, rhyming Persian prayers, interspersed by prayer poems, and in the course of the centuries the mystical prayers of Sufi masters like Mīr Dard of Delhi (d. 1785), or the long chains of invocations used in the tradition of some Sufi orders, are beautiful examples of the never-resting longing of the human heart.[60]

One of the forms found in such traditions is the prayer with the letters of the alphabet which, being a vessel into which the revelation was poured, have a sanctity of their own (see below, p. 152). Thus, one finds chains of 'alphabetical' prayers which implore God, for example *bi-dhāl dhātika* 'by the letter *dh* of Thy essence, *dhāt*', or 'By the letter *ṣād* of Thy reliability, *ṣidq*', and so on.[61]

Again, in somewhat later times, one finds the closing formula *bi-ḥaqq Muḥammadin* or *bi-sharaf Muḥammadin*, 'For Muhammad's sake' or 'For the sake of Muhammad's honour ...'. The name of the Prophet becomes, as it were, a warrant for the acceptance of prayer. Ibn Taymiyya objected to this formula; one should rather begin and close the *duʿā* with the formula of blessings for the Prophet. One can also find prayers in connection with the Koran: 'For the sake of the Koran ... I beg Thee that ...'.

During the petitionary prayer, one opens the hands, with the palms showing heavenward as though to attract the effusion of grace (or, in a more primitive interpretation, one thinks that God would be ashamed not to put something into the open hands of a begging creature). Therefore the poets see the plane tree's leaves lifted like hands to ask for God's grace.

But, like all people in the world, the Muslims too were plagued by the problem: can prayer really be heard and answered, and why does God not answer all our petitions? Some radical mystics, overstressing the concept of surrender and absolute trust in God, voiced the opinion that prayer is of no use as everything has been pre-ordained since pre-eternity. Only ritual prayer as an act of obedience is permissible.[62] However, most Muslims reminded such sceptics of the Koranic promise: 'Call upon Me, and I will answer!' (Sūra 40:62), or God's statement: 'Verily I am near, I answer the prayer of the worshipper when he prays' (Sūra 2:186).

The concept of God as a personal God, a caring and wise Lord, necessitated the dialogue between Him and His creatures – a dialogue which, naturally, was initiated by Him. When a *ḥadīth* claims that 'God does not open anyone's mouth to ask for forgiveness unless He has decreed to forgive him', then prayer is not only permitted but also required. Prayer and affliction work against each other like shield and arrow, and it is not a condition in war that one should not carry a shield, says the traditional adage.

Yet, there remains the problem that many a prayer is not answered. In this respect, Qushayri and others quote a *ḥadīth* that states that God likes to listen to the voices of those who implore Him, just as we enjoy listening to the voices of caged birds; that is why he does not fulfil their wishes immediately but keeps them at bay to enjoy their sweet voices somewhat longer ... (*AM* no. 730). This is certainly a very anthropomorphic explanation, not compatible with high theological reasoning. But since prayer often evades theological definitions and has apparently its own law of gravity, one need not be surprised that despite many rules and regulations developed even for the so-called 'free' prayer, believers concede that God accepts every sincere call – even, as Rūmī says, the prayer of the menstruating woman (who, due to her impurity, must not touch or recite the Koran). He makes this remark in the context of the story of Moses and the shepherd, when the stern, proud prophet chastised the simple lover of God who, as becomes clear, was about to reach a much higher spiritual rank than Moses himself. The true aim of prayer is, as Iqbāl says in a fine Urdu poem, not that one's wish be granted but rather that the human will be changed to become unified with the Divine will; the Divine will can then flow through the human soul, filling and transforming it, until one reaches conformity with one's destined fate.[63]

Just as free prayer can be uttered at the end of the ritual prayer, one can also often see pious people sitting after finishing the *ṣalāt*, counting their prayer beads while they repeat either a Divine name or a formula given to them by their spiritual guide. The so-called *tasbīḥ* (literally, the pronouncing of praise formulas such as *subḥān Allāh*) or *subḥa*, a thread with thirty-three or ninety-nine beads made of ritually clean material, was probably introduced from India into the central Islamic lands in the ninth century,[64] but the custom of *dhikr*, 'mentioning' or 'recollecting', goes back to the time of the Prophet. Does not the Koran – where the root *dhakara*, 'remember', occurs dozens of time – speak of 'remembering God after finishing the ritual prayer ...' (Sūra 4:103) and promise: 'Verily by remembering the Lord, hearts become quiet' (Sūra 13:28)?

This 'remembering' meant in the beginning simply thinking of God (*dhikr*) and His grace and blessings, (something a believer should constantly do), but it developed rather early into a whole system of meditation in which certain formulas were repeated thousands of times.[65] The very name of *Allāh* was probably the first formula to be used for such purposes, for after all, the Koran reminded the believers 'to remember Allah'. Furthermore, the formulas of asking forgiveness, *istighfār*, or *subḥān Allah*, or *al-ḥamdu lillāh*, were repeated many times, and the profession of faith, or at least its first part with its swinging from the negation *lā* to the affirmation *illā*, was an ideal vehicle for long meditations, all the more as it can be easily combined with breathing: *lā ilāha*, 'there is no deity', is said while exhaling, to point to 'what is not God', while the *illā Allāh* during the inhaling shows that everything returns into the all-embracing Divine Being.

The Sufis developed psychological systems to understand the working of each of the ninety-nine Divine Names lest the meditating person be afflicted by the use of a wrong name. The *dhikr* could be loud or silent; the loud one is generally used in the meetings of Sufi brotherhoods and ends in the repetition of the last *h* of *Allāh* after every other sound has slowly disappeared; this last stage resembles a deep sigh. The silent *dhikr* too has been described as a journey through the letters of the word *Allāh* until the meditating person is, so to speak, surrounded by the luminous circle of this final *h*, the greatest proximity that one could hope to reach.[66]

The *dhikr* should permeate the entire body and soul,[67] and the mystics knew of refined methods of slowly opening the centres of spiritual power in the body – the five or seven luminous points, *laṭā'if.* These techniques, along with the proper movements or attitude in sitting and the correct breathing, have to be learned from a master who knows best how the hearts of the disciples can be polished. For the *dhikr* has always been regarded as a means of polishing the mirror of the heart – this heart which can so easily be covered with the rust of worldly occupations and thoughts; constant *dhikr*, however, can remove the rust and make the heart clear so that it can receive the radiant Divine light and reflect the Divine beauty. How much even a simple *dhikr* permeates the whole being became clear to me in a Pakistani home: after a stroke, the old mother was unable to speak but repeated – one may say breathed – the word *Allāh* hour after hour.

During the *dhikr*, special positions of the body are required. One often places one's head upon one's knees – the knees are, as Abū Ḥafṣ 'Omar as-Suhrawardī writes, 'the meditating person's Mt Sinai' where one receives the manifestation of Divine light as did Moses.[68] How widespread this thought was is understood from Shāh 'Abdul Laṭīf's great Sindhi *Risālō*, in which this eighteenth-century Sufi poet in the lower Indus Valley compares the knees of the true Yogis, and that means, for him, the true lovers of God, to Mt Sinai where the epiphany takes place.

Prayer, as the Muslims knew, is an answer to God's call. Western readers are best acquainted with Rūmī's story of the man who gave up prayer because he never received an answer but then was taught by God that in every 'O Lord!' of his, there are 100 'Here I am at your service!' from God's side (*M* III 189ff.). This story, translated for the first time in 1821 into Latin by the German theologian F. D. A. Tholuck,[69] helped Nathan Söderblom and those who studied his works to understand that Islam too knows the concept of the *oratio infusa*, the prayer of grace; but few if any authors were aware that this idea had occurred in Muslim literature long before Rūmī. There are a number of *ḥadīth* dealing with prayer as initiated by God, and mystics such as al-Ḥallāj (who sang: 'I call Thee, nay, Thou callest me') and shortly after him Niffarī (d. 965) used this concept frequently. In Rūmī's *Mathnawī*, not only does this famous story point to the secret of prayer as a Divine gift, but also the poet repeats time and again:

> Thou madest prayer grow from me, for otherwise,
> how could a rose grow out of an ash pit?
> (*M* II 2,443)

Rūmī, like other mystics within and outside Islam, knew that prayer is not fettered in words. In his elaboration of the above-mentioned *ḥadīth*, 'I have a time with God', he points to the fact that ritual prayer (and, one may add, free prayer and *dhikr* as well) is an outward form, but the soul of ritual prayer 'is rather absorption and loss of consciousness, in which all these outward forms remain outside and have no room any more. Even Gabriel, who is pure spirit, does not fit into it.'

There is only silence – sacred silence is the veritable end of prayer, as Rūmī says:

> Become silent and go by way of silence toward non-existence,
> and when you become non-existent you'll be all praise and laud.

For silence is very much part of the religious experience,[70] and, like the word, has different shades and forms. There is the 'sacred silence', which means that names and formulas must not be mentioned: neither will the person involved in true *dhikr* reveal the name which he or she invokes, nor will the non-initiated be admitted into the Ismaili Jamaatkhana where silent meditation takes place. Even the use of a sacred or foreign language in the cult is, in a certain way, silence: one feels that something else, the Numinous, speaks in words and sounds which the normal observer does not understand.

Often, silence grows out of awe: in the presence of the mighty king, the humble servant would not dare to speak. In the silent *dhikr*, the repetition of the names or formulas is completely interiorized and has no signs or words; in fact, as especially the Naqshbandis have emphasized, true worship is *khalwat dar anjuman*, 'solitude in the crowd'; that is, the continued recollection of God in one's heart while doing one's duty in the world – *dast bi-kār dil bi-yār*, 'The hand at work, the heart near the friend', as the Persian saying goes. The Koran had praised those whom neither business nor work keeps away from remembering their Lord (Sūra 24:37), who are *fi ṣalātin dā'imūn*, 'persevering in prayer' (Sūra 70:22–3).

One may think in this connection also of ascetic silence, alluded to in the last phrase of the old tripartite rule of 'little eating, little sleep, little talking' (*qillat aṭ-ṭa'ām, qillat al-manām, qillat al-kalām*) – a rule that could lead to near-complete silence in the case of some Sufis. In Turkey, silence is part of the fulfilment of certain vows, such as in the *Zakarya sofrasĭ*.

But when one speaks of silent prayer, as Rūmī does in the verse quoted earlier, his remark emerges from the feeling that the ineffable cannot be fettered in words. Many of his poems therefore end in the call *khāmūsh*, 'Quiet! Silent!' because he could not express the secret of the loving interior dialogue with the Divine Beloved. To do that, one has to learn the 'tongue of tonguelessness'.

However, it is a paradox found in many religious traditions, and certainly in Islam, that the mystics, who were so well aware of the necessity and central role of silence, wrote the most verbose books and prayers to explain that they could not possibly express their thoughts. They knew that to speak of one's experience is basically a treason to the experience; for, as Dhū'n-Nūn said, the hearts of the free (that is, the real men of God) are the tombs of the secrets, *qulūb al-aḥrār qubūr al-aṣrār*. Those who have reached the highest ranges of intimacy with the Lord keep closed the doors of expression. Was not al-Ḥallaj executed because he committed the major sin of *ifshā as-sirr*, 'divulging the secret' of loving union? That is at least how later generations interpreted his death on the gallows, pointing by this interpretation to the importance of silence.

They are here in unison with the representatives of theological silence, of the apophatic theology whose roots go back, in the Western tradition, to Dionysius Pseudo-Areopagita, whose theology has influenced Christian and Islamic mysticism over the centuries.

The mystic – verbose as he may be, with however many paradoxes he may try to pour out his experience – has yet to be silent, for he is trying to fathom the unfathomable depth of the Divine Ocean, the *deus absconditus*, and cannot speak, resembling a dumb person who is unable to tell of his dreams. The prophet, however, has to speak, must speak, must preach the *deus revelatus*. And the revelation happens in Islam through the sacred book, the Divine Word inlibrated.[71]

SACRED SCRIPTURE[72]

The centre of Islam is the Koran. Its sound, as has been said, defines the space in which the Muslim lives, and its written copies are highly venerated. In no other religion has the book/Book acquired a greater importance than in Islam, which is, most importantly, the first religion to distinguish between the *ahl al-kitāb*, those who possess a revealed scripture, and the people without such a

Book. The Koran is, for the Muslim, the *verbum visibile*, the Word Inlibrate, to use Harry Wolfson's apt expression, which corresponds to the Word Incarnate of the Christian faith.

However, it is not only the Koran, written down and recited innumerable times over the centuries; since time immemorial, the very act of writing has been considered sacred. The letters, so it was felt, had a special power, and in ancient civilizations the scribes, those who could and were allowed to handle the art of writing, formed a class in themselves: they were the guardians of sacred and secret wisdom.

The mystery of letters has inspired many Muslim thinkers, and most of them would agree with Jaʿfar aṣ-Ṣādiq (d. 765), the sixth Shia imam, who said:

> In the first place a thought surged in God, an intention, a will. The object of this thought, this intention, and this will were the letters from which God made the principal of all things, the indices of everything perceptible, the criteria of everything difficult. It is from these letters that everything is known.[73]

Even Avicenna is credited with a *risāla nayrūziyya* that deals with the letters, and mystical philosophers and poets never ceased using allusions to the letters or invented fascinating relations between letters and events, between the shape of the letters and the shape of humans, and might even see human beings as 'lofty letters' which were waiting to appear, as Ibn ʿArabī says in a well-known verse.

A *ḥadīth* according to which man's heart is between two of God's fingers was poetically interpreted as meaning that the human heart resembles a pen in God's hand with which the Creator writes whatever is necessary on the vast tablet of creation. This imagery of the human being as a pen, or else as letters, written by the master calligrapher, is commonplace in Islamic poetry, as Rūmī sings:

My heart became like a pen
    that's in the Beloved's fingers:
Tonight he may write a *Z*,
    perhaps, tomorrow, a *B*.
He cuts and prepares his pen well
    to write in *riqaʿ* and *naskh*;
The pen says: 'Yes, I'll obey,
    for you know best what to do'.
Sometimes he blackens its face,
    he wipes it then in his hair.
He keeps it now upside down,
    sometimes he works with it too …

(D no. 2,530)

Seven centuries later, Ghālib in Delhi (d. 1869) translated into Urdu poetry the outcry of the letters which rebel against God who wrote them in such strange forms: the paper shirt they are wearing (i.e. the fact that they are penned on paper) shows that they are plaintiffs, unhappy with the Divine Pen's activities. But the same poet also sighed at the thought of death – after all, he is not a letter that can be easily repeated on the tablet of time.[74]

The Arabic alphabet, in which the Koran is written, followed first the ancient Semitic sequence, that is, a, b, j, d, h, w, z etc., and is still used in this so-called *abjad* sequence when dealing with the numerical value of a letter. Beginning with *alif* = 1, it counts the single digits up to *y* = 10, the tens up to *q* = 100 and the hundreds up to *gh* = 1000, so that the complete decimal system is contained in the twenty-eight letters of the alphabet and can then be used for prognostication or for chronograms to give the dates of important events, from the birth of a prince to the deaths of pious scholars (for which Koranic quotations often offered fitting dates by their numerical value) or of politicians, chronograms for whose death were often made up from less flattering sentences.

The *Tales of the Prophets* gives various stories about the inner meaning of the *abjad* letters, which are traced back to previous prophets; the most spiritual explanation is ascribed to Jesus, according to whom each letter points to one of God's qualities: a = *Allāh*; b = *bahā Allāh*, 'God's glory'; j = *jalāl Allāh*, 'God's majesty and strength'; d = *dīn Allāh*, 'God's religion'; h = *huwa Allāh*, 'He is God'; and so on,[75] while in Ismaili cosmology *alif* stands for the *nāṭiq*, *b* for the *wāṣī*, and *t* for the *Imām*.

A very special role was attributed to the groups of unconnected letters which precede a considerable number of Koranic Sūras and whose meaning is not completely clear. Thus, many mysterious qualities were ascribed to them; they could also be seen as pointing to the special names of the Prophet such as *ṬH*, *Ṭāhā* (Sūra 20:1), or *YS*, *Yāsīn* (Sūra 36:1), or other secret abbreviations; thus the sevenfold *ḤM*, *ḥā-mīm*, was sometimes read as *ḥabībī Muḥammad*, 'My beloved Muhammad'.

These isolated letters were often used in religio–magical contexts, and along with the *sawāqiṭ al-fātiḥa*, the seven letters which do not occur in the first Sūra of the Koran, they can be found in talismans engraved in agate or carnelian.[76] Inscribed in metal bowls for healing water, they are mixed with a number of Koranic verses and/or numbers. The ailing person could thus 'drink the power' of the letters, just as in the Deccan the *basmala kā dulhāñ*, 'the bridegroom of the *basmala*', was supposed to lick off the letters of the formula *bismillāh* (see above, p. 107). Frequently used in amulets and talismans are the last two Sūras of the Koran, the *muʿawwidhatān*, 'by which one seeks refuge' (with God) from assorted evils. Another protecting word is the seemingly meaningless *budūḥ* which one sees on walls, at entrance gates and in many talismanic objects; even Ghazzālī emphasized the importance of *budūḥ* in certain cases such as childbirth.[77] *Budūḥ* corresponds to the four numbers (b = 2, d = 4, ū = 6, ḥ = 8) which form the corners of the most frequently-used magic square (the one built upon the central five and resulting in every direction in the number fifteen).

The *shahāda*, the profession of faith, likewise contains sacred power. For this reason, its words are often woven or embroidered into covers for sarcophagi or tombs, for then, it is hoped, the deceased will have no difficulties in answering the questions of the interrogating angels Munkar and Nakīr in the grave. When Koranic verses and sacred letters are used to decorate a entire shirt, it is hoped that the hero who wears it will return safely and victorious from the battlefield. In our time, one finds stickers for cars and windows with the most efficacious blessing formulas such as the *basmala*, the Throne Verse (Sūra 2:255), or the *mā shā' Allāh*, 'What God willeth', which is recited against the Evil Eye. They are also used in pendants, preferably of carnelian, embroidered on various material, repeated on tiles and printed on thousands of postcards in ever-changing calligraphic designs. This can result in strange surprises, as when an American firm offers T-shirts with a decorative design which the Muslim immediately understands as the word *Allāh* or part of the *shahāda*. (One is reminded of the medieval use in Europe of Arabic religious formulas in Kufic lettering to decorate woven fabrics or even the halo of the Virgin Mary.)[78]

In houses and sometimes in mosques, one can find the *ḥilya sharīfa*, that is, the description of the Prophet's noble bodily and spiritual qualities as recorded in the oldest sources; this Arabic text is written in fine calligraphy, usually after a famous Turkish model from the seventeenth century, and serves the Muslim as a true picture of the Prophet, whose pictorial representation is prohibited.

To Muslims who use a script different from the Arabic alphabet, such as Bengali, the very sight of Arabic letters seemed to convey the feeling of sanctity, and when Josef Horovitz observed, at the beginning of the twentieth century, how Bengali villagers would piously anoint stones with Arabic inscriptions, one could see later that people carefully picked up matchboxes with Arabic words on them lest perchance a sacred name or word be desecrated.[79] During the time that Bengal was still part of Pakistan, a movement called *ḥurūf al-qur'ān*, 'the letters of the Koran', gained momentum: Muslims wanted to write Bengali in Arabic letters to show their loyalty to the Islamic heritage, and the difference of script doubtless contributed to the break-up of Pakistan in 1971.

For wherever Islam spread to become the ruling religion, the Arabic letters formed a strong bond. To reject the Arabic alphabet means a complete break with one's religious and cultural past; Ataturk's Turkey is a telling example. Even though Arabic writing is not ideally suited to the Turkish grammar and sound systems, the large number of Arabic and Persian words and grammatical elements in the classical Ottoman Turkish language made it a natural choice to use this script from the time of the Turks' conversion to Islam. A return to Arabic letters can be observed in modern times in the former Central Asian Soviet republics, where Muslims are trying to shake off the disliked Cyrillic alphabet and reintegrate their culture into the glorious Islamic past. Tajikistan is a typical case. Attempts by individuals to write Arabic itself in Roman letters caused a wild outcry among Arabs, and a timid attempt to do the same for Urdu in Pakistan was likewise doomed to failure.

The Arabic letters in which the first copies of the Koran were noted down were rather ungainly, but in a short time the script was arranged in fine, well-measured forms, and various styles emerged in centres of Muslim government both for preserving the Koranic revelation and for practical purposes such as chancellery use, copying of books, etc.[80]

We are used to calling the majority of the heavy, angular styles of early Arabic as they were used for copies of the Koran and for epigraphical purposes 'Kufic' after the city of Kufa in Iraq, a stronghold of ʿAlī ibn Abī Ṭālib and his partisans – and ʿAlī is usually regarded as a kind of patron saint of calligraphy, so that the *silsilas*, the chains of initiation, generally go back to him. The early Korans, written on vellum, have, as Martin Lings states correctly, an 'iconic quality' to them.[81] One looks at them and seems to discover through them the living element of revelation, awe-inspiring and close to one's heart. The veneration shown to the copies which, as Muslims believe, are the originals collected and edited by the third caliph, ʿOthmān, is remarkable.

The art of calligraphy developed largely owing to the wish to write the Divine word as beautifully as possible, and the majestic large Korans in cursive writing (which was shaped artistically in the tenth century) from Mamluk and Timurid times are as impressive as the small, elegant copies of the Book made in Turkey or Iran. In Turkey, the Koran copies written by Hafiz Osman (d. 1689), the leading master in the tradition of Shaykh Hamdullah (d. 1519), were taken by pious people as equal to the original and were therefore used for prognostication. Most printed editions of the Koran in Turkey are based on Hafiz Osman's work.

The belief in the *baraka* of the Koranic letters is attested first during the battle of Siffin (657), when Muʿāwiya, fighting ʿAlī, feared defeat and asked his soldiers to place pages of the Koran on their lances – the Divine word should decide between the two Muslim leaders. One may see here an attempt to utilize the *baraka* of the Koranic letters, if not to guarantee victory then at least to avert defeat. A century later, a Sufi history about Ibrāhīm ibn Adham (d. around 777) tells that a boat was saved during a storm thanks to the pages of the Koran that were on it,[82] and stories of this kind are frequent in Muslim legend, as are similar legends about an icon or a crucifix in the Christian tradition.

In thinking of the Koranic letters and words' *baraka*, one should be careful not to spoil any page of the Koran or folios on which a part of it is written; the

Journal of the Pakistan Historical Society 39, 1 (1991) contains, after the Table of Contents, the warning:

> The sacred *aayat* from the Holy Qur'an and *ahadith* have been printed for Tabligh and for increase of your religious knowledge. It is your duty to ensure their sanctity. Therefore, the pages on which these are printed should be disposed of in proper Islamic manner.[83]

The careful preservation of pages and fragments of old Korans has led to the discovery, in 1971, of a considerable number of bags in the Great Mosque of Sanaa, Yemen, which contained thousands of fragments of early Koran copies mainly on vellum.

People have pondered the origin of scriptures that contain such power, and while in India the Vedas are regarded as having emanated, and, in other traditions, the authors are, according to legend, supernaturally begotten, a widespread belief is that of the pre-existence of the Scripture.

The Koran is pre-existent; the *umm al-kitāb* (Sūra 43:4) is preserved in the heavenly original on the *lawḥ maḥfūz*, the Well-preserved Tablet, and thus the Koran, once it appeared in this world, makes the Divine power present among humans. It is, as G. E. von Grunebaum says with a fine comparison, 'an anchor of timelessness in a changing world'.[84] Its message has no end, for, as Sūra 18:109 says: 'If the sea were ink for my Lord's words, verily the sea would be exhausted before the words of my Lord even though we would bring the like of it'. And again, each word of the Koran has an endless meaning, and the world will forever understand it anew.

For decades in the early ninth century, the struggle between the Muʿtazila and the traditionalists raged, for the Muʿtazilites, jealously insisting upon God's absolute Unity, would not allow anything to be pre-eternally coexistent with Him. The Koran, they held, was the primordial Divine message, but it was created and not, as Ibn Ḥanbal (d. 855) and the majority of the believers claimed, uncreated. The dogma of the Koran's being uncreated is maintained to this day; thus, one can correctly say that every Muslim is a fundamentalist, as this term was first used to designate those American evangelical groups who firmly believed in the divine origin of the Bible.

Whether one took the side of the Muʿtazilites or the orthodox, it was accepted that the Koran is the Divine word which was 'inlibrated' through the medium of Muhammad; and, just as Mary had to be a virgin to give birth to the Word Incarnate, thus Muhammad, it was felt, had to be *ummī*, 'illiterate', to be the pure vessel for the 'inlibration' of the Word. That was why Muslims interpreted the term *ummī* as illiterate while its original meaning was probably 'the Prophet sent to the *umma*, i.e. the gentiles'.[85] And, as he was a vessel for the revelation, 'his character, *khuluq*, was the Koran', as his wife ʿA'isha said.

The Koran is certainly not the first book ever given by God to humankind. The Torah, Psalms and Gospel are believed to have been divinely sent, and the 'four books' are the proud property of the *ahl al-kitāb* although, as the Koran holds, previous peoples have altered their revelations (Sūra 2:75 et al.). Some even know of other books, and when the Koran mentioned 'the book' which was given to Moses, i.e. the Torah (Sūra 11:110, 41:45), the so-called *ṣuḥuf*, 'pages', are also given to Abraham (Sūra 87:19). To this day, some Sufi leaders claim to have seen these pages and to be aware of their contents.

In traditional religions, the believers knew that seers and prophets either see or hear the Word. In Muhammad's case, both experiences interpenetrate: he saw Gabriel and he heard the word *iqra'*, 'Read! Recite!', although later, auditions were more frequent and also stronger than his comparatively rare visionary experiences.[86] Abū Ḥafs ʿOmar as-Suhrawardī has beautifully described the experience of those who hear the Koran as the Divine word as it behoves:

> To listen to the Koran means to listen to God; hearing becomes seeing, seeing becomes hearing, knowing turns into action, action turns into knowing – that is the 'fine hearing'.[87]

The fact that the Koran is, for the Muslim, God's word resulted in a major controversy when the phonograph was first introduced: can one recite the Koran by means of the phonograph or not? How should one in such a case perform the prescribed prostrations at the required places?[88] This controversy, which happened around the turn of the twentieth century, is today absolutely obsolete, and the adversaries of mechanical recitation would be horrified to learn that the Koran is available through radio, over loudspeaker and on tapes which can be played everywhere and at any time – which entails also that non-Muslims will listen to it. Tapes and records made at the annual competitions in Koran recitation, in which men and women participate, are now coveted items.

The Koran was revealed in clear Arabic language (Sūra 16:103, 41:44, 26:192ff.), and it is its literary superiority which is several times emphasized. The *iʿjāz*, its unsurpassable style, is its true miracle (cf. Sūra 17:88). Each of its so-called 'verses', the smaller units of which a Sūra, or chapter, consists, is an *āya*, a 'sign', a Divine miracle to prove the Prophet's veracity; the 'signs' of the Koran are his *Beglaubigungswunder*. The *iʿjāz* 'which incapacitates men and djinn' to create anything comparable to it (Sūra 17:88) also makes a translation impossible: nobody could bring into another idiom its linguistic beauty, the numerous cross-relations and the layers of meaning. The text 'was verbally revealed and not merely in its meanings and ideas'. Thus states one of the leading Muslim modernists, the late Fazlur Rahman, whose words emphasize the mysterious relations between words, sound and contents of the Book.[89]

The text, so Muslims believe, contains the solution of all problems which have arisen and still will arise. Sanā'ī, taking the first and the last letter of the Koran, namely *b* and *s*, understood from them that the Koran is *bas*, 'enough' (in Persian).[90] Unknown mysteries are hidden in the sequence of its letters. To come close to it, whether to touch it and read from it or to recite it by heart, means to enter the Divine presence, as the *ḥadīth qudsī* says: 'Someone who reads the Koran is as if he were talking to Me and I were talking with him' (*AM* no. 39).

When quoting from the Koran, one begins with the phrase *qāla taʿālā*, or *qāla ʿazza wa jalla*, 'He, Most High', or 'He, Mighty and Majestic, said ...'. When reciting the Koran or referring to it by quoting a Sūra or an *āya*, one should begin with the *basmala* after pronouncing the formula of refuge, *aʿūdhu bi 'Llāh min ash-shayṭān ar-rajīm*, 'I seek refuge with God from the accursed Satan'. Each Sūra, except for Sūra 9, begins with the *basmala*, a formula which should also be uttered at the beginning of each and every work. Thus *bismillāh karnā* simply means, in Urdu, 'to begin', and when the Turk says *Hadi bismillah* he means: 'Let's start!'

The single letters or clusters of letters in the Koran have a sanctity of their own; but, even more, certain Sūras or verses carry special *baraka* with them, primarily the *Fātiḥa*, whose use in all kinds of rites was mentioned above (p. 143). Sūra 36, *Yāsīn*, is recited for the deceased or the dying and their benefit in the world to come; it is called the 'heart of the Koran'. And the Throne Verse (Sūra 2:255) is frequently used for protective purposes. The thousandfold repetition of Sūra 112, the attestation that 'God is One, neither begotten nor begetting', is another way of protecting oneself from all kinds of evil.[91]

The pious may begin the day with briefly listening to the Koran before or after the morning prayer, for the Koran was, as it were, 'personified', and appeared in some prayers as the true intercessor for the believer:

> O Lord, adorn us with the ornament of the Koran,
> and favour us through the grace of the Koran,
> and honour us through the honour of the Koran,
> and invest us with the robe of honour of the Koran
> and make us enter Paradise through the intercession
> of the Koran
> and rescue us from all evil in the world
> and the pain of the Otherworld for the sake of the
> honour of the Koran ...
> O Lord, make the Koran for us a companion in this world
> and an intimate friend in the tomb,
> and a friend at the Day of Resurrection,
> and a light on the Bridge,
> and a companion in Paradise,

and a veil and protection from the fire,
and a guide to all good deeds
by Thy grace and kindness and favour!

This prayer was especially recited when one had performed a *khatma*, a complete recitation of the Koran, which is considered to carry with it many blessings. One can do that in one sitting or by reciting each day of the month a *juz'*, that is, one thirtieth of the whole book. Often, the reward of such *khatma* is offered to a deceased person. Thus, one may also hire professional *ḥuffāẓ* (plural of *ḥāfiẓ*) to repeat so-and-so many *khatmas* for someone's soul, or one can vow to recite or have recited a *khatma*. When a child has gone through the whole Koran, or even more when he or she (usually at a tender age) has committed the Holy Book to memory and become a *ḥāfiẓ*, a feast is given.

One has always to keep in mind that the Muslim not only sees the Divine Presence when contemplating the Koran but also feels honoured to be able to talk to God with the Lord's own words when reciting the Koran: it is the closest approximation that a pious person can hope for, indeed a 'sacramental' act.[92]

As God has revealed His will in the Koran, it is also the source of law. The problems of the abrogating and abrogated verses (*nāsikh*, *mansūkh*) have occupied theologians and jurists down through the centuries, but there is no doubt that, as Bernhard Weiß writes correctly: 'Islamic law is based on texts which are considered to be sacred and therefore as absolutely final and not subject to change'.[93] The language in which the *verbum Dei* is expressed is 'determined for all times', and it is the duty of the jurists to find out the exact meaning of the grammatical forms: when the Koran uses an imperative, does that mean that the act referred to is an obligation or is only recommended, or is the form meant merely for guidance? These are problems which have been discussed down through the centuries because their understanding is central for legal praxis.

But abrogated and abrogating sentences aside, the Koran wields absolute authority, for the heavenly Book, *al-kitāb*, is faithfully reproduced in the *muṣḥaf*, the copy, which human hands can touch and which yet contains the uncreated word. Should a scribe make a mistake in copying the Koran, the page has to be taken out and replaced. (Such so-called *muhrac* pages by major calligraphers could become collector's items in Turkey.) And just as the scholars were of divided opinion about the mechanical reproduction of the Koran's sound, the question was raised much earlier as to whether or not printing or (nowadays) photocopying was permissible. This is particularly important when it comes to *muṣḥafs* printed in non-Muslim countries, where the printing facilities and techniques were, in most cases, superior – but who would know what might happen to the text in the hand of the infidels? An article issued in South Africa last year states very clearly:

> Those responsible for sending the Arabic text of the Qur'aan to impure *kuffaar* are guilty of a major sin. They are guilty of sacrilege of the Qur'aan. They are guilty of defiling and dishonouring the Qur'aan and Islam by their dastardly act of handing copies of the Qur'aan to *kuffaar* who are perpetually in the state of *hadth* and *janaabat* [minor and major impurity].[94]

The conviction that whatever is between the two covers is God's word led, understandably, to a strong bibliolatry. It is said that the vizier Ibn al-Furāt (d. 924) did not sleep in a house where a Koran was kept, out of respect for the sacred word,[95] and even though not too many people would go so far, the *muṣḥaf* should still be nicely wrapped and kept in a high place, higher than any other book. Sometimes it is hung from the ceiling or from the door frame (which secures its blessing for anyone who enters), and it can also be kept above the marital bed. The *muṣḥaf* is kissed (that accounts for the comparison of the beloved's flawless face with a beautiful *muṣḥaf*), and in Persian poetry the black tress that hangs over the radiant cheek of the beloved could be compared to an impudent Hindu who stretches his foot over the *muṣḥaf* – a double sacrilege, as the Hindu has no right to touch the Book, and as the *muṣḥaf* must never be touched with the foot.[96]

The reverence for the *muṣḥaf* led to the high rank of the calligrapher who specialized in writing the Koran: he is the quintessential Muslim artist, for everything else, including architecture, could be done by a non-Muslim, while God's word had to be written by a pious believer who was constantly in the state of ritual purity.

The high veneration of the Koran could lead to exaggerations, and as early as the tenth century, Niffarī, the Iraqi mystic, heard in his auditions that God is far beyond the fetters of words and letters, and that the Muslims of his time were caught in, as Père Nwyia puts it, 'the idolatry of letters', that is, they seemed to worship the letters of the Book while missing its spirit.[97] Did not the Koran become, as Clifford Geertz says with a daring formulation, 'a fetish radiating *baraka*' instead of being a living power, rather the heartbeat in the community's life?[98] But in all scriptures, the reification began as soon as the revelation was written down; as Schleiermacher says in the second of his *Reden über die Religion*, 'scripture is a mausoleum'. The free-floating revelation was cut off with the Prophet's death, and what he had brought was encased in the words on vellum or later on paper – and yet, to recur to these written and recited words was the only way to understand God's eternal will, and therefore scripturalism was deemed necessary for the preservation of Muslim identity.

When the scattered pieces of the revelation which had been noted down on every kind of material available to the believers were collected and organized by the caliph ʿOthmān (reigned 644–56), the exegesis began, for the very compilation of the text and its arrangement can be seen as a kind of first exegesis. The arrangement of the Sūras was done according to the length; they were preceded by the short *Fātiḥa* and closed, after Sūra 112 which contains the quintessential statement about God's Unity, with the two prayers for Divine succour against evil powers. This arrangement makes it difficult for non-Muslims to find their way through the Scripture, because it is not arranged according to the historical sequence in which the revelations appeared; to begin from the last, short Sūras which contain some of the earliest revelations is easier for the untutored reader than to start with the very long Sūra 2 with its numerous legal instructions. ʿOthmān's text is as close to the original wording as can be, even though seven minor reading variants are canonically accepted. But despite the great care that ʿOthmān took in arranging the sacred words, the Shia later accused him of having excluded numerous revelations in which ʿAlī's and his family's role was positively mentioned; and the Shia theologian Kulaynī in the tenth century even claimed that the *muṣḥaf Fāṭima*, the copy in the hands of the Prophet's daughter, was three times larger than the ʿOthmanic recension. On the other hand, the Kharijites, ethical maximalists that they were, found 'the most beautiful story' that is Sūra 12, which deals with Yūsuf's life, too worldly for a sacred book.

The history of Muslim exegesis has been studied by a number of important European scholars,[99] beginning with Theodor Nöldeke (d. 1930), who for the first time in the West attempted to write a history of the Koran, which was enlarged many times afterwards. Ignaz Goldziher's (d. 1921) *Richtungen der islamischen Koranauslegung* is still a classic when it comes to the different strands of exegesis as they developed down through the centuries among traditionalists, mystics, rationalists, Shia commentators and modernists. Helmut Gätje composed a useful reading book in which the different exegetical methods are offered to Western readers, and J. M. S. Baljon has devoted studies to modern exegesis, in particular in the Indo-Pakistani subcontinent, not to mention the great number of scholars who approached the Book from different vantage points, whether by trying to retrieve the Christian and Jewish influences or by mercilessly doubting the inherited traditions concerning the revelation; valuable studies about the formal aspects of the Koran stand beside statistics of certain terms as a basis for reaching a better understanding of the key concepts of Islam.

> But, as Nāṣir-i Khusraw writes:
> A difficult task is to seek the *ta'wīl* [esoteric interpretation] of the Book –
> It is a very easy thing to read down this Book![100]

That is in particular true for the 'unclear', *mutashābihāt* verses which are open to different interpretations, contrary to those with clear and fixed meaning (Sūra 3:7).

There were several ways to overcome dogmatic or other difficulties when interpreting the Koran, for the Arabic script in its earliest forms did not distinguish between a number of consonants by using diacritical marks, nor were signs for vocalization used. One has, in this respect, to remember that the early Kufic Korans probably mainly served as visual help for the many who knew the sacred text by heart and perhaps only every now and then needed a look at the consonantal skeleton; they would easily know whether a sequence of consonants that looked like *ynzl* had to be read as *yanzilu*, 'he comes down', or *yunazzilu* or *yunzilu*, 'he sends down', or *yunzalu* (passive).

Scholars distinguish, in the field of dogmatic exegesis, the *tafsīr*, explanation, and the esoteric *ta'wīl*, literally 'bringing back to the root', which was predominantly practised in Shia and Sufi circles. The first comprehensive *tafsīr* was compiled by the great historian Ṭabarī (d. 923), and among leading exegetes of the Middle Ages one has to mention az-Zamakhsharī (d. 1144), who, though an excellent philologist, was sometimes criticized for his tendency to use Muʿtazili argumentations.

Without going into details, one can say that Koranic exegesis provided the basis for almost all scholarly undertaking in the medieval world. The philologists had to explain the words and grammatical structures, all the more as the number of Neo-Muslims whose mother tongue was not Arabic increased constantly to surpass the number of Arabic speakers by far. Historians studied the historical setting of the Koranic stories and the history of the prophets. Allusions to natural sciences entailed the necessity of discovering their exact meaning (recently, a book about the plants of the Koran was published in Delhi). To find the direction of the correct *qibla*, to ponder the way of the stars which are placed for guidance into the firmament (Sūra 6:97) or the animals whose characteristics have to be understood, and, much more than all the sciences connected with 'the world', the eternal questions of free will and predestination, of the rights and duties of human beings, of the relationship between God and His creation could and should all be derived from the Koran. Thus, we would agree with Louis Massignon's statement that the Koran is indeed the key to the Muslims' *Weltanschauung*.

While the theologians, the *mutakallimūn*, tried to use rational discourse, through which they attempted to solve the major problems of the Koran's interpretation, the esoteric scholars, though not denying the importance of reason, found infinite possibilities for interpreting the Divine word by turning, so to speak, into another channel of revelation. It is probably an exaggerated statement that one of the early Sufis could find 7,000 meanings in a single verse of the Koran (for, as God is infinite, His words must also have infinite meanings), but the deep love of the Sufis for the revelation is an attested fact. The long-expected edition of Sulamī's *Tafsīr* will shed light on much of early Sufi exegesis.

They knew that it needed patience to understand the true meaning, for the Koran is, as Rūmī once said, like a bride who hides herself when one wants to unveil her in a hurry.[101] Rūmī has also pointed out how the exoteric and esoteric meaning of the Koran go together:

> The Koran is a double-sided brocade. Some enjoy the one side, some the other one. Both are true and correct, as God Most High wishes that both groups might have use from it. In the same way, a woman has a husband and a baby; each of them enjoys her in a different way. The child's pleasure comes from her bosom and her milk, that of the husband from kisses and sleeping and embrace. Some people are children on the path and drink milk – these enjoy the external meaning of the Koran. But those who are true men know of another enjoyment and have a different understanding of the inner meanings of the Koran ...[102]

In Shia circles, a tendency to interpret certain verses as pointing to the Prophet's family is natural, and verses like Sūra 48:10, which deals with the treaty of Hudaybiya (629), were given special weight, as one can see from Nāṣir-i Khusraw's autobiographical poem, in which he describes his true conversion when he understood the meaning of the contract 'when God's hand was above their hands'.[103]

Mystics often explained specific verses or shorter Sūra as pertaining to the Prophet, whether by understanding the unconnected letters at the beginning as sacred names of his (see above, p. 157) or in the interpretation of the oath formulas of Sūra 92 and 93, which were seen as references to his black hair ('By the night!) and his radiant face ('By the morning light!'). As early as in the days of the commentator Muqātil (d. 765), the 'lamp' mentioned in the Light Verse (Sūra 24:35) was seen as a symbol for the Prophet through whom the Divine Light radiates into the world.

A good example of the different explanations of a single Sūra is Sūra 91: 'By the sun when it shines, and the moon that follows, and the day when it opens, and the night when it darkens ...!' A Shia *tafsīr* sees in the sun and its radiance the symbol of Muhammad, the moon that follows is ʿAlī, the day when it opens is ʿAlī's sons Ḥasan and Ḥusayn, and the darkening night is the Omayyads who deprived ʿAlī and his family of the caliphate. The Sufi ʿAynul Quḍāt (d. 1131), however, saw in the sun the Muhammadan light that comes out of the beginningless East while the moon is the 'black light' of Satan that comes out of the endless West.[104]

True *ta'wīl*, the esoteric interpretation, was and is, by necessity, connected with the spiritual master who alone has full insight into the mysteries of faith.[105] For the Shia, it is the imams and their representatives on earth; in Ismaili Shia, it is the infallible Hazir Imam. But the entire Koran was in fact only seldom subjected to *ta'wīl*; one rather selected verses in which one tried to follow the meaning of the revelation into its ultimate depths and to take care of the different aspects, *wujūh*, of the words. In most cases – and certainly in that of the Sufis – one tried to strike a balance between exoteric and esoteric sense, while in certain Shiite groups the exoteric sense was barely considered important, and layer after layer of 'inner sense' was discovered.

The early Muslims, and among them in particular the ascetics out of whom the Sufi movement grew, lived constantly in the Koranic text, which led to what Père Nwyia has called 'the Koranization of the memory',[106] that is, they saw everything in the light of the Koran. This permanent awareness of the Koranic revelation was a reason for the fact that, to this day, even everyday language not only in Arabic but also in the other Islamic idioms is permeated by allusions to or short quotations from the Koran. It is next to impossible to grasp fully the whole range of allusions and meanings in a classical poem or piece of high prose without understanding the numerous allusions to Koranic figures, sentences or prescriptions. This is true even for fully secular themes or pieces: a single word can, as it were, conjure up a whole plethora of related terms and create a very special atmosphere, which the uninitiated reader, whether Western or secularized Muslim, often misses.

But while pious souls and mystically-minded scholars tried to delve into the depth of the revelation, attempts at a 'rational' interpretation were always being made. The Muʿtazilite al-Jubbāʾī is mentioned as one of the first to try a kind of demythologization.[107] However, rationalizing attempts at explaining the Koran became more important towards the end of the nineteenth century, doubtless under the increasing influence of modern Western scholarship. That is in particular true for Muslim India. Sir Sayyid Aḥmad Khan, the reformer of Indian Islam (d. 1898), was sure that 'the work of God cannot contradict the Word of God' (he wrote 'work of God' and 'Word of God' in English in the Urdu text of his treatise), and although this was a statement voiced as early as the eleventh century by al-Bīrūnī (see above, p. 16), Sir Sayyid went far beyond the limits of what had hitherto been done in 'interpreting' the Koran.[108] He tried to do away with all non-scientific concepts in the Book, such as djinns (which were turned into microbes) or angels, which are spiritual powers in man and not external winged beings. His traditional colleagues branded him therefore a *nēcharī*, 'naturalist'.

Some decades later, the former rector of the al-Azhar University in Cairo, Muṣṭafā al-Marāghī, wrote:

> True religion cannot conflict with truth, and when we are positively convinced of the truth of any scientific remark which seems to be

> incompatible with Islam, this is only because we do not understand correctly the Koran and the traditions. In our religion, we possess a universal teaching which declares that, when an apodictic truth contradicts a revealed text, we have to interpret the text allegorically.

The problem for modern Muslim exegetes is the constant change in the development of natural sciences, and while exegetes at the turn of the twentieth century and later tried hard to accommodate Darwinism to Koranic revelation, now some people try to find the H-bomb or the most recent discoveries of chemistry or biology in the Koran.[109] This process of 'demythologization' is very visible, for example in a translation-cum-commentary of the Koran issued by the Aḥmadiyya (at a time when this movement was still considered to be part of the Islamic community). In the exegesis of the powerful eschatological description in Sūra 81, 'And when the wild animals are gathered', the commentator saw a mention of the zoos in which animals would live peacefully together in later ages.

But one should be aware that the Koran is not a textbook of physics or biology but that its basic élan is moral, as Fazlur Rahman rightly states,[110] and it is the moral law that is immutable while the discoveries of science change at an ever-increasing speed.

Besides the dogmatic exegesis which by necessity follows the changes of times, one finds the historical–critical exegesis. That means, for the Muslim, studying the *asbāb an-nuzūl*, the reasons why and when a certain revelation was given. Thus, a remark at the beginning of the Sūra (*makkī* or *madanī*) indicates the place where the piece was revealed. The sequence of the revelations was thereby established to a large degree of correctness, and Western scholars have sometimes even arranged their translations of the Koran in this sequence (thus Bell's translation). A historical–critical exegesis of the type to which the Old and New Testaments have been subjected during the last 150 years means, for the Muslim, that the Koranic words concerning the falsification by Jews and Christians of their respective Scriptures (Sūra 2:75 et al.) is now proven by scientific method; however, in the case of the Koran, such criticism is considered impossible because the Koran is preserved as it was when its text was sent down upon the Prophet: the Divine word cannot be subjected to critical approach as it has never changed.

The discussions turn around the problem of whether the Koran rules the times as 'an anchor of timelessness', to take up G. E. von Grunebaum's formulation once more, or whether it should rather be interpreted according to the exigencies of time. Iqbāl speaks in his *Jāvīdnāma* of the *ʿālam al-qurʾān*, the 'world of the Koran' which reveals more and more possibilities every time one opens the Book; and, as reading and reciting the Koran is a dialogue with God, the true speaker of the Word, the possibilities of understanding are as infinite as is God Himself, and He and His word may appear to the reader in a new way, as though the meditating person's eyes and ears were opened for a new understanding every time. The Moroccan scholar ʿAziz Lahbabi has expressed it thus: 'Not the text in itself is the revelation but that which the believer discovers every time afresh while reading it'.

It is possible to change the exegetical methods or to change the emphasis in order to convey the message of the Koran to modern people, but a change of the God-given text is impossible. To recite the Koran, the Word Inlibrate, is, so to speak, a sacramental act because it is in the Word that God reveals Himself – or His will – to humanity.

This 'sacramental' quality of the Koran also accounts for the rule that basically no translation of the Koran is permissible or possible, not only because of the linguistic superiority, *iʿjāz*, (see above, p. 156) of the Koran, but also because the meaning may be coloured by the personal approach or predilection of the translator even if he gives only, as Muslims say carefully, 'the meaning of the glorious Koran'. Not only does a comparison of English, French and German translations leave the Western reader confused and bewildered, but even when reading translations into Islamic languages such as Persian, Turkish, Urdu, Sindhi or Pashto, one becomes aware of these problems.[111] It is the inadequacy of translations which has caused and still causes so many misunderstandings about the Koran and its message, especially when sentences are taken out of context and set absolute; for, according to the Muslims' understanding, not only the words and *āyāt* but also the entire fabric of the Koran, the interweaving of words, sound and meaning, are part and parcel of the Koran. Furthermore, for the great esoteric interpreters of the Koran such as Ibn ʿArabī, the apparent 'unconnectedness' of words and *āyāt* reveals in reality a higher order which only those understand who have eyes to see – that is, who read the Koran through *taḥqīq*, direct experience, not through *taqlīd*, dogmatic imitation.[112]

One 'external' remark remains: as a sacred text must never be sold (as little as the teacher who instructs children in the Koran should be 'officially' paid), one calls the price of a Koran in Turkey *hediye*, 'gift', and thus one finds the beautifully printed copies with the remark: 'Its gift is [so-and-so many] lira'.

The Koran's role as the centre of Muslim life is uncontested, important as the veneration of the Prophet may have become in Muslim piety. Nevertheless, besides the canonical, unerring Scripture, one also finds a considerable number of secondary literary works in the Islamic world. A special group is the so-called *ḥadīth qudsī*, Divine words revealed outside the Koran.[113] This genre became rather widespread among the Sufis, although the earliest sources are not specifically related to mystical circles. Yet, some of the most important sentences of mystical Islam appear first as *ḥadīth qudsī*, such as the famous Divine saying:

kuntu kanzan makhfiyyan, 'I was hidden treasure and wanted to be known, therefore I created the world' (*AM* no. 70). The growth of such 'private revelations', as one may call them, seems to continue up to the twelfth century, for there were many mystics who experienced what they understood as direct Divine revelation. The works of Niffarī, with their long chains of Divine addresses, are a case in point, but the inspirational process is repeated time and again in Sufi poetry and prose. Nevertheless, after 1200, one looks in vain – as it seems to me – for new examples of *ḥadīth qudsī*.

More important for the general history of Islam, however, is the *ḥadīth* in itself. In order to explain the Koran and elaborate the statements given in its text, one needed a solid set of interpretations, of examples from the Prophet, the unerring leader of his community. How did he understand this or that *āya* of the Koran? How did he act in a certain case? His sayings and those of his companions about his actions and his behaviour were collected and retold from early days onwards so as to help the community to learn how he had acted under this or that circumstance.

What did he like to eat? How did he clean himself? What did he do if a servant was disobedient? These and thousands of other problems arose before the believers because, as the Prophet was the *uswa ḥasana*, the 'beautiful model' (Sūra 33:21), Muslims wanted to emulate his example and to follow him in every respect. The further the community was in space and time from the Prophet's time, the more weight was given to the *ḥadīth*, and it is small wonder that the number of *ḥadīth* grew steadily. The proper chain of *isnād* is central for the verification of a *ḥadīth*, as the *isnād* is important in all Islamic sciences. The *isnād* in *ḥadīth* had to look like this: 'I heard A say: I heard B say: I heard from my father that C said: I heard from ʿA'isha that the Prophet used to recite this or that prayer before going to bed'. The veracity of the transmitters had to be investigated: could B indeed have met C, or was he too young to have been in contact with him, or did he perhaps never visit C's dwelling-place? The *ʿilm ar-rijāl*, the 'Science of the Men' (although there are quite a few women among the transmitters), developed into an important branch of scholarship; but in the mid-ninth century the most trustworthy, often-sifted *ḥadīth* were collected, and among the six canonical collections that of Bukhārī and, following him, Muslim occupy the place of honour.[114] To complete the recitation of the *Ṣaḥīḥ al-Bukhārī* (*khatm al-Bukhārī*) was considered nearly as important as the completion of the recitation of the Koran although, of course, not as blessed as the *khatm al-qur'ān*. In Mamluk Egypt, to give only one example, the *khatm al-Bukhārī* during the month of Ramaḍān was celebrated sumptuously in the citadel of Cairo.[115]

In the later Middle Ages, numerous selections from the classical collections of *ḥadīth* were prepared. To make them less cumbersome, the *isnād* were generally left out. Collections like Ṣaghānī's (d. 1252) *Mashāriq al-anwār* and Baghawī's (d.

around 1222) *Maṣābīḥ as-sunna* were copied all over the Muslim world and were taught not only in theological colleges but also in the homes of the pious.[116]

Yet, the collections of *ḥadīth* were sometimes met with criticism: was it necessary to waste so much ink on writing down traditions instead of establishing a living connection with the Prophet? Thus asked some medieval Sufis, and while certain currents among the Sufis – especially the Suhrawardiyya – gave *ḥadīth* studies a very eminent place in their teaching, others, like the Chishtiyya in India, were less interested in this field. At the beginning of modern Islamology in Europe, the works by Ignaz Goldziher created an awareness of the development of *ḥadīth*: what he highlighted was that the collections, instead of reflecting Muhammad's own sayings, rather reflected the different trends in the expanding Muslim world, and this fact accounts for the difference among the traditions, some of which advocated, for example, predestination while others dwelt upon free will. Political movements – which always means 'politico–religious' in early Islam – used *ḥadīth* to defend or underline their own position. Thus, harmonization of conflicting *ḥadīth* was an important duty of the scholars.[117]

Many Muslims objected sharply to this dismantling of the sacred Prophetic traditions, and yet, before Goldziher and probably unknown to him, the Indian Muslim Chirāgh ʿAlī of Hyderabad had refused *ḥadīth* almost wholesale and criticized it even more acerbically than did Goldziher. Only some *ḥadīth* connected with strictly religious topics were binding for the community, but there was no need to follow all the external rules that had become hallowed in the course of thirteen centuries. Chirāgh ʿAlī was one of the followers of Sir Sayyid, the '*nēcharī*' reformer, and this may be one of the reasons why the traditionalist *ahl al-ḥadīth* reacted so sharply against Sir Sayyid's reformist attempts. The maintenance of *ḥadīth* in toto seemed to guarantee, for the *ahl al-ḥadīth*, the integrity and validity of the Islamic tradition. Later, it was Ghulām Parwēz in Pakistan who, with an almost Barthian formulation, declared that 'the Koran is the end of religion' and rejected all of *ḥadīth*, an act that led him, to be sure, to a very idiosyncratic interpretation of the Scripture. Parwēz's compatriot Fazlur Rahman tried another way: his concept of the living *sunna* taught the Muslim not to imitate mechanically the words of the tradition but rather to keep to the spirit of the *sunna*; the knowledge of how the first generations of Muslims understood and interpreted the way in which the Prophet acted should enable modern Muslims to interpret the *sunna* according to the exigencies of their own time.

Thus the problem of the validity of *ḥadīth* continues to be one of the central problems that beset modern Muslims, and it seems that especially in minority areas *ḥadīth* is still one of the strongholds of Muslim identity. Collections of *Forty Ḥadīth* – sometimes with poetical translation – were often arranged and frequently calligraphed 'for the sake of blessing', *tabarrukan*.[118]

The first generations of Muslims were afraid of writing down sayings of the Prophet lest their text be confused with that of the Koran. In later times, a *ḥadīth* – which is called, like everything connected with the Prophet, *sharīf*, 'noble' – was introduced with the formula *qāla ṣallā Allāh ʿalayhi wa sallama*, 'He – may God bless him and give him peace – said'. This eulogy for the Prophet, which should actually be uttered after each mentioning of his name and is often printed either in full or in abbreviation over his name, distinguishes the *ḥadīth* also visibly from the words of the Koran.

Less 'orthodox' and generally accepted than these collections in Arabic is another group of secondary scriptures, which belongs to the mystical tradition. Jāmī (d. 1492) called Mawlānā Rūmī's *Mathnawī* 'the Koran in the Persian tongue', a remark perhaps inspired by the remark of Rūmī's son, Sultān Walad, that 'the poetry of God's friends is all explanation of the mysteries of the Koran'.[119] Much of Rūmī's lyrical and didactic poetry indeed betrays its inspirational character. In a much more outspoken way, Ibn ʿArabī saw his own *Futūḥāt al-Makkiyya* as an inspired book: 'I have not written one single letter of this book other than under the effect of Divine dictation ... It was not from my personal choice that I retained that order ...'. In fact, Ibn ʿArabī felt a genuine relationship between his *Futūḥāt* and the Koran, and the amazing cross-relations between the chapters of the *Futūḥāt* and Koranic Sūras have been lucidly explained by M. Chodkiewicz (1992).[120] More than five centuries after Ibn ʿArabī, the mystical poet of Delhi, Mīr Dard, made similar claims concerning his Persian prose works and his poetry, and stated repeatedly that he had nothing to do with the arrangement of the verses nor with the exact number of paragraphs in his *risālas*.[121]

In the Arab world, Būṣīrī's *Burda* in honour of the Prophet and the healing properties of his cloak was surrounded by a special sanctity and was repeated, written and enlarged innumerable times everywhere between North Africa and southern India (see above, p. 36). Perhaps even greater is the veneration of Jazūlī's *Dalāʾil al-Khayrāt*, the collection of blessings over the Prophet, to which miraculous powers were ascribed.

In Sindhi, the *Risālō* of Shah ʿAbdul Laṭīf (d. 1752) is probably the most sacred book in the entire literary tradition, and its stories and verses have influenced Sindhi literature both in its Muslim and its Hindu branches for more than two centuries.

Among the 'secondary sacred books', one should not forget that in the Ismaili tradition the *ginān*, poems in different idioms of the western subcontinent (Sindhi, Gujarati, Kuchhi, Panjabi) and written in a special secret alphabet, Khojki, are regarded as the inspired work of the Ismaili pirs of the fourteenth and fifteenth centuries and have been recited for centuries in the Ismaili community of the subcontinent. A historical analysis of these poems, which reflect the deep mystical tradition of Indian Sufism, is still viewed with mistrust by the traditionalist Ismailis even in Canada and the USA.[122]

Texts of *mawlids*, poems recited during the Prophet's birthday and interspersed with Koranic quotations, have assumed a sacred quality in many countries, and whether a Turk listens to the recitation of Süleyman Çelebi's *mevlûd-i sharif* or a singer in Kenya recites a *mawlūd* in Swahili, the feeling of being close to the heavenly abodes prevails everywhere.

Books that deal with the Prophet's qualities, such as Qāḍī ʿIyāḍ's (d. 1149) *Kitāb ash-shifā*, were regarded as a talisman to protect a house from evil, and even texts of the catechisms could inspire such feeling. A certain person, so it is told, was seen being punished in his grave by Munkar and Nakīr because he had not read the *ʿaqīda sanūsiyya*,[123] the central dogmatic formulary of the later Middle Ages. Even *shajaras*, spiritual lineages of Sufis, could serve as amulets owing to their inherent power.

Finally, one can also mention the rare phenomenon of 'heavenly letters' which, as their recipients claimed, had been sent from the Unseen to admonish the Muslim community to persevere and fight in the way of God, as happened during the Mahdist movement in East Africa and the Sudan.

The importance of the written word was, however, often de-emphasized – what is the use of studying *Kanz Qudūrī Kāfiya*, the traditional works on *ḥadīth*, religious law and Arabic grammar as taught in the *madrasas*? Should one not rather wash off all books or cast them in a river, as some Sufis indeed did? What matters is the vision of the Divine Beloved, and not only the Indo-Pakistani critics of these scholarly works but also the Turkish minstrel Yunus Emre knew that *dört kitabin manasï bir aliftedir*, 'The meaning of the four sacred books lies in one *alif*', that is, the first letter of the alphabet, which points with its numerical value of 1 to the One and Unique God. And the legends telling that many of the great Sufi poets were illiterate, as was the Prophet, are taken as a proof that they derived their knowledge not from books but from the fountainhead of all knowledge, from God. Thus, Qāḍī Qādan could sing:

> *Lōkāñ ṣarf u naḥw, muñ muṭāliʿa supriñ*
> Leave grammar and syntax to the people –
> I contemplate the Beloved![124]

NOTES

1. For the different interpretations of the Day of the Covenant, see R. Gramlich (1983a), 'Der Urvertrag in der Koranauslegung'; he shows that the formulation to which most Muslims (and certainly the poets and mystics) are used occurs in its classical form first in Junayd's *Kitāb al-mīthāq*.
2. Lamia al-Faruqi (1979), 'Tartīl'.
3. Baqlī (1966), *Sharḥ-i shaṭḥiyāt*, pp. 377–8.

4. J. C. Bürgel (1992), 'Ecstasy and order: two structural principles in the *ghazal*-poetry of Jalāl al-Dīn Rūmī'.
5. Nāṣir-i Khusraw (1929), *Dīvān*, p. 672.
6. G. van der Leeuw (1956), *Phänomenologie der Religion*, § 58, deals with secret languages; one could add that in some communities women have developed a special language. That is particularly important for women living in seclusion; a typical example is *rēkhtī*, the women's dialect of Urdu.
7. S. D. Goitein (1966), *Studies*, p. 7.
8. The same argumentation is still used by Shāh Walīullāh; see J. M. S. Baljon (1986), *Religion and Thought of Shāh Walī Allāh*, p. 109.
9. See A. Schimmel (1982a), *As through a Veil*, ch. 4. The classic study for Urdu is Maulvi 'Abdul Ḥaqq (1953), *Urdu kī nashw u namā meñ ṣūfiyā-i kirām kā kām*; see also the examples in R. Eaton (1978), *Sufis of Bijapur, 1300–1700.*
10. C. H. Becker (1932), *Islamstudien*, vol. 2, p. 199.
11. *Yeni Yunus Emre ve doğuşları* (1951), and *Doğuşlar* 2 (1965). Turgut Akkaş's *Özkaynak* was a short-lived journal in the 1950s in which the author – incidentally a banker – published his inspired mystical verses. Slightly earlier, a high-ranking Turkish official had published his inspirational poems, which were commented upon by Ömer Fevzi Mardin (1951), *Varidat-i Süleyman şerhi.* The genre of *varidāt* was common in Indo-Muslim literature, thus in Mīr Dard's poetry; see A. Schimmel (1976a), *Pain and Grace*, part 1.
12. Nāṣir-i Khusraw (1929), *Dīvān*, p. 245.
13. G. van der Leeuw (1956), *Phänomenologie der Religion*, § 85, referring in this context to Paul Tillich's remark that 'Only what essentially is concealed, and accessible by no mode of knowledge whatsoever, is imparted by revelation'.
14. K. Cragg (1984), '*Tadabbur al-Qur'ān*: reading and meaning', p. 189f.
15. I. Goldziher (1928), 'Verheimlichung des Namens'.
16. R. Gramlich (1976), *Die schiitischen Derwischorden*, vol. 2, p. 30f.
17. The literature about the Divine Names is very large: see Abū Ḥāmid al-Ghazzālī (1971), *Al-maqṣad al-asnā fī sharḥ ma'ānī asmā Allāh al-ḥusnā* (transl. in R. McCarthy (1980), *Freedom and Fulfillment*, appendix III); Ibn 'Aṭā' Allāh (1961), *Miftāh al-falāḥ wa miṣbāḥ al-arwāḥ*; idem (1981), *Traité sur le nom 'Allāh'* (Introduction ... par M. Gloton); al-Qushayrī (1969), *Sharḥ asmā' Allāh al-ḥusnā*; G. C. Anawati (1965), 'Un traité des Noms divins: Fakhr al-Dīn al-Rāzī's *Lawāmi' al-baiyināt fī'l asmā' wa'l-ṣifāt.* See also Daniel Gimaret (1988), *Les Noms Divins en Islam, Exégèse lexicographique et théologique.* The Most Beautiful Names could be elaborated in poetry, as C. H. Becker (1932) has shown for the Arab world (*Islamstudien*, vol. 2, p. 106f.). A superbly and beautifully produced book, *The Attributes of Divine Perfection*, by the Egyptian calligrapher Ahmad Moustafa (1989), is in particular worthy of mention. Many of the modern leaders of Sufi fraternities have published their own books or booklets on the Divine Names and their use and power.
18. For the role of the Divine Names in creation, see H. S. Nyberg (1919), *Kleinere Schriften des Ibn al-'Arabī*, p. 92ff.; W. C. Chittick (1989), *The Sufi Path of Knowledge*; H. Corbin (1958), *L'imagination créatrice dans le Soufisme d'Ibn Arabi.* See also the important ch. 22 in F. Meier (1990a), *Bahā-i Walad.*
19. A. Schimmel (1989), *Islamic Names.* Jafar Sharif (1921), *Islam in India*, p. 255, deals with the numerical values and the astrological connections of proper names.
20. *Yunus Emre Divanı* (1943), p. 562, no. CCXXXIII.
21. Iqbāl (1924), '*Jawāb-i shikwah*', in *Bāng-i Darā*, p. 231.
22. A. Fischer (1944), 'Vergöttlichung und Tabuisierung der Namen Muhammads'. See also R. Y. Edier and M. J. L. Young (1976), 'A list of appellations of the Prophet Muhammad'.
23. G. E. von Grunebaum and Roger Caillois (eds) (1966), *The Dream and Human*

Society, contains a number of highly interesting contributions by Islamicists such as F. Meier, H. Corbin and Fazlur Rahman. See also H. Gätje (1959), 'Philosophische Traumlehren im Islam'. Devin DeWeese (1992), 'Sayyid ʿAlī Hamadhānī and Kubrawī hagiographical tradition', gives a number of accounts about the dreams of the Sufi master Hamadhānī (d. 1385), especially on pp. 143–7. Ibn Sīrīn's book on the interpretation of dreams was translated into German by Helmut Klopfer (1989), *Das arabische Traumbuch des Ibn Sīrīn*.

24. I. Goldziher (1921), 'The appearance of the Prophet in dreams'. Aṣ-Ṣafadī (1979), *Al-Wāfī bi'l-wafayāt*, part 12, mentions under no. 47 that a Christian saw the Prophet in his dream, 'and he became a Muslim and learned the Koran by heart' to become a leading Islamic scholar.
25. Thus Shādhili's dream as told by Jāmī (1957), *Nafaḥāt al-uns*, p. 373.
26. C. Snouck Hurgronje (1923), 'De laatste vermaning van Mohammad aan zijne gemeende', about an appearance in Rabīʿ al-awwal 1297/1880.
27. A few examples from different geographical areas are: John Renard (1993), *Islam and the Heroic Image. Themes in Literature and the Visual Arts*; L. Brakel (1977), *The story of Muhammad Hanafiyya. A medieval Muslim Romance*, transl. from the Malay; D. Shulman (1982), 'Muslim popular literature in Tamil: The *tamimcari malai*'; and E. S. Krauss (1913), 'Vom Derwisch-Recken Gazi-Seidi. Ein Guslarenlied bosnischer Muslime aufgezeichnet, verdeutscht und erläutert'.
28. Margaret A. Mills (1991), *Rhetoric and Politics in Afghan Traditional Story-telling*.
29. The oldest legends are connected with the Prophet and his companions; see R. Paret (1930), *Die legendäre Maghazi-Literatur*; Jan Knappert (1985), *Islamic legends. Histories of the heroes, saints, and prophets of Islam*. The genre of *Heiligenlieder*, songs in honour of Muslim saints, is widespread. For some Arabic examples, see Enno Littmann (1951), *Islamisch–arabische Heiligenlieder*, and idem (1950), *Ahmed il-Badawi: Ein Lied auf den ägyptischen Nationalheiligen*.
30. Words of wisdom are often attributed to Luqmān (based on Sūra 31); in the Persianate tradition, the wise vizier Buzurjmihr appears as a model of wisdom in many stories and poems.
31. S. H. Nasr (1992), 'Oral transmission and the Book in Islamic education: the spoken and the written word'.
32. For the importance of the *malfūẓāt*, 'utterances' of Indian Sufi masters for the knowledge of medieval Muslim life, see K. A. Niẓāmī (1961), '*Malfūẓāt kā tārīkhī ahammiyat*'.
33. Typical examples are the cryptic letters by the Sufi master Junayd, as well as the few fragments preserved from al-Ḥallāj's letters. Aḥmad Sirhindi (d. 1624) tried to revive normative Islam in India through hundreds of letters which he sent to the grandees of the Mughal empire as well as to members of his own family. See Ahmad Sirhindi (1968), *Selected Letters*, ed. … by Dr Fazlur Rahman. Several collections of letters have been made available in translation, such as Sharafuddin Maneri (1980), *The Hundred Letters*, transl. Paul Jackson SJ; Ibn ʿAbbād ar-Rondī (1986), *Letters on the Sufi Path*, transl. by J. Renard; and ad-Darqāwī (1961), *Letters of a Sufi Master*, transl. by Titus Burckhardt. An interesting collection of modern letters is Mohammad Fadhel Jamali (1965), *Letters on Islam, written by a father in prison to his son*.
34. Rūzbihān Baqlī (1966), *Sharḥ-i shaṭḥiyāt*, is the classic work in this field. See also Carl W. Ernst (1985), *Words of Ecstasy in Sufism*.
35. A. Schimmel (1982a), *As through a Veil*, ch. 4. See also idem (1971), 'Mir Dard's Gedanken über das Verhältnis von Mystik und Wort'.
36. J. Pedersen (1947), 'The Islamic preacher: *wāʿiẓ, mudhakkir, qāṣṣ*'; Angelika Hartmann (1987), 'Islamisches Predigtwesen im Mittelalter: Ibn al-Ǧauzī und sein "Buch der Schlußreden" 1186 AD'; Patrick D. Gaffney (1988), 'Magic,

miracle and the politics of narration in the contemporary Islamic sermon'.

37. Ibn al-Jawzī (1971), *Kitāb al-quṣṣāṣ wa'l-mudhakkirīn*, ed. and transl. by Merlin L. Swartz; the preacher about whom he remarks is the famous mystic Aḥmad Ghazzālī (d. 1126).
38. A. Mez (1922), *Die Renaissance des Islam*, p. 319.
39. Iqbāl makes an interesting remark (1961) in the *Stray Reflections*, no. 37: 'To explain the deepest truths of life in the form of homely parables requires extraordinary genius. Shakespeare, Maulana Rum (Jalaluddin) and Jesus are probably the only illustrations of this rare type of genius.'
40. C. E. Padwick (1960), *Muslim Devotions*, p. 131; A. Schimmel (1983), 'The Sufis and the *shahāda*'.
41. A. J. Wensinck (1932), *The Muslim Creed*, deals with the development of the credal formulas.
42. Muhammad Yusuf Kokan (1974), *Arabic and Persian in Carnatic (1700–1950)*, pp. 25, 360ff. The founder of the madrasa was the Nawwab of Arcot, Ghulam Ghaus Khan Bahadur. The Muslim theologians, however, claimed that one 'could not support a cause advocating earning a livelihood rather than supporting religion'.
43. The basic work on prayer is still Friedrich Heiler (1923), *Das Gebet*. For the spiritual aspects of Muslim prayer, see Constance E. Padwick (1960), *Muslim Devotions*. See also E. E. Calverley (1925), *Worship in Islam*. The short (unattributed) article 'The significance of Moslem prayer' in *MW* 14 gives a good insight into the feelings of Muslims. See also S. D. Goitein, 'Prayer in Islam', in *Studies*, pp. 79–89; A. Schimmel (1958), 'The idea of prayer in the thought of Iqbāl'; and idem (1967), 'Maulānā Rūmī's story on prayer'.
44. F. Meier (1986), 'Die Segenssprechung über Mohammed im Bittgebet und in der Bitte'; J. Robson (1936), 'Blessings on the Prophet'; Mohammed Ilyas Burney (1983), *Mishkaat us-salawaat: A Bouquet of Blessings on Muhammad the Prophet.*
45. T. Canaan (1935), 'The curse in Palestinian folklore'.
46. J. Pedersen (1914), *Der Eid bei den Semiten in seinem Verhältnis zu verwandten Erscheinungen, sowie die Stellung des Eides im Islam.* One of the most famous oath formulas of the Prophet was: 'By Him in Whose hand Muhammad's soul is!'
47. A Sufi might even tell his disciples: 'Swear an oath by me', as did Sayyid 'Ali Hamadhānī. See Devin DeWeese (1992), p. 248.
48. A. Schimmel (1959), 'Das Gelübde im türkischen Volksglauben' (based on Hikmet Tanyu's dissertation, *Ankara ve çevresindeki adak yerleri*).
49. Kriss and Kriss-Heinrich (1962), *Volksglaube in Islam*, vol. 2, ch. 3.
50. G. van der Leeuw (1957), *Vom Heiligen in der Kunst*, p. 23.
51. Compare the story told in Hujwīrī (1911), *Kashf al-maḥjūb*, pp. 233–4.
52. 'The prayer in the community is twenty-seven degrees more valuable than the prayer of a solitary person', says a *ḥadīth*. Twenty-seven, the third power of the sacred Three, has a special importance.
53. Iqbāl (1930), *The Reconstruction of Religious Thought in Islam*, ch. 5, especially p. 93.
54. Suhrawardī (1978), *'Awārif* (transl. R. Gramlich), p. 266.
55. C. E. Padwick (1960), *Muslim Devotions*, p. 89.
56. For special uses of the *Fātiḥa*, see W. A. Cuperus (1973), *Al-Fātiḥa dans la pratique religieuse du Maroc.*
57. F. Meier (1990a), *Bahā-i Walad*, p. 250.
58. H. Ritter (1952), 'Muslim mystics' strife with God'.
59. Some collections of Muslim prayers are available in translation, among them Abdul Hamid Farid (1959), *Prayers of Muhammad*; Zayn al-'Abidin 'Ali ibn al-Ḥusayn (1988), *Al-ṣaḥīfat al-kāmilat as-saǧǧādiyya. The Psalms of Islam*, transl. … by William C. Chittick; Kenneth Cragg (1972), *Alive to God*; idem (1955), 'Pilgrimage

prayers'; idem (1957), 'Ramadan prayers'; A. Schimmel (1978b), *Denn Dein ist das Reich*, enlarged edition as *Dein Wille geschehe* (1992); Al-Ghazali (1992), *Invocations and Supplications: Kitāb al-adhkār wa'l-da' wāt* ..., transl. ... by Kojiro Nakamura; Al-Gazzali (1990), *Temps et prières. Prières et invocations. Extraits de l'Iḥyā' 'ulūm al-Dīn*, trad. ... par P. Cuperly; 'Abdullāh Anṣārī (1978), *Munājāt: Intimate Conversations*, transl. by Wheeler M. Thackston Jr.

60. A. Schimmel (1976b), 'Dard and the problem of prayer'.
61. Kriss and Kriss-Heinrich (1962), *Volksglaube im Islam*, vol. 2, p. 92.
62. Christian W. Troll (1978), *Sir Sayyid Ahmad Khan, a re-interpretation of Islamic theology*. According to Sir Sayyid, God is pleased with personal prayer as with other forms of service, but He does not necessarily grant the servant's petition. Sir Sayyid is here close to the Mu'tazilite viewpoint that God tells His servants to invoke Him because He demands the attitude of adoration from them.
63. Iqbāl (1937), *Żarb-i Kalīm*, p. 267.
64. For the history of prayer beads, see W. Kirfel (1949), *Der Rosenkranz*; Helga Venzlaff (1975), *Der islamische Rosenkranz*. M. S. Belguedj (1969), 'Le chapelet Islamique et ses aspects nord-africains', mentions, as do Kriss and Kriss-Heinrich (1960, 1962), that the *tasbīḥ* is, in a certain way, sanctified by the constant recitation of Divine Names or religious formulas and is thus considered to possess healing power and special *baraka*.
65. For the *dhikr*, see L. Gardet (1972–3), 'La mention du Nom divin, *dhikr*, dans la mystique musulmane'. Most works on Sufism contain descriptions of various kinds of *dhikr*; see A. Schimmel (1975a), *Mystical Dimensions of Islam*, pp. 167–78 for references.
66. The description of the heart's journey through the letters of *Allāh* is given in 'Andalīb (1891), *Nāla-i 'Andalīb*, vol. 1, p. 270.
67. F. Meier (1963), 'Qušairīs *Tartīb as-sulūk*', is an impressive description of how the *dhikr* permeates the whole being. A contemporary description of the experience of *dhikr* in the forty days' seclusion is by Michaela Özelsel (1993), *Vierzig Tage. Erfahrungen aus einer Sufi-Klausur*.
68. Suhrawardī (1978), *'Awārif* (transl. R. Gramlich), p. 125; Shah 'Abdul Laṭīf (1958), *Risālō*, 'Sur Ràmakali' V, verse 1, 2.
69. F. D. A. Tholuck (1821), *Ssufismus sive theosophia persarum pantheistica*, p. 12.
70. For the problem, see G. Mensching (1926), *Das heilige Schweigen*.
71. An excellent definition of the difference between the 'prophetic' and the 'mystic' approaches to God is in Iqbāl (1930), *The Reconstruction of Religious Thought in Islam*, beginning of ch. 5. In the *Payām-i mashriq* (1923), p. 186, Iqbāl sings in a *ghazal* written in imitation of Rūmī's poem D no. 441:

    They said: 'Close your lips and do not tell our mysteries!'
    I said: 'No! To shout *Allāhu Akbar* – that is my wish!'

72. For the importance of script and writing, see A. Bertholet (1949), *Die Macht der Schrift in Glauben und Aberglauben*; F. Dornseiff (1922), *Das Alphabet in Mystik und Magie*; Jean Canteins (1981), *La voie des Lettres*. For the Koran, see Thomas O'Shaughnessy (1948), 'The Koranic concept of the Word of God'; Ary A. Roest Crollius (1974), *The Word in the Experience of Revelation in the Qur'an and Hindu Scriptures*.
73. G. Vajda (1961), 'Les lettres et les sons de la langue arabe d'après Abū Ḥātim Rāzī'.
74. Ghālib (1969b), *Urdu Dīwān*, no. 1. See also A. Schimmel (1978a), *A Dance of Sparks*, ch. 4, and, in general, Schimmel (1984a), *Calligraphy and Islamic Culture*.
75. Kisā'ī (1977), *The Tales of the Prophets*, p. 60ff.
76. A. Jeffery (1924), 'The mystic letters of the Koran'. According to E. W. Lane

(1978 ed.), *Manners and Customs*, p. 256f., the Koranic verses most frequently used for healing and helping purposes are Sūra 8:14; 10:80; 16:70; 17:82; 26:79–81; and 41:45. For Shia uses of the Koran (many of which are the same as among Sunnites), see B. A. Donaldson (1937), 'The Koran as magic'.

77. R. McCarthy (1980), *Freedom and Fulfillment*, p. 110.
78. R. Sellheim (1968), 'Die Madonna mit der *šahāda*'.
79. J. Horovitz (1907), 'A list of published Mohammedan inscriptions of India', vol. 2, p. 35.
80. For a discussion, see G. Schoeler (1992), 'Schreiben und Veröffentlichen. Zur Verwendung und Funktion der Schrift in den ersten islamischen Jahrhunderten'.
81. M. Lings (1976), *Quranic Calligraphy and Illumination.* See also A. Schimmel (1984a), *Calligraphy and Islamic Culture*, passim.
82. 'Aṭṭār (1905), *Tadhkirat al-awliyā*, vol. 1, p. 105.
83. This notice is apparently based on the recent *Shariat Act* in Pakistan, where § 295B reads:

    > Whoever wilfully defiles, damages or desecrates a copy of the Holy Qur'an or of an extract therefrom or uses it in any derogatory manner or for any unlawful purpose shall be punishable with imprisonment for life.

84. G. E. von Grunebaum (1969), *Studien*, p. 32. For the 'world of the Koran', see Iqbāl (1932), *Jāvīdnāma*, line 5700ff.
85. Samuel M. Zwemer (1921), 'The illiterate Prophet'; I. Goldfeld (1980), 'The illiterate Prophet (*nabī ummī*). An inquiry into the development of a dogma in Islamic tradition', emphasizes the rather slow development of the interpretation of *ummī* in the 'mystical' sense. As in the case of the 'mystical' interpretation of Sūra 7:172 concerning the 'Primordial Covenant', the crystallization of such deeper 'mystical' interpretations seems to be achieved around the beginning of the tenth century AD/fourth century AH – similar to the dogmatization of Christological formulas at the start of the fourth century AD in Christianity.
86. William A. Graham (1987), *Beyond the Written Word. Oral Aspects of Scripture in the History of Religion*, shows very clearly the twofold character of revelation and the important role of oral transmission in the case of the Koran.
87. Suhrawardī (1978), *'Awārif* (transl. R. Gramlich), p. 41.
88. C. Snouck Hurgronje (1923), *Verspreide Geschriften*, vol. 2, p. 438 (year of reference: 1899); 'A *fatwa* on broadcasting the Koran: 5.10.1933', in *MW* 24 (1934), p. 180. For the role of proper recitation, see Lamia al-Faruqi (1979), 'Tartīl'; also Labib as-Said (1975), *The Recited Koran.* Transl. and adapted by Bernhard Weiss, M. A. Rauf, and Morroe Berger.
89. Fazlur Rahman (1966), ch. 2.
90. Sanā'ī (1962), *Dīvān*, p. 309.
91. *Sūra Luqmān* is good for pregnant women; *Sūrat al-Fatḥ* (48) and *Sūra Muzzammil* (73) avert illness and calamities.
92. W. C. Smith (1960), 'Some similarities and differences between Christianity and Islam', p. 57.
93. Bernhard Weiss (1984), 'Language and law. The linguistic premises of Islamic legal thought'.
94. *The Muslim Digest*, Durban, South Africa, May–June 1991, p. 29, repr. from *The Majlis*, Port Elizabeth, South Africa, no. 8.
95. A. Mez (1922), *Die Renaissance des Islam*, p. 328.
96. For this imagery, see A. Schimmel (1992b), *A Two-colored Brocade*, pp. 309, 373–4, note 11.

97. For the problem, see Schimmel (1975a), *Mystical Dimensions of Islam*, Appendix 1. The term is taken from P. Nwyia's penetrating analysis (1970) of Niffarī's experiences which he wrote down in his *Mawāqif wa Mukhāṭabāt* (1935), in *Exégèse coranique*, 'Des images aux symboles d'expérience', part II, 'Niffarī', especially p. 370. Nwyia shows the repercussions of the problem of the doctrine that the Koran is God's uncreated word in the debate between the Muʿtazila and the traditionalists.
98. C. Geertz (1971), *Islam Observed*, p. 73.
99. For the history of the Koran and Koranic exegesis, see the Bibliography under Ayoub, Baljon, Gätje, Goldziher, Nagel, Nöldeke, Rippin and Watt. The best survey is Angelika Neuwirth (1987), 'Koran', in Gätje (ed.), *Grundriss der arabischen Philologie*. See also T. Nagel (1983), 'Vom Qur'an zur Schrift. Bells Hypothese aus religionsgeschichtlicher Sicht'. For an approach from the vantage point of literary criticism, see A. Neuwirth (1981), *Studien zur Komposition der mekkanischen Suren*; and idem (1991), 'Der Horizont der Offenbarung. Zur Relevanz der einleitenden Schwurserien für die Suren der frühmekkanischen Zeit'.
100. Nāṣir-i Khusraw (1929), *Dīvān*, p. 446.
101. *Fīhi mā fīhi*, ch. 35.
102. *Ibid.*, ch. 43.
103. Nāṣir-i Khusraw (1929), *Dīvān*, in (1993) tr. A. Schimmel, *Make a Shield from Wisdom*, pp. 44, 46.
104. Sachiko Murata (1992b), *The Tao of Islam*, p. 262.
105. For the problem of mystical interpretation, see P. Nwyia (1970), *Exégèse coranique*; G. Böwering (1979), *The Mystical Vision of Existence in Classical Islam*; A. Habil (1987), 'Traditional esoteric commentaries'. For a special topic, see P. Bachmann (1988), 'Ein *tafsīr* in Versen. Zu einer Gruppe von Gedichten im *Dīwān* Ibn al-ʿArabīs'.
106. P. Nwyia (1972), *Ibn ʿAṭā' Allāh et la naissance de la confrérie šāḏilite*, p. 46.
107. C. Huart (1904), 'Le rationalisme musulman au IVe siècle'. A. Mez (1922), *Die Renaissance des Islam*, p. 188ff. gives a survey of the different currents among the interpreters of the Koran and the scholars during the ninth and tenth centuries, mainly in Baghdad.
108. Aziz Ahmad and G. E. von Grunebaum (eds) (1970), *Muslim Self-Statement*, p. 34.
109. Ibid., p. 171, where the position of Ghulām Aḥmad Parvēz and his *Koranic Lexique Technique* are discussed.
110. Fazlur Rahman (1966), *Islam*, p. 32.
111. For some examples of interpretation in a rather little-known language, see A. Schimmel (1963b), 'Translations and commentaries of the Qur'ān in the Sindhi language'.
112. M. Chodkiewicz (1992), 'The *Futūḥāt Makkiyya* and its commentators: some unresolved enigmas', p. 225.
113. William A. Graham (1977), *Divine Word and Prophetic Word in Early Islam.*
114. Abū ʿAbdullāh Muḥammad al-Bukhārī (1863–1902), *Kitāb jāmiʿ aṣ-ṣaḥīḥ*, 4 vols, ed. L. Krehl and W. Juynboll, transl. M. M. Khan (1978–80), *Sahih al-Bukhari*, 6 vols. Another useful work is Tabrīzī (1964–6), *Mishkāt al-maṣābīḥ*, 4 vols, transl. James Robson.
115. I. Goldziher (1915a), 'Chatm al-Buchārī'. Ibn Iyās (1933), *Badā'iʿ az-zuhūr*, mentions this custom in vol. 4 at almost every Ramaḍān; robes of honour were distributed to the readers who had completed this task.
116. A. J. Wensinck (1936–71), *Concordances et indices de la tradition musulmane*, enables the scholar to orient himself in the vast 'ocean' of *ḥadīth.*

117. I. Goldziher (1888–90), *Muhammedanische Studien*, was the ground-breaking Western study in *ḥadīth* criticism. For Chirāgh Ali, see Aziz Ahmad and G. E. von Grunebaum (1970), *Muslim Self-Statement*, pp. 49–59. A survey of modern approaches can be found in G. A. H. Juynboll (1969), *The Authenticity of Tradition Literature. Discussions in Modern Egypt.*
118. Such collections can consist of forty *ḥadīth* about the usefulness of writing, about piety or about the pilgrimage, or forty *ḥadīth* transmitted by forty men by the name of Muḥammad, or by forty people from the same town, etc. Learning such a collection by heart was considered to entail many blessings. See A. Karahan (1954), *Türk Islam edebiyatīnda Kīrk Hadis.*
119. Sultān Walad (1936), *Valadnāma*, p. 53ff. Rūmī's biographer, Sipahsālār, also quotes this statement.
120. M. Chodkiewicz (1992), 'The *Futūḥāt Makkiyya* and its commentators: some unresolved enigmas'.
121. For Mīr Dard's claims in this field, see A. Schimmel (1976a), *Pain and Grace*, p. 117ff.
122. Ali S. Asani (1991), *The Bhuj Niranjan. An Ismaili Mystical Poem*; idem (1992), *Ismaili Manuscripts in the Collection of Harvard College Library.*
123. M. Horten (1917a), *Die religiöse Gedankenwelt der gebildeten Muslime im heutigen Islam*, p. xxiii.
124. *Qāḍī Qādan jō kalām* (1978), no. 1.

V

Individual and Society

(My mercy embraces all things, and I will show it) to those who are God-fearing and pay the alms-tax and those who believe in Our signs.

Sūra 7:156

THE HUMAN BEING

'Man's situation is like this: an angel's wing was brought and tied to a donkey's tail so that the donkey perchance might also become an angel thanks to the radiance of the angel's company.'

Thus writes Mawlānā Rūmī in *Fīhi mā fīhi* to describe the twofold nature of the human being, a duality not of body and soul but of possibilities, a situation meditated upon down through the centuries whenever Muslims discuss the human condition. On the one hand, the Koran speaks in various places of the high and noble rank of man: did not God breathe into Adam from His own breath to make him alive (Sūra 15:29)? Did He not teach him the names, thus enabling him to rule over the creatures and – as the mystics would continue – to understand the working of the Divine Names as well (Sūra 2:31)? Man was appointed *khalīfa*, 'representative' either of the angels or, according to another interpretation, of God (Sūra 2:30), despite the critical remarks of the angels who foresaw his disobedience. But God spoke: *karramnā*, 'We have honoured the children of Adam' (Sūra 17:70). And humans are the only creatures who accepted the *amāna*, the good which God wanted to entrust to the world but which mountains and heavens refused to carry (Sūra 33:72); man, however, accepted it despite his weaknesses. Is it not astounding, asks Nāṣir-i Khusraw, that the weak human being was chosen over the animals? Only to him were warners and prophets sent, while camels and lions, so much stronger than he, were not blessed with such revelations but are also not held responsible for their actions.[1]

The frequent use in the Koran of the term *sakhkhara*, 'to submit, place under someone's order', reminds the reader of man's position as the God invested ruler over the created beings. Man's high position was then emphasized by the *ḥadīth* according to which God created Adam *ʿalā ṣūratihi* (AM no. 346), 'according to His form' (although the 'His' has also been read as 'his', i.e. Adam's intended form). The Sufis became increasingly fond of the *ḥadīth man ʿarafa nafsahu faqad ʿarafa rabbahu* (AM no. 529), a saying that could be and frequently was interpreted as the possibility of finding the deepest mystery of God in oneself. It could also be understood in a more general sense: the North African Sufi al-Murṣī (d. 1287) says 'he who knows his own lowliness and inability recognizes God's omnipotence and kindness', and Rūmī elaborates the same idea in the moving story of Ayāz: the Turkish officer Ayāz, beloved of the mighty sultan Maḥmūd of Ghazna (d. 1030), entered every morning a secret closet where he kept his worn-out frock and torn shoes. That was all he owned before Maḥmūd showered his favours upon him, and by recognizing his own unworthiness and poverty he gratefully understood the master's bounty (*M* V 2,113ff.).

The human being could, however, also become the *asfal as-sāfilīn*, 'the lowest of the low' (Sūra 95:5), and while one is constantly reminded of one's duty to strive for the education of one's soul, the danger is always present that the animal traits may become overwhelming in one's lower self: greed, ire, envy, voracity, tendency to bloodshed and many more negative trends make the human being forget his heavenly origin, his connection with the world of spirit. For this reason, the Ikhwān aṣ-ṣafā as well as some Sufi writers have thought that these animal qualities will become manifest on Doomsday in the shapes of dogs, donkeys and the like, for the *ḥadīth* says that everyone will be resurrected according to the state in which he or she dies (*AM* no. 40; see above, p. 28).

To explain the mystery of man is impossible: man is, as Rūmī says with a comparison that prefigures John Donne's expression, 'a mighty volume': the external 'words' fit with this world, the inner meaning with the spiritual world. For man, created from dust and returning to dust (Sūra 30:20, 37:53), gains his true value only through the Divine light that shines through the dust, the Divine breath that moves him.

As Ayāz was a slave of Maḥmūd, the human being is first and foremost a slave of God, and the feeling that one is nothing but a slave, *'abd*, makes the poet or the artist, the petitioner as well as the prince, sign his or her letters and works with terms like *al-faqīr*, 'the poor', *al-ḥaqīr*, 'the lowly' and similar terms, while in high speech one used to refer to oneself, in Persian or Ottoman Turkish, as *banda*, 'the servant'.

The use of *'abd* for the human being goes back to numerous verses of the Koran, in which human beings and in particular prophets are called *'abd*, as well as to the repeated statements that everything was created to serve God. Furthermore, the Primordial Covenant (Sūra 7:172), when God addressed future humanity with the words: *alastu bi-rabbikum*, 'Am I not your Lord?', to which they answered: 'Yes, we testify to that', implies that they, acknowledging God as the eternal Lord, accepted, logically, their role as God's servants until they are asked on the Day of Judgment whether they had remained aware of God's being the one and only Lord whom they had to obey.

But the Koran also offers the basis for interpreting the word *'abduhu*, 'His [i.e. God's] slave', as the highest possible rank that man can reach: was not the Prophet called *'abduhu*, 'His slave', in the two Koranic sentences that speak of his highest experiences, namely in Sūra 17:1, which alludes to his nightly journey ('praised be God who travelled at night with His slave ...'), and in Sūra 53:10, which contains the vision in which God 'revealed to His slave what He revealed'? That means for the Muslim that 'God's servant' is the highest rank to which one can aspire; and, based on centuries of praise bestowed on Muhammad as *ʿabduhu*, Iqbāl has summed up these feelings once more in his great hymn in honour of the Prophet in his *Jāvīdnāma*.

There is only one situation when the human being is freed from bondage: that is in the case of the mentally deranged, who are not 'burdened' by the obligations of law; they are, as the poets liked to say, 'God's freed people'. Therefore, one finds that ʿAṭṭār, in his Persian epics, puts all rebellious words against the Creator, the outcry of the debased and the unhappy, into the mouths of madmen: they will not be punished for their unbridled behaviour.[2]

But while the believer always feels himself or herself to be God's servant, mystical Islam, especially in later centuries, has developed the idea of *al-insān al-kāmil*, the Perfect Man, who is manifested in the Prophet but whose rank is the goal of the true mystical seeker. Great is the number of Sufi leaders who claimed to be, or whose disciples saw them as, the Perfect Man, and the contrast between the feeling of humility as *ʿabd* and the claim to have reached the stage of the Perfect Man amazes the reader of later mystical texts time and again. The extreme contrast between these two possible interpretations of humanity has led a number of scholars to claim that Islam has no 'humanism' in the European sense of the word: man is not the normative being, the one whose rights are central in interhuman relations and who works freely in the spirit of realization of the 'human values', but appears either as the lowly slave or as the 'inflated' Perfect Man.[3]

The Koran has spoken of man's creation in several instances, most importantly in the first revelation Sūra 96. Man was created from dust and then an *ʿalaq*, a blood clot, and the miracle of the begetting and growth of a child is mentioned several times. The first human, Adam, was created from clay, and later mythological stories have elaborated this creation in poetical images. It is said, for example, that Adam was kneaded for forty days by God's two hands before the Creator breathed His breath into the clay vessel (*AM* no. 632). Iblīs refused to fall down before him because he did not perceive the Divine breath in Adam but looked only to the dust-form and, being created from fire, felt superior to him.

The human being is made up, as can be understood from the story of creation, of body and soul, and the different parts of the spiritual side of humans are mentioned in varying forms (see below, p. 183). The *rūḥ*, 'spirit', and *nafs*, 'soul', are central as the truly spiritual aspects that keep humans in touch with the higher realities, but the body is indispensable for this life. It is made up of four elements and is perishable as everything composite; it returns to dust, but will be reassembled on Doomsday. And although many pious people have expressed their aversion to the body, this old donkey or camel, to neglect the body or kill it by exaggerated mortification is nevertheless not acceptable, for the body is needed for the performance of ritual duties and should be kept intact to serve for positive purposes, even though the mystics would rather call it a town in which the soul feels like a stranger. The human body in its totality also carries power, *baraka*.

One of the most important centres of power is the hair. It has therefore to be covered. Not only women should veil their hair, but also men should not enter the Divine presence with bare head (cf. above, p. 94). To tear one's hair is a sign of utter despair, as women do in mourning rites: the *marthiyas* which sing of the tragedy of Kerbela often describe the despair of the women in Ḥusayn's camp who came to the fore, their hair dishevelled.

The *nāṣiya*, the 'forelock', which is mentioned twice in the Koran (Sūra 96:15, cf. Sūra 11:56), belongs to the same cluster of objects: to grasp someone (or an animal) by the forelock means to grasp his (or its) most power-laden part, that is, to overcome him completely.

The offering of the new-born child's first hair during the *ʿaqīqa* should be remembered in this context as well as the hair-offering of certain dervishes and the taboos connected with hair during the pilgrimage.

Sanctity is also contained in the beard: 'The beard is God's light', as a saying goes. Thus Indian Muslims would sometimes dip the beard of an old, venerable man in water, which was then given to ailing people to drink and was especially administered to women in labour.[4]

When the hair as such is considered to be so filled with *baraka*, how much more the Prophet's hair and beard![5] Muslim children in Sind had formerly to learn the exact number of the Prophet's hairs, while in the Middle East some authors 'knew' that 33,333 hairs of the Prophet were brought to the Divine Throne.[6] Taking into consideration the importance of hair and beard, one can also understand, at least to a certain extent, the role of Salmān al-Fārisī in Muslim piety: he, the barber, was the one who could touch the Prophet's hair and beard, and from earliest times one reads that a few hairs of the Prophet, sewn into a turban, served as a protecting amulet. Hairs of the Prophet are preserved in varous mosques: the Mamluk sultan Baybars (reigned 1266–77) gave a hair of the Prophet for the *miḥrāb* of the Khānqāh Siryāqūṣ, the Sufi hospice near Cairo,[7] and riots broke out in Srinagar, Kashmir, some years ago when *Ḥaz ratbāl*, 'Its Excellency the Hair', was stolen; this hair was honoured by building a fine mosque in the city around it. Usually, such a hair is preserved in a fine glass vessel which is wrapped in dozens of fragrant silk covers, as in the Alaettin Mosque in Konya, where it was hidden in a wall. But generally, non-Muslims (and in Bijapur's Athar Mahal also women) are not allowed into a room that contains such a treasure. Some Muslims believe that these hairs can grow and multiply: as the Prophet, they contend, is alive, so also is his hair. And as the romantic lover in the West carried his beloved's curl as a kind of amulet, hairs from the beard of a venerated Muslim saint can serve the same purpose.

Like the hair, the nails have special properties, which is evident from the prohibition of paring the nails during the *ḥajj*. There are special days recommended for paring one's nails, and the comparison used by Persian and Urdu poets who likened the crescent moon to a fingernail (which does not sound very poetical to Westerners) might have a deeper reason than simply the external shape.

As the soul is often thought to be connected with the breath (one need only think of God's 'breathing' into Adam), the nose and the nostrils play a considerable role in popular belief; to sneeze means, as ancient Arabic sources as well as Turkish folk tales mention, to be quickened from death (the morning, too, 'sneezes' when it dawns). Alternatively, by sneezing one gets rid of the devil, who was hiding in the nostrils: hence the custom of uttering a congratulatory blessing to a sneezing person. The role of the nose as a sign of honour and rank, as understood from many Arabic and Turkish expressions, also explains why one of the ways to deprive a culprit of his or her honour is to cut off his or her nose, a common punishment until recently.[8]

Breathing is connected with the soul. It is therefore life-giving and healing (as was, for example, Jesus' breath: Sūra 3:49). In an ingenious *ta'wīl*, the Suhrawardī saint Makhdūm Nūḥ of Hala (Sind) (d. 1591) interpreted the 'girl buried alive' of Sūra 81:8 as the breath that goes out without being filled with the *dhikr*, the recollection of God.

The importance of saliva is well known in religious traditions. When a saint spits into the food, it brings blessings, and when the Prophet or a saint (whether in reality or in a dream) puts some of his saliva into somebody's mouth, the person will become a great poet or orator.[9] The saliva of the beloved is compared to the Water of Life owing to its *baraka*, and *mawlid* singers in Egypt – to quote an example from modern times – sing of the 'licit wine of the Prophet's saliva'.[10]

It is a similar case with perspiration. Women in the environment of the Prophet – so it is told – would collect his perspiration to use it as a perfume, and the legend that the rose grew from drops of the Prophet's perspiration which fell to Earth during his nightly journey shows the *baraka* of this fragrant substance.

Blood too can be a carrier of soul substance, and the avoidance of blood in ritual and food is likely to go back originally to the fear of the soul power contained in the blood.

Head and feet are respected, and it is especially the cult of the feet or the footprint which is remarkably developed in Islamic folklore: touching the feet of a venerable person is an old custom to show one's devotion and humility (to 'become the dust for the beloved's feet' is a widespread wish in Oriental poetry). The veneration of the Prophet's footprint has been attributed to influences from

India, where Vishnu's or the Buddha's feet are highly honoured; but the most enthusiastic poems about the Prophet's sandals, as well as the earliest mention of the cult of his footprint, came from the Arab world. The cult of the Prophet's sandal was substituted for the cult of his foot some time after his death. Maqqarī's (d. 1624) voluminous Arabic work is a treasure trove of poems and pictures of this cult.[11]

The feet of normal believers are also filled with power, and whether the Sufi kisses his master's foot or the son that of his mother, the wish to humiliate oneself before the power inherent even in the lowest part of the person's body can be sensed. That becomes very clear from the custom of *dōsa*: the shaykh of the Sa'diyya *ṭarīqa* (and in Istanbul formerly also of the Rifā'iyya) would walk or even ride over the bodies of his followers who were lying flat on the ground; thus they were blessed by his feet's power.[12]

I mentioned, at the beginning, the belief in the Evil Eye (see above, p. 91), and the negative power of the 'look' mentioned in the Koran (Sūra 68:51f.) is something to be reckoned with. However, the eye has not only dangerous properties; rather, the look of the saintly person may bless the visitor, and there are numerous miracles ascribed to the blessings of someone's 'look'. Sudden conversions are ascribed to the single glance of the spiritual master, and so are healing miracles.[13] The rule that women should strictly avoid eye contact with strangers reminds us of the danger of the glance; women therefore often wear dark glasses to cover their eyes.

As the body is filled with power, certain bodily states in which one loses, as it were, some 'power' have to be rectified by a major purification. Such states include the sexual act or any loss of semen, as well as death. No food should be cooked for three days after a death; the neighbours will bring everything required to the home. Pregnant women should not be present during the memorial rites for a family member (women in general never participate in a funeral).[14] They are also not allowed, during pregnancy, into a saint's shrine. The time for purification after parturition or death is forty days, the traditional period of waiting and changing for the better.

The spiritual elements of the human being are classified in various ways, but Muslims always know that there is the spirit, *rūḥ*, and the soul, *nafs*. The spirit generally appears as the paternal, that is, begetting and impressing power, while the soul is usually taken as the female, receptive part. The spirit, as part of the all-pervading Spirit, is one, but the 'mothers' are different for every being.[15] The problem of whether or not bodies and spirits were created at the same time is answered differently; philosophers and mystics usually agree that the spirits were created before the bodies.[16] The tensions between soul and body, or spirit and body, are alluded to in numerous stories, especially by Rūmī, whose psychology is, however, not very consistent. For him, as for many mystics, the most important part of one's spiritual aspects is the heart, the organ through which one may reach immediate understanding of the Divine presence: a veritable heart, as many mystics hold, has to be born, or else it has to be cleaned of the rust of worldliness to become a pure vessel, a clean house, a radiant mirror for the Divine Beloved. Rūmī even compares the birth of the truly spiritual parts of the human being to the birth of Jesus from the Virgin Mary: only when the birth pangs – sufferings and afflictions – come and are overcome in loving faith can this 'Jesus' be born to the human soul.[17]

Both terms, 'spirit' and 'soul', have airy connotations: *rūḥ* and *rīḥ*, 'wind', *nafs* and *nafas*, 'breath': thus the importance of the breath as a vehicle of the soul can be understood, as can the frequent symbol of the 'soul bird', the airy, flighty part of human beings.

The classification of the soul is based upon the Koran, and the three definitions of the *nafs*, found in three different places, served the Muslims to form a general theory of the development of the soul. The *nafs ammāra* (Sūra 12:53), the 'soul that incites to evil', is 'the worst of all enemies' (*AM* no. 17), but it can be educated by constant fight – the veritable 'Greater *jihād*' – against its base qualities to become the *nafs lawwāma* (Sūra 75:2), a concept not far from Western 'conscience', and finally it is called back to its Lord after reaching the state of *nafs muṭma'inna*, 'the soul at peace' (Sūra 89:27). When the word *nafs* is used without qualification, it denotes the 'self' or the reflexive pronoun, but in literary texts, especially in Persian and Turkish, it is usually the *nafs ammāra*, the negative qualities of the lower self, which is then symbolized in various shapes, from a black or yellow dog to a disobedient woman or a restive horse.

Everyone is made of body and soul-spirit; everyone also participates more or less in the above-mentioned 'powers', and yet, despite the emphasis in Islam upon the equality of all believers, who are distinguished only by the degree of their God-fearingness and piety, some people are filled with more *baraka* than others.[18] Myths are woven around ancient prophets and saints who are thought to be blessed with longevity: Noah lived for 900 years, and there is the strange figure of Ratan, a Muslim saint who was discovered in the twelfth century in India and claimed to tell authentic *ḥadīth* as he had lived in the company of the Prophet; the *ḥadīth* collected from him are the *rataniyyat*.[19] In *futuwwa* circles, Salmān al-Fārisī is credited with a lifespan of 330 years.[20] Legendary saints of times long past were sometimes imagined to be gigantic; the phenomenon of the tombs of the *naugaza*, people 'nine cubits long', is well known in Muslim India.

But to come to actual human beings as one encounters them day by day, one has to single out as prime carriers of *baraka* the parents about whom the Koran (Sūra 17:23) orders: 'You shall not worship any but Him, and be good to the parents whether one or both attain old age with you'.

Every elderly man can represent the father figure and often functions as the role model for the son. The families are extremely close-knit, as everyone knows who has lived with Muslim families. Yet, in the Koran, Abraham is the model of those who sever the family bonds by turning from idol-worship to the adoration of the One God (Sūra 6:74): true religion supersedes ancestral loyalties (and one can be shocked when hearing how recent converts to Islam sometimes mercilessly consign their non-Muslim parents to Hell).

The child grows under the mother's protection and remains in her house, with the women, until he is seven years old. A beautiful tradition inculcates love of and respect for the mother in the believer's heart: 'Paradise lies under the feet of the mothers' (*AM* no. 488) is a famous *ḥadīth*, and when the Prophet was asked: 'Who is the most deserving of loving kindness, *birr*?', he answered: 'Your mother!' and repeated this thrice, only then mentioning the father. The role of pious mothers in the formation of Sufis and other pious people is a well-known fact and proves that they were given not only a religious education but, more than that, an example by their mothers, and remained beholden to them all their lives (see also below, p. 198).

In many early civilizations, the leader or king is blessed by a special power which is called in the Iranian tradition the *khwarena*. The *farr*, 'radiance', with which Emperor Akbar was surrounded according to his court historiographer Abū 'l-Faz l, is – philologically and in its meaning – this very royal charisma. Normative Islam does not know the concept of Divine or sacred kingship; the leader in traditional Sunni life is the caliph, the successor of the Prophet as leader of the community in prayer and war, who has no religious authority and is bound, like every other Muslim, to the commands of the *sharīʿa* and their interpretation by the *ʿulamā*. The goal of the caliphate was not, as can sometimes be read, to establish 'the kingdom of God' on Earth but rather to look after the affairs of the community and defend the borders against intruders or, if possible, extend them to enlarge the 'House of Islam'. The caliph was regarded as a 'religious' leader only at a later stage in history, namely when the Ottoman caliph (whose office was in itself, seen historically, a construction without real historical justification) was described as the 'caliph of the Muslims' at the time when the Crimea, with its Muslim Tatar inhabitants, was ceded to Russia in 1774; at this point, the Ottoman sultan-caliph was called to act as the 'religious' head of the Muslim community. This concept induced the Indian Muslims after the First World War to rally to the *khilāfat* movement, in an attempt to declare the Ottoman caliph their spiritual head while they were still smarting under British colonial rule. But the *khilāfat* movement, in which many Muslims emigrated – or tried to emigrate – to Afghanistan and Turkestan, finally broke down when Ataturk abolished the caliphate in 1924.

While the Sunnite caliph is at best a symbol of the unity of Muslims (as was the case during the later centuries of the Abbasid caliphate of Baghdad, which was terminated by the Mongols in 1258), the concept of divine rulership can be found to a certain extent in Shia Islam. The return of the leader of a community after a long time in hiding is an old theme in human history, and this motif was first applied to ʿAlī's son from a wife other than Fāṭima, Muḥammad ibn al-Ḥanafiyya (d. 700). The widespread belief in the return of the hero, who is usually thought to live in a cave, grew among the Shiites to culminate, in the Twelver Shia, in the concept of the hidden Imam who will return at the end of time 'to fill the world with justice as it filled with injustice'. The Divine light which the imams carry in them gives them a position similar to that of a 'sacred king', but the theme is even more pronounced in the Ismaili tradition, where not the hidden but the living Imam is the centre of the community: the *ḥāzir imām* is not only the worldly but also the spiritual leader through whom the light shines forth and whose *darshan*, the 'looking at him', is believed to convey spiritual blessings to those present. Hence, the term 'sacred kingdom' has been used for Ismaili Islam, while this concept is totally alien to the Sunnite tradition.[21]

A similar aversion to a Divinely inspired or religiously exceptional clergy is typical of Sunnite Islam. There is no priest in Islam in the traditional sense of someone to administer the sacrament, for the only sacrament, *sit venia verbo*, is the recitation of the Koran in which the individual listens and responds to the words of the Lord.

The central role in the community at large belongs to the *ʿulamā*, the lawyer-divines and interpreters of the *sharīʿa*; for, as the *ḥadīth* says, 'the *ʿulamā* are the heirs of the prophets'; they are responsible for the maintenance of the Divine Law and the tradition. Thus they have contributed to the stability of the *umma*, the Muslim community,[22] even though they are also blamed, especially in modern times, as those who resist modernization and adaptation to the changing values and customs of the time because they see the dangers inherent in breaking away from the sacred tradition while they themselves are, probably, not acquainted with the opportunities that a fresh look into tradition may offer the Muslims who have to find a feasible approach to the modern world.

One could speak of a kind of clergy, for example under the Fatimids; and Ismaili Islam, especially among the Aga Khanis or Khojas, has a considerable number of ranks in the religious hierarchy, from the *dāʿī*, the missionary, and the *ḥujjat*, the 'proof', down to the *mukhi*, who is responsible for the organization of the local communities. (Interestingly, women can also be appointed to any echelon of these offices.) Yet, it sounds strange to a traditionist ear when a leading religious functionary of the Ismaili Bohora community (who has a 'worldly' profession as well) says: 'I was trained to become a minister'.

The *mujtahid* in the Twelver Shia can perhaps be called a cleric, as he helps to spread the wisdom of the hidden imam, guiding the community in legal decisions based on a deeper religious insight.

The most important figure with religious charisma, the model and the beloved whose presence and the thought of whom spreads blessing, is, without doubt, the prophet. To be sure, more than a century ago, Aloys Sprenger remarked sarcastically: 'In Germany, one has deprived the word "prophet" of all is meaning and then claimed that he, Muhammad, is a prophet'.[23] Sprenger is certainly wrong from the phenomenological viewpoint; for, as much as Muhammad's contemporaries were prone to compare him to the *kāhin*, the Arabic soothsayer, or to the *shāʿir*, the poet, who by means of his magic knowledge was able to utter satires against the enemies and thus wound them, as it were, with the arrows of his powerful words; and as much as Western critics have been concerned not only with the Prophet's numerous marriages late in his life but also with his political role in Medina, which seemed to overshadow his religious vocation – yet his way is exactly that of a prophet according to the definition in the history of religions. For the prophet is called and has no choice; he has to speak whether he wants to or not (cf. Sūra 96, the Divine order: 'Read!' or 'Recite!').

Islam differentiates between two kinds of prophets: the *nabī*, who receives a revelation, and the *rasūl*, who *must* preach the message; he is the lawgiver who speaks according to the Divine order.[24] The miracles which the prophet shows are called *muʿjiza*, 'something that incapacitates others to repeat or imitate them'; they prove not so much his power but rather the power of the Lord whose messenger he is, and while *muʿjizāt* have to be openly shown, the miracles of the saints, *karāmāt*, should be kept secret. The prophet is also a political personality, for he is concerned with and responsible for his people's fate in this world and the world to come: the archetypal ruler among the prophets is Sulaymān (Solomon), the 'prophet-king'.

The contents of the prophet's message are basically ethical and culminate in absolute obedience to God, who reveals His will through him. Often, the prophet is an *Unheilsprophet*: he has to warn people of the impending disaster if they do not listen, for only the rest will be saved. The tales of the earlier prophets which appear in the Koran time and again bear witness to this aspect of prophethood.

The prophet has to be a vessel for the Divine word, hence the importance of the interpretation of the word *ummī* as 'illiterate' even though its primary meaning is different. But he must be illiterate lest his knowledge be stained by intellectual activity such as collecting and adapting previous texts and stories. One could also see him as a mirror that takes in itself the immediate celestial communication; the concept of the *ḥajar baht*, the absolutely pure polished stone, belongs to this set of images.

The prophet – so the theologians emphasize – has to possess *ʿiṣma*, that is, he has to be without sin and faults; for, had he sinned, sin would be a duty for his community. As the *Sanūsīya*,[25] the widespread dogmatic catechism stresses further, the prophet *must* bring the message and cannot hide it. Furthermore, *ṣadāqa*, 'veracity', is a necessary quality of a prophet: he cannot tell lies. Without these essential qualities, one cannot be called a true prophet; but it is possible that a prophet may be subject to human accidents such as illness.

The Koran mentions twenty-eight prophets by name; parallels to the twenty-eight lunar stations and the letters of the Arabic alphabet could easily be discovered. Other traditions speak of 313 prophets, and the plethora of 124,000 prophets also occurs. However, there can be only one God-sent messenger at a time. Each of the previous messengers prefigures in a certain way the final prophet, Muhammad; their actions are basically identical with his, for all of them are entrusted with the same Divine message. There is no problem for the Muslim in recognizing prophets not mentioned in the Koran, provided that they have lived before Muhammad (e.g. the Buddha, or Kungfutse), because Muhammad is called in Sūra 33:40 the *khātam an-nabiyyīn*, the 'Seal of the prophets'. He was also understood as the paraclete promised to the Christians, because the word *aḥmad*, 'most praiseworthy', in Sūra 61:5 was interpreted as a translation of *perikletos*, which was thought to be the word intended by *parakletos*.[26]

Although Muhammad himself is called in the Koran a human being who, however, had to be obeyed (Sūra 3:32 et al.), and always emphasized that he was nothing but a messenger, the *baraka* inherent in him was nevertheless so immense that his descendants through his daughter Fāṭima were likewise endowed with a special sanctity, whether one thinks of the politico–religious leaders of Sharifian descent in Morocco or of the *sayyids*, whose veneration is particularly strong in Indo–Pakistan; they have to observe special taboos, and their daughters are not allowed to marry a non-*sayyid*.

While the respect for *sayyids* and *sharīfs* is common to Sunni and Shia Muslims (though much more pronounced among the Shiites), emphasis on the companions of the Prophet is natural in Sunni circles. The Shia custom of *tabarra'*, that is, distancing oneself from the first three caliphs and even cursing them, is considered a grave offence by Sunnis, for after all, even though the Shia claimed that they had usurped the caliphate from ʿAlī, the only legitimate heir to the Prophet, one has still to remember that Abū Bakr was the father of Muhammad's youngest wife ʿA'isha, and ʿOmar was the father of his wife Ḥafṣa, while ʿOthmān was married to two of the Prophet's daughters and is therefore called *dhu'n-nūrayn*, 'the one with the two lights'. Especially in India, Sunni theologians wrote treatises in favour of the first three caliphs and even of Muʿāwiya, the founder of the Omayyad caliphate, in order to counteract the Shia propaganda.

The designation of Muhammad as the 'Seal of the prophets' included for Muslim theologians the impossibility of the appearance any other religion and a

Divinely-inspired *sharīʿa* after Muhammad's death. Movements that claimed a continuing revelation, such as the Bābī-Bahai movement in Iran at the beginning of the nineteenth century, or the Ahmadiyya in the Panjab at the turn of the twentieth century, were declared as heresies and, in the case of the Aḥmadiyya, as non-Islamic as late as 1974.[27] Hence the merciless persecution in Iran of the Bahais, whose claim to possess a new revelation violated the dogma of Muhammad as the final bearer of Divine revelation.

Iqbāl phrased the concept of the finality of Muhammad's prophetic office in an interesting way which, interpreted wrongly, could lead to heated arguments.

> The birth of Islam ... is the birth of inductive intellect. In Islam, prophecy reaches its perfection in discovering the need of its own abolition.[28]

According to popular belief, the Prophet was sent not only to humankind but also to the angels to honour them. But connected with the theme of the 'Seal' was the question: what would happen if there were human beings on other stars, in other hitherto unknown worlds? This question, which disquieted some Muslims at the time when they became aware of new discoveries in astronomy in the early nineteenth century, resulted, in India, in a fierce theological debate between Faz l-i Ḥaqq Khayrābādī and Ismāʿīl Shahīd (d. 1831). Could God create another Muhammad in such a case? Ghālib, the poet of Delhi, wrote a line which was quoted with approval by Iqbāl in his *Jāvīdnāma*:

> Wherever the tumult of a world arises,
> there is also a *raḥmatan li 'l-ʿālamīn*, 'Mercy for the worlds'.[29]

For God will not leave any community without prophetic guidance, and humanity was never without prophets until the time of Muhammad.

Prophetology took a different turn among the Shia and in particular in the Ismaili community. The six days of creation (Sūra 25:60 et al.) were connected with six cycles of prophets: Adam, Noah, Abraham, Moses, Jesus and Muhammad; the seventh one will bring resurrection. Each of the seven prophets brings the *sharīʿa*, the Divine Law, which is then preserved by the *wāṣī*, the 'heir'; that was in Moses' case Hārūn, in Muhammad's case ʿAlī.

The human Prophet, the *uswa ḥasana*, 'beautiful model' (Sūra 33:21) of his followers, was soon surrounded by innumerable miracles, and when attributes like *karwānsālār*, 'the caravan leader', or in Bengal 'helmsman to the far shore of Truth' point to this quality as the guide of the community and are therefore generally acceptable, the development of his role as the first thing ever created, as the pre-eternal light that was between the Divine Throne and the Divine Footstool, leads into gnostic speculations disliked by more sober Sunni theologians. When the Koran calls Muhammad *raḥmatan li 'l-ʿālamīn*, poets symbolized him as the great cloud that brings *raḥma* (rain, mercy) to the dried-up hearts; the short allusion to his nightly journey (Sūra 17:1) was elaborated in most colourful verbal and painterly images, and although the Koran and Islam in general strictly reject a soteriology of a Christian type,[30] Muhammad appears more and more as the intercessor who will intercede for the grave sinners of his community (cf. *AM* no. 225), and millions of believers have trusted and still trust in his *shafāʿa,* his intercession.

He appears as the longed-for bridegroom of the soul, and just as theology sees the virtues of all previous prophets embodied in him, mystically-inclined poets knew also that the beauty of all of them appears in his beauty. At an early point in history, the *ḥadīth qudsī* claimed '*Laulāka* ...' (*AM* no. 546), 'but for your sake I would not have created the horizons' (i.e. the world). Surrounded by numerous names – similar to the Divine *asmāʾ al-ḥusnā* – he is separated from God only by one letter, as his heavenly name *Aḥmad* shows: when the *m* of *Aḥmad* disappears, there remains only *Aḥad*, The One, as a *ḥadīth qudsī* states.[31] Later Sufis composed complicated treatises about the *ḥaqīqa muḥammadiyya*, the 'Muhammadan archetype', the suture between God and Creation; and although in early Sufism the goal was *fanā fī Allāh,* annihilation in God, it is in later times the *fanā fī ʾr-rasūl,* the annihilation in the Prophet which constitutes the highest goal, for one can reach the *ḥaqīqa muḥammadiyya* while the *deus absconditus* in Its essence remains forever beyond human striving. The Prophet, as many people believe, is alive and guides his community through dreams; he can vindicate people who visit his tomb in Medina.

Several Sufi brotherhoods which called themselves *ṭarīqa muḥammadiyya* emerged in the eighteenth and early nineteenth centuries, although the term goes back to the Middle Ages; they taught the *imitatio muḥammadi,* not only in the external practices that were reported about him but also in the deeper layers of faith. At a time when Western influences were increasingly endangering the traditional Muslim world, the example of the Prophet who, as Muslims believed, would appear in *dhikr* sessions devoted to the recitation of blessings upon him, seemed to be an important stronghold against the threat of Westernization, for he is – as Kenneth Cragg says – 'the definitive Muslim'.

Even though the traditionalists never liked the exaggeration of his veneration, which so permeated popular and high Islam, everyone agrees that it is Muhammad who defines the borders of Islam as a separate religion. It is the second half of the profession of faith, 'Muhammad is His messenger', which distinguishes Islam from other religions; when Iqbāl says in his *Jāvīdnāma*:

> You can deny God but you cannot deny the Prophet,

he has expressed the feeling of the Muslims for the man who brought the final and decisive Divine message. Therefore *sabb ar-rasūl*, 'slandering of the Prophet', is one of the worst crimes, liable, according to some authorities, to capital punishment – one has to keep this in mind to understand the Muslims' reaction to Salman Rushdie's *Satanic Verses*.

There is no end to Muhammad's external and spiritual greatness. Frithjof Schuon[32] has represented him in an interesting model, using his earthly and his heavenly names, *Aḥmad* and *Muḥammad*, to show the two sides in him:

Muḥammad	Aḥmad
connected with the *laylat al-qadr*, the night of the first revelation of the Koran;	connected with the night of the heavenly journey;
representing the Prophet's role as *ʿabd* 'slave', which manifests His *jalāl* side;	is given the description of *ḥabīb*, 'friend, beloved; and thus represents the *jamāl* side of God;
he is the active messenger, *rasūl*.	he is the 'unlettered' *ummī*, the passive recipient of the message.

Positive activity and receptivity, *mysterium tremendum* and *mysterium fascinans*, descent of the Divine word and ascent into the Divine presence, are thus understood from the Prophet's two major names. One can expand the scheme and say, with the traditional scholars and Sufis, that every prophet also carries in himself the quality of the saint, and that the prophet is connected with 'sobriety' and *qurb al-farāʾiḍ*, 'the proximity to God reached through faithful adherence to the religious duties', while the saint, *walī*, is characterized by 'intoxication' and *fanā*, annihilation as a result of the *qurb an-nawāfil*, 'proximity reached by supererogative works', a state based upon a *ḥadīth qudsī*: 'My servant does not cease drawing closer to Me by means of supererogative works … until I become his hand with which he grasps, his eye by which he sees, his ear by which he hears …' (AM no. 42).

The question of the superiority of the Prophet or the saint was discussed several times in medieval Islam, but it was generally agreed that the Prophet, thanks to his twofold quality, was superior.

The *walī*, the friend or 'protégé' of God, is, in the beginning, in some respect comparable to the monk in other religious traditions, but 'there is no monkery, *rahbāniyya*, in Islam', as a famous *ḥadīth* states (AM no. 598), for 'the *jihād* [war for religious causes] is the monkery of my community' (AM no. 599). Monkery was something specifically Christian, and Jesus often appears as the loving ascetic who has no place to put his head and finds no rest even when seeking refuge in a jackal's den: God throws him out from every place of repose to draw him to Himself.

The early ascetics knew their Christian neighbours, hermits in the mountains of Lebanon or Syria, or in the deserts of Egypt, and among these ascetics as well as in later, institutionalized Sufism, practices similar to those in other monastic communities occurred, the most important one being poverty and total obedience to the spiritual leader.[33] The Prophet's word *faqrī fakhrī*, 'My poverty is my pride' (*AM* no. 54), was their guiding principle. But the third vow besides poverty and obedience which the Christian monk would make, namely celibacy, could never become part of Sufi life. Chastity in a wider sense can be seen in the strict following of the rules of behaviour, in the meticulous accepting of even the strictest orders of the *sharīʿa*. Celibacy, however, was ruled out by the very example of the Prophet.

Part of Sufi life was, again similar to monastic groups in other traditions, meditation and constant recollection of God, *dhikr*, as was the *rābiṭa*, the spiritual relation between master and disciples. Unconditioned love of and obedience to the spiritual guide was a *conditio sine qua non*, ending with the complete merging into the shaykh's identity.[34] The *tawajjuh*, the strict concentration upon the master, is compared by a modern Sufi to the tuning of a television set: one has to be on the same wavelength to enjoy a fruitful relation with the master, who then can spread his *himma*, his spiritual power, over the disciple and not only guide but also protect or heal him (hence the numerous stories of the master appearing in a faraway place when the disciple needs his help). The *shaykh* or *pīr* could be compared in his soul-nourishing activity not only to a father but also to a loving mother who, as it were, breast-feeds her spiritual child.[35]

While the prophet is called by an irresistible Divine order and forced to speak, the saint is slowly transformed by Grace. The term for 'saint' is *walī Allāh*, 'God's friend'; it is 'the friends of God who neither have fear nor are sad', as the Koran (Sūra 10:62) describes them. The term does not refer, in Islam, to a person canonized by a special religious rite; the Sufi saint develops, one could say, after being initiated into the spiritual chain. The simple concept of the 'friends of God' was elaborated into a complicated hierarchy of saints as early as around 900. In this hierarchy, the *quṭb*, 'pole, axis', stands in the centre; around him the world seems to revolve as the spheres revolve around the Pole Star. At least, around him revolve the groups of four *nuqabā*, seven *abrār*, forty *abdāl*, 300 *akhyār*, etc., among whom the seven *abrār* or forty *abdāl* play a special role: in North Africa, some Muslims sing hymns to the 'seven men of Marrakesh', that is, the seven protecting saints of the city whose tombs are visited to this day, so that a 'seven-man-pilgrimage' is also well known in that area, while the Turkish *Kïrklarelī* is 'the area of the Forty'.

The saints are hidden from the world; they are, as the *ḥadīth qudsī* states, 'under My domes' (*AM* no. 131), and therefore even the most unlikely person may be a saint. The virtue of hospitality, so central in Oriental culture, comprises also the poorest and most disgusting visitor, for – who knows – perhaps he is one of God's hidden friends, for *wilāya* can even exist independent of the moral qualities of the recipient.

Those Sufis who have traversed the path as *sālik* 'wayfarer', can become masters of others; those who have been 'dragged away' (*majdhūb*) in a sudden rapture, *jadhba*, are not suitable as teachers, as they lack practical experience of the stations on the path and its pitfalls; an 'enraptured' Sufi, *majdhūb*, is often someone who is demented under the shock of too strong a spiritual 'unveiling'.

One of the pitfalls on the path is pride in one's supernatural gifts. The Sufis are credited with innumerable miracles of the most diverse kinds, but to rely upon these miracles, which are called *karāmāt*, 'charismata', can induce them to ostentation and thus provoke a serious setback. Therefore, a crude saying was coined to warn them against 'miracle-mongering' (as later writers would say): 'Miracles are the menstruation of men', that is, they hinder true union with the Divine Beloved due to the individual's impurity.

Among the 'saints', one finds the most diverse characters: wild and irascible like the *'ajamī* saints of whom the Egyptians are afraid; saints whose word makes trees dry up and people die; and others who radiate kindness and beauty, harmony and sweetness, and can take upon them the burden – illness or grief – of others. They often claim to be beyond good and evil, as they have reached the fountainhead of everything and are united with Divine will in such a way that they can do things that look inexplicable from a theological viewpoint, comparable to Khiḍr when he shocked Moses by his three seemingly criminal acts (Sūra 18:66ff.).

They are the true 'men of God' 'who take the arrow back into the bow', as Rūmī says with an allusion to the Koranic address to the Prophet: 'You did not cast when you cast ...' (Sūra 8:17). To Rūmī we owe the finest poetical description of the 'man of God':

The man of God is drunken without wine,
The man of God is full without roast meat.
The man of God is all confused, distraught,
The man of God needs neither food nor sleep.
...
The man of God, he is a boundless sea,
The man of God rains pearls without a cloud.
...
The man of God: nor heresy, nor faith,
The man of God knows not of wrong or right
...

But those who still cling to hope and fear are comparable to the *mukhannath*, 'catamite', while the lowest class of worldlings are just 'women'. This does not however, exclude, the possibility that women can be counted among the 'true men of God', as the hagiographers state.

The Sufi leaders are usually given honorific titles, such as *Pīr-i dastgīr*, 'the Pir who takes you by the hand', or *Bandanawāz*, 'he who cherishes the slaves' (i.e. humans); and as a general term for high-ranking religious leaders is *makhdūm*, 'the one who is served', a special saint can be called *makhdūm-i jahāniyān*, 'he who is served by all inhabitants of the world'. Often, they are spoken of in the plural: a Sufi in Central Asia is usually referred to as *īshān*, 'they', while Ḥasan *Abdāl* and Niẓāmuddīn *Awliyā* bear nicknames that mean 'substitutes' (the groups of the seven or forty) or 'saints'.

But it is natural that the lofty ideals of earlier times were often watered down, and the complaints of true spiritual leaders about the numerous impostors who made their living by telling stories to credulous people and who paraded in Sufi dress, purporting to demonstrate miracles, began as early as the eleventh century. Rūmī satirizes these self-styled Sufis with shaved heads and half-naked bodies who pose as 'men of God':

> If every naked person were a 'man',
> garlic too would be a man …
> (*D* no. 1,069)

An ancient belief claims that the human being – provided that one possessed *baraka* during one's life – becomes an even stronger source of *baraka* after death. Despite the general warning against tomb-worship, the saying: 'Seek help from the people of the tombs' is also attributed to the Prophet, and it was customary among the Sufis and members of the *futuwwa* sodalities to visit the cemetery first when entering a town in order to pray for the deceased.

Such a power is, naturally, greatest in the case of the saintly people, and therefore it is small wonder that almost every place in the Muslim world contains a tomb or a mausoleum. Sir Thomas Arnold has told the famous story about the poor Pathans who smarted under the sad fact that they had no tomb in their village; thus they invited a passing *sayyid* to stay with them, regaled him and 'made sure of his staying in the village by cutting his throat', so that they could erect a beautiful mausoleum for him in order to enjoy the blessings that radiated from his last resting place.[36] The statement of an Indian Muslim historian can probably be generalized for the subcontinent:

> Many important infidels of the region entered the fold of Islam because of the blessing of the tomb of that embodiment of piety.[37]

Thus it is not surprising that many saints have several tombs or memorial sites (see above, p. 55).

The role of the 'mighty dead' in Islamic history is great, despite the Sunni aversion to it, and when G. van der Leeuw describes burial as a sort of seed-sowing, he seems to translate Rūmī, who asks, in his great poem on travelling:

> Did ever a grain fall into the earth that did not bring rich fruit?
> Do you believe that the grain 'man' will be different?
>
> (*D* no. 911)

Not only simple people who hoped for the fulfilment of their wishes visited and still visit saints' tombs; Muslim rulers, too, often came for political reasons to enhance their power thanks to the saint's *baraka*. The mausoleum of Muʿīnuddīn Chishtī in Ajmer is a famous case in point.[38]

Mausoleums may preserve, in a special room, some relics of the saint – his turban, his prayer beads and the like – and in modern shrines one can also find his spectacles or his dentures, all filled with *baraka*. The *baraka* can also be inherited: the marabouts in North Africa, as studied in particular by Clifford Geertz and Ernest Gellner, are the most prominent example of this phenomenon; and for the average Moroccan it holds true that 'Islam is what the saints do'.[39] The role of the inherited *baraka* of Indo–Pakistani Pīr families belongs here too.

If the term *walī Allāh*, 'God's friend', is generally applied to what we translate as 'saints', it is used in a more specific way and in an absolute sense for ʿAlī. The formula "ʿAlī is the friend of God', *ʿAlī walī Allāh*, was added to the bipartite profession of faith when Shah Ismaʿil had introduced the Twelver Shia as the state religion in Iran in 1501. There are great structural similarities between the *quṭb*, the Pole or Axis, of Sufism and the Imam as understood by the Shia. For the Shiite, the presence of the imam – whether in the flesh or (since the disappearance of the twelfth imam in 874) in the unseen, *ghayba* – is deemed necessary, for it is the imam from ʿAlī's and Fāṭima's offspring who is blessed with divinely-inspired religious knowledge and has absolute teaching authority: like the Prophet, he enjoys *ʿiṣmat*, immunity from error.

ʿAlī ibn Abī Ṭālib was surrounded with the highest honours, which led to his near-deification among the sect of the *ʿAlī-Ilāhī*, and strange legends are woven around him. In popular piety, he is sometimes called 'lord of the bees' because bees helped him in battle; and his proficiency in war, which is connected with the wondrous sword Dhū 'l-fiqār, is as much praised as his wisdom. The Prophet not only called him 'the gate to the city of wisdom' but also said: 'Whose master, *mawlā*, I am, ʿAlī is also his master, *mawlā*'; and religious songs praising *Mawlā ʿAlī* abound at least in the Indian subcontinent. In him, the ideal of the glorious young hero, *fatā*, was embodied. Members of his family were surrounded by myths: not only was the ancient belief in the *rajʿa*, the return of the hidden leader of the community, applied to them, but also dusk was interpreted by some pious

Shiites as the blood of Ḥusayn. The martyrdom of Ḥusayn offered them the passion motif, which added a special hue to Shia piety.

To be sure, the motif of martyrdom also exists in Sunni Islam, for the Koran speaks extensively of the sufferings of the prophets preceding Muhammad, as does the oft-quoted saying *ʿashaddu balāʾan al-anbiyāʾ* (*AM* no. 320), 'Those who are afflicted most are the prophets, then the saints, and then the others rank by rank'. The Koran stated that 'those slain in the way of God are not dead but alive' (Sūra 3:169), and that applies mainly to those slain in *jihād*.

Those whom the Sufis, and following them many orientalists, regard as the famous martyrs are usually considered heretics by the orthodox: these are Sufis such as al-Ḥallāj (d. 922), the young Persian mystic ʿAynul Quḍāt (d. 1131) and the philosopher-mystic Suhrawardī (d. 1191) (who is not called *shahīd*, 'martyr', but *maqtūl*, 'killed'); the Ḥurūfī poet Nesimi (d. 1405) in the Turkish environment, the Mughal prince Dārā Shikōh and his friend the poet Sarmad (d. 1659 and 1661 respectively). Owing to their unusual, non-conformist attitude, all of them have attracted, as Hamid Algar states with some dismay, the interest of scholars much more than has the normative Sunni believer.

One of these 'normative' believers has to be mentioned: it is the so-called *mujaddid*, the 'renovator' who is supposed to appear at the turn of every century of the hegira to interpret afresh the Sunni tradition.[40] The concept becomes more central – understandably – in the course of time, the further the days of the Prophet and the companions were away, and although there is a considerable number of people who are considered, by this or that trend in Sunni Islam, to be a *mujaddid*, one name immediately comes to mind: that is the 'renovator of the second millennium', *mujaddid-i alf-i thānī*, Aḥmad Sirhindī (d. 1624). Coming from the *sharīʿa*-minded Naqshbandi Sufi tradition, he tried, at the beginning of the second millennium of the hegira, the turn of the sixteenth to the seventeenth century AD, to reform Indian Islam, which he felt had been polluted by adapting to many Indian, pagan customs. Emperor Akbar's attempt to create a *dīn-i ilāhī*, an eclectic religion that comprised all the 'positive' elements of the religions in his vast empire, aroused the wrath of orthodox Muslims (as reflected in Bada'onī's historical work *Muntakhab at-tawārīkh*). By means of letters, Aḥmad Sirhindī tried to call back the Mughal nobility to the true highway that leads to salvation. His followers were probably not aware of Sirhindī's extremely high claims for himself and his three successors, for he felt himself to be the *qayyūm*, the one through whom the motion of the world continues – a rank higher even than that of the *quṭb* in mystical Islam. Sirhindī's posthumous influence extended over large parts of the central and eastern Muslim world, and the letters of the *imām rabbānī*, the 'Imam inspired by the Lord', have been translated into several Islamic languages.

Later lists of *mujaddids* continued the sequence with a number of famous religious scholars, such as al-Kūrānī, who propagated Sirhindī's teachings in the later seventeenth century; and even Ṣiddīq Ḥasan Khan (d. 1885), the prince-consort of Bhopal and active member of the orthodox *ahl-i ḥadīth* movement in India, was seen by some as a *mujaddid*.

The 'man of God' was always mentioned as the ideal of the true believers, but one should beware of taking 'man' here as gender-related. As Rūmī says:

> If one could become a 'man' by virtue of beard and testicles,
> every buck has enough hair and beard!
>
> (*M* V 3,345)

A woman can equally be a 'man of God', for 'when a woman walks on the path of God she cannot be called woman', as ʿAṭṭār says about the great woman saint Rābiʿa of Basra (d. 801). Yet, the prejudice that women are second-rate creatures and that they have no soul is still very much alive, and especially the mass media in the West like to dwell upon these topics.[41]

The Koran certainly ameliorated the woman's position compared to previous times. She receives a share of any inheritance, though less than a man, for she is supposed to be maintained by her husband, who had to pay the dower. More than that, she had the right to administer her own wealth and whatever she might earn or inherit during her lifetime; there is no *Gütergemeinschaft* (joint ownership of property) in marriage. Against these positive developments (of which many uneducated women barely know, for their rights were curtailed in many cases by the *ʿulamā*), women are not fully emancipated politically and legally, and are considered half of the man: one needs two male but four female witnesses at court, and the blood money for a woman is half of that for a free man. Marriage is arranged, and, as marriage of cousins is frequent (and easy to practise in large family units), the first wife is usually referred to, in Arabic, as *bint ʿammī*, 'my cousin'.

Polygamy is permitted (Sūra 4:3f.), so that the man can marry up to four legitimate wives; but from the condition that these wives have to be treated absolutely equally, modernists have deducted that this is a hidden suggestion to adhere to monogamy – for who could be absolutely just not only in material sustenance but also in affection? Slave-girls can serve as concubines, and if they bear a child to their master they become free. Numerous caliphs in the Muslim world were sons of slave-girls, who thus wielded a considerable influence upon politics. Divorce is easy and can be pronounced by the husband (Sūra 2:229); after the third *ṭalāq*, the expression of the divorce formula, the divorce is final, and the man can remarry the same wife only after she has been married to and divorced from another man. Women can include a paragraph into the marriage contract that under certain circumstances (mental illness; impotence of the husband) they have the right to ask for divorce. Temporary marriage is permitted in Shia law; it can last from a few hours to months and years; children from such marriages are legitimate.[42]

The strange idea that women have no soul according to Islam can immediately be discarded when one reads the numerous Koranic sentences in which the term 'those who do right, men or women' (Sūra 16:97) occurs, or where *muslimūn wa muslimāt, mu'minūn wa mu'mināt*, 'Muslim men and women, believing men and women' are mentioned together. Women have to fulfil all religious duties like men: they must perform the ritual prayer, although they are not encouraged to pray in the congregation on Fridays; they fast and go on pilgrimage (in company of a relative, not alone); and it is only during the days of their impurity that they cannot participate in cultic acts – but they have to make up the loss at a later point or, in the case of fasting, by substitute acts.

It would indeed be amazing if Islam were a religion that is against women. As much as later developments may give this impression, the Prophet himself said in a famous *ḥadīth*, which was taken by Ibn ʿArabī as the centre of meditation for his chapter on Muhammad in the *Fuṣūṣ al-ḥikam*: 'God made dear to me from your world women and perfume, and my consolation is in prayer' (*AM* no. 182). Muhammad's first wife, the mother of his children, was Khadīja, 'the mother of the faithful', whom he loved dearly and who was his greatest supporter during the crises triggered by the shock of the first revelations. Before the Wahhabi rule in Saudi Arabia with its strict prohibition of 'tomb-worship', the Meccans used to go to Khadīja's mausoleum and ask for help *bi-barakat sittinā*, 'by the blessing of our lady!'[43]

The position of the Prophet's youngest daughter, Fāṭima, was raised in Shia piety: the mother of the martyred imams became a kind of *mater dolorosa*, interceding for those who weep for Ḥusayn.[44] While her importance in Shia life cannot be overstated, the Shia thoroughly dislike the Prophet's youngest wife, ʿA'isha, the daughter of Abū Bakr, who was to become the first caliph (thus usurping ʿAlī's rightful position, as the Shia held). Young ʿA'isha, a mere child when she was married, was certainly a strange element among the other women – divorced and widowed – whom the Prophet had married after Khadīja's death in 619. A considerable number of *ḥadīth* about the Prophet's personal habits are related on ʿA'isha's authority, and often the Prophet's address to her – '*Kallimīnī ya Ḥumayrā*, Talk to me, oh little reddish one!' – is quoted to show his fondness of her (*AM* no. 47). Later (656), she played an important political role, riding out on her camel to lead her companions – against ʿAlī.

Women from the following generations appear in legend and piety, such as Sakīna, Imam Ḥusayn's daughter, or Sitt Nafīsa (d. 824), whose mausoleum in Cairo is much visited and whose birthday was celebrated in Mamluk times by the sultan. The mausoleum of Zaynab Umm Hāshim is likewise a centre of popular piety for the Egyptians: this lady is regarded as a kind of director of the day-to-day affairs in the heavenly government (now called, with a 'democratic' term, *dīvān ash-shūrā*), and thus proves resourceful when called for one's daily needs.

The Koran mentions or alludes to only a few women in sacred history: Eve's part in the Fall is not mentioned in the Scripture but was elaborated in the *Tales of the Prophets* to show her negative role in man's seduction;[45] Asiya is the believing wife of Pharaoh who saved the infant Moses; Hajar, the mother of Isma'il, is closely connected with the Kaaba; but pride of place belongs to Maryam, the only one mentioned by name and extolled as the virgin mother of Jesus.

I mentioned the importance of the mothers in the biographies of great Sufis and pious scholars, and could add the pious wives or daughters of Sufi masters, such as Qushayrī's wife, the daughter of Abū 'Alī ad-Daqqāq (d. 1015). It is not surprising to find a good number of women who were saints in their own right, all over the Islamic world, not only the noble ladies from the Prophet's family but also princesses or poor, unlettered women – from Princess Jahānārā, the daughter of the Mughal emperor Shāh Jahān (d. 1681) to the poor, love-intoxicated Lallā Mīmūna in Morocco; from Pisili Sultan, 'she with the kitten', and Karyağdi Sultan, 'Miss It Has Snowed' in Anatolia, to Būbū Rāstī in Burhanpur (d. after 1620), who was a sought-after commentator of classical Persian mystical poetry; from Rābi'a of Basra (d. 801)[46] to Fāṭima of Cordoba (d. after 1200) who, despite her great age, deeply influenced young Ibn 'Arabī, not forgetting the great number of more or less unknown women saints in Palestine – there is no lack of saintly women. Sometimes they are simply grouped together, like the *Haft 'afīfa*, 'the seven pure ones' in Sind; and, just as a female visitor is not admitted inside certain shrines, male visitors are kept outside the shrines or enclosures where saintly women rest.

In the Middle Ages, convents for women existed in Cairo and elsewhere; there, women could spend a span of time, for example after a divorce when they had to wait three months and ten days until they could remarry, or after the death of their husband. Such convents were led by a *shaykha* who also preached to the inmates and led them in prayer. Women appear now and then as preachers, or reciters of religious poetry, and some even taught *ḥadīth* publicly (such as Karima of Marw in Mecca).

Benazir Bhutto's appointment as prime minister of Pakistan amazed many in both Muslim and Western countries, yet there were quite a few precedents of a woman ruling a country (provided that she does not claim to be *imam* in the political sense, or caliph!) such as Raz ia Sultana in Delhi (1236–40) and a few years later Shajarat ad-Durr (1246–50) in Egypt, and, last but not least, the famous Begums of Bhopal, who ruled over the central Indian province in female succession for nearly a century from the 1830s onwards.

The Koran (Sūra 24:31) states that the Prophet's wives should 'cover their ornaments', a sentence that has been interpreted in different ways – it resulted in the complete veiling of hair, face, body and hands (a notable Pakistani woman professor even used to wear gloves lest an inch of her skin be visible). Originally, the order to cover oneself decently was meant to make a distinction between noble women and the servants and lower-class women who went out with little more but the necessary clothing; it was a distinction, not an onerous duty. In rural areas, veiling was barely possible, as the women had to work in the fields or woods. The strictest taboos were imposed on *sayyid* women, because it was held that the rules given to the Prophet's wives should be applied to them – and, as always in such cases, they were exaggerated and hardened over the course of the centuries: a pious woman would leave her husband's house only on the bier (and she has to be buried somewhat deeper than a man).

The insistence upon woman's deficiencies (a term very much used also in the Christian Middle Ages) reveals the ascetic fear of women's power, and the ascetics in early Islam saw in women something horrible but – alas! – necessary. The *sunna*'s insistence on married life left them between their wish to sever completely the bonds with this world (a world that appeared to them, as it did to their Christian contemporaries, as a ghastly old hag, always ready to seduce and then to devour her unfortunate lovers) and a normal and normative family life. Marriage, to be sure, is no sacrament but a simple contract in which the bride is represented by her *wālī*, 'representative'.

The institution of marriage is beautifully called one of God's wonderful signs, *ayāt*, in the Koran (Sūra 30:21) and is explained, in the *Tales of the Prophets*, by God's creation of Eve, where God is said to address Adam: 'I gathered My grace in My handmaiden Eve for you, and there is no favour, O Adam, better than a pious wife'. And when they were married, the angels showered coins from Paradise over them,[47] as is done in traditional wedding processions (and to this day weddings have remained an occasion to show off, connected with incredible expenses which often impoverish a family).

Man's right (Sūra 4:34) to beat his wife for any misconduct by her has coloured the general image of suffering wives, and the *ḥadīth* quoted by Ghazzālī, and well known also in India, that 'If it were permitted to fall down before anyone but God, women should prostrate before their husbands' certainly does not convey the idea of equality between the partners. Nor does Rūmī's comparison of married life to an educational process in which the man wipes off his impurities onto the woman speak of a very lofty state – and yet marriage could also become a symbol for creation in general and for worship. For Ibn 'Arabī, everything that transforms, *muḥīl*, is a father, and that which is transformed, *mustaḥīl*, a mother, while the act of transformation is a marriage, *nikāḥ*. The Prophet is credited with the sayings: 'The best of you is the one who is best to his wife ...' (*AM* no. 57) and 'When he kisses her it is as if he has kissed the pillar of the Kaaba ...'. These and similar praises of married life are found in a Persian treatise on the 'Mysteries of Marriage', to which Sachiko Murata has recently drawn attention.[48] And the very frank descriptions of the happiness of sexual union in Bahā-i Walad's life form, as it were, a bridge between actual marriage and the experience of mystical union. Mawlānā Rūmī, although turning at times to the ascetic aversion to women (despite his own happy marriage to a remarkable woman, Kīrā Khātūn, whom he married after his first wife's death), has found the most beautiful description of women's secret: when commenting (*M* I 2,413f.) upon the Prophet's word that 'many a woman prevails over the intelligent' (cf. *AM* no. 57), he suddenly turns from criticism to praise of women:

> She is a ray of God, she is not that 'sweetheart' –
> She is a creator – one would almost say: she is not created!

One reason for the deteriorating image (and, as a corollary, position) of women was the old ascetic equation between women and the *nafs*, the lower soul, *nafs* being a feminine term. As the *nafs* incites one to evil (Sūra 12:53), woman, too, tries to divert man from his lofty goals – or so it was thought. However, as the Koran points to the different stages of the *nafs*, one could also apply this image to women, and the mystical interpretations of the legends, for example of the Indus Valley, by poets of the western subcontinent are fine examples of the purification of the women who walk on the hard path to the Divine as a true 'man of God'. Thus the parallel with the feminine, receptive quality of the true seeker's soul becomes evident once more.

Furthermore, not only is the *nafs* feminine, but Ibn 'Arabī – who admitted of the possibility of women entering the higher echelons of the mystical hierarchy – found that the word *dhāt*, 'essence', is also feminine. Thus, the feminine aspect of the innermost essence of God was revealed in women. As the discoverer of the 'Eternal Feminine', the great Andalusian mystical thinker, in whose life not only his female teachers but also the beautiful Persian lady who inspired his Arabic verse are worthy of mention, could become the ideal interpreter of the Prophet's positive statement about 'women and scent'. That he was accused of a predilection for 'parasexual symbolism' is an understandable reaction from traditionalist circles.[49]

SOCIETY

The *ideal* Islamic society is, according to Louis Massignon and, following him Louis Gardet, 'an egalitarian theocracy of lay members', whatever that means. The community of the believers is central in normative Muslim thought, hence the aversion of some Muslims to the Western interest in exotic figures such as Sufis and the like, as they do not represent the norms and ideals of the *umma* because the *umma* is built according to the Prophet's divinely-inspired vision of the perfect society.[50] The 'good life', the life of a Muslim that should bring him or her happiness here and in the Hereafter, should be organized to its least relevant detail in accordance with the rulings of revelation as interpreted by competent authorities.[51]

The Koran describes the Muslim community as *ummatan wusṭā* (Sūra 2:143), a 'middle' community, that is, a group of people who wander the middle path between extremes, just as the Prophet often appears as the one who avoided both Moses' stern, unbending legalism and Jesus' overflowing mildness; for, as the oft-quoted *ḥadīth* says, 'The best thing is the middle one' (*AM* no. 187). The members of this group are the *ahl as-sunna wa 'l-jamāʿa*, those who follow the *sunna* established by the Prophet and subscribe to the rules and regulations that determine the believer's life. They are brothers (and sisters) in and thanks to their faith (Sūra 9:11, 33:5, 49:10); rather, they are 'like a single soul' (*AM* no. 109), therefore they are obliged to support each other on the path of salvation by ordering the good and prohibiting the evil, *amr bi 'l-maʿrūf wa nahy ʿan al-munkar*. That means that, by being a member of this *umma*, one will find the way to heaven and be – it is hoped – protected from Hell. The beautiful legend of the Prophet's pledge to intercede for his community belongs here; when on Doomsday everyone is overwhelmed by horror and calls out *nafsī, nafsī*, 'I myself, I myself [want to be saved]', Muhammad will call out *ummatī, ummatī*, 'My community, my community [shall be saved]'. Therefore, the members of his *umma* feel part of the *umma marḥūma* (*AM* no. 79), the community upon which forgiveness is and will be showered, *inshā Allāh*.

For modern thinkers such as Iqbāl, the *umma* becomes the true witness to *tauḥīd*: One God, one Prophet, one Koran, one direction of prayer.[52] The *umma* is, as the same poet-philosopher sings in his *Asrār-i khudī* ('Secrets of the Self'), like a rose with many petals but one fragrance, and this fragrance is the Prophet's guiding presence and the *umma's* love for him.

The importance of the *umma* is clear from the fact that the principle of *ijmāʿ*, 'consensus' – which was originally the consensus of the religious scholars of a certain time – was expanded to comprehend the whole community. As Georg Santillana writes:

> When the Muslim community agrees to a religious practice or rule of faith it is, in a certain manner, directed and inspired by God, preserved from error, and infallibly led towards the truth ... by virtue of a special grace bestowed by God upon the community of believers.

We may call this the *baraka* of the *umma*.

The Muslim knows that beatitude and hope of eternal bliss lies in worshipping and serving God, as the Koran repeatedly states; but true *ʿibāda*, 'worship', can be realized in full only in the *umma*, by participating in the five daily prayers, the Friday service, the two feasts and the pilgrimage, as well as by paying the *zakāt*. These duties constitute the fabric of the ideal Muslim life. For the Muslim is not only part of the *ahl as-sunna wa 'l-jamā'a* but also of the *ahl al-qibla*, those who turn in prayer towards the Kaaba.

The role of the 'middle community' has been emphasized in a work by the Egyptian author Tawfīq al-Ḥakīm, who speaks of the *ta'āduliyya*,[53] the attempt to strike the right middle path between extremes, and this quality of *ta'āduliyya* – so it is thought – has inspired the general tolerance of the *umma* in religious concepts: as long as one accepts the binding truth of the Koranic commands and prohibitions, one remains part of the *umma* even though one breaks the commandments; it is the denial of the absolute validity of the Koranic revelation that would make a person an infidel. One should also be very careful to practise *takfīr*, declaring someone as a *kāfir*, 'infidel, unbeliever', for the *ḥadīth* says: 'He who declares a Muslim to be an unbeliever is himself an unbeliever', an adage unfortunately lost on some modern, aggressive groups among Muslims. H. A. R. Gibb could state, in this respect:

> No great religious community has ever possessed more fully the catholic spirit or been more ready to allow the widest freedom to its members provided only that they accepted, at least outwardly, the minimum obligations of the faith.[54]

The schisms that have occurred time and again in history were concerned mainly with practical and political issues, not so much with doctrinal problems.

The feeling of belonging to the *umma marḥūma* makes, it was claimed, every Muslim a missionary who wants his friends to walk on the same highway towards eternal happiness on which oneself is walking. One can even explain the concept of *jihād* in this way: the aim of *jihād*, the 'striving in the way of God', i.e. war against infidels (the concept of 'holy war', as *jihād* is nowadays usually translated, is un-Islamic!), is the expansion of the *dār al-Islām* and is thus, as G. E. von Grunebaum formulates it, an instrument to unite the world in the *pax islamica*.[55] This may sound utopian and incompatible with the harsh political realities; but we are dealing here with ideals and thought patterns.

The concept of the *umma* has sometimes erroneously been identified with 'nation'. This, however, is a grave misunderstanding. It is telling that before the partition of the Indian subcontinent in 1947, most tradition-bound *'ulamā*, such as those of Deoband and related schools of thought, refused the idea of Pakistan as a Muslim state, as this seemed to contradict the true concept of the *umma*. In a similar line of thought, one can argue that in classical times the caliph was never a 'head of state' in the modern sense but the head of the *umma* at large wherever the Muslims lived;[56] for the medieval 'states' were generally governed by princes or sultans, who would call themselves by titles like *nāṣir ʿamīr al-muʾminīn*, 'helper of the Prince of the Believers', or the like. The later interpretation of the caliphate as something 'spiritual' is probably derived from this overarching concept.

The problem of the right government has been discussed by theologians and philosophers down through the centuries without reaching a conclusive form. The parts of the *sharīʿa* dealing with the ideals of statecraft remained generally theoretical, and the practice looked quite different. The decades-long struggle for a constitution in Pakistan which should be Islamic *and* modern is a reflection of these difficulties. One thing, however, is clear from history: it is better – according to general opinion as well as theological reasoning – to accept the rule of the *dhū shawka*, a ruler who has grasped power (even despotically), than to let the country disintegrate into anarchy.

The ideal of the all-embracing *umma* in which differences of race and colour were unknown, as the Koran defined the community of the believers, had to be realized in a constantly expanding 'state' in which an increasing number of new, non-Arab converts who had accepted Islam had to ally themselves with one of the Arab tribes as a *mawlā*, 'client'; and only as 'adopted' members of the Arab community could they gain full 'citizen status', not so much by embracing Islam and believing in the One God and His Prophet. It is understandable that the *mawālī* soon realized the paradox of this situation and rebelled; the system broke down with the growing numbers, especially of Persians, who often became the true guiding lights of intellectual progress in medieval Islam.

Another problem with which the *umma* had to deal was that of the *dhimmī*, the *ahl al-kitāb*, 'People of the Book', that is, the Jews, Christians, Sabians and later also Zoroastrians who were placed under the protection, *dhimma*, of the Muslim government and had to pay a special tax (cf. Sūra 9:29) but who had the right of self-government under their respective religious leaders (rabbi, bishop and the like), although they were not admitted as witnesses in Muslim courts. They were also exempt from military service. The government rarely interfered with their affairs, and they could occupy almost any profession: the large number of Christian and Jewish physicians, translators and secretaries in the administration (where, for example, the Copts boasted centuries of experience to put at the Muslim rulers' disposal) is a well-known feature of medieval and post-medieval life. The fact that many of the Jews who had been expelled from Spain in 1492 chose to settle in the Ottoman Empire, where they enjoyed freedom to live and to practise their skills, shows the tolerance of the Muslim government as compared to that of Christian Spain.[57] To this day, Muslim countries have high-ranking officials from the Christian or, in Pakistan, the Parsee community who are fully integrated as High Court judges or ambassadors (to mention only some examples from Pakistan; Egypt's Boutros-Ghali is another example of a non-Muslim serving in a most responsible position).

To be sure, Muslims reverted time and again to the Koranic warning: 'Don't take Jews and Christians as friends!' (Sūra 5:51), and edicts were issued that the *dhimmīs* should distinguish themselves from the Muslims by dress and demeanour. The first known edict that ordered the Jews to wear honey-coloured veils and belts was issued in 849, and the yellow colour remained associated with them down through the centuries (as it was the case in Europe). When early Persian poets described an autumnal landscape, they thought that the trees 'put on a Jewish garment ...'[58]

Conversions of the *dhimmīs* were not encouraged in early times for financial reasons: a special tax, as well as the land tax which they had to pay, was a welcome addition to the treasury. Yet, conversions were rather frequent. The concept of *dhimmī* was extended to Buddhists and Hindus when Muḥammad ibn al-Qāsim conquered Sind in 711–12, a measure which meant that Muslims did not need to lead *jihād* against the native inhabitants of the country, which would have been next to impossible for the tiny group of Muslims settling in the western subcontinent.[59] Conversions in the fringe areas of Islam especially in India but also in Central Asia and, somewhat later, in Africa, were largely due to the activities of the Sufi orders, not – as usually claimed – by 'fire and sword' or by 'forced circumcision'. The exact mechanics of conversion, however, are not yet fully understood and explained.[60]

Similar to the attitude of the earliest Arab conquerors towards the *mawālī*, the new Muslims of Hindu background in India were regarded by some traditionists as second-class citizens: the historian Baranī (d. after 1350) harshly ruled out the possibility of a *naw musulmān*'s occupying a responsible position in the state. The true Muslim was (now no longer the Arab but) the Turk, for the successful Muslim conquerors of the north-western subcontinent from the days of Maḥmūd of Ghazna (reigned 999–1030) had been predominantly Turks.[61] In general, too, many Muslims tended to regard the convert with a certain distrust because they suspected that his conversion was mainly due to practical – financial or political – reasons, not for the love of Islam. (Conversions for the love of a human being occurred too; as a Muslim girl is not allowed to marry a non-Muslim, such conversions play a role perhaps even more in our time than earlier as result of the mobility of social groups, educational facilities, and the like.)

The community, embracing Muslims of different political and dogmatic approaches to the central truth as well as the *ahl al-kitāb* and other small groups, was thus far from uniform. In the long run, even something like Muslim 'castes' developed, especially in India.[62] Occupational stratification was common, and the relations among members of certain classes or groups continue to this day. 'Horrible – my aunt was buried close to a *mirzā* [member of the Turco-Persian nobility in Indo-Pakistan!] – what a disgrace for a *sayyid* lady!' I heard this remark in Lahore in 1983.

But how to deal with those non-Muslims who were also not *ahl al-kitāb*? The problem of *jihād*, the 'striving on the way of God', was and still is one of the greatest obstacles for non-Muslims to understanding Islam. Some of the Sūras revealed in Medina deal with the problem of warring for the sake of the true faith, but this is to be understood primarily as the fight against aggressors and apostates. Yet, the fact that Muhammad, in the course of his prophetship, became increasingly sure that he was sent not only to the Arabs but to the *ʿālamīn*, all the inhabitants of the world, involved a missionary claim; and thus, in the end, it was revealed to him: 'Fight against those who do not believe in God nor in the Last Day, who prohibit not what God and His messenger have prohibited, and who refuse allegiance to the true faith from among those who have received the Book, until they humbly pay tribute out of hand' (Sūra 9:29). The translation of *jihād* as 'holy war', as is now current even among Muslims, cannot be justified on philological grounds; the term 'Holy War' was first coined in medieval Europe for the undertakings of the Crusaders. Rules for the treatment of prisoners, women and children are given, but one should always keep in mind that *jihād* is not a 'Pillar of Islam'; rather, it is a *farḍ al-kifāya*, a duty to which the community in general is called. As Sūra 2:256 states: 'There is no compulsion in religion', it was impossible to declare *jihād* as one of the absolutely binding pillars of Islam.

A *ḥadīth* makes the Prophet say: 'The difference of opinion in my community is a sign of Divine mercy'. This *ḥadīth*, however, does not intend the different opinions and strata inside the variegated *umma* but rather the differences between the legal schools which came into existence in the first two centuries of Islam. Their leaders developed legal systems based on the Koran and *sunna,* and added – as was necessary in a time of fast expansion of Islam into areas with completely different values and traditions – the principle of analogy, *qiyās*, which enabled the jurists to decide cases according to precedents. One may also add *ra'y*, speculation and use of independent judgment. The systematization of the given data and their elaboration constituted the field of *fiqh*, 'understanding and pondering', that is, the human interpretation of the Divinely-given *sharīʿa*.

The legal schools (sometimes wrongly described as 'sects') are called *madhhab*, 'the way on which one goes', a word which is nowadays sometimes used for 'religion' in its historical aspects (*ta'rīkh al-madhāhib* means at times simply 'History of religions', for *dīn*, 'religion par excellence', is only *one*). The *madhāhib* differ generally only in minor points, such as the position of the hands in prayer, the necessity of ablution after touching a non-related woman's skin, and questions in personal status law. Out of a larger number of legal currents, such as the school of al-Awzāʿī (d. 774) and the Ẓāhirites, four have remained active to this day. The Hanafites are followers of Abū Ḥanīfa an-Nuʿmān, whose *madhhab* is generally accepted in Turkish areas, including northern India, and is regarded as being most prone to a rather 'free' interpretation of the law. Mālik ibn Anās (d. 795) is regarded as the representative of the traditionalist school of Medina; the Malikites are mainly found in the western part of the Muslim world. Ash-Shāfi'ī (d. 820) takes a stance between the two earlier masters; his school is probably the most widespread one, while the fourth school is connected with the stern traditionist Aḥmad ibn Ḥanbal (d. 855). The Hanbalites are characterized by adhering unswervingly to the words of Koran and *sunna*, disallowing human reason to solve problems. Out of this group grew, later, the Wahhabis, who rule today in Saudi Arabia and deny all *bidʿa*, innovations, in the legal sphere.

The *madhāhib* are not hermetically closed. One can refer to a lawyer from a *madhhab* different from one's own if one sees this as useful, and members of the same family can belong to different legal schools. But once one has chosen a *madhhab*, one has to follow the rulings found by the previous generations. This *taqlīd*, 'imitation', was meant to ensure that the spirit in which earlier lawyers had solved a problem was kept intact, but it soon deteriorated into a narrowing traditionalism: the *ʿulamā* and *fuqahā* (those who deal with the *fiqh*) were no longer permitted to use their own intelligence to investigate the Koran and *sunna* but were bound, instead, to accept the results originally arrived at and hallowed by general acceptance, *ijmāʿ*. As Islamic *fiqh* comprises not only legal but also religious and what we would call 'profane' acts and duties of the believer, *ijmāʿ* carried over many medieval customs and ideas which, in themselves, were only derivations and not actually based on the veritable roots of *fiqh*, i.e. Koran and *sunna*. *Fiqh* also established, on a Koranic and *sunna* basis, the personal status law and the duties of the human being towards God as well as towards fellow humans, and defined transgressions and the different kinds of punishment according to strict rules. One should keep in mind that it is in law that the position of the human being is defined and interpreted, not in theology (as largely in Christianity); the law establishes exactly who is *mukallaf*, 'burdened', with performing which duty.

Thus, the institution of *ijmāʿ*, once thought to open the way for a development of the Muslim patterns of life, slowly became an impediment to new developments because, from around AD 1000 onwards, it was held that the gate of *ijtihād*, 'free investigation into the sources', was closed. Yet, time and again, individuals opened this gate for themselves, and the aversion to *taqlīd* became more and more outspoken among modernists, who perceive the dangers of fossilization of the community and its way of life and rightly believe that a fresh investigation into the *uṣūl al-fiqh* would serve Muslims to find a way to prosper in modern times as they once prospered. One has also to keep in mind that the gap between the *sharīʿa* and the *sharīʿa*-based legal systems on the one hand and that of customary and 'secular' law had been steadily widening – the caliphs had not only the *qāḍīs*, who administered and judged according to the *sharīʿa*, but also lawyers concerned with non-religious law, by which many of the punishments were handled and state taxes imposed.

One speaks of seventy-two or seventy-three 'sects' inside Islam, one of which is the *firqa nājiya*, the 'group that will be saved'. Yet, one cannot call 'sects' in the classical sense of the word the numerous religious and theological groups which lived side by side down through the centuries. Again, Gibb's remark comes to mind:

> It would not be to go too far beyond the bounds of strict truth to say ... that no body of religious sectarians has ever been excluded from the orthodox community but those who desired such an exclusion and as it were excluded themselves.[63]

True 'sects' appear, however, at a very early point in Muslim history, beginning with the battle of Siffin in 657, when one group of ʿAlī's partisans retreated from the battlefield because their leader accepted his adversary Muʿāwiya's suggestion to leave the decision to a divinely-ordained arbitrium. The Kharijites (from *kharaja*, 'to walk out, secede') were the first group to shape themselves into what they felt to be the ideal Muslim community. They were ethical maximalists, overstressing the *ʿamr bi 'l-maʿrūf*, and have rightly been called the Puritans of Islam. By declaring an infidel anyone who commits a major sin, they limited the community and cruelly fought against those who did not accept their rigid ethical standards. This attitude led Muslims to ponder the problem of the relation between faith and works – to what extent do works influence faith? Can faith increase or decrease by works? This, again, was connected with the question of the right leader of the community – should Muhammad's successor be from his family, his clan, or was it solely piety that determined the choice? The Kharijites advocated the opinion that, according to the Koranic words 'The one most honoured by God among you is the most pious' (Sūra 49:13), only piety counted, and coined the famous sentence that the most pious could be the true caliph even though he be an Abyssinian slave – because he has the necessary moral qualities.

Such extremist views could not possibly be accepted by the *umma wusṭā*, and after several battles the Kharijites slowly receded into fringe areas such as North Africa and Oman. Under the name Ibadis, they continued to live in North Africa, and their teaching offered a practical framework for dynastic, especially Berber, rebellions which flared up from time to time in the Maghrib.

The problem of faith and works as well as that of predestination versus free will occupied the minds of several theological groups, who answered the question of whether a person committing a grave sin was still a Muslim in different ways, or decided to leave the judgment to God, who alone knows what is in human hearts. Out of these discussions grew the Muʿtazila, who was to cause major theological discussions in the late eighth and ninth centuries, centring upon God's unity and his justice (see below, p. 222). Yet, even these theological movements cannot be termed 'sects'.

One can say, with undue simplification, that the battle of Siffin was indeed the event that gave birth to the two major sects of Islam, the Kharijite on the one hand and the Shia on the other.[64] While the Kharijites stressed the ethical qualities of the leader of the community, the *shīʿat ʿAlī*, "ʿAlī's party', insisted upon the inherited sacred quality of the leader. One can juxtapose the positions concerning authority in Shia and Sunni Islam, which softened the Kharijite approach to achieve once more the golden mean, as follows:

Sunnite	Shia
Adhering to the Prophet's words and example. Authority is contractual.	Authority is inherent in the leader by virtue of an inherited sacred knowledge.
The leader of the community is, at least in theory, elected from Muhammad's clan Quraysh. The caliph has no teaching and interpreting authority.	The imam's rule is God-given and necessary.
The caliph is the leader of the community in prayer and war.	The imam possesses a luminous substance.

That means that, according to Sunni opinion the caliph is the first of the believers, while the imam in the Shia tradition is distinguished by the inherited sanctity of Prophetic descent.

The Shia split into numerous groups. Zayd, son of the only surviving son of Ḥusayn, Zayn al-ʿAbidīn, is the imam after whom the Zaydiyya or Fiver Shia is called, who ruled in the Middle Ages in Tabaristan and until the 1960s in Yemen. They profess an active imamate and expect the leader to fight and defend his community. Every Alid, whether from Ḥasan's or Ḥusayn's progeny, can become the imam; no secret inherited knowledge is involved.

While the Zaydites teach active participation in the fight against injustice, many Shiites consider the *miḥan*, the 'tribulations', part and parcel of Shia life. As many members of the Alid family were persecuted (under the Abbasids the persecution was sometimes stronger than under the Omayyads, because the Abbasids had to fear the dynastic claims of their Alid relatives), suffering plays an important role in the Shia mentality, and many believe that mourning for those that have suffered or were martyred has a redemptive quality. This attitude has been contrasted – though not completely correctly – with the 'success-oriented' Sunnites.

Shia leaders practised the *daʿwā*, the rebellious call to revolution to avenge the injustice done to their imams, but in order to survive they were allowed to use *taqiya*, 'dissimulation' of their true faith (based on Sūra 3:29). Later Shia authors tended to include in their historical surveys many people who are known as Sunnis; but, according to the Shia view, these poets, literati or whatever, must have been Shiites who practised *taqiya* to survive in the inimical Sunni environment. This tendency becomes stronger after the Twelver Shia was introduced as the state religion in Iran in 1501 by the young Ismāʿīl the Safavid, scion of a Shia Sufi family in Ardabil. If leading mystical poets like ʿAṭṭār and Rūmī had not been Shia, how could one accept and love them?[65] And, as there is among many Sunnites a certain *tashayyuʿ ḥasan*, a tendency to express one's love for the Prophet's family and descendants, such an interpretation was not difficult.

Two aspects of Shia life are connected with the very beginning of the sectarian development in Islam, that is, with the question of the caliphate. These are *tabarraʾ* and *walāyat* – to refuse the first three caliphs (who were often cursed from the pulpits) and to cling faithfully to the true *walī Allāh*, ʿAli and his descendants, the imams who alone can guide the community thanks to their inspired wisdom.

The idea that the Mahdi from the Prophet's family will appear at the end of time 'to fill the world with justice as it is filled with injustice' is a dogma in Shia Islam, while Sunnites accept this idea only sporadically – yet the numerous Mahdi figures who emerged in the Muslim lands every now and again to fight against injustice show that the concept was widespread. Suffice it to mention the Mahdi of Jaunpur (d. 1505), who preached a mystically-tinged Islam with strong reliance upon *dhikr* instead of prayer, or the belligerent Mahdi of the Sudan (d. 1885), who caused so much horror among Europeans and who became a symbol of the Muslim fight against the colonial powers (thus in a moving chapter in Iqbāl's *Jāvīdnāma*).

While the so-called Twelver Shia, whose twelfth and last imam disappeared as a child in 874, constitutes the mainstream of Shia Islam and largely shaped intellectual and spiritual life in Iran and parts of India, not to mention smaller pockets in Syria and other countries, the Ismaili currents split off with a dispute over the seventh Imam, the son of Jaʿfar aṣ-ṣādiq (d. 765), one of the most influential scholars and sages, whose important role in mystical tradition as well as law is also accepted in Sunni Islam. Instead of his son Mūsā al-Kāẓim (through whom the chain of the Twelver continues), the line was continued to Ismāʿīl ibn Muḥammad. The different branches of the so-called Ismaili movement have incorporated much of gnostic thought, with ʿAlī's role becoming more and more important until even a kind of deification was reached (thus among the Nuṣayris and ʿAlī Ilāhīs, called *ghulāt*, 'exaggerators', even in Shia sources).

The Ismaili movement, to which medieval Islam owes highly important philosophical speculations, assumed its visible shape in the Fatimid caliphate in Egypt (969–1171). The glory of eleventh-century Cairo was described by the great Ismaili philosopher-poet Nāṣir-i Khusraw in his *Safarnāma*, the 'Travelogue', and in some of his autobiographical poems. The movement split with the death of the caliph al-Mustanṣir (reigned 1036–94), once more over the question of succession. One group accepted the birth rights of Mustanṣir's elder son Nizār, while others were in favour of the younger son Mustaʿlī, who succeeded his father in Egypt. His *dāʿīs* went to Yemen, where one still finds Ismaili villages and which was regarded as the basis of the true *daʿwā*. Yemenite scholars were brought to India to teach in the families whose ancestors were converted to Ismaili Islam from the late twelfth century onwards. This group, centred mainly in Bombay and Gujarat, is called Bohoras ('traders') and constitutes to this day a wealthy trading community. They still follow the legal code established by the Fatimid jurist Qāḍī Nuʿmān.[66] The highest authority among the Daudi Bohoras is His Holiness Sayyidna, whose ancestor came to India in the mid-sixteenth century; his rule can be compared almost to that of a pope (without celibacy, of course). His commands are to be obeyed exactly, otherwise excommunication is practised. Lately, Sayyidna has promulgated an even harder line in accordance with the increasing fundamentalist tendencies in mainstream Islam. A smaller group, the Sulaymanis, who remained faithful to the Yemeni connection, were and still are a remarkably progressive community. They played a role in politics: Badruddin Tayyabjee, first Muslim president of the Indian National Congress; A. A. A. Fyzee with his interesting modern interpretation of Islam; and Atiya Begum, the fighter for women's education in the first decades of the twentieth century, were part of the Sulaymani Bohora community.

Followers of Nizār, who was brought to the Persian fortress of Alamut, where his line continued, acted also as *dāʿīs* in the Indian subcontinent and converted a considerable number of Hindus in Sind and Gujarat. Smaller pockets of this faction are found in Syria (once the seat of the mysterious *shaykh al-jabal*, the Old Man of the Mountain, of Crusader fame); eastern Iran, northern Afghanistan and Central Asia have small Ismaili groups, and an important area where the Ismailis are the true political leaders is Hunza in the Karakoram region of Pakistan, close to the area of Badakhshan where Nāṣir-i Khusraw spent the last fifteen or twenty years of his life. The leader of the Ismailis, who had received the tithe from his followers everywhere, left Iran for India in 1839 to join his community in Bombay and adjacent areas; he was given the title Aga Khan. His grandson, the famous Sultan Muhammad Aga Khan III, was able, during his long reign, to transform the so-called Khoja groups into a modern community in which, for example, education of women is given a very special place; he also encouraged the migration to East Africa of numerous families from Sind, Gujarat and the Panjab. Most of them, however, have recently left Africa in the wake of racial unrest and persecution of minorities to settle in the west, mainly in Canada.

Contrary to the Twelver Shia, the Khojas do not emphasize the suffering of the imams or indulge in commemorating the event of Kerbela; rather, they feel blessed by the presence of the Aga Khan, the *ḥāẓ ir imām* through whose firmans they receive Divine guidance. Like the Bohoras, the Khojas have a highly structured organization, a true hierarchy with defined duties for everyone. The literature of both groups comes to light only slowly due to the secrecy with which the beliefs are surrounded; the *ginān*s of the Khojas (see above, p. 168) reflect a deep mystical piety in which all the longing of the soul is directed towards the Imam through whom the Divine light radiates.[67]

Another group inside Islam, which is not 'sectarian' in the strict sense of the word but whose ideals have influenced the Muslim community deeply, is the Sufi *ṭarīqa*, a term translated as 'order, brotherhood, fraternity'.[68] Ernest Gellner has called the establishment of Sufi *ṭarīqas*, which began in the mid-twelfth century, 'a reformation in reverse', because the Sufi orders created a quasi-church with the *shaykh* or *pīr* forming the centre around whom the different strata of members were – more or less – organized.[69] Early Sufism was ascetic and certainly very averse to the world and what is in it; government was generally equated to evil and corruption. Later, the Sufis assumed, wittingly and unwittingly, an immense political power. The Sufi *shaykh* was thought to have a direct influence on political events and material destiny of the realms where his spiritual authority was exercised. That is true not only in India but also for Sufi *ṭarīqas* in many other parts of the Muslim world. Offence against a *shaykh* could be regarded as a reason for a ruler's downfall or a mighty person's sudden misfortune: thus some Sufis explained the Mongol invasion of Iran and the adjacent countries in 1220 and the following decades in part due to the misbehaviour of some Muslim rulers towards the 'friends of God'.[70]

The faces of the Sufi orders differ widely; one finds rural and urban orders, and the teachings of the different *ṭarīqas* appeal to every stratum of society. Some *ṭarīqas* are connected, at least loosely, with certain professions: the Mevleviyya (which never crossed the borders of Ottoman Turkey) attracted artists, poets and calligraphers, and represented the sophisticated educational level; the Turkish Bektashis, strongly inclined towards the Shia and notorious for admitting women to all their meetings, were the order that worked with the Ottoman elite troops, the Janissaries, and thus lost some influence after the Janissaries' fall in 1829; and adherence to the Shādhiliya with its sober, refined literature was often preferred by members of the upper middle class, who felt attracted by the emphasis on quietude, purity and meditation without begging and ecstatic rites, as these are so often part of dervish orders. It is typical that one of the Shādhiliyya's offspring, the Darqāwiyya, has attracted several important Western converts to Islam. On the other hand, the musical sessions of the Indian Chishtis are the joy of those who try to find God through the mediation of sacred music. Ecstatic groups with wild *dhikr* meetings and a tendency to perform dangerous-looking miracles, like eating glass or taking out their eyes, live beside others who practise silent *dhikr* and retire in nightly vigils from the outside world to find strength for their daily occupation, in which they may be highly successful (the Naqshbandis and their subgroups are among these). Others work for the benefit of the community as do the Muridin of Ahmadu Bambu in Senegal;[71] and while medieval history knows of a number of Sufi rebels against the government (Qāḍī Badruddīn of Simavna (d. 1414) in Ottoman Turkey, Shāh ʿInāyat of Jhōk in Sind in the early eighteenth century)[72] or, like Sharīatullāh, against the rich landlords in Bengal, other Sufi families are very involved in politics.[73]

In short, the influence of Sufism is visible in almost every walk of life, for – as Marshall Hodgson writes – 'they developed a picture of the world which united the whole *dār al-Islām* under a comprehensive spiritual hierarchy of *pīrs*'.[74]

However, the Sufis have been and still are harshly criticized for introducing foreign, 'pagan' customs into Islam and polluting the pure, simple teachings of the Koran and the Prophet by adopting gnostic, 'thoroughly un-Islamic' ideas. Strange dervishes, wandering mendicants in exotic attire, or half-naked faqirs were the first representatives of 'Sufism' which Western travellers encountered and from whom they gained the impression that Sufism was something alien to Islam, a weird movement of drug-addicts who did not know anything of the legal and theological foundations of Islam. The inner values of Sufism were discovered only slowly. But the degeneration of Sufism in general and the quest for more political than spiritual power was undeniable, so much so that many Western observers considered Sufism the greatest barrier to a modern development in Islam. Muslim thinkers like Iqbāl joined them, claiming that *molla*-ism and *pīr*-ism were the greatest obstacles to truly Islamic modern life, and that the influence of 'pantheistic' ideas in the wake of Ibn ʿArabī's teachings and the ambiguous symbolism of – mainly Persian – poetry and the decadence that was its result (or so he thought) were 'more dangerous for Islam than the hordes of Attila and Genghis Khan'.[75] And yet, Iqbāl's own interpretation of Islam owes much to the intense love of God and the Prophet that are typical of classical Sufism.

Out of Sufism, and often parallel with it, grew another movement, called *futuwwa*. *Futuwwa*, the quality of the *fatā*, the virtuous young hero, is based, as its adherents say, on the example of ʿAlī, the true *fatā*. The leaders of the *futuwwa* groups also reminded their followers of the appearance of the term in the Koran, where Abraham (Sūra 21:60) as well as the Seven Sleepers (Sūra 18:10) are called *fatā* or (plural) *fityān*. *The futuwwa* groups apparently developed in the late tenth century and were a kind of sodality permeated by Sufi ideas. Some members of the movement sometimes turned against the establishment, and its offshoot, the *ʿayyārūn*, can be compared to the classical mafia. The Abbasid caliph an-Nāṣir (1182–1220) gave the movement a proper organization and sent out the Sufi leader Abū Ḥafṣ ʿOmar as-Suhrawardī to invite the princes of adjacent areas to join the *futuwwa*, thus creating, as it were, a political network of allegiances. Its initiation ritual was apparently more formal than that in many Sufi orders; the novice was girded and invested with special trousers, *sarāwīl al-futuwwa*, and had to drink salty water, a sign of loyalty, perhaps endowed with a certain apotropaic power. Franz Taeschner has described the details of this initiation and translated handbooks from medieval Arabic and Turkish so that one can form an almost complete insight into this hierarchically-organized *Männerbund* whose members were subject to stern ethical roles – only men from respectable families and professions were accepted.[76]

The *futuwwa* sodalities were connected with the artisans' guilds, although the problem of whether and how guilds are at all related to Sufism and *futuwwa* has been debated intensely among scholars. The guilds – if we can use this term – had a patron saint, and as late as in 1953 the cotton-carder, *ḥallāj*, in Istanbul who cleaned my mattress told me proudly the story of his patron saint, the martyr-mystic al-Ḥallāj. The guilds and sodalities such as the *Akhi*, who represented the Turkish offshoot of the *futuwwa*, impressed visitors from other countries, as can be understood from Ibn Baṭṭūṭa's travelogue: he was highly grateful to the *Akhis* in Anatolia, whose honesty and hospitality he praises.

All the groups were involved, in one way or another, in defending the *dār al-islām*, and the political changes brought about by colonial powers had to be met by new interpretations. For instance, was an Indian province now under British rule considered to be *dār ul-ḥarb*, which could entail that no Friday prayer could be performed?[77] The problem of Muslim minorities in a non-Muslim majority area is to this day difficult to solve, especially in the West. Can they, as minorities, play an important role in society? How are they to prove that they are real Muslims?[78] Can their approach to education help to ward off the dangers of backwardness of which the Muslims are often accused? Innumerable questions have arisen which were never discussed in previous centuries but which may lead to a fresh self-understanding for Muslims.[79] For most reformers have reminded their co-religionists of Sūra 13:12: 'Verily God does not change the fate of a people until they change what is in themselves'.

The new Muslim presence in the West also requires an increased dialogue, but it is unfortunate that, often, abstract theological and philosophical issues are raised instead of seeking the vital meeting point, namely the concept of God and the human soul's relation to Him. Wilfred Cantwell Smith was right when he remarked that, in such meetings and in conferences about Islam and Christianity, 'much talk about Islam can be heard but very little about God …'.[80]

NOTES

1. Nāṣir-i Khusraw (1929), *Dīvān*, p. 214.
2. See the numerous examples in H. Ritter (1955), *Das Meer der Seele.*
3. H. H. Schaeder (1925), 'Die islamische Lehre vom Vollkommenen Menschen'; L. Massignon (1947), 'L'Homme Parfait en Islam et son originalité eschatologique'. See also H. S. Nyberg (1919), *Kleinere Schriften des Ibn al-ʿArabi*, p. 99ff., and Tor Andrae (1918), *Die person Muhammads in glauben und lehre seiner gemeinde* for the development of Muhammad as the Perfect Man.
4. Jafar Sharif (1921), *Islam in India*, p. 22.
5. S. M. Zwemer (1947), 'Hairs of the Prophet'. The cult of the Prophet's hair was apparently more prominent among Turks and Indian Muslims than among the Arabs.
6. R. Burton (1851), *Sindh*, p. 135. G. Schoeler (1990), *Arabische Handschriften, Teil II*, no. 94 (Ms. or. oc. 2319), a *futuwwetnama* with an explanation of the ceremony of shaving off one's hair.
7. J. A. Williams (1984), 'The Khānqāh of Siryāqūṣ', p. 118.
8. T. Kowalski (1924), 'Nase und Niesen im arabischen Volksglauben und Sprachgebrauch'.
9. About spitting, see also E. Doutté (1908), *Magie et religion*, p. 440.
10. Information from Dr Kamal Abdul Malik, Toronto, from his PhD thesis about songs in honour of the Prophet.
11. Maqqarī (1916), *Fatḥ al-mutaʿāl fī madḥ an-niʿāl*; Anastase Marie de St Elie (1910), 'Le culte rendu par les musulmans aux sandales de Mahomet'.
12. See *EI*, s.v. *dawsa*, and, for Istanbul, *MW* 13 (1923), p. 185.
13. About the glance, see R. Gramlich (1976), *Die schiitischen Derwischorden*, vol. 2, p. 209; for more examples, idem (1987), *Die Wunder der Freunde Gottes.*
14. Jafar Sharif (1921), *Islam in India*, p. 19.
15. S. Murata (1992b), *The Tao of Islam*, p. 144.
16. H. S. Nyberg (1919), *Kleinere Schriften des Ibn al-ʿArabi*, p. 125. The idea was common among the mystics; see A. Schimmel (1975a), *Mystical Dimensions of Islam*, p. 192, and the numerous references in, for example, Rūmī's work.
17. *Fīhi mā fīhi* (1952), end of ch. 5.
18. The classification of 'people with *baraka*' used here follows F. Heiler's (1961) model (*Erscheinungsformen und Wesen der Religion*, p. 365ff.). Quite different is the number of 'people of Eminence' as described by Shāh Walīullāh, where one find the *ḥakīm*, 'wise man, philosopher', the *walī*, 'friend of God', the caliph, the *muḥaddath*, 'one to whom God has spoken', the *fard*, 'singular man', the *mujaddid*, 'renewer', the *ʿulamā*, the philosophers, and the *mutakallimūn*, 'scholastic theologians', that is, people distinguished more by knowledge than by *baraka*. See J. M. S. Baljon (1986), *Religion and Thought of Shāh Walī Allāh Dihlawī (1703–1762)*, ch. 9, p. 116ff.
19. J. Horovitz (1910), 'Baba Ratan, the Saint of Bhatinda'.
20. F. Taeschner (1979), *Zünfte*, p. 439.
21. H. S. Morris (1958), 'The Divine Kingship of the Aga Khan: a study in theocracy in East Africa'; P.-J. Vatikiotis (1966), 'Al-Ḥākim bi-Amrillah, the God-king idea realized'.
22. Fazlur Rahman (1966), *Islam*, p. 169.
23. A. Sprenger (1869), *Das Leben und die Lehre des Muhammad*, 2nd ed., vol. 1, p. ix.
24. Fazlur Rahman (1958), *Prophecy in Islam.*

25. For the *ʿaqīda sanūsiyya*, see Frederick J. Barney (1933), 'The creed of al-Sanūsī'. German translation and commentary of the *ʿaqīda* in R. Hartmann (1944), *Die Religion des Islam*, pp. 43–50.
26. The number of books about the Prophet published by Muslims and non-Muslims is much too great to be mentioned. For a brief survey, see A. Schimmel (1988), *And Muhammad is His Messenger*, bibliography. For a moderate Western view, see W. M. Watt (1961), *Muhammad, Prophet and Statesman*, as well as his numerous other works. Also of particular interest are M. Hamidullah (1959), *Le Prophète de l'Islam*, and Martin Lings (1983), *Muhammad.*
27. Y. Friedmann (1989), *Prophecy Continuous. Aspects of Ahmadi Religious Thought and its Medieval Background.*
28. Iqbāl (1930), *The Reconstruction of Religious Thought in Islam*, p. 126; cf. A. Schimmel (1963a), *Gabriel's Wing*, p. 168f. See also Fazlur Rahman (1966), *Islam*, p. 220.
29. Daud Rahbar (1966), 'Ghālib and a debatable point of theology'.
30. Fazlur Rahman (1966), *Islam*, p. 247. Nevertheless, although the Koran is the veritable centre of Islamic faith and the *dharma* the central concept in Buddhism, both the Prophet and the Buddha each gained a position much higher than that of a simple carrier of revelation or preacher of the right path, and both of them were endowed with a soteriological and a cosmic aspect.
31. For this development, see Tor Andrae (1918) *Die person Muhammads*, and A. Schimmel (1988), *And Muhammad is His Messenger.*
32. Frithjof Schuon (1989), *In the Face of the Absolute*, p. 230; and idem (1987), 'The spiritual significance of the substance of the Prophet'.
33. Tor Andrae (1948), *I Myrtenträdgarden* (English translation by Birgitta Sharpe (1987), *In the Garden of Myrtles)*, deals with the earliest phase of Sufism.
34. Bikram Nanda and Mohammad Talib (1989), 'Soul of the soulless: an analysis of Pīr–Mūrid relationships in Sufi discourse', p. 129.
35. J. ter Haar (1992), 'The spiritual guide in the Naqshbandi order', p. 319.
36. Sir Thomas Arnold (1909), 'Saints, Muhammadan, India', *ERE*, vol. 11, the story of the Pathan, p. 72.
37. C. Troll (ed.) (1989), *Muslim Shrines in India*, p. 7.
38. Carl W. Ernst (1992a), *Eternal Garden*, is a good survey of the relations between the shrines in Khuldabad/Deccan and the rulers.
39. C. Geertz (1971), *Islam Observed*, p. 51.
40. Y. Friedmann (1971), *Shaykh Ahmad Sirhindi. An Outline of His Thought and a Study of His Image in the Eyes of Posterity*. For later definitions of the *mujaddid*, see J. O. Hunswick (1984), 'Ṣāliḥ al-Fullānī (1752/3–1803). The career and teachings of a West African *ʿālim* in Medina'.
41. The number of books and articles about Muslim women increases day by day. A solid introduction is Wiebke Walther (1980), *Die Frau im Islam.*
42. S. Murata (1987), *Temporary Marriage in Islamic Lands.*
43. C. Snouck Hurgronje (1925), *Verspreide Geschriften*, vol. 5, p. 60.
44. Ali Shariati (1981), *Fatima ist Fatima*. Fāṭima was also Iqbāl's ideal, as becomes clear from his *Rumūz-i bēkhudī* (1917).
45. Kisā'ī (1977), *Tales of the Prophets*, p. 44f.
46. Margaret Smith (1928), *Rābiʿa the Mystic and her Fellow Saints in Islam.*
47. Kisā'ī (1977), *Tales of the Prophets*, p. 33.
48. S. Murata (1992a), 'Mysteries of marriage – notes on a Sufi text'.
49. Fazlur Rahman (1966), *Islam*, p. 146.
50. T. Naff (1984), 'The linkage of history and reform in Islam'.
51. G. E. von Grunebaum (1958), *Muhammedan Festivals*, p. 5.
52. About Iqbāl's view of the *umma*, see A. Schimmel (1963a), *Gabriel's Wing*, pp. 64–5.

53. The concept of *wasaṭ*, 'middle', was praised in both normative (Ibn Taymiyya) and mystical literature in Islam. See Merlin L. Swartz (1973), 'A seventh-century AH Sunni creed: the *'Aqīqa Wāsiṭiyya*': 'Doctrinal error or heresy results when one element of the truth is elevated to the whole, so that the integrity and dialectical tension that ought to exist between the parts of the whole are destroyed' (p. 96). That means that the healthy equilibrium in the *umma* is the most important thing.
54. H. A. R. Gibb (1949), *Mohammedanism*, p. 119. The Santillana quote is also from this book (pp. 96–7).
55. G. E. von Grunebaum (1969), *Studien*, p. 26, note 5, referring to a Turkish statement of 1959.
56. 'Alī 'Abdur Rāziq, quoted in K. Cragg (1965), *Counsels in Contemporary Islam*, p. 70.
57. For a special case, see B. Braude and B. Lewis (eds) (1982), *The Christians and Jews in the Ottoman Empire. The Functioning of a Plural Society.*
58. Khāqāni (1959), *Dīvān*, pp. 133, 428; Mas'ūd ibn Sa'd-i Salmān of Lahore (1960), *Dīvān*, p. 471.
59. Derrick N. Maclean (1989), *Religion and Society in Arab Sind*, especially p. 41f.
60. Sir Thomas Arnold (1896), *The Preaching of Islam*, is still the basic introduction to this topic, although the question of conversion has been discussed frequently during the last decades.
61. Żiyāuddīn Baranī (1860–2; 1957), *Tārīkh-i Fērōzshāhī*, deals with this problem. See also A. Schimmel (1974), 'Turk and Hindu, a poetical image and its application to historical fact'.
62. Satish C. Misra (1963), *Muslim Communities in Gujarat*; Imtiaz Ahmad (1978), *Caste and Social Stratification among Muslims in India*; idem (ed.) (1976), *Family, Kinship and Marriage among Indian Muslims.*
63. H. A. R. Gibb (1949), *Mohammedanism*, p. 119.
64. H. Halm (1988) *Die Schia*, English translation (1992), *The Shia*; Allamah Sayyid Muḥammad Ḥusayn Ṭabāṭabā'ī (1975), *Shiite Islam*; S. A. A. Rizvi (1985), *A Socio-intellectual History of the Isna Ashari Shiis in India*; A. Falaturi (1968), 'Die Zwölfer-Schia aus der Sicht eines Schiiten'.
65. Shushtari (1975), *Majālis al-mu'minīn*, is a good example of this tendency. For the problem, see Habibeh Rahim (1988), *Perfection Embodied. The Image of 'Alī ibn Abī Ṭālib in Non-Shia Persian Poetry.*
66. For a very critical statement about this sect, see Asghar Ali Engineer (1980), *The Bohras.*
67. Farhad Daftary (1992), *The Ismailis*; Azim Nanji (1978), *The Nizari Ismaili Tradition in the Indo-Pakistani Subcontinent*; S. H. Nasr (ed.), (1977) *Ismaili contributions to Islamic Culture*; Ismail K. Poonawala (1977), *Bibliography of Ismaili Literature.*
68. For a general survey, see A. Schimmel (1975a), *Mystical Dimensions of Islam.* J. Spencer Trimingham (1971), *The Sufi Orders in Islam*, is a wide-ranging survey. For Iran, see R. Gramlich (1965–81), *Die schiitischen Derwischorden Persiens*, a work that by far surpasses its rather limited title and gives an introduction into beliefs and customs of some orders. See further O. Depont and X. Coppolani (1897–8), *Les confréries religieuses musulmans*; A. Popovic and G. Veinstein (eds) (1986), *Les ordres mystiques dans l'Islam*; R. Lifchetz (ed.) (1992), *The Dervish Lodge: Architecture, Art, and Sufism in Ottoman Turkey*; R. Eaton (1978), *Sufis of Bijapur, 1300–1700*; J. Paul (1991), *Die politische und soziale Bedeutung der Naqšbandiyya in Mittelasien im 15. Jahrhundert*; John K. Birge (1937), *The Bektashi Order of Dervishes*; Sorayya Faroqhi (1981), *Der Bektaschi-Orden in Anatolien*; A. Gölpĭnarlĭ (1953), *Mevlâna'dan sonra Mevlevilik.*
69. E. Gellner (1972), 'Doctor and Saint', p. 255.

70. L. Lewisohn (ed.) (1992), *The Legacy of Medieval Persian Sufism*, p. 30. Christiaan Snouck Hurgronje (1923), *Verspreide Geschriften*, vol. 3, p. 190ff., speaks of the influence of different Sufi *ṭarīqas* on the Ottoman Sultan ʿAbdul Hamīd.
71. D. B. Cruise O'Brien (1971), *The Mourides of Senegal.*
72. F. Babinger (1943), *Die Vita des Schejch Bedr ed-Dīn Maḥmūd.* The Turkish leftist poet Nazīm Hikmet devoted a group of powerful poems to Bedreddin. For the less well-known Sindhi rebel, see A. Schimmel (1969), 'Shāh ʿInāyat of Jhōk'.
73. Sarah F. D. Ansari (1992), *Sufi Saints and State power. The Pirs of Sind, 1843–1947.* See also H. T. Lambrick (1972), *The Terrorist.*
74. Marshall G. S. Hodgson (1974), *The Venture of Islam*, vol. 3, pp. 211–2.
75. Iqbāl, Foreword to *Muraqqaʿ-i Chughtay*, a collection of paintings by Abdur Rahman Chughtay; his aversion to 'Sufism' is evident from his verdict against Ḥāfiẓ in the first edition of the *Asrār-i khudī* (1915) and his numerous poems against the 'Sufi'.
76. H. Thorning (1913), *Beiträge zur Kenntnis des islamischen Vereinswesens auf Grund von* Basṭ madad at-taufīq, was the first study of the *futuwwa* phenomenon. See also A. Gölpīnarlī (1962), *Islam ve Türk illerinde fütüvvet tes kilatī ve kaynaklarī.* The most comprehensive collection of studies is F. Taeschner (1979), *Zünfte und Bruderschaften im Islam.*
77. Not all Indian Muslims were critical of British sovereignty; rather, Sir Sayyid Aḥmad Khan and his friend Ḥālī were grateful for the blessings of the Raj, which protected them against the growing political aspirations of the Hindus. See also Maulana Muhamed Ali's speech for the *khilāfat* Movement 1920, in Aziz Ahmad and G. E. von Grunebaum (eds) (1970), *Muslim Self-Statement*, p. 112.
78. F. Meier (1991), 'Über die umstrittene Pflicht des Muslims, bei nicht-muslimischer Besetzung seines Landes auszuwandern'. American Muslims have sometimes compared their situation to that of the Prophet's companions who emigrated to the Christian country of Abyssinia.
79. The *Journal of Muslim Minorities Affairs*, issued in Jeddah, is an important publication in this field.
80. Quoted in S. D. Goitein (1966), *Studies*, p. 30.

VI

God and His Creation; Eschatology

And of His signs is that He created you from dust, and you became humans, all spread around.

Sūra 30:20

'To reflect on the essence of the Creator ... is forbidden to the human intellect because of the severance of all relations between the two existences.' Thus wrote Muḥammad ʿAbduh, the Egyptian modernist theologian.[2] Islam has generally held the opinion that it is sinful to apply human reason to God. The *ḥadīth* states: 'Think about the creation, but do not think about the Creator' (*AM* no. 439). One has to accept the way in which He describes Himself in the Koran, for according to Ismāʿīl Rājī al-Fārūqī, 'The Qur'an expresses God's inconceptualizability in the most emphatic manner'.[3]

Ancient religions had tried to circumscribe the Numinous power in various ways. The High God was recognized as causing and maintaining creation, and could be symbolized as father or, less frequently in historic times, as mother. Functional deities were in many religions responsible for the different events in Nature and in life: in the high religions many of them were 'sublimated', as it were, into saints who are thought to perform similar functions – hence the aversion of traditional Muslims to saint-worship, which, as they feel, imperils the pure, true monotheism whose confession is the duty of the believers.

Religions of antiquity also saw Fate as an impersonal power behind the events, and ancient Arabic as well a good part of Persian poetry reflects that fear of the revolving sky which, like a millstone, crushes everything. Who can escape the movement of the *haft āsiyā*, the 'seven mills', as the spheres are sometimes called in Persian? Who is not trampled down by the black and white horses which draw the chariot of the sky? Who knows what cruel Time has in its store, on its loom? The feeling that a merciless Fate reigns over the world surfaces time and again in literature,[4] and yet there is a deep difference between this fatalism, which the Oriental world inherited from earlier systems of thought, and the belief in the active God who cares for His creatures and who knows best what is good in any moment of life even though His wisdom is often incomprehensible to human minds and one wonders what He intends. To be sure, there are enough statements, especially in the *ḥadīth*, in which God's omnipotence seems to be expressed through a seemingly feelingless fate, such as the famous *ḥadīth qudsī*: 'Those to Paradise and I do not care, and those to Hell and I do not care' (*AM* no. 519). Predestination of this kind seems illogical, even downright cruel, to a modern mind, but it expresses a strange, irrational relation between the human 'slave' and the Lord; a relation which Tor Andrae, the Swedish Islamicist and Lutheran bishop has described thus: 'Belief in predestination is the deepest and most logical expression of interpreting the world and human life in a purely religious way'.[5] This statement translates well the Muslim's understanding of God's omnipotence and absolute Lordly power.

History of religions knows of different ways to describe God or, at least, to try to understand Him. There are the *via causalitatis*, the *via eminentiae* and the *via negationis*. All three can be comfortably applied to Islam, although the first one seems to be predominant in the Koranic message. Among His names, *al-khāliq, al-bārī, al-muṣawwir*, 'the Creator, the Shaper, the Form-giver' stand besides others that point to His care for His creatures, such as *ar-rāziq*, 'the Nourisher'. He is *al-muḥyī al-mumīt*, the One 'who gives life and who gives death'. 'Every day He is in some work' (Sūra 55:29), that is, He never rests, and 'slumber or sleep do not touch Him' (Sūra 2:255). Just as He has placed His signs 'in the horizons and in themselves' (Sūra 41:53), He also 'taught Adam the names' (Sūra 2:31), and furthermore 'He taught the Koran' (Sūra 55:2). That means that He taught everything, for the Koran contains the expression of His will, while the names endow humankind with the power over everything created as well as with an understanding of the Divine Names through which His creative power manifests itself.

One could transform the words of the *shahāda* that 'there is no deity save Him' into the statement that there is no acting Power but Him, for all activities begin from Him: He began the dialogue with humanity in pre-eternity by asking in the Primordial Covenant *alastu bi-rabbikum*, 'Am I not your Lord?' (Sūra 7:172), and He inspires prayer and leads people on the right path if He so wishes. Yet the supreme cause of everything perceptible is not perceptible Itself.

As much as tradition and the Koran use the *via causalitatis* to point to God's power, they also use the *via eminentiae*, that is, they show that He is greater than everything conceivable. This is summed up in the formula *Allāhu akbar*, 'He is greater (than anything else)'; and He is 'above what they associate with Him' (Sūra 59:23).

But His is also the absolute Beauty, even though this is not stated explicitly in the Koran. Yet, the *ḥadīth* 'Verily God is beautiful and loves beauty' (AM no. 106) was widely accepted, especially by the mystically-minded, and when daring Sufis claimed that the Prophet had said: 'I saw my Lord in the most beautiful form', they express the feeling that longing for this Absolute Beauty is part of human life.

God is absolute Wisdom, and the Muslim knows that there is a wisdom in everything. For 'God knows better (than anyone)', *Allāhu aʿlam*, as is repeated in every doubtful case. Therefore, God should not be asked why this or that happened, and ʿAlī's word: 'I recognized my Lord through the annulment of my intentions' (AM no. 133) reflects this mentality: the Lord's strong hand should be seen even in moments of disappointment and despair, for, as the Koran states (Sūra 21:23), 'He is not asked about what He does'. This feeling has inspired Rūmī's poetical version of Adam's prayer in the *Mathnawī* (M I 3,899ff.):

If You treat ill Your slaves,
    if You reproach them, Lord –
You are the King – it does
    not matter what You do.
And if You call the sun,
    the lovely moon but 'scum',
And if You say that 'crooked'
    is yonder cypress slim,
And if You call the Throne
    and all the spheres but 'low'
And if You call the sea
    and gold mines 'needy, poor' –
That is permissible,
    for You're the Perfect One:
You are the One who can
    perfect the transient!

God's will is higher than any human will, but this description does not mean, as Fazlur Rahman says, that we have to do with a 'watching, frowning and punishing God nor a chief Judge, but a unitary and purposive will creative of order in the universe'.[6] Thus, the constant use of *mā shā' Allāh*, 'what God wills' or, even more, *inshā Allāh*, 'if God wills', does not refer to any whim of the Lord but rather to His limitless power.

God is the One who dispenses absolute Justice, so much so that one of the most penetrating books on Islamic theology is called 'God of Justice'.[7] However, overemphasis on His justice, *ʿadl*, as was practised by the Muʿtazilites, could conflict with His omnipotence, because His justice was judged according to human understanding of 'justice', which is not applicable to God. The description of God as the *khayr al-mākirīn*, 'the best of those who use ruses' (Sūra 3:54, 8:30), and the entire problem of His *makr*, 'ruse', belongs to the realm of His omnipotence; it cannot be solved by human reasoning.[8]

God is the absolute Truth, *al-ḥaqq*. It is therefore not surprising that the term *ḥaqq* was later used by the Sufis to point to the innermost essence of God, who was experienced as the sole Reality, something beyond all definitions – and before the *ḥaqq*, all that is *bāṭil*, 'vain', disappears (Sūra 17:81).

God is higher than everything – not only in His will, justice or knowledge, but He is also supreme mercy and love, even though the quality of love is rarely if ever mentioned in the Koran (cf. Sūra 5:59, end) but is reflected in His name, *al-wadūd* (Sūra 11:90). Yet, mercy and compassion are expressed in His two names which precede every Sūra of the Koran, namely *ar-raḥmān ar-raḥīm*, 'the All-Merciful the All-Compassionate'. They come from the root *r-ḥ-m*, which also designates the mother's womb, and thus convey the warm, loving care of the Creator for His creatures. These words, repeated whenever the Muslim begins something with the *basmala*, 'inspired to the Muslim a moderate optimism',[9] and Islamic scholars have spoken, in the same context, of God's 'providential mercy balanced by justice'. Later traditions emphasize that God acts in the way that human beings think He would – 'I am with My servant's thought', says the *ḥadīth qudsī*, to point out that the one who trusts in God's forgiveness will not be disappointed.[10] Rūmī tells the story of Jesus and John the Baptist; while the latter was constantly brooding in fear and awe, Jesus used to smile because he never forgot God's loving care and kindness, and therefore he was dearer to God.[11]

The *via eminentiae* can be summed up in the statement that, as God's perfections are infinite, 'there is no perfection compared to which there is not a still greater perfection in God and with God', and rightly did an oft-quoted Arabic verse say:

> Praised be He by whose work the intellects become confused;
> praised be He by whose power the heroes are incapacitated!

This exclamation of utter confusion leads to the third way of describing God, the *via negationis*:

> Whatever you can think is perishable –
> that which enters not into any thought, that is God,

says Rūmī, in a verse (*M* II 3, 107) that sums up the feeling about God. Human thought is a limitation, and when the theosophical mystics of the school of Ibn ʿArabī tried to describe Him in terms that point simultaneously to His transcendence and His immanence, this is nothing but a faint attempt to describe Him, the *deus absconditus*, whom one can approach at best by 'seizing the hem of His Grace', that is, to describe one of His manifestations which cover His Essence like garments, like veils. How is one to speak about the One who is absolutely transcendent and yet is closer to mankind than their jugular vein (Sūra 50:16), so that the mystics found Him at the end of the road, in the 'ocean of the soul' and not in the mosque, not in Mecca or in Jerusalem? Poems have sung of Him in colourful images, in paradoxes, negations and affirmations which, however, do nothing but hide the transcendent Essence, for He is, so to speak, the 'Super-Unknowable'.

On the philosophical side, the Ismailis have tried to maintain His transcendence by using a double negation freeing the idea of God from all association with the material and removing Him also from the association with the non-material. God is thus neither within the sensible world nor within the extrasensible.[12]

He is, in the Koranic expression, 'the First and the Last, the Inward and the Outward' (Sūra 57:3), and the mystery of His being is summed up in Sūra 59:23–4:

> He is God besides whom there is no deity, the One who knows the visible and the invisible. He is the Merciful, the Compassionate. He is God, besides whom there is no deity, the King, the Holy, the Giver of Peace, the Faithful, the Protector, the Mighty, the Overpowering, the Very High. Praised be God who is above what they associate with Him. He is God, the Creator, the Form-giver; His are the Most Beautiful Names. He is praised by what is in the heavens and on Earth and He is the Mighty, the Wise.

Similarly, the Throne Verse (Sūra 2:255) has served to describe Him to a certain degree, and the concept of His Throne on which He dwells (Sūra 7:54; 10:3 et al.) and which comprises Heaven and Earth has evoked many commentaries, from realistic descriptions to visions of a seat of chrysolite or ruby[13] to the mystical interpretation that the true Divine Throne is the human heart, for the *ḥadīth qudsī* promises: 'My heaven and My Earth do not comprise Me, but the heart of My faithful servant comprises Me' (*AM* no. 63).

The God as revealed in the Koran is a living God, who has invited mankind to call Him and He will answer (Sūra 40:62, cf. 2:186), an active, creating and destroying, maintaining and guiding God who is yet beyond any human understanding. He is, in a certain way, a 'personal' God, for He has addressed humankind and revealed Himself to them, but the term *shakhṣ*, 'person', cannot be applied to Him.

When looking at the active, powerful Lord of the Koran, one wonders how scholastic theologians could define Him in rational terms: the *ʿaqīda sanūsiyya*, a dogmatic creed from the fifteenth century which was largely used among Muslims, describes God with forty-one qualities, *ṣifāt*. Six are basic qualities of which the first and essential one is existence, then further pre-eternity (*azaliyya*), eternity (*abadiyya*), His being different from what has become in time, His self-subsistence and the fact that He needs neither place nor originator.

He has a further seven necessary qualities which are: Power, Will, Knowledge, Life, Hearing, Seeing and Speech, and seven accidental qualities, that is: His being powerful, being willing, being knowing, being living, being hearing, being seeing and being speaking (this differentiation emerged from early theological discussions between the Muʿtazilites and traditionists about His attributes).[14]

Against these twenty qualities are posited twenty others that are impossible, that is, the contrary of the previous ones: He cannot be not-hearing or not-eternal. His forty-first quality is that it is possible for Him to do or not to do everything possible. Thus the living God as described in the Koran was transformed into a set of definitions with which the normal believer could not establish a true relationship. But definitions of this kind became a central part of normative thinking.

On the other hand, the *ḥadīth qudsī* in which God appears as a 'hidden treasure who wanted to be known' became the focal point among mystically-minded Muslims. But while God is usually seen and experienced as the One who does not need anything, *al-ghanī*, 'the Self-sufficient, Rich', the moving myth of the Divine Names who longed to manifest themselves and to be reflected in the world leads to the feeling that God (at least on the level of the *deus revelatus*) needs the creatures and that, in the last instance, God and man are as it were interdependent – an idea often found in mystical speculations everywhere in the world but, understandably, contrary to the convictions of traditionist Muslims who maintained God's supreme rulership and self-sufficiency.

God has been described as the *wājib al-wujūd*, 'He whose existence is absolutely necessary' and upon whom everything relies. One could also transform the simple statement of the *shahāda* into the phrase *la mawjūda illā Allāh*, 'There is nothing existent save God', for He is the only One upon whom existence can be predicated, and He is the only One who has the right to say 'I'.[15]

The concept of *waḥdat al-wujūd*, 'Unity of Existence' as formulated by the commentators of Ibn ʿArabi, would be expanded (by losing its necessary sophisticated connotations!) into the simple statement *hama ūst*, 'everything is He', which was used in Persian mystical poetry, for example in ʿAṭṭār's verse, before Ibn ʿArabī's time and which permeates later Sufi thought in the entire Persianate world. But those who used it usually forgot that the opposite of unity of Existence is *kathrat al-ʿilm*, 'the multiplicity of knowledge', that is, the infinite number of created things which are reflections of God's knowledge and hence different from His Essence.[16]

God is the *prima causa*, and there are no secondary causes: He works through what looks like secondary causes just as a tailor works with a needle or a calligrapher works with a pen, and thus it is He who is the real Creator of the design. Again, as He has a name by which He called Himself in the Koran, that is, Allah, He is, as Iqbāl states, an Ego, the highest all-embracing Ego in which the smaller egos of the created universe live like pearls in the ocean, and who contains infinite possibilities in a Presence that transcends created time.

The tension between Divine transcendence and immanence, between theologically defined impersonality and experienced personality, is reflected in a variety of sayings, verses and extra-Koranic Divine words. The *ḥadīth qudsī* 'My Heaven and My Earth do not comprise Me but the heart of My faithful servant comprises Me' (*AM* no. 63) points to this problem. He is incomparable, beyond every possibility of being grasped by human thought, and the human being, His slave, cannot talk about Him but by *taʿṭīl*, keeping Him free from all human comparisons and not admitting the slightest possibility of an *analogia entis*; but when one thinks that He made Adam His *khalīfa*, His vicegerent on Earth, and made him alive with His breath, one uses *tashbīh*, comparison with human concepts. Both aspects reflect the Divine, for man is both slave and representative, and God's attributes of majesty, *jalāl,* and beauty, *jamāl,* which are related to each other like man and woman, as it were, form the fabric of the created universe. The tendency of pairing concepts, of speaking in polarities, seems typical of Islamic thought. The Creator is one, but He reveals Himself both in ethical concepts (as orthodoxy sees Him) and in aesthetic concepts (according to the Sufis' experiences). Infidelity and faith, *kufr* and *īmān* are, as Sanā'ī sings, 'only doorkeepers at the sanctuary of His Unity and Oneness'.[17]

Although the 'looks do not reach Him' (Sūra 6:103), we know of Ibn 'Arabī's vision of the letter *h*, the last and essential letter of *Allāh*, which points to His *huwiyya*, 'He-ness' – He, who had revealed His words in the letters of the Koran, could be 'seen' only in a symbol taken from the letters, from the Book.[18]

Perhaps, one may say with the poets, He can be seen with the heart's eye:

I saw my Lord with my heart's eye and asked:
'Who are You?' He answered: 'You'.[19]

God's Absolute Oneness seems to make it impossible for a human being to profess that there is 'no deity but God', for the very act of pronouncing this formula already means establishing duality – as Anṣārī says:

No-one confesses the One as the One,
for everyone who confesses Him as the One denies Him.

The mystics knew that (as Dārā Shikōh phrases it):

From saying 'One' one does not become a monotheist –
The mouth does not become sweet from saying 'sugar'.[20]

Human existence was seen by these radical monotheists as 'a sin to which nothing is comparable' – only the One exists. Yet, one should distinguish here between the overwhelming spiritual vision of the lover who sees nothing but the beloved and hides his names in all names that he or she mentions – as did Zulaykhā, according to Rūmī's wonderful description at the end of the *Mathnawi* (*M* VI 4,023ff.) – and between the attempt to 'explain' this experience, to fetter it in philosophical terms and conceptualize it in high-soaring systems which confuse the reader (and here I intend the traditionist as well as the intoxicated lover) more than they enlighten him.

From whichever angle one tries to understand the All-powerful, the All-majestic and All-merciful One God, one should certainly listen carefully to the verse in which Sanā'ī has God speak:

Whatever comes to your mind that I am that – I am not that!
Whatever has room in your understanding that I would be like this –
I am not like this!

Whatever has room in your understanding is all something created –
In reality know, O servant, that I am the Creator![21]

The Koran speaks of God as Creator, Sustainer and Judge; but how can one imagine His creative activity?[22]

Ancient religions sometimes speak of created beings as 'begotten' by the deity, a concept which, on the level of mystical and philosophical speculation, might be described as 'emanation' – an idea not unknown among Muslim philosophers and mystical thinkers. Creation could also be seen as the deity's victory over the chaos: God is the One who shapes and forms a previously existent matter to fit it into His wise plan. Finally, there is the *creatio ex nihilo*, a creation owed to the free will of God and hence emphasized by the prophetic religions.

The Koran states that God created the world in six days (Sūra 57:4 et al.) without getting tired, but there is also the idea of a constant creation out of nothing: the long deliberations in Rūmī's work about *'adam*,[23] a concept perhaps to be translated best as 'positive Not-Being' capable of accepting form, show how much he, like other mystical thinkers, pondered the mystery of Creation, which might be taken as an actualization of contingent 'things'. Such ideas led Ibn 'Arabī and his followers to the mythical definition that God and the non-existent things are as it were male and female, and the existent thing that results can be regarded as a 'child'.[24] Rūmī speaks in similar connections of the 'mothers', for everything touched by a creative force engenders something that is higher than both.

But in whatever way one wants to explain creation, one knows from the Koran that He needs only say *Kun*, 'Be! and it is' (Sūra 2:117 et al.). For He creates by His Power, as normative theology states.

More than that: the Koran insists that the world has a deep meaning, for 'He has not created it in jest' (Sūra 21:16). That is why it obeys Him and worships Him with everything that is in it (Sūra 51:56). And yet, it was also felt – in the succession of Ibn 'Arabī – that God takes the created universe back into Himself to 'exhale' it again; in infinitesimally short moments, the world is as it were created anew, and nothing exists that is not subject to constant though invisible change. Poets and thinkers sing endless hymns of praise to the Creator whose work amazes everyone who has eyes to see, and they ask in grand poems:

Who made this turquoise-coloured turning dome
without a window or a roof, a door?

Who granted stripes to onyx from the Yemen?
From where comes fragrance of the ambergris?[25]

All the miracles that the seeing eye perceives in the created universe point to the necessity of God's existence; they are His signs, *āyāt*, which he placed into the world (cf. Sūra 41:53).[26]

The events in the created world are effects of the Creator's direct involvement: whatever happens is not the result of causality but rather the *sunnat Allāh*, the Divine custom which can be interrupted at any moment if He decrees so. That is why one has to say *in shā Allāh*, because one is aware that God can change things and states in the wink of an eye. One also does not praise the artist when admiring a work of art or some special performance but exclaims *mā shā Allāh* (Sūra 18:39) or *subḥān Allāh* to praise the One whose wondrous activity shows itself through His creatures; and the pious author will describe his successful actions as *minan*, 'Divine gifts' for which he owes gratitude.

God is One, but with creation, duality comes into existence, and from duality, multiplicity grows. The mystics found an allusion to this truth by discovering that the Divine address *kun*, written in Arabic *kn*, consists of two letters and is comparable to a two-coloured rope, a twist, which hides the essential unity from those who are duped by the manifold manifestations. Polarity is necessary for the existence of the universe, which, like a woven fabric, is capable of existence only thanks to the interplay of God's *jalāl* and *jamāl*, the *mysterium tremendum* and the *mysterium fascinans*, by inhaling and exhaling, systole and diastole. *Azal*, eternity without beginning, and *abad*, eternity without end, are the poles between which the world pulsates; Heaven and Earth, *ghayb*, 'unseen', and *shahāda*, 'the visible things' (cf. Sūra 9:94), point to this dual aspect of the created universe as do the concepts of *lawḥ*, the Well-preserved Tablet (Sūra 85:22), and *qalam*, the primordial Pen (Sūra 68:1), which work together to write the creatures' destiny.

The idea that God created the world by His word in one moment or, according to another counting, in six days, was paralleled by the mystical concept of the 'hidden treasure'. Ibn ʿArabī developed the myth of the longing Divine Names which, utterly lonely and so to speak 'non-existent', that is, not yet actualized in the depths of the Divine, longed for existence and burst out in an act comparable to Divine exhalation. The Names manifested themselves in the universe, which thus became their mirror; contingent being received existence as soon as it was hit by the Name which was to be its *rabb*, 'Lord'. Creation is thus a work of Divine love, but also of Divine self-love – God longed to see His beauty in the mirror of the created things.[27]

The breath by which this manifestation took place is the *nafas ar-raḥmān*, the 'breath of the Merciful', which is, so to speak, the substance of Creation: pure Mercy and pure Existence are, as it were, the same in the visions of the Ibn ʿArabī school.

The sudden outbreak of the Divine breath may be called a mystical parallel to the modern Big Bang theory; in either case, one cannot go behind that moment, and the Divine that caused it remains absolutely transcendent while we see 'as through a looking-glass'. Non-discerning people admire only the highly decorated reverse side of the mirror (medieval steel mirrors were often artistically decorated); they enjoy 'the world' without recognizing the face of the mirror which can reflect the eternal beauty. By doing so, they are clearly branded as infidels because, according to the Koran, the world, *dunyā*, is embellished for the infidels (Sūra 2:212). While the Muslims are called to see God's marvels in creation as pointing to Him, and to listen to the adoration of everything created, they are also warned, in the Koran, not to rely upon the *dunyā*, 'this world', which is usually contrasted with *al-ākhira*, the Otherworld, the Hereafter. This world, so the Koran states, was created for play and jest (Sūra 57:20). The pleasure derived from the world and its use is but small (Sūra 4:77 et al.), for the world cheats humankind (Sūra 3:185 et al.) – that is why it appears in traditional images often as a cunning, lecherous old hag who attracts lovers to kill them afterwards. For the *dunyā* is the power which can divert humans from the Hereafter (Sūra 87:16), and those who prefer it to the future life (Sūra 2:86, 4:74) or love it more (Sūra 14:3, 16:107) are warned and called upon to repent.[28]

Therefore, this world was often blamed by the sage; Ibn Abī Dunyā's book *Dhamm ad-dunyā* is a good example of this genre. Sufi handbooks abound in such blame, and the aversion to the 'world' permeates much of Sufi-minded literature.

On the other hand, one should keep in mind that the world – even if it be worth only a gnat's wing (*AM* no. 645) – is God's creation, and gives human beings an environment where they can perform worship and improve its conditions: 'do not ruin the world after it has been set straight' (Sūra 7:56), warns the Koran, and modern Muslims have taken this *āya* as a command to work for the improvement of the environment, for one will be asked how one has practised one's responsibility in the world. For this reason, the normative believer disliked overstressed mortification and that kind of *tawakkul*, 'trust in God', which left no room for activity:[29] Rūmī, practically-minded as he was, states that 'negligence' is also necessary, for if everyone were busy only with ascetic pursuits and works that lead to the Hereafter, how would the world continue and thrive as God had ordered it?

And more than that: the world – again according to Rūmī – is like a tent for the king, and everyone performs his or her work in embellishing this tent: tentmaker and weaver, ropemaker and those who drive in the pegs or the nails are engaged in some work, and their work is their praise for God whose glorification they intend by performing their various occupations. And those who love his world because it proves God's creative power and contains the signs that point to Him are, as Ghazzālī holds, the true monotheists.[30]

The myth of the 'hidden treasure' was widely circulated among the Sufis. But there is still another creation myth which was not as generally accepted. It is the vision of Suhrawardī the Master of Illumination, according to whom Creation came into existence by means of the sound of Gabriel's wings: the archangel's right wing is sheer light, oneness, mercy and beauty, while his left wing has some darkness in it and points to multiplicity, Divine wrath and majesty; it is directed towards the created universe which, in turn, is maintained through innumerable ranges of angels through whom the primordial light, the Divine Essence *kat' exochén*, is filtered down into the universe and finally reaches humankind.[31]

Suhrawardī's angelology is a central piece of his philosophy, but angels are an important part of creation in general and thus play a great role in the religious cosmos of the Muslims.[32] Sūra 35 is called 'The Angels', and, in Sūra 2:98, people are mentioned who 'are enemies of God and the angels, the messengers and of Gabriel and Michael'. Thus, belief in the angels is part of the Muslim creed.

Angels are treasurers of God's mercy; they are imagined to be luminous beings but will die at the end of time, to be resurrected immediately and transferred to Paradise. Angels, so Muslims believe, accompany the mortals at every step (Sūra 13:11), but they do not enter places where a picture or a dog is found. They spread the shade of their wings over saints and martyrs or, in Shia tradition, the imams. They have different occupations: thus four, or eight of them carry the Divine Throne (Sūra 69:17), but their main duty is constant worship; adoration is their food and drink, silence is their speech; yet each group of angels which is engaged in ritual prayer performs only one of the prayer positions. They have no free will, and are obedient: only once, so the Koran tells, did they question God's wisdom, that is, when He announced His intention to create Adam and appoint him as *khalīfa*, 'vicegerent' (Sūra 2:30). But after acquiescing to God's will and command, they prostrated themselves before the newly-created Adam. The brief remark (Sūra 2:102) about the disobedient and rather frivolous angels Hārūt and Mārūt offered imaginative exegetes good story material.

Two angels, the *kirām kātibīn* (Sūra 82:11), sit on the human being's shoulders to note down his actions and thoughts. But there are also nineteen angels under the leadership of one Malik who are in charge of Hell (Sūra 74:30).

Tradition and the Koran know of four archangels. The first is Michael (whose wings, as Muslims believe, are all covered with emeralds); he is in charge of the distribution of nourishment to all creatures, and it was he who taught Adam to answer the greeting of peace with the words *wa raḥmatu Allāhi wa barakātuhu*, 'And God's mercy and blessings be upon you'. Michael, so it is told, never laughed after Hell was created.

Most prominent in the Koran is Gabriel who is also called *ar-rūḥ al-amīn*, 'the faithful spirit' (Sūra 26:193), and even *rūḥ al-quds*, 'the holy spirit' (Sūra 2:87, 5:110, 16:102). He lives by looking at God, and he is the messenger in charge of the prophets: as he taught Adam the alphabet and agriculture, he instructed Noah in how to build the ark, offered assistance to Abraham when he was flung into the blazing pyre, and taught David to weave coats-of-mail. But more importantly, he was the one who placed God's word into the Virgin Mary so that she could give birth to Jesus, the Word Incarnate, and likewise brought the revelation to Muhammad, the unstained vessel for the Word Inlibrate. Gabriel accompanied the Prophet on his heavenly journey, but had to stay back at the *sidrat al-muntahā* (*AM* no. 444) 'like a nightingale that is separated from his rose', as the Turkish poet Ghanizade sang in the seventeenth century.[32] The idea that only the Prophet could transgress the limits of the created universe and enter the immediate Divine Presence induced thinkers and especially mystics to equate Gabriel with intellect (or Intellect) – for intellect can lead the seeker in the way towards God, unfailingly and dutifully, but is not allowed into the bridal chamber of Love.

The third archangel, not mentioned by name in the Koran but very popular in Muslim tradition, is Isrāfīl, who will blow the trumpet that starts the Resurrection. For this reason, poets liked to compare the thunder's sound in spring to Isrāfīl's trumpet, which inaugurates the resurrection of flowers and plants from the seemingly dead dust. Others, not exactly modest, have likened their pen's scratching to Isrāfīl's trumpet because they hoped, or assumed, that their words might awaken their slumbering compatriots and cause a 'spiritual resurrection'. Even the word of a saint or the beloved could be compared to Isrāfīl's trumpet because of its reviving qualities.

The most dreaded archangel is 'Azrā'īl, the angel of death, who, as Muslims tell, was the only angel who dared to grasp clay for Adam's creation from four parts of the earth, and who will tear out the human soul at the appointed hour and place, gently in the case of a believer, painfully in the case of a sinner. However, as mystics claimed, he has no power over those who have already 'died before dying' by annihilating themselves in God.

There is a host of angels with strange-sounding names which are used in incantations and magic prayers, and in Suhrawardī's philosophy, angels are seen as the celestial selves of humans. In the later mystical tradition, an angel *Nūn* appears, connected with the Pen (cf. Sūra 68:1).

An initial encounter with the angel at the beginning of the spiritual path is common to all visionary recitals, especially in the Persianate world, and Iran has contributed the angelic being Sarōsh to medieval Muslim angelology (at least in the eastern lands of Islam). Sarōsh, an old Zoroastrian angelic being, appears as parallel to Gabriel; but while the archangel brings the Divine word, the religious revelation to prophets, Sarōsh appears usually as inspiring poets.

As important as the angels may be, man is still higher than they because he can choose between good and evil and is capable of development, while the angels are perfect but static, bound to be good. The daring expression that the true lover of God can 'hunt angels' occurs in Rūmī's and sometimes in other mystics' Persian verse. It was taken up, in the twentieth century, by Iqbāl, for whom angels are but a lowly prey for the true believer who is 'the falcon of the lord of *lawlāk'*, that is, of the Prophet. Iqbāl has often poetically described how the angels gaze at the Perfect Man and praise him and his position in the universe.[34]

Angels are created from light; other spiritual beings, however, are created from fire (Sūra 15:27, 55:15). These are the djinns and devils. Sūra 72 deals with the djinns. They can embrace Islam, and Muslims believe that marriages between djinns and humans are possible and legally permitted – perhaps the name of the grammarian Ibn Djinnī (d. 1002) points to this belief. Sulaymān, king and mighty prophet, ruled over the djinn as he ruled over all kinds of creatures, and numerous incantations and talismans against spirits of sorts are prepared in his name, for he was able to imprison some particularly nasty specimens of that race in bottles which he then sealed and cast into the ocean. The 'fairy in the bottle' has lived on to this day in fairytales, romances and television films.

Among the spirits, Iblīs, *diabolus*, Satan, occupies a special place. He too is God's creature, and never appears as God's enemy or an anti-divine power. He was the teacher of the angels, credited with thousands of years of perfect obedience, but his pride made him claim to be superior to Adam (Sūra 38:76) as fire is superior to clay. His refusal to fall down before Adam, a logical outcome of his pride, was nevertheless interpreted differently: according to al-Ḥallāj and his followers, Iblīs preferred to obey God's eternal will that nobody should prostrate himself before anything but Him, and not His outspoken command to fall down before Adam. Caught between Divine will and command, he emerges as a tragic figure and became the model of the true lover who would rather accept his beloved's curse than disobey his will[35] – an idea that even reached the remote Indus Valley, where Shāh ʿAbdul Laṭīf sang: *ʿāshiq ʿazāzīl* – "ʿAzāzīl [i.e. Satan] is the true lover'.[36]

This interpretation was, however, restricted to a very small group of Sufis, for usually Iblīs represents the one-eyed intellect who did not see the Divine spark in Adam but only the form of clay.

Nāṣir-i Khusraw, speaking of the 'devils of [his] time', that is, the people who seem to corrupt the true faith, thinks that nowadays devils are of clay rather than of fire – an idea that is also found in Iqbāl's highly interesting satanology. Iqbāl considers Iblīs as a necessary force in life, because only by fighting him in the 'greater Holy War' can one grow into a perfect human being. In a remarkable poetical scene in the *Jāvīdnāma*, Iqbāl translated Iblīs's complaint that man is too obedient to him and thus constantly blackens his, Satan's, books while he longs to be vanquished by the true Man of God to find rescue from the Divine curse. Iblīs makes life colourful as the *jihād* against him gives human life a meaning; and, as Iqbāl says in a very daring Urdu verse, Iblīs 'pricks God's side like a thorn', while his 'old comrade' Gabriel and the angels are complacent and obedient and thus do not contribute much to make life interesting or worth living.[37]

Iqbāl's approach to Iblīs is probably inspired by a famous *ḥadīth* in which the

Prophet, asked how his *shayṭān*, his 'lower soul' fared, answered: *aslama shayṭānī*, 'My *shayṭān* has surrendered himself [or: has become a Muslim] and does only what I order him'. That means that, by educating one's lower faculties by sublimating the *nafs*, one can achieve positive results just as a converted thief will make the best policeman because he knows the tricks of the trade and how to deal with insubordinate people. That is why Iqbāl's Iblīs longs to be trained and educated by a true believer.

Iblīs, similar to Goethe's Mephistopheles, remains under God's command and can be overcome by human striving. This idea, as well as the fact that Islam does not accept the concept of original sin, led a number of critics to the conclusion that Islam does not take seriously the problem of evil. This seems to be a somewhat questionable viewpoint. Even without the concept of original sin and all the problems that result from it, culminating in the necessity of redemption, the thought of man's weakness, sinfulness and his tendency to prefer the ephemeral pleasures of this world to the good ordained by God permeates the Koran, and evil is certainly a problem which is discussed, even if only in the emphasis on *istighfār*, 'asking for forgiveness', and the numerous prayers in which generations of Muslims have confessed their sins, shivering in fear of God's punishment and yet hoping for His grace because the gate of repentance remains open until the sun rises from the West (*AM* no. 390). This attitude becomes clear when one thinks of the eschatological part of the revelation. It is absolutely clear from the Koran that the world is transient – everything that is in it will perish save God's countenance (Sūra 28:88; cf. 55:26f.).

Is death not sufficient as a warner? The Muslims asked this repeatedly; every day, one sees how humans, animals, plants and even the firm-looking mountains die and decay. Hence the only thing that really matters is to prepare oneself for the day when one will meet one's Lord. For: 'Everyone will taste death' (Sūra 29:57 et al.). Ghazzālī's *Iḥyā' 'ulūm ad-dīn* is nothing but a slow preparation for the moment when one has to face God. The way to that dreaded moment is facilitated – so Ghazzālī may have pondered – by guiding the Muslim through the traditional forty steps (in the forty chapters of his book) and teaching the requirements for a life that, as one may hope, will lead to heavenly bliss. All knowledge, as Muslims know, is only accumulated to prepare the human being for the Hereafter. Only those who have longed all their life to meet with their spiritual Beloved may look forward to death, for 'death is the bridge that leads the lover to the Beloved'[38] and 'Death is the fragrant herb for the believer' (*AM* no. 364).

When the Muslim passes through the last agony, the profession of faith is recited into his or her ears so that he or she can answer the questions which Munkar and Nakīr, the angels in the grave, will ask; for those who answer correctly, the grave will be wide and lofty, while sinners and infidels will suffer in the narrow, dark hole and be tormented by snakes and scorpions. Praying a *Fātiḥa* for their soul or planting a tree on the site of the grave may alleviate their pain.[39]

The status of the dead between death and resurrection has been variously described: one encounters the idea of the soul's sleep until resurrection, as also the idea of a foretaste of the future life. 'The tomb is one of the gardens of Paradise or one of the holes of Hell' (*AM* no. 433). Dream appearances in which the deceased tells what happened to him or her sound as if one already had a full knowledge of one's future fate without the general Judgment.

But what is this death? Muslims know that 'everything hastens towards a fixed term' (Sūra 13:2). Are people not asleep and do they not awake when they die (*AM* no. 222), as the Prophet said? The feeling that this life is nothing but a dreamlike preparation for the true life in the world to come permeates much of pious thought. However, one should not think that this dream has no consequences – the *ḥadīth* states clearly that 'this world is the seedbed for the next world' (*AM* no. 338), and one will see the interpretation of one's so-called 'dream' in the morning light of eternity. Death could thus be seen as a mirror of one's actions: at this moment, one will see whether one's face is ugly or beautiful, black or white; it is, to use Swedenborg's expression, 'the unveiling of the true Self'. Death is the fruit of life; it is, as one says in Persian, *baghalparwarde*, 'brought up in one's armpit' so that one will experience the death which one has prepared, unwittingly, during one's lifetime. Rūmī has often dwelt upon these ideas in his verse, and the poems in popular literature that sing of the spinning or weaving of one's gown for the wedding day, that is for the death or resurrection, symbolize the same idea. Those who love God would sing again with Rūmī:

> If death's a man, let him come close to me
> that I can take him tightly to my breast.
> I'll take from him a soul, pure, colourless:
> He'll take from me a coloured frock, that's all.

Death could also be seen as a homecoming – be it the nightingale's return to the rose-garden, or the drop's merging into the ocean, its true home.

Death can be seen as spiritual nuptials, and the term *ʿurs* for the memorial days of a saint's death expresses this feeling. At such an *ʿurs*, people would come to the site of a saintly person's mausoleum to participate in the dead person's increased spiritual power, although the Prophet warned of the danger of 'turning a grave into a festive site'. The correct way of visiting tombs, says Shāh Walīullāh, who quotes this *ḥadīth*, is to read the Koran, pray for the deceased, give alms or manumit a slave in the name of the deceased – that will be credited to his or her soul.[40]

If individual death suffices as a warning, then the Koranic revelations about the Day of Judgment are meant to strengthen this warning. There is an astounding number of descriptions of the Day, the Hour and the Knocking One in the earliest revelations, which continually point to this horrible event in new, ever more powerful words, sentences and whole Sūras.[41] Perhaps the hour is closer than the distance between two fingers (*AM* no. 350)? Perhaps it will even happen tomorrow ...

Sūra 81 is one of the strongest descriptions:

> When the sun shall be darkened,
> when the stars shall be thrown down,
> when the mountains shall be set moving,
> when the pregnant camels shall be neglected,
> when the savage beasts shall be mustered,
> when the seas shall be set boiling,
> when the souls shall be coupled,
> when the buried infant shall be asked for what sin she was slain,
> when the scrolls shall be unrolled,
> when Heaven shall be stripped off,
> when Hell shall be set blazing,
> when Paradise shall be brought nigh,
> then shall a soul know what it had produced.
>
> (transl. A. J. Arberry)

The Meccans, practically-minded as they were, did not take seriously the threats of the impending Judgment, let alone the idea of a resurrection; but not only the growth of the human foetus in the womb but also the 'resurrection' of plants from the dead earth should be proof enough. That accounts for the abundance of spring poems in which the imagery of resurrection is used, for in spring the trees will be covered with the green silken robes of Paradise.

Many mythological tales and many allegorical stories were woven around the events before and during Resurrection, such as the return of Jesus and the arrival of the Mahdi. But the central image is that of a terrible confusion on a day that is hundreds of years long. In Islamic languages, the term *qiyāmat*, 'resurrection', often means something incredibly confused – *kĭyamet koptu* in Turkish is 'everything was upside down, was in a terrible state'. The poets, on the other hand, often complain that a day without the beloved is 'longer than the day of Resurrection'.

Popular tradition claims that death will be slaughtered in the shape of a ram. This is one of the numerous fanciful tales, but there is much Koranic foundation for other details of the Day of Judgment: first of all, no soul can carry the burden of another soul (Sūra 2:48), for everyone is responsible for his or her actions and, as tradition has it, every limb will testify for or against its owner. The actions which the angel-scribes have noted down in the books will be given in everyone's left or right hand – left for the sinners, right for the pious. These books can be blackened from sins, but are white and radiant thanks to pious and lawful action; likewise, the sinners have black faces and the blessed have white ones (Sūra 3:106 et al.).

Poets have sometimes expressed their hope for forgiveness in an image taken from the art of calligraphy: as Oriental ink is soluble in water, they hoped, metaphorically, to wash off the black letters in their book of actions with tears of repentance.

Scales will be put up (Sūra 21:47 et al.), and, as Sūra 99 states even more emphatically, when the earth opens, everyone will see what he or she has done, even if it is as small as a mustard seed. The Balance is, so to speak, an eschatological symbol of justice and equilibrium. It is, however, not completely clear what is actually being weighed on the scales – is it the actions themselves, the book or the person? One has also to face the Bridge, which is thinner than a hair and sharper than a sword's edge. Rūmī has taken up the ancient Iranian concept of the *daēna* who will meet the soul at the Bridge to guide it – in the shape of a beautiful young girl in case of a pious person, but as an old ugly hag when a sinner arrives. He ingeniously combines this idea with the Koranic descriptions of death and Judgment.

> Your good ethical qualities will run before you after your death –
> Like ladies, moon-faced, do these qualities proudly walk ...
> When you have divorced the body, you will see houris in rows,
> 'Muslim ladies, faithful women, devout and repenting ladies'.
>
> (Sūra 66:5)
>
> Without number will your characteristics run before your bier ...
> In the coffin these pure qualities will become your companions,
> They will cling to you like sons and daughters,
> And you will put on garments from the warp and woof of your works of obedience ...
>
> (*D* no. 385)

In popular traditions, it was assumed that good acts turn into light and that everything assumes a tangible form: sinners may appear as dogs or pigs according to their dirty habits, while the believers' virtues will come to intercede for them; mosques appear as 'boats of salvation' or as white camels to those who have regularly prayed with the community; the rams sacrificed at the *ʿīd al-aḍḥā* will carry the person who offered them across the bridge; the Koran and Islam come as persons, Friday as a young bridegroom, and prayer, fasting or patience will all be there to intercede for those who have cared for them and performed works of obedience.[42] Children who died in infancy will bring their parents to the paradisiacal meadows lest they feel lonely; and, most importantly, the Prophet will come with the green 'banner of praise', *liwā al-ḥamd*, to intercede for the sinners in his community (*AM* no. 225).

While normal believers will be interrogated in the grave, the martyrs will enter Paradise directly and await resurrection in special places, for they 'are alive with their Lord' (Sūra 3:169).

The compensation of good and evil posed a problem at some point, because the Muʿtazilites claimed that God *must* punish the sinner and reward the pious, which is a position incompatible with the faith in the omnipotent Lord, who must not be asked what He does (Sūra 21:23) – and who could know whether he or she will be among those who are saved?

The world to come is, no doubt, an intensification of this world. Therefore both mistakes and virtuous deeds appear incredibly enlarged in the form of punishments or compensations. Time and again, the Koran points to terrible details of the punishments in Hell, and it was easy for the commentators and even more for the popular preachers to embellish the Koranic data. When in the Koran Hell is mentioned, for example as calling out *Hal min mazīd*, 'Is there no more?' (Sūra 50:30), then it is described in popular tradition as a dragon with 30,000 heads, each of which has 30,000 mouths, and in each mouth are 30,000 teeth, etc. The central characteristic of Hell is the fire, a fire that rages and burns people, whose skin is renewed again and again to make them suffer infinitely (Sūra 4:56). The food of the inhabitants of Hell is the fruits of poisonous trees, *zaqqūm* (Sūra 44:43), and their drink is all kinds of dirty stuff, such as *dhū ghuslayn* (as Naṣir-i Khusraw repeatedly states), that is, water in which ablution has been performed twice, therefore very dirty water.[43]

The descriptions of Hell led the believers to speculate on whether or not these torments would be eternal, for Sūra 11:108–9 says: 'The damned enter the Fire ... to remain therein as long as Heaven and Earth exist, except if God should decree otherwise', a word that opens doors to different interpretations.

While the Muʿtazilites regarded eternal punishment in Hell as a logical corollary of God's justice, and Abū Ḥanīfa had claimed that 'Heaven and Hell are realities never to disappear', later scholars drew the reader's attention to Sūra 28:88, which states that 'everything is perishing save the countenance of God', and to its parallel in Sūra 55:26. That implies, one would think, that even Heaven and Hell, being created, will perish and cease to exist – and might not God 'decree otherwise' (Sūra 11:108)? According to a later *ḥadīth*, one could find consolation in the thought that 'there will be a day when the floor of Hell is humid and cress will grow out of it' – for there cannot be a limit to God's power and mercy. Did He not make seven gates for Hell but eight doors for paradise to show that His mercy is greater than His wrath (cf. *AM* no. 64)?

Some thinkers seem to transform Hell into a kind of purgatory. Rūmī's statement in *Fīhi mā fīhi* points to a wholesome aspect of Hell, strange as it may sound to us:

> The inhabitants of Hell will be happier in Hell than they were on Earth because there they remember their Lord.

While all religions seem to compete in describing the horrifying and gruesome aspects of Hell, it seems much harder to describe the joys of Paradise.

The 'sensual' images of Paradise in the Koran have angered Christian theologians for centuries: the ideal of 'gardens under which river flow' (Sūra 2:25 et al.) might be acceptable (and has influenced the architecture of mausoleums surrounded by watercourses), but the large-eyed virgins, the luscious fruits and drinks, the green couches and the like seemed too worldly to most non-Muslim critics.[44] Such symbols, of course, are prone to invite crude elaborations, and some descriptions in theological works, let alone popular visions of Paradise, take the brief Koranic words too much at face value and indulge in images of 70,000 rooms with 70,000 beds in each of them, each with 70,000 pillows on each of which 70,000 virgins are waiting, whose beauty and tenderness is then further depicted. One could, however, interpret the houris and the fruits as symbolizing the greatest happiness, that of perfect union with the Beloved, and of the ancient belief that one can attain union with the Holy by eating it (see above, p. 107).

While the descriptions of Paradise were materialized and clumsified by imaginative people, one of the true concerns of the pious was the question of whether or not one could see God in paradise. While the Muʿtazilites categorically denied such a possibility, the traditional Muslim view was that it is possible, at least at intervals, and the *ḥadīth* 'and your Lord is smiling' was applied to the inexhaustible happiness caused by the inexplicable experience called the 'smile' of Divine Beloved.

But the Koran also offers another picture of Paradise, namely that it is filled with laud and praise of God while the blessed exchange the greetings of peace (Sūra 10:10–11; cf. also 36:58). Based on this Koranic Sūra, Abū Ḥafs ʿOmar as-Suhrawardī spoke of the country of Paradise which consists of fields whose plants are praise and laud of God;[45] and a century after him, the Turkish bard Yunus Emre sang in the same style:

S ol cennetin ĭrmaklarĭ
akar Allah deyu deyu ...
The rivers all in Paradise
they flow and say Allah Allah ...[46]

The all-too-human descriptions of Paradise and their endless variations in the works of fanciful preachers and poets were criticized by both philosophers and mystics. The philosophers partly denied bodily resurrection (Avicenna) or taught that a simulacrum would be supplied (Averroes),[47] or stated that only the soul survives; rather, only the souls of highly-developed thinkers and knowledgeable people will live on, while the simple souls, like grass, are destroyed at death. These ideas, in a different key, resurface in Iqbāl's philosophy.

The Sufis criticized people who rely on the hope of Paradise or fear of Hell and need these feelings, as it were, to stimulate them to worship. Rābiʿa (d. 801) was probably the first to voice her criticism, and wanted 'to put fire to Paradise and pour water into Hell' so that these two veils might disappear. Why turn to such veils? After all, human beings are created for God. Alluding to the story that Adam left Paradise because he ate the forbidden fruit or, in Islamic tradition, the grain, one writer asks:

> Why would you want to settle in a place which your father Adam sold for a grain?[48]

Paradise, says Yunus Emre, is a snare to catch human hearts, while five centuries later in Muslim India, Ghālib called the traditional 'Paradise which the mullah covets: a withered nosegay in the niche of forgetfulness of us who have lost ourselves ...'.[49]

In certain trends, the degrees, *darajāt*, to which the Koran allusively speaks (Sūra 17:21; cf. also *AM* no. 306), are understood not as different gardens in Paradise but as alluding to the transmigration of the soul. This interpretation occurs among the early Shia and the Ismailis.

But how to define these degrees? They seem to point to the fact that what the Muslim awaits in the Hereafter is not a static, unchanging immortality:

> If our salvation means to be free from quest,
> the tomb would be better than such an afterlife –

says Iqbāl.[50] As God's perfections are infinite, the climax is also infinite. Tor Andrae in Sweden wrote: 'To live means to grow – if future life is a real life, then it is impossible that it could be eternally unchangeable, happy bliss'.[51] At the same time, Iqbāl, who was not aware of Andrae's work, interpreted old images of Paradise and Hell in modern terms: according to him, man is only a candidate for personal immortality (an idea which was sharply attacked by several Muslim theologians).

For Iqbāl, Hell is the realization of one's failure in one's achievements, while Heaven is a 'growing without diminishing' after the individual, who has strengthened himself sufficiently, has overcome the shock of corporeal death.[52] Then a new phase begins, entering into ever-deeper layers of the Infinite, for 'Heaven is no holiday'.[53] Once the journey to God is finished, the infinite journey in God begins.

NOTES

1. A general work is A. Schimmel and A. Falaturi (eds) (1980), *We Believe in One God. The Experience of God in Christianity and Islam.*
2. Quoted in K. Cragg (1965), *Counsels in Contemporary Islam*, p. 38.
3. Quoted in K. Cragg (1984), '*Tadabbur al-Qur'ān*', p. 187.
4. H. Ringgren (1953), *Fatalism in Persian Epics*; idem (1955), *Studies in Arabic Fatalism*; W. M. Watt (1948), *Free Will and Predestination in Early Islam.*
5. Quoted in F. Heiler, *Erscheinungsformen* (1961), p. 514.

6. Fazlur Rahman (1966), *Islam*, p. 45.
7. Daud Rahbar (1960), *God of Justice*, is the classic.
8. Eric L. Ormsby (1984) *Theodicy in Islamic Thought*; H. Zirker (1991), 'Er wird nicht befragt ... (Sūra 21:24). Theodizee und Theodizeeabwehr in Koran und Umgebung'.
9. Frederick M. Denny (1984), 'The problem of salvation'.
10. F. Meier (1990b), 'Zum Vorrang des Glaubens und des "guten Denkens" vor dem Wahrheitseifer bei den Muslimen', deals with 'thinking good of God'.
11. *Fīhi mā fīhi*, ch. 12.
12. Azim Nanji (1987), 'Isma'ilism', p. 187.
13. M. Horten (1917b), *Die religiöse Gedankenwelt des Volkes*, p. 70.
14. Frederick J. Barney (1933), 'The creed of al-Sanūsī'; R. Hartmann (1992), *Die Religion des Islams* (new ed.), pp. 55–8.
15. P. Nwyia (1970), *Exégèse coranique*, p. 249.
16. William Chittick (1992), 'Spectrums of Islamic thought: Sa'id al-Din Farghānī on the implications of Oneness and Manyness'. The contrast between *waḥdat al-wujūd* and *kathrat al-'ilm* also occurs in earlier times; see R. Gramlich (1983b), *At-tajrīd fī kalimat at-tanḥīd. Der reine Gottesglaube*, p. 12.
17. Sanā'ī (1950), *Ḥadīqat al-ḥaqīqa*, p. 60.
18. There may have been other visions as well, such as that of Bahā-i Walad, who 'saw His forgiveness like a whiteness composed of pearls': Bahā-i Walad (1957), *Ma'ārif*, vol. IV, p. 33.
19. al-Ḥallāj (1931), *Dīwān, muqaṭṭa'* no. 10.
20. Quoted in Bikrama Jit Hasrat (1953), *Dara Shikuh: Life and Works*, p. 151, quatrain no. xix. The Anṣārī quote is from S. Langier de Beaurecueil, *Khwādja 'Abdullāh Anṣārī (396–481 h/1006–1089) Mystique Hanbalite*, 1965.
21. Sanā'ī (1962), *Dīwān*, p. 385.
22. S. H. Nasr (1964), *An Introduction to Islamic Cosmological Doctrines*; H. Halm (1978), *Kosmologie und Heilslehre der frühen Isma'iliyya.*
23. See A. Schimmel (1978c), *The Triumphal Sun*, s.v. *'adam.*
24. S. Murata (1992b), *The Tao of Islam*, p. 148.
25. Nāṣir-i Khusraw (1924), *Dīwān*, p. 254; p. 48.
26. Fazlur Rahman (1966), *Islam*, p. 121.
27. H. Corbin (1958), *L'imagination créatrice*, deals with this 'longing of the Names' and related problems. See also H. S. Nyberg (1919), *Kleinere Schriften des Ibn al-'Arabi*, p. 85.
28. A fine survey of the use of *dunyā* is in R. Gramlich (1976), *Die schiitischen Derwischorden*, vol. 2, p. 91ff.
29. B. Reinert (1968), *Die Lehre vom* tawakkul *in der klassischen Sufik*, shows the different aspects of 'trust in God' and its exaggerations.
30. Ghazzālī (1872), *Iḥyā' 'ulūm ad-dīn*, part IV, p. 276.
31. Suhrawardī (1935), *Awāz-i parr-i Jibrīl*: 'Le bruissement de l'aile de Gabriel', ed and transl. by H. Corbin and P. Kraus. For Suhrawardī's angelology in general, see H. Corbin (1989), *L'homme et son ange.*
32. W. Eickmann (1908), *Die Angelologie und Dämonologie des Korans im Vergleich zu der Engel- und Geisterlehre der Heiligen Schrift.* Toufic Fahd (1971), 'Anges, démons et djinns en Islam'.
33. This story is based on a *ḥadīth* (AM no. 444); an English translation appears in A. Schimmel (1988), *And Muhammad is His Messenger*, p. 116.
34. Iqbāl (1937), *Zarb-i Kalīm*, p. 133; idem (1936), *Bāl-i Jibrīl*, pp. 92, 119; idem (1927), *Zabūr-i 'ajam*, part 2, p. 16. For the topic, see Schimmel (1963a), *Gabriel's Wing*, pp. 208–19.
35. Peter J. Awn (1983), *Satan's Tragedy and Redemption: Iblis in Sufi Psychology*; see also

Schimmel (1963a), *Gabriel's Wing*, pp. 208–19. For a traditional approach, see P. Eichler (1929?), *Die Dschinn, Teufel und Engel im Koran.*

36. Shāh ʿAbdul Laṭīf (1958), *Risālō*, 'Sur Yaman Kalyān', ch. V, line 24.
37. Iqbāl (1936), *Bāl-i Jibrīl*, p. 192f. See Schimmel (1963a), *Gabriel's Wing*, pp. 208–19.
38. Quoted in Abū Nuʿaym al-Iṣfahānī (1967), *Ḥilyat al-awliyā*, vol. 10, p. 9.
39. Irene Grütter (1956), 'Arabische Bestattungsbräuche in frühislamischer Zeit'; César W. Dubler (1950), 'Über islamischen Grab- und Heiligenkult'. F. Meier (1973), 'Ein profetenwort gegen die totenbeweinung', deals with the problem of whether or not the dead are suffering when their relatives and friends cry after their death.
40. A useful survey of all the names by which Resurrection and Judgment are known is 'Resurrection and Judgement in the Kor'an'.
41. The literature about Muslim eschatology is quite large: see D. S. Attema (1942), *De mohammedaansche opvattingen omtrent het tijdstip van den Jongsten Dag en zijn voortekenen*; Al-Ghazālī (1989), 'The remembrance of death and the Afterlife …', transl. by J. T. Winter; R. Leszyinski (1909), *Muhammadanische Traditionen über das Jüngste Gericht*; L. Massignon (1939), 'Die Auferstehung in der mohammedanischen Welt'; ʿAbd ar-Raḥīm ibn Aḥmad al-Qāḍī (1977), *Islamic Book of the Dead*; al-Ḥāriṯ ibn Asad al-Muḥāsibī (1978), *Kitāb at-tawahhum: Une vision humaine des fins dernières*; Taede Huitema (1936), *De Voorspraak (shafāʿa) in den Islam*; Thomas O'Shaughnessy (1969), *Muhammad's Thoughts on Death*; idem (1986), *Eschatological Themes in the Qurʿan*; Jane Smith and Yvonne Haddad (1981), *The Islamic Understanding of Death and Resurrection.* For a far-reaching problem, see M. Asín Palacios (1919), *La escatologia musulmana en la Divina Comedia.*
42. M. Horten, *Die religiöse Gedankenwelt des Volkes*, p. 253, also p. 74.
43. M Wolff (1872), *Mohammedanische Eschatologie, nach den aḥwālu'l-qiyāma, arabisch und deutsch*; J. Meyer (1901–2), *Die Hölle im Islam.*
44. C. LeGai Eaton (1982), *Islam and the Destiny of Man*, last chapter, contains a remarkably 'sensual' description of Paradise, which seems amazing in a book written recently by a British Muslim, which is otherwise highly recommendable for modern readers.
45. Suhrawardī (1978), *ʿAwārif* (transl. R. Gramlich), p. 297.
46. *Yunus Emre Divanï* (1943), p. 477.
47. Fazlur Rahman (1966), *Islam*, p. 119.
48. Samʿānī, quoted in S. Murata (1992b), *The Tao of Islam*, p. 65.
49. Ghālib (1969b), *Urdu Dīwān*, p. 9.
50. A. Schimmel (1963a), *Gabriel's Wing*, pp. 273–306.
51. Tor Andrae (1940), *Die letzten Dinge*, p. 93ff., especially p. 99.
52. In his notebook of 1910, *Stray Reflections* (1961), Iqbāl noted (no. 15): 'Personal immortality is not a state, it is a process … it lies in our own hands'.
53. Iqbāl (1930), *The Reconstruction of Religious Thought*, p. 123. See also Schimmel (1963a), *Gabriel's Wing*, pp. 119–23.

VII

How to Approach Islam?

And We shall show them Our signs in the horizons and in themselves.

Sūra 41:53

In which language does the modern Muslim express himself, his faith and his ideals? That is a question not only of philology but also of a general attitude, visible in modern art, audible in modern music, reflected in modern literature and thus a question that concerns every aspect of life.[1]

The use of broadcasting not only for the recitation of the Koran but also for giving legal decisions, *fatwā* (as is the case for example in Yemen); the fact that in Cairo a *walī* heals by telephone every Friday between 9 and 11 a.m.; and the reactions to spaceships and computer technology make us ask: how can the modern Muslim, faced with the overwhelming success of Western technology, find a way to accept and cope with the time-honoured teachings of traditional *tafsīr* and *ḥadīth* in modern times? Is not a science, *ʿilm*, which is basically geared toward a preparation of human beings for the Hereafter, obsolete and to be discarded?

To silence opponents, sceptics and worried souls, it is often proclaimed that Islam is self-sufficient, that it owes nothing to other religions and philosophical systems but rather that it endowed the West with scholarly discoveries during the dark 'Middle Ages'; and that Islam alone contains the final truth, as Muhammad was the Seal of Prophets. This answer, usually given by so-called fundamentalists, leaves most Western seekers and quite a number of Western-educated Muslims unsatisfied, simple and convincing as it is.

To be sure, nobody nowadays would agree with the poisonous remark written by an unsuccessful missionary to the Muslims and published in *The Moslem World* (12, 1922, p. 25):

> Even if a savage found a full satisfaction in animism, or a semi-civilized man in Islam, that does not prove that either animism or Islam could meet the need of civilized man.

The extreme wealth of Islamic literatures, of works of art, of psychological insight as developed over the centuries in Sufism; the refined though (for an outsider's understanding) complicated network of legal and ritual prescriptions: all this is being discovered slowly in the West, and attempts to understand and interpret Islam, especially in its mystical dimensions, for modern Westerners are increasing, as is the number of converts in Europe and America.

Scholars and politicians used to ask whether Islam can be 'reformed', and whether it has to be reformed. During my years at the Ilâhiyat Fakültesi in Ankara, where we worked to introduce young Muslim theologians to the techniques of modern critical scholarship and European thought-systems to enlarge their horizons, one question surfaced time and again: is there no Luther available for Islam? Turkish students as well as modernist thinkers have often mentioned the example of Luther as a possible 'saviour' for present-day Muslims (while Iqbāl, well read in European history, saw him as a negative force responsible for the break-up of Christian Europe!). However, as Islam has no structure comparable to that of the Roman Catholic Church, and no centralized source of authority such as the Pope, it is next to impossible to imagine a single person emerging and 'freeing' Islam from what Fazlur Rahman has called 'the dead weight of time'. Islam was at its beginning a reform movement which brought a fresh approach to life into the medieval world but became increasingly surrounded over the centuries by an ever-hardening crust of legalistic details, of traditions, scholia, commentaries and supercommentaries under which the original dynamic character of the revelation, the innovative impetus of the Prophet, seemed to disappear, so much so that Lord Cromer, more than a century ago, made the famous remark that 'reformed Islam is no longer Islam'.[2]

But, like any other religion, Islam has been growing in a constant dialectic movement which, in contemporary parlance, would be called the interplay of Chaos and Order – the *sunna* was always 'disquieted' by the introduction of *bidʿas*, innovations. That was particularly true when Islam expanded to the furthest corners of Asia and Africa and, naturally enough, took over a more or less significant part of indigenous traditions. The *ʿurf*, custom, or *ʿādat* law, according to the different countries gained its place besides the *sharīʿa* law. Normative Islam as laid down in the books of classical theologians and jurists and taught in the madrasas, the use of the 'letters of the Koran' and the sacred Arabic language, and the conscious following of the Prophet's example as expressed in the *ḥadīth* characterized the *umma* wherever Islam reached. All these factors helped to create a picture of a uniform, even 'monolithic' Islam; and yet a large variety of popular forms grew, especially due to Sufism with its emphasis, mainly on the folk level, on the veneration of saints. This trend often appeared to the normative believers as mere idol-worship, as a deviation from the clear order to strict monotheism which had to be defended against such encroachments of foreign elements, which, however, seemed to satisfy the spiritual needs of millions of people better than legal prescriptions and abstract scholastic formulas. But *tawḥīd*, strictest monotheism, is the quintessence of Islam along with the acknowledgment that this religion was established in its temporal manifestation by Muhammad – hence the tendency to go back, in cases of doubt, to the days of the Prophet, the ideal time, indeed the fullness of time, which was and should remain the model for the generations to come.[3] Muhammad is the centre of history; his is the middle way between stern legalism as manifested through Moses and world-renouncing asceticism and loving mildness embodied in Jesus; he constitutes, as mystics would say, the means in which *ghayb*, the Invisible, and *shahāda*, the visible and tangible, meet, and is thus the Perfect Man *kat' exochén*.

The *shahāda* in its two parts is the foundation of Islam, and a Muslim is a person who pronounces it and accepts the validity of the *sharīʿa* as the God-given path to walk on.

But there is the need for a deeper ethical dimension, *īmān*, 'faith', which has been expressed in very many writings, most notably (and the best-known of which are) those by al-Ghazzālī. The very definition of *muslim* and *mu'min*, or *islām* and *īmān* (cf. Sūra 49:14), shows that besides the formal acceptance of the religion of 'surrender' there has to be inner faith, and the introduction of the third term, *iḥsān*, 'to do good', or, as a Sufi master in Hyderabad/Deccan explained to us, 'to do everything as beautifully as possible' because God watches over each and every human act, brings a deep personal piety to the fore. Everything should be done in absolute sincerity, *ikhlāṣ*, without any admixture of selfishness or 'showing off'. Then, even the simplest action will bear good fruits. This attitude seems to be expressed in the Prophet's answer to the question: 'What is virtue?', to which he replied: 'Virtue is that in which the heart becomes peaceful'. Not so much an external legal decision, *fatwā*, is the thing that matters, but: 'Ask your heart for a *fatwā*' (*AM* no. 597).

The fact that Muslim thinkers always want to go back to the Prophet's time has led many observers to believe that Islam became fossilized as a result of the strict clinging to externals. Yet, modernists have constantly drawn their co-religionists' attention to the Koranic statement: 'Verily, God does not change a people's condition unless they change what is in them' (Sūra 13:12), for, as has been seen (above, p. 220), predestination, which looms large in the Koran and even more in *ḥadīth*, is only one of the two ways of giving a meaning to one's life. The belief in a predestined order in the universe is, in its deepest meaning, the human attempt to take God seriously as the only acting power and to surrender completely to Him and His wisdom. However, the Muslims were also very much aware that the acceptance of a kind of mechanical working of Fate can lead to laziness and is often used as an excuse for one's own faults instead of ascribing one's good actions to God and blaming oneself for one's faults and sins. After all, the Koran (Sūra 4:79) states clearly: 'Whatever of good befalls you is from God, and whatever of evil befalls you, it is from yourself'. The *ḥadīth*: *qad jaffa 'l-qalam*, 'The Pen has dried up' (*AM* no. 92), should therefore not be interpreted as meaning that everything and every human act was written once for all time but rather, as Rūmī insists, that there is one absolutely unchanging law, that is, good actions will be rewarded while evil will be punished.

To be sure, there was always an unsolved aporia between the belief in predestination and that in free will, but the *ḥadīth* according to which 'this world is the seedbed of the Hereafter' (*AM* no. 338) was meant to spur the believers to good actions as did the Koranic emphasis on doing good, for Divine Justice will place even the smallest act on the balance (cf. Sūra 99).

For some thinkers, the problem of free will and predestination meant that the human being will be judged according to his or her capacity:

> One does not beat an ox because he does not sprout wings,
> but beats him because he refuses to carry the yoke ...
> (*M* V 3,102)

Predestination could thus be explained as the development of one's innate talents: one cannot change them but can work to develop them as beautifully as possible until the *nafs*, which once was 'inciting to evil' (Sūra 12:53), is finally tamed and, strengthened by its steady struggle against adversities and temptations, reaches inner peace so that it can return to its Lord (Sūra 89: 27–8).

Nevertheless, there has always been a certain emphasis on those *ḥadīth* that defend absolute predestination, culminating in the oft-repeated *ḥadīth qudsī*: 'Those to Paradise, and I do not care, and those to Hell, and I do not care' (*AM* no. 519).

God appears in poetical parlance as the Master Calligrapher who writes man's fate 'on his forehead' (*sarnivisht* in Persian, *alīn yazīsī* in Turkish), or else He appears as the great Weaver or the Playmaster whose hands hold the strings of the puppets in the great theatre of the world and move them according to His design to cast them, in the end, again into the 'dark box of unity'. And there were and still are outcries against the seemingly 'unjust' acts of God, whether in 'Aṭṭār's dramatic prayers or in more flippant style in 'Omar Khayyām's *rubāʿiyāt* and, half-jokingly, in Turkish Bektashi poetry. Perhaps the finest definition of free will is that by Rūmī:

> Free will is the endeavour to thank God for His beneficence (M I 929).

For gratitude – often contrasted with *kufr*, 'ingratitude, infidelity' – is a quality highlighted in the Koran (cf. Sūra 42:43). True gratitude, which draws more and more graces upon the believer, is manifested in the loving acceptance of whatever God sends. By gratefully accepting one's 'fate', the human may reach, ideally, uniformity with God's will and thus realize what modernists have called *jabr maḥmūd*, a 'higher predestinarianism' in loving surrender to whatever God has decreed.

This kind of lofty thought is, understandably, not as common as it ideally should be. Modern times have brought such a shift in the religious consciousness not only of Muslims but also everywhere else that it is small wonder when in much of modern literature in the different languages of the Muslim world Islam, either in its official or in its popular form, appears as the attitude of old-fashioned, middle-class or simple people (a kind of attitude formerly called, often condescendingly, 'the faith of the old women of the community').[4] The excesses of 'saint-worship' are banded just as much as 'molla-ism', the attitude of the hardline religious orthodoxy, of lawyer-divines or religious teachers, whose behaviour is often incompatible with the ideals that they preach. In poetry, one may find, at least for a moment, a return to figures of the mystical tradition such as al-Ḥallāj who, however, are interpreted as representatives of a free, loving religiosity and are posited against narrow orthodoxy or, even more, depicted as rebels against the 'establishment' or a government considered to be a traitor to the ideals of true Islam.[5] An additional problem is that the majority of modern, educated Muslims are used to thinking in either English or French and have to find a new language to express their ideas which, again, are largely coloured by their acquaintance with Western literary models rather than with classical Islamic ones. For many Muslims are now born in a completely un-Islamic environment, and often come from a background that has nothing in common with the traditional Islamic settings. The various strands of Muslims – either born Muslims or converts – in the USA, the Indians and Pakistanis in the UK, the Turks in Germany and the Algerians in France offer the most divergent approaches to what seems to them 'true Islam' as well as to the problem of the *umma*; and recent Western converts again add new shades of understanding to the picture, shades that alternate between theosophical mysticism and strictest observant, normative Islam.[6] They no longer read and write in the classical languages of the Islamic world, and when their brethren and sisters in the Middle East do, they perhaps try to couch their message in an antiquated Arabic style, or else shape their native tongues (Persian, Urdu, even more Turkish) to cope with the exigencies of our time.

For the influence of European languages in both vocabulary and syntax, let alone thought patterns, on the 'Islamic' languages creates a literary idiom quite different from the classical one, so that many of the precious and meaningful images or expressions of previous times are irretrievably lost. Alternatively, allusions to and terms from the religious traditions are used in such a skilful way that the non-Muslim reader barely recognizes the 'blasphemous' meaning that a seemingly harmless sentence or image may contain.

But usually, the younger generation both of Western-educated Muslims in the East and those who have grown up in the West know precious little of their own tradition; everyone who has taught classical literature in Arabic, Turkish, Persian or Urdu to native speakers of these languages experiences this break with the tradition. And it is understandable that 'fundamentalism', with its return to and stern observance of time-honoured models, emerges as a reaction to such overly Westernizing trends.

Westernization goes together with a diminishing knowledge of the sacred language, Arabic, but also with attempts to de-Arabicize the Islamic world. A tendency expressed decades ago by Turkish reformers such as Zia Gökalp is typical of such movements, whose fruits are seen, for example, in the secularization of Turkey (where, however, a strong feeling for Islamic values continues beneath the Westernized surface). Similar approaches can also be found in India in the work of scholars like A. A. A. Fyzee, while Iqbāl advocated a return to the central sanctuary, to Mecca, which should go together with a revival of the original, dynamic and progressive Islam. And what will be the post-modernist perceptions of Islam of which the brilliant Pakistani anthropologist Akbar S. Ahmad speaks?[7]

Nathan Söderblom once defined the use of the negation in the 'prophetic' and the 'mystical' type of religion: the 'prophetic No' is exclusive, as is the *lā ilāha illā 'Llāh* in the *shahāda*: '*No* deity save God'; and whatever is against this absolute truth is dangerous, prohibited, sinful and, as the Muslim would say, has to be cut off 'with the sword of *lā*' (which in its graphic form somewhat resembles a two-edged sword). The 'mystical No', on the other hand, is inclusive, and that is expressed in the transformation of the *shahāda* into the words, *lā maujūda illā Allāh*, 'there is nothing existent but God', who includes everything.

This twofold orientation of Islam towards the *ẓāhir* and the *bāṭin*, the exoteric 'prophetic' and the esoteric 'mystical' stance, has continued down through the centuries. It is clearly visible in Indian Islam, for example where one finds the 'Mecca-oriented' normative piety of the theologians who still felt 'in exile' in the subcontinent although their families had lived in India for hundreds of years, while the 'India-oriented' current emphasized the compatibility of Islam with the indigenous traditions and achieved amazing synthetic results, for example in mystical folk poetry.

It is also possible to see the inner-Islamic tensions expressed in terms of 'nomos-oriented' and 'eros-oriented' religion: normative Islam is, no doubt, nomos-oriented, built upon the Law in which God's will is revealed, and therefore averse to movements and people that seem to break out of the sacred limits of the Law to indulge in practices not exactly compatible with the norms. That is especially the case in a large part of Sufism, which expressed itself in poetry, music and even dance with an emphasis on feeling and 'tasting' – in short, in ecstatic movements which are typical of the eros-oriented (in the widest sense of the term) attitude. 'Sober' Sufis often tried to strike a balance between both aspects and to show that they were inseparably intertwined and that every unusual spiritual progress or event had to be weighed against the balance of the Law. For *sharīʿa*, 'Law', and *ḥaqīqa*, 'Divine Truth', belong together just as the *shahāda* in its first part points to the Divine Reality and in its second part to the Law. Similarly, according to Qushayrī's remark, the sentence in the *Fātiḥa*, *iyyāka naʿbudu*, 'Thee we worship', points to the Law, while its continuation, *iyyāka nastaʿīn*, 'To Thee we turn for help', refers to the Divine Reality.[8]

The Law promises, perhaps even guarantees, the human being's posthumous salvation, while in the mystical trends the tendency is to 'touch' the Divine here and now, to reach not so much a blessed life in the Hereafter (which is only a kind of continuation of the present state) but rather the immediate experience of Love. The Sufis' ecstatic experiences and at times unbridled utterances could lead to death (both mystical death and execution by the government), while normative theology shows the way to perfect happiness during one's life by dutifully following the right path and obeying God's laws. The poets expressed this contrast by speaking of 'gallows and *minbar*': the mystical lover will die for his love; the sober preacher will call people to obedience from the *minbar*, the pulpit; and yet gallows and pulpit are made from the same wood.[9]

When William James claims that 'sobriety says No while drunkenness says Yes', this statement is very applicable to the 'prophetic' and the 'mystical', the exclusive and the inclusive No in Islam or, as we saw earlier (see above, p. 191), to the juxtaposition of *qurb al-farā'iḍ*, the proximity reached by the punctual fulfilment of ritual duties, which is the prophets' way, and *qurb an-nawāfil*, the proximity reached by supererogative works, which is the way of God's friends, the *awliyā*.

Again, while the Prophet said: 'We do not know Thee as it behoves!', the Sufi Bāyezīd Bisṭāmī called out: '*Subḥānī*', 'Praise to me!' If we are to believe legend, it was the contrast between these two utterances that awakened Mawlānā Rūmī to the spiritual life. Rūmī, so it is told, fainted when listening to Shams's shocking question about whether Bāyezīd or the Prophet was greater, a question based on the two men's respective sayings that express the human reactions to the meeting with the Divine. The tensions between the two poles of religious experience, that of the prophet, who knows his role as humble 'servant', and that of the mystic, who loses himself in loving union, became clear to him.

There are, however, many different reactions of Muslims to the experience of the Numinous besides these two basic forms. There is unending awe, an awe like the one felt when one approaches the mighty Lord, the King of all kings – such an awe is an attitude expressed best in prayer and reflected in prayer poems.

Awe before the *mysterium tremendum* is natural, but one has also to reckon with fear – fear of the terrible Day of Judgment; fear when thinking of God's Justice with which one will be confronted on that day; fear of His 'ruses', the sudden changes by which He confuses those who are all-too-secure on the way and then meet with unexpected hardships; and if a wanderer may be too advanced to fear God's ruses, one may still fear being deprived of God's presence, of the consoling feeling that He is watching here and now and that He is eternal when everything else will perish; and the mystic who has 'found' the Divine beloved may fear being separated from Him, a thought more terrible than Hellfire.

But there is also hope, the hope of the merciful God's endless capacity for forgiving one's sins and mistakes. Fear and hope, as the traditional saying claims, are 'the two wings by which the soul flies towards God', for too much fear stifles and paralyzes the soul, and too much hope can make humans frivolous and oblivious to their duties. Yet, hope always has the upper hand, as is understood from the *ḥadīth qudsī* that one should 'think well of God' (see above, p. 223).

On a different level, fear and hope are expressed in the stages of *qabḍ* and *basṭ*, depression and elation; that is, the anguish of the soul, which feels like 'living in a needle's eye', when nothing is left but hope against all hope, and the elation during which the jubilant soul seems to encompass the entire universe, sees the world in radiant colours and sings of divine joy. These stages alternate in the course of one's life. The impression which the reader obtains is that the state of *basṭ* seems to dominate in mystical circles – how else is one to explain the thousands of ecstatic verses that translate the happiness of the lover who feels united with all and everything? Yet, the state of *qabḍ*, depression, is considered more valuable in the 'sober' traditions, for, while living through the dark night of the soul, one has to realize that there is only God to whom one can turn, and thus the ideal of pure worship of the One can be achieved better.

As important as awe, fear and hope are, in Islam the encounter with God will nevertheless be most frequently called 'faith'. Unquestioning faith in His power and wisdom requires the belief in the positive meaning of everything He decrees in His eternal wisdom, negative as it may seem. For people sometimes hate something, and yet they will discover its positive aspects later on (cf. Sūra 2:216). Such faith can be considered the most characteristic quality of the true believer. So also is *tawakkul*, absolute 'trust in God'. *Tawakkul* was developed into a multi-layered science of its own among the early Sufis, but could not be maintained in its pure form, for that would have formed a complete impediment to any practical work, not to mention to the believer's duties and responsibilities towards society. But, as an ideal, it remained a factor that largely coloured the Muslim's life.[10]

Love is certainly not an attitude which one expects to find on the general map of Islam, and the use of the term and the concept of love of God, or reciprocal love between God and humans, was sharply objected to by the normative theologians: love could only be love of God's commands, that is, strict obedience. Yet, it remained the central issue with the mystically-minded, whose love was directed first exclusively to God (one of whose names is *al-wadūd*, 'the Loving', in Sūra 11:90; 85:14) but then turned more and more to God's beloved, *ḥabīb*, namely the Prophet, love for whom became a highly important ingredient in Muslim life. And in many ecstatic love poems written in the Islamic, particularly the Persianate, world, one can barely discern whether the beloved object addressed is God, the Prophet, or a human being in whom the poet sees Divine beauty manifested.

Love engenders gratitude and peace of mind: the concept of *iṭmi'nān*, the resting peacefully in God's will, plays a distinctive role in the Koran. 'Is it not that the hearts find peace by remembering God?' (Sūra 13:28). It is this peace and stillness reached through constant recollection of God which characterizes the soul's final stage. The concept of this peace and stillness, which is a sign of *yaqīn*, the 'absolute certainty', has been combined with the legend of the opening of Muhammad's breast when he experienced a soothing coolness and quietude. One finds a beautiful interpretation of his event and the ensuing peaceful serenity in an unexpected source, namely in a sentence of the German author Jean Paul (d. 1825), who writes:

> Als Gott (nach der Fabel) die Hände auf Muhammad legte, wurd' ihm eiskalt; wenn ein unendlicher Genuß die Seele mit dem höchsten Enthusiasmus anrührt and begabt, dann wird sie still und kalt, denn nun ist sie auf ewig gewiß.

> When God, according to the legend, placed His hands upon Muhammad, he turned as cold as ice; when an infinite pleasure touches the soul and inspires her with the highest enthusiasm, she becomes quiet and cold, for now she is certain in eternity.

This quiet, cool certainty of having reached the goal seems perhaps to contrast with the fiery, restless seeking and the never-resting striving on the path, and yet it is often mentioned by deeply religious people.

Similarly, observers have often emphasized the Muslim's seriousness in demeanour and general attitude, a seriousness typical of nomos-oriented religions; yet the inner joy does not lack either: the Sufi Abū Saʿīd-i Abū' l-Khayr is probably the most radiant example of the joy which, as Fritz Meier has lucidly shown, is an integral part of true Sufi life.[11]

Out of such an inner joy grows the praise and laud of God which permeates the whole universe. As the first Sūra of the Koran begins with the words *al-ḥamdu lillāh*, 'Praise be to God', thus praise of God fills the created world, audible to those who understand the signs. Is not Muhammad's very name derived from the root *ḥ-m-d*, 'to praise'? Thus he will carry the 'banner of praise' in the field of Resurrection when those who constantly praise the Lord will be, as popular tradition has it, the first to enter Paradise.[12]

Gerardus van der Leeuw has offered different typologies of religion, and one may wonder which one may be most suitable for Islam. When it comes to the human attitude to God, one would certainly say that Islam is the 'religion of servitude' to God: the term *ʿabd*, 'slave', for the human being points to this truth, as does the idea that *ʿabduhu*, 'God's servant', is the highest rank that a human being can reach (see above, p. 179). This servitude, in which all of creation is united, is best expressed in the prostration in ritual prayer.

One can also speak of a 'religion of the Covenant', though it is not as outspoken as in Judaism, where the Covenant is the true heart of religion (a fact mentioned several times in the Koran). Yet, the Primordial Covenant (Sūra 7:172) is the metahistorical foundation of the relation between God and humankind: they have promised to acknowledge Him as the Lord and King at the time before times, and thus are bound to obey Him to the Day of Judgment – again as His servants.[13]

Another concept is that of 'friendship with God', connected in particular with Abraham, who is called *khalīl Allāh*, 'God's friend'. But such friendship and close bond of relation is much more important in the use of the term *walī* (plural *awliyā'*). This word, which occurs often in the Koran, points to the relation between the Divine Lord and His friends, or perhaps better 'protégés', who are under His protection and 'have neither fear nor are they sad' (Sūra 10:62). The whole development of the hierarchy of the *awliyā'*, the 'friends of God' in Sufism, belongs to this sphere. Furthermore, the Shia term for ʿAlī, *walī Allāh*, singles out the Prophet's cousin and son-in-law as the one who was especially honoured by God's protective friendship which He shows to those whom He elects.

G. van der Leeuw speaks of the 'religion of unrest' when discussing ancient Israel, but this term can be applied as well to Islam, for God is never-resting Will: 'neither slumber nor sleep seize Him' (Sūra 2:255), and 'He is constantly in some work' (Sūra 55:29).

The concept of a 'religion of unrest', often forgotten in times when scholastic definitions seemed to overshadow and even conceal the picture of the living and acting God of the Koranic revelation, has been revived in the twentieth century by Iqbāl, who never tired of emphasizing that Islam is a dynamic force and that it is the Living God of the Koran whom the Muslims should remember and to whom they should turn instead of indulging in Hellenizing mystico-philosophical ideas of a mere *prima causa* which has receded completely from active involvement in the world. Indeed, many orientalists and religious historians, especially during the nineteenth century, have regarded Islam as a purely deistic religion. But many mystics had stressed the living and never-resting activity of God: the story that Rūmī tells both in his *Dīvān* (D no. 1,288) and in *Fīhi mā fīhi* (ch. 27) is a good example of this point. One winter day, a poor schoolmaster saw a bear (apparently dead) drifting down a river in spate and, incited by the school-children to grab this wonderful fur coat, jumped into the water but was grasped by the bear. Called back by the frightened children, he answered: 'I'd love to let the fur coat go, but it does not let me go!' Thus, Rūmī concludes, is God's mercy, love and power, which do not leave the poor human beings but follow them untiringly to draw them near. Already, three centuries earlier, the Iraqi mystic Niffarī (d. 965) had symbolized God's never-resting will to save His creatures in a parable that was rightly compared to Francis Thompson's *Hound of Heaven.*[14]

For God's power shows itself in His will, and He wills that humanity be saved; once humans understand that, then faith, obedience and gratitude issue naturally from this knowledge.

It is the concept of will and obedience which, in van der Leeuw's scheme, is typical of ancient Israel's religious stance. But again, the model fits Islam perfectly. Where in the Old Testament failures and mishaps are ascribed to the people's lack of obedience, the same is true in Islam. The Koran (Sūra 3:152) blames the Muslim defeat in the battle of Uhud (625) upon the hypocrites and the disobedient Muslims: misfortune is a punishment for disobedience. Two of the most eloquent modern expressions of this feeling are Iqbāl's Urdu poems *Shikwa* and *Jawāb-i Shikwa*, 'Complaint' and 'God's answer to the complaint' (written in 1911–12), in which the Muslims, lamenting their miserable situation in the modern world, are taught by God's voice that it is their own fault: they have given up obedience and neglected their ritual duties, so how can they expect God to guide them after straying off the straight path? Did not the Koran often mention the fate of ancient peoples who disobeyed God and His messengers? Thus, in every historical catastrophe, the Muslim should discover an *ʿibra*, a warning example for those who believe and understand.

According to van der Leeuw's model, Islam is the 'religion of Majesty and Humility' – a beautiful formulation which certainly hits the mark, as the whole chapter on Islam reveals his insight into Islam's salient features. Surrender, *islām*, to the Majesty beyond all majesties is required, and Temple Gairdner, as cited by van der Leeuw, despite his otherwise very critical remarks about Islam, speaks of 'the worship of unconditioned Might'. Islam, according to another Christian theologian quoted by van der Leeuw, 'takes God's sovereignty absolutely seriously', and Muslims believe in God's power and might without any suspicion or doubt. Lately, J. C. Bürgel has tried to show how Islamic culture develops out of the tension between God's omnipotence and the unceasing human attempt to create a power sphere of one's own.[15] It is the attitude of unquestioning faith which, as van der Leeuw says, makes Islam 'the actual religion of God'. And it may well be that this feeling of God's absolute omnipotence, which is the basis of Muslim faith at its best (and which is slightly criticized by van der Leeuw), shocks and even frightens human beings in a time of increasing distance from 'God', of secularization, of loss of the centre.

The historian of religion would probably be surprised to see that Muslims have also called Islam the 'religion of Love', for Muhammad, so they claim, appropriated the station of perfect Love beyond any other prophet, since God took him as His beloved – *Muḥammad ḥabībī*. Therefore, Muhammad is regarded as the one who shows God's love and His will and thus guides humanity on the straight path towards salvation, as the Koran states: 'Say: If you love God then follow me, so that God loves you' (Sūra 3:31). He brought the inlibrated Divine

Word in the Koran, and he preached the absolute unity of God around which theology, philosophy and mystical thought were to develop.

One can well understand that the words of the two-part *shahāda* are the strong fortress in which the believer finds refuge; but nothing can be predicated upon God Himself: 'He was and is still as He was'.

For the pious Muslim, *islām* shows itself everywhere in the universe – in the blood circulation, the movement of the stars in their orbits, in the growth of plants – everything is bound by *islām*, surrender and subordination to the Divinely-revealed Law. But this *islām* – as at least Mawlānā Mawdūdī holds – then became finalized in historical Islam as preached by Muhammad.[16] The differentiation which is made in Urdu between *muslim*, someone or something that practises surrender and order by necessity, and *musulmān*, the person who officially confesses Islam, is typical of this understanding. And this differentiation also underlies Goethe's famous verse in the *West-Östlicher Divan*:

> Wenn Islam Ergebung in Gottes Willen heißt –
> In Islam leben und sterben wir alle.

(If Islam means surrender to God's will, then all of us live and die in Islam).

Historians have compared the Divine voice that was heard in Mecca to that of a lion roaring in the desert, and have often seen Islam as a typical religion of the desert, overlooking the fact that Islam was preached first and developed later in cities: in the beginning in the mercantile city of Mecca, later in the capitals of the expanding empire. 'City' is always connected with order, organization and intellectual pursuits, while the desert is the dangerous land where spirits roam freely and where those possessed by the madness of unconditioned love may prefer to dwell; those who do not follow the straight path between two wells will perish there.

It is the city that offers us a likeness of Islam, which can be symbolized as a house, based on the Koranic expression *dār al-Islām*.[17] It looks indeed like a house, a strong Oriental house, built of hard, well-chiselled stones and firmly resting on the foundation of the profession of faith and supported by four strong pillars (prayer, alms tax, fasting and pilgrimage). We may observe guards at its gate to keep away intruders and enemies, or see workmen with hammers and swords to enlarge parts of the building lest the shifting sand-dunes of the desert endanger it. We admire the fine masonry but find it at first glance rather simple and unsophisticated. But when entering the large building, we see lovely gardens inside, reminiscent of Paradise, where watercourses and fountains refresh the weary wayfarer. There is the *ḥarīm*, the women's sacred quarters, where no stranger may enter because it is the sanctuary of love and union.

The house is laid out with precious carpets and filled with fragrance. Many different people bring goods from the seven climates and discuss the values of their gifts, and the Master of the house admonishes everyone to keep the house clean, for after crossing its threshold and leaving one's sandals outside, one has entered sacred space.

But where is one to find the builder and owner of the house? His work and His orders give witness to His presence, awesome and fascinating at the same time, but human reason cannot reach Him, however much it exerts itself and tries to understand in which way He will protect the inhabitants of the House of Islam, of the house of humanity.

Perhaps Rūmī can answer the human mind's never-ending question as to how to reach Him who is the Merciful and the Powerful, the Inward and the Outward, the First and the Last, the One who shows Himself through signs but can never be comprehended:[18]

> Reason is that which always, day and night, is restless and without peace, thinking and worrying and trying to comprehend God even though God is incomprehensible and beyond our understanding. Reason is like a moth, and the Beloved is like the candle. Whenever the moth casts itself into the candle, it burns and is destroyed – yet the true moth is such that it could not do without the light of the candle, as much as it may suffer from the pain of immolation and burning. If there were any animal like the moth that could do without the light of the candle and would not cast itself into this light, it would not be a real moth, and if the moth should cast itself into the candle's light and the candle did not burn it, that would not be a true candle.
>
> Therefore the human being who can live without God and does not undertake any effort is not a real human being; but if one could comprehend God, then that would not be God. That is the true human being: the one who never rests from striving and who wanders without rest and without end around the light of God's beauty and majesty. And God is the One who immolates the seeker and annihilates him, and no reason can comprehend Him.

NOTES

1. The number of works about different aspects of modern Islam increases almost daily. Some useful studies are: John J. Donohue and John L. Esposito (eds) (1982), *Islam in Transition: Muslim Perspectives*; Gustave E. von Grunebaum (1962), *Modern Islam. The Search for Cultural Identity*; Werner Ende and Udo Steinbach (eds) (1984), *Der Islam in der Gegenwart*; Wilfred Cantwell Smith (1957), *Islam in Modern History*; idem (1947): *Modern Islam in India* (2nd ed.); and Rotraut Wielandt (1971), *Offenbarung und Geschichte im Denken moderner Muslime.*
2. C. H. Becker (1910), 'Der Islam als Problem'; Johann Fück (1981a), 'Islam as a historical problem in European historiography since 1800'. About different

ways of dealing with Muhammad in earlier times, see Hans Haas (1916), *Das Bild Muhammads im Wandel der Zeiten.*

3. Johann Fück (1981b) 'Die Rolle des Traditionalismus im Islam'; Sheila McDonough (1980), *The Authority of the Past. A Study of Three Muslim Modernists*; Richard Gramlich (1974b), 'Vom islamischen Glauben an die "gute alte Zeit"'.
4. See, for example, M. M. Badawi (1971), 'Islam in modern Egyptian literature'.
5. Thus Ṣalāḥ ʿAbd aṣ-Ṣabūr (1964), *Ma'sāt al-Ḥallāj*; English translation by K. J. Semaan (1972), *Murder in Baghdad.* See also A. Schimmel (1984b), 'Das Ḥallāğ-Motiv in der modernen islamischen Dichtung'.
6. About modern movements and problems in America, see Earle Waugh, Baha Abu-Laban and Regula B. Quraishi (eds) (1983), *The Muslim Community in North America*; Khalid Duran (1990), 'Der Islam in der Mehrheit und in der Minderheit'; idem (1991), '"Eines Tages wird die Sonne im Westen aufgehen". Auch in den USA gewinnt der Islam an Boden'.
7. Akbar S. Ahmad (1992), *Postmodernism and Islam. Predicament and Promise.*
8. Qushayrī (1912), *Ar-risāla,* p. 261; the same idea in Hujwīrī (1911), *Kashf al-maḥjūb*, p. 139.
9. The expression is used in Nāṣir-i Khusraw (1929), *Dīvān*, p. 161; also in idem, tr. A. Schimmel (1993), *Make a Shield from Wisdom*, p. 78.
10. See B. Reinert (1968), *Die Lehre vom* tawakkul *in der klassischen Sufik.*
11. F. Meier (1976), *Abū Saʿīd-i Abū'l Ḫair.* Leben und Legende.
12. The glorification of God which, according to the Koran, permeates the universe had led early Muslims to the idea that 'a fish or a bird can only become the victim of a hunter if it forgets to glorify God' (Abu'l-Dardā, d. 32h/652). See S. A. Bonebakker (1992), 'Nihil obstat in storytelling?' p. 8.
13. R. Gramlich (1983a), 'Der Urvertrag in der Koranauslegung'.
14. Niffarī (1935), *Mawāqif wa Mukhāṭabāt*, ed. and.transl. by A. J. Arberry, *Mawqif* 11/16.
15. J. C. Bürgel (1991), *Allmacht und Mächtigkeit*, passim.
16. Mawlānā Mawdūdī's views, often published in Urdu and translated into English, are summed up in Khurshid Ahmad and Z. I. Ansari (eds) (1979), *Islamic Perspectives.* In this volume, the article by S. H. Nasr, 'Decadence, deviation and renaissance in the context of contemporary Islam', pp. 35–42, is of particular interest. See further Muhammad Nejatullah Siddiqi's contribution, 'Tawḥīd, the concept and the prospects', pp. 17–33, in which the author tries to derive the necessity of technology for communication, organization and management in the religious and worldly areas from the central role of *tawḥīd.* An insightful study of the problems is Fazlur Rahman (1979), 'Islam: challenges and opportunities'.
17. For the 'House', see Juan E. Campo (1991), *The Other Side of Paradise*, and A. Petruccioli (1985), *Dār al-Islam.* Titus Burckhardt has attempted to show the truly 'Islamic' city in his beautiful book (1992) on *Fes, City of Islam.*
18. *Fīhi mā fīhi*, end of ch. 10.

Bibliography

ʿAbd ar-Raḥīm ibn Aḥmad al-Qāḍī, *Islamic Book of the Dead, a Collection of* ḥadīth *concerning the Fire and the Garden*. Norwich: Divan Press, 1977.

ʿAbd aṣ-Ṣabūr, Ṣalāḥ, *Ma'sāt al-Ḥallāj*. Beirut: Dār al-ādāb, 1964. English translation by K. J. Semaan, *Murder in Baghdad*. 1972.

ʿAbdul Ḥaqq, Maulvi, *Urdū kī nashw u numā meñ ṣūfiyā-i kirām kā kām*. Karachi 1953; Aligarh 1967.

ʿAbdul Laṭīf, Shāh, *Risālō*, ed. by Kalyan Adwani. Bombay: Hindustan Kitabghar, 1958.

Abū Nuʿaym al-Iṣfahānī, *Ḥilyat al-awliyā*, 10 vols. Cairo: Dār al-kitāb al-ʿarabī, 2nd ed. 1967.

Adams, Charles J., 'The history of religions and the study of Islam', in Joseph M. Kitagawa (ed.) (1967), *The History of Religion*, pp. 177–93.

Addas, Claude, *Ibn ʿArabī: La quête du Soufre Rouge*. Paris: Editions du Seuil, 1988.

Ahmad, Akbar S., *Postmodernism and Islam. Predicament and Promise*. London 1992.

Ahmad, Imtiaz (ed.), *Family, Kinship and Marriage among Indian Muslims*. Delhi: Manohar, 1976.

—— *Caste and Social Stratification among Muslims in India*, 2nd ed. Delhi: Manohar, 1978.

Ahmad Khan, Sir Sayyid, *Maqālāt-i Sir Sayyid*, 13 vols. Lahore: Majlis-i taraqqī-yi adab, 1961.

Aksel, Mehmet, *Türklerde Dini Resimler*. Istanbul: Elif Yayĭnlarĭ, 1967.

Albright, William F., 'Islam and the religions of the ancient Orient'. *JAOS* 60 (1955), pp. 283–301.

Ali, Mrs Meer Hassan, *Observations on the Mussulmauns of India: Descriptive of their manners, customs, habits, and religious opinion, made during a twelve years' residence in their immediate society*, 2 vols. London: Parbury, Allen & Co., 1832; repr. Delhi: Idāra-yi Adabiyat-i Delhi, 1973.

Ambros, Arne A., 'Gestaltung und Funktionen der Biosphäre im Koran'. *ZDMG* 140, 2 (1990), pp. 290–325.

Ameer Ali, Syed, *The Spirit of Islam*. 1891. Repr. London: London University paperback, 1965.

Anawati, Georges C., 'Un traité des Noms divins: *Fakhr al-Dīn al-Rāzī's Lawāmiʿ al-baiyināt fi'l-asmā' wa'l-ṣifātʿ*, in G. Makdisi (ed.) (1965), *Arabic and Islamic Studies*, pp. 36–52.

ʿAndalīb, Nāṣir Muḥammad, *Nāla-i ʿAndalīb*, 2 vols. Bhopal 1309h/1890–1.

Andrae, Tor, *Die person Muhammads in glauben und lehre seiner gemeinde*. Stockholm: Vorstedt og söner, 1918.

—— *Mohammad: Sein Leben und sein Glaube*. Göttingen: Vandenhoek und Ruprecht, 1932; repr. 1977. English translation by Theophil Menzel, *Muhammad: The Man and His Faith*. London: Allen and Unwin, 1956.

—— *Die letzten Dinge*, German translation by Hans Heinrich Schaeder. Leipzig: J. C. Hinrichs, 1940.

—— *I Myrtenträdgården.* Stockholm: Bonniers, 1948. English translation by Birgitta Sharpe, *In the Garden of Myrtles.* Albany: SUNY Press, 1987.

Anṣārī, ʿAbdullāh, *Munājāt: Intimate Conversations*, transl. by Wheeler M. Thackston Jr. New York: Paulist Press, 1978.

Ansari, Sarah F. D., *Sufi Saints and State Power. The Pirs of Sind, 1843–1947.* Cambridge: South Asian Studies 50, 1992.

Arnold, Sir Thomas, *The Preaching of Islam.* London 1896, 2nd ed. 1913, repr. 1985.

—— 'Saints, Muhammadan, India'. *ERE,* vol. 11, 1909, pp. 68–73.

—— *Painting in Islam.* Oxford: Clarendon Press, 1928; with a new foreword by Basil W. Robinson, New York: Dover Publications, 1965. Last ed. with an introduction by J. A. Saiyid. Lahore: Shirkat-i qalam (no date).

Asani, Ali S., *The Bhuj Niranjan. An Ismaili Mystical Poem.* Cambridge, MA: Harvard Center for Middle Eastern Studies, 1991.

—— *Ismaili Manuscripts in the Collection of Harvard College Library.* Boston, MA: Hall, 1992.

—— 'Bridal symbolism in the Ismaili *ginān* literature', in Robert Herrera and Ruth Link-Salinger (eds), *Mystics of the Book: Themes, Topics, and Typologies.* Bern/Frankfurt: Peter Lang, 1993.

Asín Palacios, Miguel, *La escatologia musulmana en la Divina Comedia.* Madrid: Real Academia Española, 1919.

ʿAṭṭār, Farīduddīn, *Tadhkirat al-awliyā*, ed. by Reynold A. Nicholson, 2 vols. London: Luzac and Leiden: Brill, 1905, 1907.

—— *Muṣībatnāma*, ed. by N. Wiṣāl. Tehran: Zawwār, 1338sh/1959. Translated into French by Isabelle de Gastines, *Le livre de l'épreuve.* Paris: Flammarion, 1981.

—— *Dīvān-i qaṣā'id wa ghazaliyāt*, ed. by Saʿīd-i Nafīsī. Tehran: Sanā'ī 1339sh/1960.

—— *Manṭiq uṭ-ṭayr*, ed. by Javād Shakūr. Tehran: Kitābfurūshi-ye Tehran, 1341sh/1962.

Attema, D. S., *De mohammedaansche opvattigen omtrent het tijdstip van den Jongsten Dag en zijn voortekenen.* Amsterdam 1942.

Awn, Peter J., *Satan's Tragedy and Redemption: Iblis in Sufi Psychology.* Leiden: Brill, 1983.

Ayalon, David, 'On the Eunuchs in Islam'. *Jerusalem Studies in Arabic and Islam* (1979), pp. 67–124.

Ayoub, Mahmoud, *Redemptive Suffering in Islam.* The Hague: Mouton, 1978.

—— *The Qur'an and Its Interpreters.* Albany: SUNY Press, 1984 (ongoing).

Ayverdi, Samiha, *Istanbul Geceleri*, Istanbul 1952.

—— *Ibrahim Efendi'nin Konağı.* Istanbul: Fatih Cemiyeti, 1964.

Aziz Ahmad and G. E. von Grunebaum, *Muslim Self-Statement in India and Pakistan (1857–1968).* Wiesbaden: Harrassowitz, 1970.

Babinger, Franz, *Die Vita des Schejch Bedr ed-Dīn Maḥmūd von Chalid b. Isma'il b. Schejch Bedr ed-Din Maḥmūd.* Leipzig: Harrassowitz, 1943.

Bachmann, Peter, 'Ein *tafsīr* in Versen. Zu einer Gruppe von Gedichten im *Dīwān* Ibn al-ʿArabīs'. *Der Islam* 65 (1988), pp. 38–55.

Badaoni, Abdul Qādir, *Muntakhab at-tawārīkh*, 3 vols, ed. by W. Nassau Lees, Maulvi Kabiruddin and Maulvi Ahmad Ali. Calcutta: Bibliotheca Indica, 1864–9. English translation by George A. Ranking, W. H. Lowe and Wolseley Haig, repr. Patna: Academia Asiatica, 1972.

Badawi, Muhammad Mustafa, 'Islam in modern Egyptian literature'. *Journal of Arabic Literature* 2 (1971).

Bahā-i Walad, *Maʿārif*, ed. by B. Furūzānfar. Tehran: University, 1336sh/1957.

Bakharzī, Yaḥyā, *Awrād al-aḥbāb wa fuṣūṣ al-ādāb*, ed. by Iraj Afshār. Tehran: University, 1345sh/1966.

Baljon, J. M. S., *Modern Muslim Koran Interpretation (1880–1960).* Leiden: Brill, 1961.

—— *A Mystical Interpretation of Prophetic Tales by an Indian Muslim: Shāh Walī Allāh's* ta'wīl al-aḥādīth. Leiden: Brill, 1973.

—— *Religion and Thought of Shāh Walī Allāh Dihlawī (1703–1762)*. Leiden: Brill, 1986.
Baloch, N. A. (ed.), *Munāqiba*. Hyderabad/Sind: Sindhi Adabi Board, 1960.
—— (ed.), *Maulūda*. Hyderabad/Sind: Sindhi Adabi Board, 1961.
Bannerth, Ernst, 'Lieder ägyptischer *meddāḥīn*'. *WZKM* 56 (1960), pp. 9–20.
—— *Islamische Wallfahrtsstätten Kairos*. Cairo: Österreichisches Kulturinstitut, 1973.
Baqlī, Rūzbihān, *Sharḥ-i shaṭḥiyāt*, ed. by Henry Corbin. Tehran/Paris: Maisonneuve, 1966.
Baranī, Żiyāuddīn, *Tārīkh-i Fērōzshāhī*, ed. by Sayyid Aḥmad Khan. Calcutta: Bibliotheca Indica, 1860–2; new ed. by Shaykh Abdur Rashid, Aligarh: University, 1957.
Barney, Frederick J., 'The creed of al-Sanūsī'. *MW* 23 (1933), pp. 46–55.
Basheer, Suliman, ''Ashūrā. An early Muslim fast'. *ZDMG* 141, 2 (1991), pp. 281–316.
Basset, Henri, *Le culte des grottes au Maroc*. Algiers 1920.
Bausani, Alessandro, *Persia Religiosa. Da Zaratustra a Baha'ullah*. Milan: Il Saggiatore, 1959.
Becker, Carl Heinrich, 'Der Islam als Problem'. *Der Islam* 1 (1910), pp. 1–21.
—— *Islamstudien*, 2 vols. Leipzig: Quelle und Meyer, 1924, 1932.
—— 'Die Kanzel im Kultus des alten Islam', in *Islamstudien*, vol. 1 (1924), pp. 450–71.
Beelaert, Anna Livia F. A., 'The Ka'ba as a woman – a topos in classical Persian literature'. *Persica* 13 (1988–9), pp. 107–23.
Belguedj, M. S., 'Le chapelet Islamique et ses aspects nord-africains'. *REI* 1969, 2, pp. 291–322.
Bennigsen, Alexandre, and Chantal Quelquejay, *Le Soufi et le commissaire*. Paris: Editions du Seuil, 1988.
Bertholet, Alfred, *Die Macht der Schrift in Glauben und Aberglauben*, Berlin: Akademie-Verlag, 1949.
Bijlefeld, Willem, 'A Prophet and more than a prophet? Some observations on the use of the Qur'ānic terms "Prophet" and "Apostle"'. *MW* 49 (1959), pp. 1–28.
—— 'Islamic Studies within the perspective of the history of religions'. *MW* 62 (1972), pp. 1–11.
Birge, John K., *The Bektashi Order of Dervishes*. Cambridge: Cambridge University Press, 1937; repr. London: Luzac, 1965.
Birkeland, Harris, *The Legend of the Opening of Muhammad's Breast*. Oslo: Nordske Videnskaps Academi, in commission J. Dywood, 1955.
Blackman, Winifred, 'Sacred trees in modern Egypt'. *Journal of Egyptian Archeology* 11 (1925), pp. 56–7.
Bleeker, C. Jouco, *Inleiding tot een Phaenomenologie van den godsdienst*. Assen: Van Gorcum, 1934.
Bombaci, Alessandro, 'The place and date of birth of Fuzuli', in C. E. Bosworth (ed.) (1971), *Iran and Islam*. Edinburgh: Edinburgh University Press, pp. 91–107.
Bonebakker, Seger A., 'Nihil obstat in storytelling?' *Mededelingen van de Afdeling Letterkunde* 55 (new series). Amsterdam: Academy of Sciences, 1992.
Bousquet, G.-H., *Les grandes pratiques rituelles de l'Islam*. Paris 1949.
—— 'La pureté rituelle en Islam'. *RHR* 138 (1950), pp. 53–71.
—— 'Des animaux et de leur traitement selon le Judaïsme, le Christianisme et l'Islam. *Studia Islamica* (1958), pp. 31–48.
Bousset, Wilhelm, 'Die Himmelsreise der Seele'. *ARW* 4, (1901), pp. 136–69, 228–73.
Böwering, Gerhard, *The Mystical Vision of Existence in Classical Islam: The Qur'anic Hermeneutics of the Sufi Sahl at-Tustarī (d. 283/896)*. Berlin: de Gruyter, 1979.
Brakel, L., *The Story of Muhammad Hanafiyya. A Medieval Muslim Romance*, translated from the Malay. The Hague: Nijhoff, 1977.
Braude, B., and Bernard Lewis (eds), *The Christians and Jews in the Ottoman Empire. The Functioning of a Plural Society*, 2 vols. New York 1982.

Braune, Walther, *Der islamische Orient zwischen Vergangenheit und Zukunft*. Bern: A. Francke, 1960.

Bravmann, René A., *African Islam*. Washington, DC: Smithsonian Institute, 1983.

Brockelmann, Carl, 'Allah und die Götzen. Der Ursprung des islamischen Monotheismus'. *ARW* 21 (1922), pp. 99–121.

Browne, Edward Granville, *A Literary History of Persia*, 4 vols. Cambridge: Cambridge University Press, 1902–24, several reprints.

Bruijn, J. T. P. de, *Of Piety and Poetry. The Interaction of Religion and Art in the Life and Works of Ḥakīm Sanāʾī of Ghazna*. Leiden: Brill, 1984.

Brunel, René, *Le monachisme errant dans l'Islam: Sidi Heddi et les Heddawa*. Paris: Larose, 1955.

Bukhārī, Abū ʿAbdullāh Muḥammad al-, *Kitāb jāmiʿ aṣ-ṣaḥīḥ*, 4 vols, ed. by Ludolf Krehl and W. Juynboll. Leiden: Brill, 1863–1902. Translated by M. M. Khan, *Sahih al-Bukhari*, 6 vols. Lahore: Ashraf, 1978–80.

Burckhardt, Titus, 'The symbolism of the Mirror'. *Symbolon* 4 (1954).

—— *Fes, City of Islam*. English translation by William Stoddart, Cambridge: Islamic Texts Society, 1992.

Bürgel, J. Christoph, 'Sanāʾī's Jenseitsreise der Gottesknechte als *poesia docta*'. *Der Islam* 60, 1 (1983), pp. 78–90.

—— *The Feather of Sīmurgh*. New York: New York University Press, 1988.

—— *Allmacht und Mächtigkeit*. Munich: Beck, 1991.

—— 'Ecstasy and order: two structural principles in the *ghazal*-poetry of Jalāl al-Dīn Rūmī', in L. Lewisohn (ed.) (1992), *The Legacy of Mediaeval Persian Sufism*, pp. 61–74.

Burhānpūrī, Rashīd, *Burhānpūr kē Sindhī Awliyā*. Karachi: Sindhi Adabi Board, 1957.

Burney, Mohammad Ilyas, *Mishkaat us-Salawaat: A Bouquet of Blessings on Muhammad the Prophet*, transcribed into Roman script and translated into English by M. A. Haleem Ilyasi. Hyderabad/Deccan 1983.

Burton, Richard, *Sindh, and the Races that Inhabit the Valley of the Indus*. London 1851; repr. Karachi: Oxford University Press, 1973.

Būṣīrī, Abū ʿAbdallāh Muḥammad al-, *Die Burda*, ed. and transl. by C. A. Ralfs, with metrical Persian and Turkish translation. Vienna: Hof- und Staatsdruckerei, 1860.

Busse, Heribert, 'Jerusalem and the story of Muhammad's night journey and ascension'. *Jerusalem Studies in Arabic and Islam* 14 (1991), pp. 1–40.

Cachia, Pierre, and Alford Welch (eds), *Islam – Past Influence and Present Challenge*. Edinburgh: Edinburgh University Press, 1979.

Calverley, Edwin Elliot, *Worship in Islam*. Madras 1925.

Campo, Juan E., 'Shrines and talismans – domestic Islam in the pilgrimage paintings of Egypt'. *Journal of the American Academy of Religion* 55 (1987), pp. 285–305.

—— *The Other Side of Paradise. Explorations into the Religious Meanings of Domestic Space in Islam*. Columbia, SC: University of South Carolina Press, 1991.

Canaan, Taufiq, 'The curse in Palestinian folklore'. *JPOS* 15 (1935), p. 235ff.

Canteins, Jean, *La voie des Lettres*. Paris: Albin Michel, 1981.

Cerulli, Enrico, *Il Libro della Scala e la questione dei fonti arabo–spagnole della Divina Commedia*. Città del Vatican: Biblioteca Apostolica Vaticana, 1949.

Chelhod, Joseph, 'La *baraka* chez les Arabes ou l'influence bienfaisante du sacré'. *RHR* 148 (1955), pp. 68–88.

—— *Les structures du sacré chez les Arabes*. Paris: Maisonneuve et Larose, 1964; 2nd ed. 1986.

Chelkowski, Peter J. (ed.), *Taʿziye (Ritual and Drama in Iran)*. New York: New York University Press, 1979.

Chittick, William C., 'The five Divine Presences from al-Qūnavī to al-Qayṣari'. *MW* 72, 2 (1982), pp. 107–28.

—— *The Sufi Path of Love*. Albany: SUNY Press, 1985.

—— *The Sufi Path of Knowledge*. Albany: SUNY Press, 1989.
—— 'Spectrums of Islamic thought: Saʿīd al-Dīn Farghānī on the implications of Oneness and Manyness', in L. Lewisohn (ed.) (1992), *The Legacy of Mediaeval Persian Sufism*, pp. 203–18.
Chodkiewicz, Michael, 'The *Futūḥāt Makkiyya* and its commentators: some unresolved enigmas', in L. Lewisohn (ed.) (1992), *The Legacy of Mediaeval Persian Sufism*, pp. 219–232.
Combs-Schilling, M. E., *Sacred Performances. Islam, Sexuality, and Sacrifice*. New York: Columbia University Press, 1989.
Corbin, Henry, *L'imagination créatrice dans le Soufisme d'Ibn Arabi*. Paris: Maisonneuve, 1958; English translation by Ralph Manheim. Princeton: Princeton University Press, 1969.
—— 'La configuration du Temple de la Kaʿba comme secret de la vie spirituelle'. *Eranos Jahrbuch* 34 (1965); English translation in Corbin (1986), *Temple and Contemplation.*
—— *L'homme de lumière dans le soufisme iranien*, 2nd ed., Paris: Librairie de Medicis, 1971; English translation by Nancy Pearson. Boulder, CO: Shambhala, 1979; German translation by A. Schimmel, *Die smaragdene Vision*. Cologne: Diederichs, 1987.
—— 'Réalisme et symbolisme des couleurs en cosmologie Shiite'. *Eranos-Jahrbuch* 41 (1972). English translation in Corbin (1986), *Temple and Contemplation.*
—— *Cyclical Time and Ismaili Gnosis*, translated by Ralph Manheim. London: Kegan Paul, 1983.
—— *Temple and Contemplation*. Translated by Philip Sherrard. London/New York: Kegan Paul International, 1986.
—— *L'homme et son ange*. London: Kegan Paul, 1989.
Cragg, Kenneth, 'Pilgrimage prayers'. *MW* 45 (1955), p. 269.
—— 'Ramadan prayers'. *MW* 47 (1957) p. 210.
—— *The Call of the Minaret*. New York: Oxford University Press, 1964.
—— *Counsels in Contemporary Islam*. Edinburgh: Edinburgh University Press, 1965.
—— *Alive to God* (Prayers). London 1972.
—— '*Tadabbur al-Qur'ān*: reading and meaning', in A. H. Green (ed.) (1984), *In Quest of an Islamic Humanism*, pp. 181–95.
Crawley, A. E., '*Mirror*', in *ERE*, vol. 8 (1908), p. 695f.
Crollius, Ary A. Roest, *The Word in the Experience of Revelation in the Qur'an and Hindu Scriptures*. Rome: Documenta missionalia, 1974.
Cuperus, W. A., *Al-fātiḥa dans la pratique religieuse du Maroc*. PhD dissertation, Utrecht 1973.
Currie, P. M., *The Shrine and Cult of Muin al-Din Chishti of Ajmer*. Oxford: Oxford University Press, 1989.
Daftary, Farhad, *The Ismailis*. Cambridge: Cambridge University Press, 1992.
Damīrī, Kamāluddīn Muhammad ad-, *Kitāb al-ḥayawān*, 2 vols. Cairo 1305h/1887. Repr. Cairo: Mustafa al-Babi al-Halabī, 1956.
Darqāwī, ad-, *Letters of a Sufi Master*, translated by Titus Burckhardt. London 1961.
Dawlatshāh, *Tadhkirat ash-shuʿarā*, ed. by M. Abbasi (based on E. G. Browne's edition of 1900). Tehran (no date).
Denny, Frederick M., 'The problem of salvation in the Quran: key terms and concepts', in A. H. Green (ed.) (1984), *In Quest of an Islamic Humanism*, pp. 196–210.
Depont, O., and X. Coppolani, *Les confréries religieuses musulmans*, 2 parts. Algiers 1897–8; repr. 1987.
Dermenghem, Emile, *L'écloge du vin – poème mystique d'Omar ibn al-Faridh, et son commentaire par Abdulghani an-Nabulusi*. Paris: Véga, 1931.
—— *Le culte des saints dans l'Islam maghrébin*. Paris: Gallimard, 1954.
DeWeese, Devin, 'Sayyid ʿAlī Hamadhānī and Kubrawī hagiographical tradition', in L. Lewisohn (ed.) (1992), *The Legacy of Mediaeval Persian Sufism*, pp. 121–58.

Digby, Simon, 'The Sufi Shaykh and the Sultan: a conflict of claims to authority in medieval India'. *IRAN* 28 (1990), p. 71ff.
Donaldson, Bess Allen, 'The Koran as magic'. *MW* 27 (1937), pp. 254–66.
—— *The Wild Rue. A Study of Mohammedan Magic and Folklore in Iran.* London: Luzac, 1938; repr. Princeton, NJ: Arno Press, 1973.
Donohue, John J., and John L. Esposito (eds), *Islam in Transition: Muslim Perspectives.* New York: Oxford University Press, 1982.
Dornseiff, Franz, *Das Alphabet in Mystik und Magie.* Berlin 1922.
Doutté, Edmond, *Magie et religion dans l'Afrique du Nord.* Algiers: Adolphe Jourdan, 1908.
Dubler, César W., 'Über islamischen Grab-und Heiligenkult'. *Schweizer Archiv für Volkskunde* 4 (1950), pp. 1–23.
Duran, Khalid, 'Der Islam in der Mehrheit und in der Minderheit', in W. M. Watt, A. Schimmel et al. (eds) (1990), *Islam*, vol. 3, pp. 422–51.
—— '"Eines Tages wird die Sonne im Westen aufgehen". Auch in den USA gewinnt der Islam an Boden'. *CIBEDO* 5/2 (1991), pp. 33–59.
During, Jean, *Musique et mystique dans les traditions d'Iran.* Leuven: Bibliotheca Iranica, 1989.
Eaton, Charles LeGai, *Islam and the Destiny of Man.* London: George Allen and Unwin, and Cambridge: Islamic Texts Society, 1982. German translation by Eva-Liselotte Schmid, *Der Islam und die Bestimmung des Menschen.* Cologne: Diederichs, 1987.
Eaton, Richard, *Sufis of Bijapur, 1300–1700.* Princeton, NJ: Princeton University Press, 1978.
Edier, R. Y., and M. J. L. Young, 'A list of appellations of the Prophet Muhammad'. *MW* 66 (1976), pp. 259–62.
Eglar, Zekiye, *A Punjabi Village in Pakistan.* New York: Columbia University Press, 1960.
Eichler, Paul, *Die Dschinn, Teufel und Engel im Koran.* Berlin: Buchhandlung Klein, 1929?
Eickmann, W., *Die Angelologie und Dämonologie des Korans im Vergleich zu der Engel- und Geisterlehre der Heiligen Schrift.* New York 1908.
Eliade, Mircea, *Images and Symbols. Studies in Religious Symbolism.* New York: Sheed and Ward, 1952.
Ende, Werder, and Udo Steinbach (eds), *Der Islam in der Gegenwart.* Munich: Beck, 1984.
Engineer, Asghar Ali, *The Bohras.* Sahibabad: Vikas, 1980.
Ernst, Carl W., *Words of Ecstasy in Sufism.* Albany: SUNY Press, 1985.
—— *Eternal Garden. Mysticism, History, and Politics at a South Asian Sufi Center.* Albany: SUNY Press, 1992a.
—— (1992b), 'The symbolism of birds and flight in the writings of Rūzbihān Baqlī', in L. Lewisohn (ed.) (1992), *The Legacy of Mediaeval Persian Sufism*, pp. 353–66.
Esin, Emel, *Mecca the Blessed, Medina the Radiant.* New York: Crown Publishers, 1963.
Ess, Josef van, *Der* Ṭaylasān *des Ibn Ḥarb. 'Mantelgedichte' in arabischer Sprache.* Heidelberg: Sitzungsberichte der Akademie der Wissenschaften, 1979.
Ettinghausen, Richard, 'Persian ascension miniatures of the fourteenth century', in *L'Oriente e l'Occidente nel medioevo.* Rome, Accademia dei Lincei, 1957, pp. 360–83.
Fahd, Toufic, 'Anges, démons et djinns en Islam'. *Sources Orientales* 8, Paris: Editions du Seuil, 1971.
—— 'Génèse et cause des couleurs d'après L'Agriculture Nabatéenne', in R. Gramlich (ed.) (1974), *Islamwissenschaftliche Abhandlungen*, pp. 78–95.
Falaturi, Abduljawad, 'Die Zwölfer-Schia aus der Sicht eines Schiiten', in E. Graef (ed.) (1968) *Festschrift für Werner Caskel*, pp. 63–96.
Farhadi, A. G. Rawan, 'Le *majlis* de al-Ḥallāj, de Shams-i Tabrezi, et du Molla de Roum'. *REI* (1954).
Farid, Abdul Hamid, *Prayers of Muhammad.* Karachi 1959.
Faroqhi, Sorayya, *Der Bektaschi-Oden in Anatolien.* Special issue of the *WKZM.* Vienna 1981.
Faruqi, Lois Lamiya Ibsen al-, 'Tartīl', in Khurshid Ahmad and Z. I. Ansari (eds) (1979), Islamic Perspectives, pp. 105–20.

—— *Islam and Art.* Islamabad: National Hijra Council, 1985.
Fayṭūrī, Muḥammad al-, 'Āshiq min Ifrīqiyya. Beirut: Dār al-ādāb, 1970.
Fazlur Rahman. *Prophecy in Islam.* New York/London: Allen and Unwin, 1958.
—— *Islam.* New York/Chicago: Holt, Rinehart and Winston, 1966; and several other editions and reprints.
—— 'Islam: challenges and opportunities', in P. Cachia and A. Welch (eds) (1979), *Islam*, pp. 315–30.
Fischer, August, 'Vergöttlichung und Tabuisierung der Namen Muhammads', in Richard Hartmann and Helmuth Scheel (eds), *Beiträge zur Arabistik, Semitistik und Islamkunde.* Leipzig: Harrassowitz, 1944.
Fischer, Wolfdietrich, *Farb-und Formbezeichnungen in der Sprache der arabischen Dichtung.* Wiesbaden: Harrassowitz, 1965.
Fleischhammer, Manfred (ed.), *Arabische Kultur und Islam im Mittelalter* (collected articles by J. Fück). Leipzig: Böhlau, 1981.
Fohrer, Georg, *Der Heilige Weg.* Dissertation, Düsseldorf 1939.
Friedmann, Yohanan, *Shaykh Ahamd Sirhindi. An Outline of His Thought and a Study of His Image in the Eyes of Posterity.* Montreal/London: McGill University Press, 1971.
—— 'Qiṣṣa Shakarwarti Farmāḍ'. *Israel Oriental Studies* 5 (1975), pp. 233–58.
—— *Prophecy Continuous. Aspects of Ahmadi Religious Thought and its Medieval Background.* Berkeley, CA: University of California Press, 1989.
Fück, Johann (1981a), 'Islam as a historical problem in European historiography since 1800', in M. Fleischhammer (ed.), *Arabische Kultur und Islam im Mittelalter*, pp. 317–27.
—— (1981b) 'Die Rolle des Traditionalismus im Islam', in M. Fleischhammer (ed.), *Arabische Kultur und Islam*, pp. 214–34.
Furūzānfar, Badīʿuzzamān, Aḥādīth-i Mathnawi. Tehran: University, 1334sh/1955 (abbreviated *AM*).
Gaffney, Patrick D., 'Magic, miracle and the politics of narration in the contemporary Islamic sermon'. *Religion and Literature* 20, 1, Spring 1988, pp. 111–37.
Gardet, Louis, 'Les noms et les statuts. Le problème de la foi et des oeuvres in Islam'. *Studia Islamica* 5 (1956), p. 61ff.
—— *L'islam. Religion et communauté.* Paris: Desclées du Brouwer, 1967. German translation: *Islam.* Cologne: P. C. Bachem, 1968.
—— 'La mention du Nom divine, *dhikr*, dans la mystique musulmane'. *Revue Thomiste* (1972–3).
Gätje, Helmut, 'Philosophische Traumlehren im Islam'. *ZDMG* 109 (1959), pp. 258–85.
—— 'Zur Farbenlehre in der muslimischen Philosophie'. *Der Islam* 43, 4 (1967), pp. 280–301.
—— *Der Koran und seine Auslegung.* Zurich/Stuttgart: Artemis, 1971. English translation by Alford Welch, *The Qur'an and its exegesis.* Berkeley/Los Angeles: University of California Press, 1976.
—— (ed.), *Grundriß der arabischen Philologie*, vol. 2, Wiesbaden: Reichert, 1987.
Gaudefroy-Demombynes, Maurice, *Le pèlerinage à la Mecque.* Paris 1923; repr. 1977.
—— *Muslim Institutions*, translated from the French by John P. MacGregor. London: George Allen and Unwin, 1950; 3rd ed. 1961.
Geertz, Clifford, *Islam Observed.* Chicago, IL: Chicago University Press, 1971.
Gellner, Ernest, 'Doctor and Saint', in Nikki Keddie (ed.), *Scholars, Saints, and Sufis.* Berkeley/Los Angeles: University of California Press, 1972, p. 307–26.
Gēsūdarāz, Sayyid Muḥammad, *Jawāmiʿ al-kilam*, ed. by Hafiz Muhammad Hamid Siddiqi. Cawnpur 1356h/1937.
Ghālib, Mirza Asadullah, *Kulliyāt-i fārsī*, 17 vols. Lahore: University, 1969.
—— *Urdu Dīwān*, ed. by Ḥāmid Aḥmad Khan. Lahore: University, 1969b.
Ghallab, Mohammad, *Les Survivances de l'Egypte antique dans le folklore Egyptien moderne* Paris 1929.

Ghazzālī, Abū Ḥāmid al-, *Iḥyā' 'ulūm ad-dīn.* 4 vols. Bulaq 1289h/1872.
—— *Al-maqṣad al-asnā fī sharḥ ma'ānī asmā Allāh al-ḥusnā,*, ed. by Fadlou Shéhadi. Beirut: Dar al-Machreq, 1971. A translation appears in R. McCarthy (1980), *Freedom and Fulfillment,* appendix III.
—— 'The Remembrance of death and the Afterlife'. Book XL of *The Revival of the Religious Sciences,* translated with an introduction and notes by J. T. Winter. Cambridge: Islamic Texts Society, 1989.
—— (Al-Ghazzali) *Temps et prières. Prières et invocations. Extraits de l'Iḥyā' 'ulūm al-Dīn,* trad. de l'arabe ... par P. Cuperly. Paris 1990.
—— (Al-Ghazali) 'Invocations and Supplications: Kitāb al-adhkār wa'l-da'wāt'. Book IV of *The Revival of the Religious Sciences, Iḥyā' 'Ulūm al-Dīn,* translated with an introduction and notes by Kojiro Nakamura, 2nd ed. Cambridge: Islamic Texts Society, 1992a.
—— (Al-Ghazali) *The Ninety-nine Beautiful Names of God.* Translated with notes by David B. Burrell and Nazih Daher. Cambridge: The Islamic Texts Society, 1992b.
Ghazzālī, Aḥmad, *Sawāniḥ. Aphorismen über die Liebe,* ed. by Hellmut Ritter. Istanbul/ Leipzig: Brockhaus, 1942. English translation by Nasrullah Pourjavady, *Inspirations from the World of Pure Spirits.* London: Octagon, 1986. German translations by Richard Gramlich, 1977, and Gisela Wendt, 1978.
Gibb, Hamilton A. R., *Whither Islam?* London: Gollancz, 1932.
—— *Mohammedanism.* London: Oxford University Press, 1949; several reprints.
—— 'The structure of religious thought in Islam', in Stanford Shaw and William R. Polk (eds), *Studies on the Civilization of Islam,* London: Routledge and Kegan Paul, 1962, pp. 176–218.
Gimaret, Daniel, *Les Noms Divins en Islam. Exégèse lexicographique et théologique.* Paris: Editions du Cerf, 1988.
Goethe, Johann Wolfgang von, *West-Östlicher Divan.* Herausgegeben unter Mitwirkung von Hans Heinrich Schaeder von Ernst Beutler. Leipzig: Dieterichsche Verlagsbuchhandlung, 1943. (First published Stuttgart: Cotta, 1819.)
Goitein, Shlomo Dev, 'Beholding God on Friday'. IC 34 (1960) pp. 163–8.
—— *Studies in Islamic History and Institutions.* Leiden: Brill, 1966.
Goldammer, Kurt, 'Wege aufwärts und Wege abwärts'. *Eine Heilige Kirche* 22 (1940), pp. 25–6.
Goldfeld, Isaiya, 'The Illiterate Prophet (*nabī ummī*). An inquiry into the development of a dogma in Islamic tradition'. *Der Islam* 57 (1980), pp. 58–67.
Goldziher, Ignaz (1915a), 'Linguistisches aus der Literatur der muhammadanischen Mystik'. ZDMG 26 (1877), pp. 764–85.
—— 'Le sacrifice de la chevelure des Arabes'. RHR 14 (1886), p. 49f.
—— *Muhammedanische Studien,* 2 vols. Halle: Niemeyer, 1888–90. Translated by C. R. Barber and S. M. Stern, *Muslim Studies,* 2 vols. Chicago, IL: Aldine, 1966, 1971.
—— 'Der Seelenvogel im islamischen Volksglauben'. *Globus* 1903, pp. 301–4.
—— 'Wasser als dämonenabwehrendes Mittel'. ARW 13 (1910), p. 20.
—— 'Chatm al-Buchārī'. *Der Islam* 6 (1915–16), p. 214.
—— (1915b), 'Die Entblößung des Hauptes'. *Der Islam* 6 (1915–6), pp. 301–10; additions by Hellmut Ritter, *Der Islam* 8 (1918), p. 156.
—— *Richtungen der islamischen Koranauslegung.* Leiden: Brill, 1920; repr. 1970.
—— 'The appearance of the Prophet in dreams'. JRAS 1921, pp. 503–6.
—— *Vorlesungen über den Islam,* 2nd ed. by Franz Babinger. Heidelberg: Carl Winters Universitätsbuchhandlung, 1925.
—— 'Verheimlichung des Namens'. *Der Islam* 17 (1928), pp. 1–3.
Gölpīnarlī, Abdulbaki, *Mevlâna'dan sonra Mevlevilik.* Istanbul: Inkilap Kitabevi, 1953.
—— *Islam ve Türk illerinde fütüvvet teşkilatī ve kaynaklarī.* Istanbul: Inkilap ve Ata, 1962.
—— *Tasavvuftan dilimize geçen terimler.* Istanbul: Inkilap ve Ata, 1977.

Graef, Erich (ed.), *Festschrift für Werner Caskel zum 70. Geburtstag am 5.3.1966.* Leiden: Brill, 1968.

Graham, William A., *Divine Word and Prophetic Word in Early Islam.* The Hague: Mouton, 1977.

—— *Beyond the Written Word. Oral Aspects of Scripture in the History of Religion.* Cambridge: Cambridge University Press, 1987.

Gramlich, Richard, *Die schiitischen Derwischorden Persiens*, 3 vols: 1. Die Affiliationen; 2. Glaube und Lehre; 3. Brauchtum und Riten. Wiesbaden: Steiner, 1965, 1976, 1981.

—— (ed.), *Islamwissenschaftliche Abhandlungen*, Fritz Meier zum 60. Geburtstag, Wiesbaden: Steiner, 1974a.

—— (1974b) 'Vom islamischen Glauben an die "gute alte Zeit"', in Gramlich (ed.) (1974a), *Islamwissenschaftiche Abhandlungen*, pp. 110–17.

—— (1983a), 'Der Urvertrag in der Koranauslegung'. *Der Islam* 60 (1983), pp. 205–30.

—— *At-tajrīd fī kalimat at-tauḥīd.* Der reine Gottesglaube. Das Wort des Einheitsbekenntnisses. Wiesbaden: Steiner, 1983b.

—— *Die Wunder der Freunde Gottes. Theologien und Erscheinungsformen des islamischen Heiligenwunders.* Stuttgart: Steiner, 1987.

—— 'Abū Sulaymān ad-Dārānī'. *Oriens* 33 (1992), pp. 22–85.

Green, Arnold H. (ed.), *In Quest of an Islamic Humanism.* Arabic and Islamic Studies in memory of Mohammad al-Nowaihi. Cairo: American University Press, 1984.

Grothues, Jürgen, *Automobile Kunst in Pakistan.* Sunderburg: Schrader, 1990.

Grotzfeld, Heinz, *Das Bad im arabisch–islamischen Mittelalter.* Wiesbaden: Harrassowitz, 1970.

Grunebaum, Gustave E. von, *Muhammedan Festivals.* Leiden: Brill and New York: Schurman, 1958; repr. London, 1992.

—— *Modern Islam. The Search for Cultural Identity.* Los Angeles/Berkeley: University of California Press, 1962.

—— *Studien zum Kulturbild und Selbstverständnis des Islam.* Zurich/Stuttgart; Artemis, 1969.

Grunebaum, Gustave E. von, and Roger Caillois (eds), *The Dream and Human Society.* Berkeley, CA: University of California Press, 1966.

Grütter, Irene, 'Arabische Bestattungsbräuche in frühislamischer Zeit', *Der Islam* 32 (1956), pp. 168–94.

Haar, J. ter, 'The spiritual guide in the Naqshbandi order', in L. Lewisohn (ed.) (1992), *The Legacy of Mediaeval Persian Sufism*, pp. 311–21.

Haarmann, Ulrich, and Peter Bachmann (eds), *Die islamische Welt zwischen Mittelalter und Neuzeit. Festschrift für Hans Robert Roemer.* Beirut and Wiesbaden: Steiner, 1979.

Haas, Hans, *Das Bild Muhammads im Wandel der Zeiten.* Berlin: Hütter Verlag, 1916.

Habil, Abdurrahman, 'Traditional esoteric commentaries', in S. H. Nasr (ed.) (1987), *Islamic Spirituality*, vol. 1, pp. 24–47.

Ḥallāj, al-Ḥusayn ibn Manṣūr al-, *Kitāb aṭ-ṭawāsīn*, ed. with the Persian commentary by Baqlī and translated by Louis Massignon. Paris: Geuthner, 1913.

—— '*Dīvān.* Essai de reconstitution par Louis Massignon'. *JA* 218 (1931), Jan–Mar, p. 1–158.

Halm, Heinz, *Kosmologie und Heilslehre der frühen Isma'iliyya.* Wiesbaden: Steiner, 1978.

—— *Die Schia.* Darmstadt: Wissenschaftliche Buchgesellschaft, 1988. English translation *The Shia.* Edinburgh: Edinburgh University Press, 1992.

Hamidullah, Muhammad, *Le Prophète de l'Islam*, 2 vols. Paris: Vrin, 1959.

Hammer, Joseph von, *Der Diwan des … Hafis*, 2 vols (translated into German). Stuttgart: Cotta, 1812–13.

Hartmann, Angelika, 'Islamisches Predigtwesen im Mittelalter: Ibn al-Ǧauzī und sein "Buch der Schlußreden" 1186 AD'. *Saeculum*, 38, 4 (1987), pp. 336–66.

Hartmann, Richard, *Die Religion des Islam. Eine Einführung.* Berlin: E. S. Mittler und Sohn, 1944; new ed. Darmstadt: Wissenschaftliche Buchgesellschaft, 1992.

Hartmann-Schmitz, U., *Die Zahl Sieben im sunnitischen Islam. Studien anhand von Koran und Hadith.* Frankfurt/Bern: Lang, 1989.
Hasrat, Bikrama Jit, *Dara Shikuh: Life and Works.* Santiniketam: Vishvabharati, 1953.
Heiler, Friedrich, *Das Gebet,* 5th ed. Munich: Reinhard, 1923; repr. 1968. Abbreviated English translation by Samuel McComb, *Prayer.* New York: Oxford University Press 1958.
—— *Erscheinungsformen und Wesen der Religion.* Stuttgart: Kohlhammer, 1961.
Hodgson, Marshall G. S., *The Venture of Islam,* 3 vols. Chicago, IL: Chicago University Press, 1974.
Hoenerbach, Wilhelm (ed.), *Der Orient in der Forschung. Festschrift für Otto Spies zum 5.4.1966.* Wiesbaden: Harrassowitz, 1967.
Horovitz, Josef, 'A list of published Mohammedan inscriptions of India'. *Epigraphica Indo-Moslemica,* vol. 2. Calcutta: Bibliotheca Indica, 1905–10.
—— 'Baba Ratan, the Saint of Bhatinda'. *Journal of the Punjab Historical Society* 2 (1910).
Horten, Max, *Die religiöse Gedankenwelt der gebildeten Muslime im heutigen Islam.* Halle: Niemeyer, 1917.
—— *Die religiöse Gedankenwelt des Volkes im heutigen Islam.* Halle: Niemeyer 1917.
Hovanassian, Richard G., and Speros Vryonis Jr (eds), *Islam's Understanding of Itself.* Malibu, CA: Undena, 1983.
Huart, Clément, 'Le rationalisme musulman au IVe siècle'. *RHR* 50 (1904).
Huitema, Taede, *De Voorspraak (shafā'a) in den Islam.* Leiden: Brill, 1936.
Hujwīrī, 'Ali ibn 'Uthmān al-Jullābī, *Kashf al-maḥjūb,* translated by Reynold A. Nicholson, London: Luzac, and Leiden: Brill, 1911; and many reprints.
Hunswick, J. O., 'Ṣāliḥ al-Fulānī (1752/3–1803). The career and teachings of a West African *'ālim* in Medina', in A. H. Green (ed.) (1984), *The Quest of an Islamic Humanism,* pp. 139–54.
Ibn Abbād ar-Rondī, *Letters on the Sufi Path,* translated and introduced by J. Renard. New York: Paulist Press, 1986.
Ibn Abī Dunyā, *Dhamm ad-dunya,* ed. by Leah Goldberg. Jerusalem: Hebrew University, 1990.
Ibn al-Jawzī, *Kitāb al-quṣṣāṣ wa'l-mudhakkirīn,* ed. and translated by Merlin L. Swartz. Beirut: Dar el-Machreq, 1971.
Ibn 'Aṭā' Allāh, *Miftāḥ al-falāḥ wa miṣbāḥ al-arwāh.* Cairo: Mustafa al-Bābī al-Ḥalabī and Sons, 1961.
—— *Kitāb al-ḥikam,* edited and translated into French by Paul Nwyia (1972) in *Ibn 'Aṭā Allāh et la naissance de la confrérie šadilite,* pp. 84–229; English translation by Victor Daner, *The Book of Wisdom.* New York: Paulist Press, 1978; German translation by A. Schimmel, *Bedrängnisse sind Teppiche voller Gnaden.* Freiburg: Herder, 1987.
—— Traité sur le nom 'Allāh'. Introduction, traduction et notes par M. Gloton. Paris 1981.
Ibn Baṭṭūta, *Riḥla,* 4 vols, ed. by C. Defrémery and B. R. Sanguinetti, Paris 1853–9. Translated by H. A. R. Gibb, *The Travels of Ibn Baṭṭūṭa,* 2 vols. Cambridge: Hakluyt Society, 1958, 1962.
Ibn Ḥazm, *Ṭawq al-ḥamāma,* ed. by D. K. Petróf. St Petersburg/Leiden: Brill, 1914. English translation by Arthur J. Arberry, *The Ring of the Dove.* London; John Murray, 1953; repr. 1981. German translation by Max Weisweiler, *Halsband der Taube.* Leiden: Brill, 1940.
Ibn Iyās, *Badā'i' az-zuhūr fī waqā'i' ad-duhūr,* vols 3–5, ed. by Paul Kahle and M. Mostafa. Istanbul and Leipzig: Brockhaus, 1931–5.
Ibn Taghrībirdī, *An-nujūm az-zāhira fī ta'rīkh Miṣr wa'l-Qāhira,* ed. by W. A. Popper, 8 vols, Berkeley, CA: University of California Press, 1920–36.
Idris, Hady Roger, 'De la notion arabo-musulmane de voie salvatrice'. *Orientalia hispanica,* vol. 1. Leiden: Brill, 1974.

Ikrām, Shaykh Muhammad (ed.), *Armaghān-i Pāk*. Karachi: Idāre-yi maṭbūʿāt, 1953.
Ipşiroğlu, M., *Das Bild im Islam. Ein Verbot und seine Folgen*. Vienna/Munich 1971.
Iqbāl, Muḥammad, *Asrār-i khudī*. Lahore: Ashraf, 1938.
—— *Rumūz-i bēkhudī*. Lahore: Ashraf, 1917.
—— *Payām-i mashriq*. Lahore: Ashraf, 1923.
—— *Bāng-i Darā*. Lahore: Ashraf, 1924.
—— *Zabūr-i ʿajam*. Lahore: Ashraf, 1927.
—— *The Reconstruction of Religious Thought in Islam*. Lahore: Ashraf, 1930; new ed. by M. Saeed Sheikh, Lahore: Institute of Islamic Culture, 1986. (The original edition is quoted.)
—— *Jāvīdnāma*. Lahore: Ashraf, 1932.
—— *Musāfir*. Lahore: Ashraf, 1933.
—— *Bāl-i Jibrīl*. Lahore: Ashraf, 1936.
—— Żarb-i Kalīm. Lahore: Ashraf, 1937.
—— *Armaghān-i Ḥijāz*. Lahore: Ashraf, 1938.
—— *Speeches and Statements*, ed. by 'Shamloo'. Lahore: Al-Mānar Academy, 1948.
—— *Stray Reflections*, ed. by Javid Iqbāl. Lahore: Ghulam Ali and sons, 1961.
Italiaander, Rolf (ed.), *Aus der Palmweinschenke. Pakistanische Erzählungen*. Tübingen: Erdmann, 1972.
ʿIyāḍ, Qāḍī, *Kitāb ash-shifā fī riʿāyat ḥuqūq al-Muṣṭafā*. Istanbul 1312h/1895.
Izutsu, Toshikiko (1971a), *God and Man in the Koran*. Tokyo: Keio Institute of Linguistic Studies, Keio University, 1964.
—— 'The basic structure of metaphysical thinking in Islam', in M. Mohaghghegh and H. Landolt (eds) (1971), *Collected Papers on Islamic Philosophy and Mysticism*, pp. 39–72.
—— 'The paradox of light and darkness in the Garden of Mystery of Shabastari', in J. P. Strelka (ed.), *Anagogic Qualities of Literature*. University Park, PA: University of Pennsylvania Press, 1971, pp. 288-307.
Jackson, Paul, 'Perceptions of the *dargāhs* of Patna', in C. W. Troll (ed.) (1989), *Muslim Shrines in India*, pp. 98–111.
Jafar Sharif, *Islam in India, or the Qanun-i Islam*, translated by G. A. Herklots, ed. by William Crooke. Oxford: Oxford University Press, 1921; repr. London/Dublin: Curzon Press, 1972.
Jamali, Mohammad Fadhel, *Letters on Islam, written by a father in prison to his son*. London: Oxford University Press, 1965.
Jāmī, ʿAbdur Raḥmān, *Nafaḥāt al-uns*, ed. M. Tawhidipur. Tehran: Saʿdī, 1336sh/1957.
—— *Dīvān-i kāmil*, ed. Hashim Raza. Tehran: Payruz, 1341sh/1962.
Jazūlī, Muhammad ibn Sulayman, *Dalā'il al-Khayrāt*. Numerous MSS and editions.
Jeffery, Arthur, 'The mystic letters of the Koran'. *MW* 14 (1924), pp. 247–60.
—— *ʿIbn al- ʿArabi's* shajarat al-kawn. Lahore: Aziz Publishers, 1980.
Jomier, Jacques, *Le maḥmal et la caravane égyptienne des pèlerins de la Mecque en XIV–XX* siècles. Cairo: *IFAO*, 1953.
Jong, Fred de, 'The iconography of Bektashiism. A survey of themes and symbolism in clerical costume, liturgical objects, and pictorial art'. *Manuscripts of the Middle East*, vol. 4. Leiden: Brill, 1989.
Juynboll, G. A. H., *The Authenticity of Tradition Literature. Discussions in Modern Egypt*. Leiden: Brill, 1969.
Kadkani, Muhammad Reza Shafii, 'Anmerkungen zum Flickenrock der Sufis'. *Spektrum Iran* 2/4, Bonn, 1989.
Karahan, Abdulkadir, *Türk Islam edebiyatında Kırk hadis*. Istanbul: Üniversite, 1954.
Keddie, Nikki R. (ed.), *Scholars, Saints, and Sufis*. Berkeley/Los Angeles: University of California Press, 1972.
Kessler, Christel, 'Mecca-oriented urban architecture in Mamluk Cairo; The Madrasa

Mausoleum of Sultan Shaʿbān II', in A. H. Green (ed.) (1984), *Islamic Humanism*, pp. 98–108.
Khāqānī, Afḍaluddīn, *Dīvān*, ed. by Żiā'uddīn Sajjādī. Tehran Zawwār, 1338sh/1959.
Khurshid Ahmad and Zafar Ishaq Ansari (eds), *Islamic Perspectives. Studies in honour of Mawlana Sayyid Abu'l-Aʿlā Mawdudi*. Leicester: The Islamic Foundation, 1979.
King, David A., 'The sacred direction in Islam. A study of the interaction of religion and science in the Middle Ages'. *Interdisciplinary Science Review* 10, 4 (1986), pp. 315–28.
Kirfel, Willibald, *Der Rosenkranz*. Walldorf: Verlag für Orientkunde, 1949.
Kisā'ī, *The Tales of the Prophets*, from the Arabic *Qiṣaṣ al-anbiyā*, translated by Wheeler M. Thackston Jr. Boston, MA: Twayne-Hall, 1977.
Kitagawa, Joseph M. (ed.), *The History of Religion. Essays in the Problem of Understanding*. Chicago, IL: Chicago University Press, 1967.
Klopfer, Helmut, *Das arabische Traumbuch des Ibn Sīrīn*. Munich: Diederichs, 1989.
Knappert, Jan, *Swahili Religious Poetry*, 3 vols. Leiden: Brill 1971.
—— *Islamic Legends. Histories of the Heroes, Saints and Prophets of Islam*, 2 vols. Leiden: Brill, 1985.
Köbert, Raimond, 'Zur Lehre des *tafsīr* über den bösen Blick'. *Der Islam* 28 (1948), pp. 110–21.
Koch, Ebba, 'Jahangir and the angels: recently discovered wall paintings under European influence in the Fort of Lahore', in Joachim Deppert (ed.), *India and the West*. New Delhi: Manohar, 1983, pp. 173–96.
Kohlberg, Etan, 'Manāhij al-ʿārifīn. A treatise on Sufism by Abū ʿAbd al-Raḥmān al-Sulamī'. *Jerusalem Studies in Arabic and Islam* 1 (1979), pp. 19–39.
Kokan, Muḥammad Yusuf, *Arabic and Persian in Carnatic (1700–1950)*. Madras: Hafiza House, 1974.
Konieczny, M. G., 'Unbeachtete muslimische Kultstätten in Pakistan'. *Baessler-Archiv*, NF XXIV (1976), pp. 197–215.
Kowalski, Tadeusz, 'Nase und Niesen im arabischen Volksglauben und Sprachgebrauch'. *WZKM* 31 (1924), pp. 193–218.
Krauss, E. S., 'Vom Derwisch-Recken Gazi-Seidi. Ein Guslarenlied bosnischer Muslime aufgezeichnet, verdeutscht und erläutert'. *Beiträge zur Kenntnis des Orients* 10 (1913), pp. 16–50.
Kriss, Rudolf, and Hubert Kriss-Heinrich, *Volksglaube im Islam*, 2 vols. Wiesbaden: Harrassowitz, 1960, 1962.
Künstlinger, David, 'Die Namen der "Gottesschriften" im Quran'. *Rocznik orientalistyczny* 31 (1937), pp. 72–84.
Labib as-Said, *The Recited Koran*. Translated and adapted by Bernhard Weiß, M. A. Rauf and Morroe Berger. Princeton, NJ: Darwin Press, 1975.
Lambrick, H. T., *The Terrorist*. London: Ernest Benn, 1972.
Lane, Edward William, *Manners and Customs of the Modern Egyptians*, 2 vols. London 1836. Repr. in one vol. London: East-West Publishers, 1978.
Lang, Hubert, *Der Heiligenkult in Marokko. Formen und Funktionen der Wallfahrten*. Passauer Mittelmeerstudien, Sonderreihe, Heft 3. Passau: Passavia Universitätsverlag, 1992.
Laugier de Beaurecueil, S., *Khwādja ʿAbdullāh Anṣārī (396–481 h/1006–1089). Mystique Hanbalite*. Beirut: Imprimerie Catholique, 1965.
Lazarus-Yafeh, Hava, *Some Religious Aspects of Islam*. Leiden: Brill, 1981.
Lech, Klaus, *Geschichte des islamischen Kultus 1, 1: Das Ramaḍān-Fasten*. Wiesbaden: Harrassowitz, 1979.
Leeuw, Gerardus van der, *In den Himel is eenen dans*. Amsterdam: H. J. Paris 1930.
—— *Phänomenologie der Religion*, 2nd ed. Tübingen: J. C. B. Mohr (Paul Siebeck), 1956. English translation by J. E. Turner, with appendices (the additions to the second German edition) by Hans H. Penner: *Religion in Essence and Manifestation*. Princeton, NJ: Princeton University Press, 1986.

—— *Vom Heiligen in der Kunst.* Gütersloh: Bertelsmann, 1957.
Lehmann, Edvard, and Johan Pedersen, 'Der Beweis für die Auferstehung im Koran'. *Der Islam* 5 (1914), pp. 54–61.
Leszynski, Rudolf, *Muhammadanische Traditionen über das Jüngste Gericht.* Gräfenhainichen 1909.
Lewisohn, Leonard (ed.), *The Legacy of Mediaeval Persian Sufism.* London: Khanqah-i Nimatullahi, 1992.
Lifchetz, Raymond (ed.), *The Dervish Lodge: Architecture, Art, and Sufism in Ottoman Turkey.* Berkeley, CA: University of California Press, 1992.
Lings, Martin, 'The Qur'anic symbolism of water'. *Studies in Comparative Religion* 2 (1968), pp. 153–60.
—— *Quranic Calligraphy and Illumination.* London: Festival of Islam Trust, 1976.
—— *Muhammad.* London: George Allen and Unwin and Islamic Texts Society, 1983; new ed. 1991.
Littmann, Enno, *Ahmed il-Badawi: Ein Lied auf den ägyptischen Nationalheiligen.* Mainz: Akademie der Wissenschaften, 1950.
—— *Islamisch–arabische Heiligenlieder.* Wiesbaden: Steiner 1951.
Lohmeyer, E., 'Vom göttlichen Wohlgeruch'. *Sitzungsberichte der Heidelberger Akademie der Wissenschaften,* philologisch-historische Klasse 1919, 9.
Long, David Edwin, *The Hajj Today: A Survey of the Contemporary Mecca Pilgrimage.* Albany: SUNY Press, 1979.
Löwinger, S., and J. de Somogyi (eds), *Ignace Goldziher Memorial.* Budapest 1947.
McCallum, Lyman, *The* Mevlidi Sherif *by Suleyman Chelebi.* London: John Murray, 1943.
McCarthy, Richard, *Freedom and Fulfillment. An annotated translation of al-Ghazālī's* al-Munqidh min aḍ-Ḍalāl *and other relevant works of al-Ghazāli.* Boston, MA: Twayne-Hall, 1980.
McDonough, Sheila, *The Authority of the Past. A Study of Three Muslim Modernists.* Chambersburg: The American Academy of Religion, 1980.
Maclean, Derrick N., *Religion and Society in Arab Sind.* Leiden: Brill, 1989.
Mahdihasan, S., 'The garb of the Sufi and its significance'. *IQBAL,* January 1960.
Mahmood, Tahir, 'The *dargāh* of Sayyid Sālār Mas'ūd Ghāzī in Bahraich: legend, tradition, and reality', in C. W. Troll (ed.) (1989), *Muslim Shrines in India,* pp. 23–43.
Makdisi, George (ed.), *Arabic and Islamic Studies in Honor of Hamilton A. R. Gibb.* Cambridge, MA: Harvard University Press, 1965.
Maneri, Sharafuddin, *The Hundred Letters,* transl. by Paul Jackson SJ. New York: Paulist Press, 1980.
Manto, S. H. 'Kālī Shalwār', in Rolf Italiaander (ed.) (1972), *Aus der Palmweinschenke.*
Maqqarī, Aḥmad ibn Muḥammad al-Maghribī al-, *Fatḥ al-muta'āl fī madḥ an-ni'āl.* Hyderabad/Deccan: Dairatul Maarif, 1334h/1916.
Mardin, Ömer Fevzi, *Varidat-i Süleyman şerhi.* Istanbul 1951.
Martin, Richard C. (ed.), *Islam in Local Contexts* (Contributions to *Asian Studies* 17). Leiden: Brill, 1982.
Massignon, Louis, *La Passion d'al Hosayn ibn Mansour, martyre mystique de l'Islam,* 2 vols. Paris: Geuthner, 1922; enlarged ed. 4 vols. Paris: Gallimard, 1975. English translation by Herbert Mason, *The Passion of al-Hallaj, Mystic and Martyr of Islam,* 4 vols. Princeton, NJ: Bollingen Series, 1982.
—— 'Die Auferstehung in der mohammedanischen Welt'. *Eranos Jahrbuch* 6 (1939).
—— 'L'Homme Parfait en Islam et son originalité eschatologique'. Eranos Jahrbuch 15 (1947), pp. 287–314.
—— 'Le temps dans la pensée islamique'. *Eranos Jahrbuch* 21 (1952).
—— 'La Cité des Morts au Caire: Qarāfa. Darb al-aḥmar'. *BIFAO* 57 (1958), p. 25ff.
—— 'L'oratoire de Marie à l'Aqça, vu sous le voile de deuil de Fatima'. *Les Mardis de Dār al-Salām.* Paris: J. Vrin, 1964, pp. 5–37.

Massignon, Louis, and Clément Huart, 'Les entretiens de Lahore'. *JA* 208 (1926), pp. 285–334.
Mas'ūd ibn Sa'd-i Salmān, *Dīvān*, ed. by Rashid Yashmi. Tehran: Payruz, 1339sh/1960.
Meier, Fritz, *Vom Wesen der islamischen Mystik*. Basel: Benno Schwabe, 1943.
—— 'Das Mysterium der Kaaba: Symbol und Wirklichkeit in der islamischen Mystik'. *Eranos Jahrbuch* 11 (1944), pp. 187–214.
—— 'Der Derwischtanz'. *Asiatische Studien* 8 (1954), pp. 107–36.
—— *Die* fawā'iḥ al-jamāl wa fawātiḥ al-jalāl *des Naǧm ad-dīn al-Kubrā*. Wiesbaden: Harrassowitz, 1956.
—— 'Ein Knigge für Sufis', in *Scritti in onore Giuseppe Furlani*. Rome 1957, pp. 457–524.
—— 'Qušairis *Tartīb as-sulūk*'. *Oriens* 16 (1963), pp. 1–39.
—— 'Ein profetenwort gegen die totenbeweinung'. *Der Islam* 50 (1973), pp. 207–29.
—— *Abū sa'īd-i Abū'l Ḫair. Leben und Legende*. Leiden: Brill, 1976.
—— 'Niẓāmī und die Mythologie des Hahnes'. *Colloquia sul poeta persiano Niẓāmī e la leggenda iranica di Alessandro Magno*. Rome: Accademia dei Lincei, 1977, pp. 55–115.
—— 'Die Segenssprechung über Mohammed im Bittgebet und in der Bitte'. *ZDMG* 136, 2 (1986), pp. 364–401.
—— *Bahā-i Walad*. Leiden: Brill, 1990a.
—— (1990b), 'Zum Vorrang des Glaubens und des "guten Denkens" vor dem Wahrheitseifer bei den Muslimen'. *Oriens* 32 (1990), pp. 1–40.
—— 'Über die umstrittene Pflicht des Muslims, bei nicht-muslimischer Besetzung seines Landes auszuwandern'. *Der Islam* 68, 1 (1991), pp. 65–86.
Mélikoff, Irène, 'Nombres symboliques dans la littérature epico–religieuse des Turcs d'Anatolie'. *JA* 250 (1962), pp. 435–45.
—— 'Le drame de Kerbela dans la littérature epique turque'. *REI* 34 (1966), pp. 133–48.
—— 'La fleur de la souffrance. Recherches sur le sens symbolique de *lâla* dans la poésie mystique turco–iranienne'. *JA* 255 (1967), pp. 341–60.
Memon, Muhammad Umar, *Ibn Taimiyya and Popular Religion*. The Hague/Paris: Mouton, 1976.
Mensching, Gustav, *Das heilige Schweigen*. Gießen: Töpelmann, 1926.
—— *Das heilige Wort*. Bonn: Röhrscheidt, 1937.
Meyer, Jonas, *Die Hölle im Islam*. Dissertation, University of Basle, 1901–2.
Mez, Adam, *Die Renaissance des Islam*, ed. by H. Reckendorf. Heidelberg: Carl Winters Universitätsbuchhandlung, 1992.
Michaud, Roland and Sabrina, *Dervishes du Hind et du Sind*. Paris: Phébus, 1991.
Mills, Margaret A., *Rhetoric and Politics in Afghan Traditional Story-telling*. Philadelphia, PA: University of Pennsylvania Press, 1991.
Misra, Satish C., *Muslim Communities in Gujarat*. New York: Asia Publishing House, 1963.
Mittwoch, Eugen, 'Muhammads Geburts- und Todestag'. *Islamica 2* (1926), pp. 397–401.
Mohaghghegh, Mehdi, and Hermann Landolt (eds), *Collected Papers on Islamic Philosophy and Mysticism*. Tehran: University, 1971.
Moini, Syed Liaqat Hussain, 'Rituals and customary practices at the Dargāh of Ajmer', in C. W. Troll (ed.) (1979), *Muslim Shrines*, pp. 50–75.
Mokri, Muhammad, *La lumière et le feu dans l'Iran ancien … et leur démythification en Islam*. Louvain: Studia Iranica, 1982.
Molé, Marijan, 'La Danse extatique en Islam', in 'Les Danses sacrées', *Sources Orientales* 6. Paris: Editions du Seuil, 1963, pp. 145–280.
Morgan, Kenneth W. (ed.), *Islam, the Straight Path. Islam interpreted by Muslims*. New York: The Ronald Press Co., 1958.
Morris, H. S., 'The Divine Kingship of the Aga Khan: a study in theocracy in East Africa'. *SWJA* 14 (1958), pp. 545–73.
Moustafa, Ahmad, *The Attributes of Divine Perfection* (Calligraphies). Jeddah: Xenel Industries, 1989.

Muḥāsibī, al-Ḥāriṯ ibn Asad al-, *Kitāb at-tawahhum: Une vision humaine des fins dernières*, edited and translated by A. Roman. Paris 1978.

Muḥsin Kākōrawī, *Kulliyāt-i na't*, ed. by Maulvi Muhammad Nur ul-Hasan. Lucknow: an-Naẓīr Press, 1324h/1904.

Mujeeb, Muhammad, *Islamic Influences on Indian Society*. Meerut: Meenakshi Prakash, 1972.

Murata, Sachiko, *Temporary Marriage in Islamic Lands*. London: The Muhammadi Trust, 1987.

—— (1992a) 'Mysteries of marriage – notes on a Sufi text', in L. Lewisohn (ed.) (1992), *Legacy of Mediaeval Persian Sufism*, pp. 343–51.

—— *The Tao of Islam*. Albany: SUNY Press, 1992b.

Naff, Thomas, 'The linkage of history and reform in Islam', in A. H. Green (ed.) (1984), *In Quest of an Islamic Humanism*, pp. 123–8.

Nagel, Tilman, 'Vom Qur'an zur Schrift. Bells Hypothese aus religionsgeschichtlicher Sicht'. *Der Islam* 60 (1983), pp. 143–65.

—— *Der Koran. Einführung, Texte, Erläuterungen*, 2nd ed. Munich: Beck, 1991.

Nahj al-balāgha, wth commentary of Muḥammad 'Abduh, ed. by 'Abdul'aziz Sayyid al-ahl. Beirut: Dār al-Andalus, 1963.

Nanda, Bikram, and Mohammad Talib, 'Soul of the soulless: an analysis of Pīr–Murid relationships in Sufi discourse', in C. W. Troll (ed.) (1989), *Muslim Shrines in India*, pp. 125–44.

Nanji, Azim, *The Nizari Ismaili Tradition in the Indo–Pakistani Subcontinent*. Delmar, NY: Caravan Books, 1978.

—— 'Isma'ilism', in S. H. Nasr (ed.) (1987), *Islamic Spirituality* vol. 1, pp. 179–98.

Nāṣir-i Khusraw, *Dīwān-i ash'ār … based on the MS edited by Ḥajjī Sayyid Naṣr Allāh Taqawī, along with Rawshanā'ināmā, Sa'ādatnāma, Risāla*. Tehran 1929; repr. Chāpkhāna-i Gīlān 1339sh/1960. Selections in *Make a Shield from Wisdom*.

—— *Make a Shield from Wisdom*. English verse translation by A. Schimmel. London: Kegan Paul, 1993.

Nasr, Seyyed Hosein, *Ideals and Realities of Islam*. London: Allen and Unwin, 1960.

—— *An Introduction to Islamic Cosmological Doctrines*. Cambridge, MA: Harvard University Press, 1964.

—— (ed.), *Ismaili Contributions to Islamic Culture*. Tehran: Imperial Academy of Philosophy, 1977.

—— 'Decadence, deviation, and renaissance in the context of contemporary Islam', in Khurshid Ahmad and Z. I. Ansari (eds) (1979), *Islamic Perspectives*, pp. 35–42.

—— (ed.), *Islamic Spirituality*, 2 vols. New York: Crossroads, 1987, 1990.

—— 'Oral transmission and the Book in Islamic education: the spoken and the written word'. *Journal of Islamic Studies* 3, 1 (1992), pp. 1–14.

Neuwirth, Angelika, *Studien zur Komposition der mekkanischen Suren*. Berlin: de Gruyter, 1981.

—— 'Koran', in P. Gätje (ed.) (1987), *Grundriş der arabischen Philologie*, vol. 2, pp. 96–134.

—— 'Der Horizont der Offenbarung. Zur Relevanz der einleitenden Schwurserien für die Suren der Frühmekkanischen Zeit', in U. Tworuschka (ed.) (1991), *Gottes ist der Orient*, pp. 3–30.

Nicholson, Reynold Alleyne, *Studies in Islamic Mysticism*. Cambridge: Cambridge University Press, 1921; repr. 1967.

Niffarī, 'Abduljabbār an-, *Mawāqif wa Mukhāṭabāt*, ed. and transl. by Arthur J. Arberry. London: Luzac, 1935.

Niẓāmī, Ilyās, *Kulliyāt-i Khamsa*, 3rd ed. Tehran: Amīr Kabīr, 1351sh/1972.

Niẓāmī, Khalīq Aḥmad, '*Malfūẓāt kā tārīkhī ahammiyat*', in Malik Ram (ed.), *Arshi Presentation Volume*. Delhi 1961.

Nöldeke, Theodor, *Geschichte des Qorans*, vol. 1. Göttingen: Dietrich, 1860. Vols 1 and 2.

2nd ed. by F. Schwally, Leipzig: Dietrich, Vol. 3: *Geschichte des Qorantextes*, by G. Bergsträßer and O. Pretzl, Leipzig: Dietrich, 1938.

Norris, H. R., 'The Ḥurūfi legacy of Faḍlullāh of Astarabad', in L. Lewisohn (ed.) (1992), *The Legacy of Mediaeval Persian Sufism*, pp. 87–98.

Nurbakhsh, Javad, *Sufi Symbolism*. London: Khaniqah-i Nimatullahi, 1988.

—— *Dogs. From a Sufi Point of View*. London/New York: Khaniqah-i Nimatullahi, 1989.

Nwyia, Paul, *Exégèse coranique et langage mystique*. Beirut: Dar el-Machreq, 1970.

—— *Ibn ʿAṭāʾ Allāh et la naissance de la confrérie šādilite*. Beirut: Dar el-Machreq, 1972.

Nyberg, Hendrik Samuel, *Kleinere Schriften des Ibn al-ʿArabī*. Leiden: Brill, 1919.

O'Brien, D. B. Cruise, *The Mourides of Senegal*. Oxford: Clarendon Press, 1971.

Oesterley, W. O. E., *The Sacred Dance*. Cambridge 1923.

Öney, Gönül, 'Das Lebensbaum-Motiv in der seldschukischen Kunst in Anatolien'. *Belleten* 32, Ankara: Türk Tarih Kurumu, 1968.

Ormsby, Eric L., *Theodicy in Islamic Thought. The Dispute over al-Ghazali's 'Best of all Possible Worlds'*. Princeton, NJ: Princeton University Press, 1984.

O'Shaughnessy, Thomas, 'The Koranic concept of the Word of God'. *Studia Biblica et Orientalia*, Rome 1948.

—— *Muhammad's Thoughts on Death*. Leiden: Brill, 1969.

—— *Eschatological Themes in the Qur'an*. Manila: Ateneo University, 1986.

Otto, Rudolf, *Das Heilige*. Munich: C. H. Beck, 1917; 28th ed. Munich: Biederstein 1947; 35th ed. 1973. English translation by John W. Harvey, *The Idea of the Holy*. London: Oxford University Press, 1924.

—— *Das Gefühl des Überweltlichen*. Munich: C. H. Beck, 1932.

Özelsel, Michaela M., *Vierzig Tage. Erfahrungen aus einer Sufi-Klausur*. Munich: Diederichs, 1993.

Padwick, Constance E., *Muslim Devotions*. London: SPCK, 1960.

Paret, Rudi, 'Die Legende von der Verleihung des Prophetenmantels (*burda*) an Kaʿb ibn Zuhair'. *Der Islam* 17 (1928), pp. 7–14.

—— *Die legendäre Maghazi-Literatur*. Tübingen: J. C. B. Mohr (Paul Siebeck), 1930.

—— *Symbolik des Islam*. Stuttgart: Kohlhammer, 1958.

Parsram, Jethmal, *Sind and its Sufis*. Madras 1924.

Paul, Jürgen, *Die politische und soziale Bedeutung der Naqšbandiyya in Mittelasien im 15. Jahrhundert*. Berlin: Klaus Schwarz, 1991.

Pedersen, Johannes, *Der Eid bei den Semiten in seinem Verhältnis zu verwandten Erscheinungen, sowie die Stellung des Eides im Islam*. Strasbourg: Karl Trubner, 1914.

—— 'The Islamic preacher: *wāʿiẓ, mudhakkir, qāṣṣ*', in S. Löwinger and J. Somogyi (eds), *Ignace Goldziher Memorial*, vol. 1. Budapest 1947, pp. 226–51.

Petruccioli, Attilio, *Dār al-Islam. Architetture del territoria nei paesi islamici*. Rome: Carucci, 1985.

Poonawala, Ismail K., *Bibliography of Ismaili Literature*. Malibu, CA: Undena, 1977.

Popovic, Alexandre, and G. Veinstein (eds), *Les ordres mystiques dans l'Islam. Cheminement et situation actuelle*. Paris 1986.

Qāḍī Qādan jō kalām, ed. by Hiran Thakur. Delhi: Puja Publications, 1978.

Qushayrī, ʿAbdul Karīm al-, *Ar-risāla al-qushayriyya fi't-taṣawwuf*. Cairo: Dār al-kūtub al-ʿarabiyya al-kūbrā, 1330h/1912.

—— *Sharḥ asmāʾ Allāh al-ḥusnā*, ed. by ʿAbdas Salām al-Ḥulwānī. Cairo 1969.

Rahbar, Daud, *God of Justice*. Leiden: Brill, 1960.

—— 'Ghālib and a debatable point of theology'. *MW* 56 (1966), pp. 14–17.

Rahim, Habibeh, *Perfection Embodied. The Image of ʿAlī ibn Abī Ṭālib in Non-Shia Persian Poetry*. PhD dissertation, Harvard, Cambridge, MA, 1988.

Rāzī, Najmuddīn Dāyā, *Mirṣād al-ʿibād min al-mabdaʾ ilāʾ l-maʿād*. Tehran 1312h/1893. Translated by Hamid Algar, *The Path of God's Bondsmen from the Beginning to the Return*. Delmar: Caravan Books, 1982.

Reinert, Benedikt, *Die Lehre vom* tawakkul *in der klassischen Sufik.* Berlin: de Gruyter, 1968.

Renard, John, *In the Footsteps of Muhammad: An Interpretation of Islam.* New York: Paulist Press, 1992.

—— *Islam and the Heroic Image. Themes in Literature and the Visual Arts.* Columbia, SC: University of South Carolina Press, 1993.

Ringgren, Helmer, *Fatalism in Persian Epics.* Uppsala: Almquist, and Wiesbaden: Harrassowitz, 1953.

—— *Studies in Arabic Fatalism.* Uppsala: Almquist, and Wiesbaden: Harrassowitz, 1955.

Rippin, Andrew (ed.), *Approaches to the History of the Interpretation of the Qur'an.* Oxford: Oxford University Press, 1988.

Ritter, Hellmut, 'Muslim mystics' strife with God'. *Oriens* 5 (1952), pp. 1–15.

—— *Das Meer der Seele. Mensch, Welt und Gott in den Geschichten des Farīduddīn 'Aṭṭār.* Leiden: Brill, 1955; 2nd ed. 1978.

Rizvi, Sayyid Athar Abbas, *A Socio-intellectual History of the Isna Ashari Shiis in India*, 2 vols. New Delhi: Manoharlal, 1985.

Robson, James, 'Blessings on the Prophet'. *MW* 26 (1936), pp. 365–71.

Roscher, Wilhelm Heinrich, 'Omphalos'. *Abhandlungen der phil.-hist. Klasse der Sächsischen Gesellschaft der Wissenschaft* 29, 9. Leipzig: Akademie der Wissenschaften, 1913, pp. 1–140.

—— 'Neue Omphalos-Studien'. Ibid. 31, 1. Leipzig: Akademie der Wissenschaften, 1915.

Rosenthal, Franz, 'Nineteen'. *Studia Biblica et Orientalia*, vol. 3. Rome 1959, pp. 304–18.

—— *Four Essays on Art and Literature in Islam.* Leiden: Brill, 1971.

Royster, James E. W., 'The study of Muhammad. A survey of approaches from the perspective of the history and phenomenology of religion'. *MW* 62 (1972), pp. 49–71.

Roy, Asim, *The Islamic Syncretistic Tradition in Bengal.* Princeton, NJ: Princeton University Press, 1983.

Rückert, Friedrich, *Grammatik, Poetik und Rhetorik der Perser*, ed. by Wilhelm Pertsch. Gotha, 1874. Repr. Osnabrück: Zeller, and Wiesbaden: Harrassowitz, 1966.

Rūmī, Jalāluddīn, *Mathnawī-yi ma'nawī*, 8 vols, ed. by Reynold A. Nicholson. Leiden: Brill, and London: Luzac, 1925–40 (abbreviated *M*, with number of volume and line).

—— *Fīhi mā fīhi*, ed. by Badī'uzzamān Furūzānfar. Tehran: University, 1952. English translation by A. J. Arberry, *Discourses of Rumi.* London: John Murray, 1961. German translation by A. Schimmel, *Von allem und vom Einen.* Cologne: Diederichs, 1988.

—— *Dīvān-i kabīr yā Kulliyāt-i Shams*, 10 vols, ed. by Badī'uzzamān Furūzānfar. Tehran: University, 1957–72 (abbreviated *D*, with number or line of poem).

Rypka, Jan, 'Der böse Blick bei Niẓāmī'. *Ural-altaiische Jahrbücher* 36 (1964), pp. 397–401.

Sa'dī, Muṣliḥuddīn, *Kulliyāt*, 4 vols, ed. by Muḥammad 'Alī Furūghī. Tehran: Eqbal, 1342sh/1963.

Ṣafadī, Ṣalāḥuddīn Ḫalīl ibn Aibek as-, *Al-Wāfī bi'l-wafayāt*, part 12, ed. by Ramaḍān 'Abdul Tawwāb. Beirut and Wiesbaden: Steiner, 1979.

St Elie, Anastase Marie de, 'Le culte rendu par les musulmans aux sandales de Mahomet'. *Anthropos* 5 (1910), pp. 363–6.

Sanā'ī, Abu'l-Majd Majdūd, *Ḥadīqat al-ḥaqīqat*, ed. by Mudarris Riz avī. Tehran: Ṭāhūrī, 1329sh/1950.

—— *Dīvān*, ed. by Mudarris Riz avī. Tehran: Ibne Sīnā, 1341sh/1962.

—— 'Sayr al-'ibād', in *Mathnavīhā*, ed. by Mudarris Riz avī. Tehran: University, 1348sh/1969.

Santillana, Georg, *Istituzioni di diritto musulmano malichite*, 2 vols. Rome 1926, 1938.

Sarrāj, Abū Naṣr as-, *Kitāb al-luma' fi't-taṣawwuf*, ed. by Reynold A. Nicholson. London: Luzac, and Leiden: Brill, 1914; and reprints.

Schaeder, Hans Heinrich, 'Die islamische Lehre vom Vollkommenen Menschen, ihre Herkunft und ihre dichterische Gestaltung', *ZDMG* 79 (1925), pp. 192–268.

—— 'Die persische Vorlage für Goethes "Selige Sehnsucht"', in *Festschrift für Eduard Spranger*. Leipzig: Hinrichs, 1942.

Schimmel, Annemarie, 'The idea of prayer in the thought of Iqbāl'. *MW* 48 (1958), pp. 205–22.

—— 'Das Gelübde im türkischen Volksglauben' (based on Hikmet Tanyu's dissertation, *Ankara ve çevresindeki adak yerleri*). *WI* (new series) 6 (1959), pp. 71–90.

—— *Gabriel's Wing. A Study into the Religious Ideas of Sir Muhammad Iqbāl*. Leiden: Brill, 1963a; repr. Lahore: Iqbal Academy, 1989.

—— (1963b), 'Translations and commentaries of the Qur'ān in the Sindhi language'. *Oriens* 16 (1963), pp. 224–43.

—— 'Der Regen als Symbol in der Religionsgeschichte', in *Religion und Religionen, Festschrift für Gustav Mensching*. Bonn: Röhrscheidt, 1966, pp. 179–89.

—— 'Maulānā Rūmī's story on prayer', in Jiří Bečka (ed.), *Yādnāma-i Jan Rypka*. Prague: Akademi, 1967.

—— 'Sufismus und Heiligenverehrung im spätmittelalterlichen Ägypten', in E. Graef (ed.) (1968), *Festschrift für Werner Caskel*, pp. 274–89.

—— 'Shāh 'Ināyat of Jhōk', in *Liber Amicorum, Festschrift für C. J. Bleeker*. Leiden: Brill, 1969, pp. 151–170.

—— 'Mir Dard's Gedanken über das Verhältnis von Mystik und Wort', in Wilhelm Eilers (ed.), *Festgabe deutscher Iranisten zur 2500-Jahrfeier Irans*. Stuttgart: Hochwacht Verlag, 1971.

—— 'Nur ein störrisches Pferd ...', in *Ex Orbe Religionum, Festschrift für Geo Widengren*. Leiden: Brill, 1972, pp. 98–107.

—— 'Turk and Hindu, a poetical image and its application to historical fact', in S. Vryonis (ed.) (1974), *Islam and Cultural Change*, pp. 107–26.

—— *Mystical Dimensions of Islam*. Chapel Hill, NC: University of North Carolina Press, 1975a. German ed., *Mystische Dimensionen des Islam*. Cologne: Diederichs, 1985.

—— *Zeitgenössische arabische Lyrik* (German translations). Tübingen: Erdmann, 1975b.

—— *Pain and Grace. A Study of Two Mystical Writers in Eighteenth-century Muslim India*. Leiden: Brill, 1976a.

—— (1976b), 'Dard and the problem of prayer', in (1976a), *Pain and Grace*, pp. 126–47.

—— 'The Celestial Garden in Islam', in Elizabeth MacDougall and Richard Ettinghausen (eds), *The Islamic Garden*. Washington, DC: Dumbarton Oaks, 1976c, pp. 13–39.

—— *A Dance of Sparks*. Delhi: Ghalib Academy, 1978a.

—— *Denn Dein ist das Reich. Gebete aus dem Islam*. Freiburg: Herder, 1978b. Enlarged ed. as *Dein Wille geschehe*. Bonndorf: Turban Verlag, 1992.

—— *The Triumphal Sun. A Study of the Life and Works of Mowlana Jalaloddin Rumi*. London/The Hague: East-West Publications, 1978c; repr. Albany: SUNY Press, 1993.

—— (1979a), 'Eros – heavenly and not-so-heavenly – in Sufism', in Affaf Lutfi as-Sayyid Marsot (ed.), *Society and the Sexes in Medieval Islam*. Malibu, CA: Undena, 1979, pp. 119–41.

—— (1979b) 'Ghālib's *qaṣīda* in honour of the Prophet', in P. Cachia and A. Welch (eds) (1979), *Islam – Past Influence and Present Challenge*, pp. 188–210.

—— *Islam in the Indian Subcontinent*. Leiden: Brill, 1980a.

—— *Märchen aus Pakistan*. Cologne: Diederichs, 1980b.

—— *As through a Veil. Mystical Poetry in Islam*. New York: Columbia University Press, 1982a.

—— *Islam in India and Pakistan* (Iconography of Religion). Leiden: Brill, 1982b.

—— *Makli Hill*. Karachi: Institute of West and Central Asian Studies, 1983a.
—— (1983b) 'The Sufis and the *shahāda*', in R. G. Hovanassian and S. Vryonis (eds) (1983), *Islam's Understanding of Itself*, pp. 103–25.
—— *Calligraphy and Islamic Culture*. New York: New York University Press, 1984a; repr. 1989.
—— (1984b), 'Das Ḥallāǧ-Motiv in der modernen islamischen Dichtung'. WI (new series) 23–24 (1984), pp. 165–81.
—— *Die orientalische Katze*. Cologne: Diederichs, 1985; enlarged ed. Munich: Diederichs, 1989.
—— *Liebe zu dem Einen. Texte aus der indo-muslimischen Mystik*. Zurich: Einsiedeln, and Cologne: Benziger, 1986.
—— *And Muhammad is His Messenger*. Chapel Hill, NC: University of North Carolina Press, 1988.
—— *Islamic Names*. Edinburgh: Edinburgh University Press, 1989.
—— *I am Wind, You are Fire*. Boston, MA: Shambhala, 1992a.
—— *A Two-colored Brocade. The Imagery of Persian Poetry*. Chapel Hill, NC: University of North Carolina Press, 1992b.
—— (1992c), 'Yusof in Mawlānā Rūmī's poetry', in L. Lewisohn (ed.) (1992), *The Legacy of Mediaeval Persian Sufism*, pp. 45–60.
—— *The Mystery of Numbers*. New York: Oxford University Press, 1993.
Schimmel, Annemarie, and A. Falaturi (eds), *We Believe in One God. The Experience of God in Christianity and Islam*. London: Burns and Oates, 1980.
Schimmel, Annemarie, and Stuart Cary Welch, *A Pocket Book for Akbar: Anvarī's* Dīvān. New York: The Metropolitan Museum, 1983.
Schoeler, Gregor, *Arabische Naturdichtung: Die* Zahriyyāt, Rabīʿiyyāt *und* Rauḍiyyāt *von den Anfängen bis aṣ-Ṣanaubarī*. Beirut and Wiesbaden: Steiner, 1974.
—— *Arabische Handschriften, Teil II* (Kataloge der orientalischen Handschriften in Deutschland). Wiesbaden: Steiner, 1990.
—— 'Schreiben und Veröffentlichen. Zur Verwendung und Funktion der Schrift in den ersten islamischen Jahrhunderten'. *Der Islam* 69, 1 (1992), pp. 1–43.
Scholz, Heinrich, *Die Unsterblichkeitsgedanke als philosophisches Problem*. Berlin 1920.
—— *Religionsphilosophie*. Berlin 1921.
Schubart, Walther, *Religion und Eros*. Munich: Beck, 1941.
Schuon, Frithjof, 'The spiritual significance of the substance of the Prophet', in S. H. Nasr (ed.) (1987), *Islamic Spirituality*, vol. 1, pp. 48–63.
—— *In the Face of the Absolute*. Bloomington, IN: World Wisdom Books, 1989.
Schwerin, Kerrin Gräfin, 'Heiligenverehrung im indischen Islam'. *ZDMG* 126 (1976).
Scott, Jamie, and Paul Simpson-Housley (eds), *Sacred Places and Profane Spaces. Essays in the Geographies of Judaism, Christianity, and Islam*. New York/Westport, CT/London: Greenwood Press, 1991.
Séguy, Marie-Rose, *The Miraculous Journey of Mahomet*. New York: Braziller, 1972.
Seligmann, Siegfried, *Der böse Blick*. Berlin 1910.
—— 'Das Siebenschläfer-Amulett'. *Der Islam* 5 (1914), pp. 370–88.
Sellheim, Rudolf, 'Die Madonna mit der *šahāda*', in E. Graef (ed.) (1968), *Festschrift für Werner Caskel*, pp. 308–15.
Shackle, Christopher, 'The pilgrimage and the extension of sacred geography in the poetry of Khwāja Ghulām Farīd', in Athar Singh (ed.), *Socio-Cultural Impact of Islam in India*. Chandigarh: Panjab University Publication Bureau, 1978, pp. 159–70.
Shariati, Ali, *Fatima ist Fatima*. Bonn: Embassy of Iran, 1981.
Sharpe, Eric J., *Nathan Söderblom and the Study of Religion*. Chapel Hill, NC: University of North Carolina Press, 1990.
Sheikh-Dilthey, Hiltrud, 'Der böse Blick'. *Der Islam* 67 (1990), pp. 140–9.
Shinar, Pesah, 'Traditional and Reformist *maulid* celebrations in the Maghrib', in M.

Rosen-Ayalon (ed.), *Studies in Memory of Gaston Wiet.* Jerusalem: Hebrew University, 1977, pp. 371–413.
Shīrwānī al-Yamani, Aḥmad ibn Muḥammad ash-, *Al-manāqib al-ḥaydariyya.* Lucknow 1821.
Shulman, David, 'Muslim popular literature in Tamil: The *tamimcari malai*', in Y. Friedmann (ed.), *Islam in South Asia.* Jerusalem: Magnus Press, 1982, vol. 2.
Shushtarī, Sayyid Nūrullāh, *Majālis al-mu'minīn*, 2 vols. Tehran: Kitab-furūshi-yi Islamiyye, 1354sh/1975.
Siddiqi, Muhammad Nejatullah, 'Tawḥīd, the concept and the prospects', in Khurshid Ahmad and Z. I. Ansari (eds) (1979), *Islamic Perspectives*, pp. 17–33.
Siddiqui, Iqtidar Husain, (1989a), 'The early Chishti dargāhs', in C. W. Troll (ed.) (1989), *Muslim Shrines in India*, pp. 1–23.
—— (1989b), 'A note on the *dargāh* of Sālār Mas'ūd in Bahraich in the light of standard historical sources', in C. W. Troll (ed.) (1989), *Muslim Shrines in India*, pp. 44–7.
Ṣiddīqui, Sājid, and Walī 'Aṣī, *Armaghān-i na't.* Lucknow: Maktaba-i din wa adab, 1962.
'The significance of Moslem prayer'. *MW* 14 (1924), pp. 49–53.
Simsar, Muhammad S., *The Cleveland Museum of Art's* Ṭūṭīname: *Tales of a Parrot.* Graz: Akademische Druck- und Verlagsanstalt, 1978.
Sirhindi, Aḥmad, *Selected Letters*, ed. and transl. with an introduction by Dr Fazlur Rahman. Karachi: Iqbal Academy, 1968.
Smith, Jane, and Yvonne Y. Haddad, *The Islamic Understanding of Death and Resurrection.* Albany: SUNY Press, 1981.
Smith, Margaret, *Rābi'a the Mystic and her Fellow Saints in Islam.* Cambridge: Cambridge University Press, 1928; repr. 1986.
Smith, Wilfred Cantwell, *Modern Islam in India.* London: Victor Gollancz, 1946. 2nd ed. Lahore 1947.
—— *Islam in Modern History.* Princeton NJ: Princeton University Press, 1957.
—— 'Some similarities and differences between Christianity and Islam. An essay in comparative religion', in James Kritzek and Bayley R. Winder (eds), *The World of Islam. Studies in Honour of Philip K. Hitti.* London/New York 1960.
Snouck Hurgronje, Christiaan, *Het Mekkaansche Feest.* Leiden: Brill, 1888.
—— *Verspreide Geschriften*, 6 vols. Leipzig: K. Schroeder, 1923–37.
—— 'De laatste vermaning van Mohammad aan zijne gemeende', in (1923), *Verspreide Geschriften*, vol. 1, p. 124ff.
Söderblom, Nathan, *Ur religionens historia.* Stockholm: P. A. Norstadt, 1915.
—— *The Living God.* The Gifford Lectures. London: Oxford University Press, 1933.
Sprenger, Aloys, *Das Leben und die Lehre des Muhammad*, 2nd ed. Berlin 1869.
Stieglecker, Hermann, *Die Glaubenslehren des Islam.* Paderborn: Schöningh, 1962; 2nd ed. 1983.
Subtelny, Maria, 'The cult of 'Abdullāh Anṣārī under the Timurids', in Alma Giese and J. C. Bürgel (eds), *'God is Beautiful and He Loves Beauty'. Festschrift for Annemarie Schimmel.* Bern: Lang, 1993.
Suhrawardī, Abū Ḥafṣ 'Umar as-, *'Awārif al-ma'ārif.* German translation by Richard Gramlich, *Die Gaben der Erkenntnisse des ....* Wiesbaden: Steiner, 1978.
Suhrawardī, Shihābuddīn, *Awāz-i parr-i Jibrīl*, 'Le bruissement de l'aile de Gabriel', ed. and translated by Henry Corbin and Paul Kraus. *JA*, July 1935.
—— *shaykh al-ishrāq, Opera metaphysica et mystica*, 3 vols, ed. by Henry Corbin. Teheran and Paris: Maisonneuve, 1945, 1952; *Oeuvres en Persan*, ed. by Henry Corbin. Teheran and Paris: Maisonneuve, 1970.
Sulṭān Bahoo, *Abyāt*, ed. and transl. by Maqbul Elahi. Lahore: Ashraf, 1967.
Sulṭān Walad, *Valadnāma*, ed. by Jalāl Humā'ī. Tehran 1315sh/1936.
Swartz, Merlin L. 'A seventh-century AH Sunni creed: the *'Aqīqa Wāsiṭiyya*', in *Humaniora Islamica*, vol. 1. The Hague: Mouton, 1973, pp. 91–131.

Ṭabāṭabā'ī, Allamah Sayyid Muḥammad Ḥusayn, *Shiite Islam*, transl. and ed. by S. H. Nasr. London: George Allen and Unwin, 1975.
Tabrīzī, *Mishkāt al-maṣābīḥ*, 4 vols, transl. by James Robson. Lahore: Ashraf, 1964–6.
Taeschner, Franz, *Zünfte und Bruderschaften im Islam. Texte zur Geschichte der futuwwa.* Zurich/Stuttgart: Artemis, 1979.
Tanyu, Hikmet, *Türklerde taşla ilgili inançlar.* Ankara: Kültür ve Turizm Bakanliği, 1979.
Thackston, Wheeler M., *The Mystical and Visionary Treatises of Suhrawardī.* London: Octagon, 1982.
Tholuck, F. D. A., *Ssufismus sive theosophia persarum pantheistica.* Berlin: Ferdinand Dümmler, 1821.
Thorning, Hermann, *Beiträge zur Kenntnis des islamischen Vereinswesens auf Grund von* Basṭ madad at-taufīq. Berlin 1913.
Tirmidhī, al-Ḥakīm at-, *Bayān al-farq bayna' ṣ-ṣadr wa'l-qalb wa'l-fu'ād wa'l-lubb*, ed. by Nicholas Heer. Cairo 1958.
Topper, Uwe, *Sufis und Heilige im Maghreb.* Munich: Diederichs, 1991.
Trimingham, J. Spencer, *The Sufi Orders in Islam.* Oxford; Oxford University Press, 1971; reprints.
Troll, Christian W., *Sir Sayyid Ahmad Khan, a Re-interpretation of Islamic Theology.* New Delhi: Vikas, 1978.
—— (ed.), *Muslim Shrines in India.* Delhi: Oxford University Press, 1989.
Tworuschka, Udo (ed.), *Gottes ist der Orient, Gottes ist der Okzident.* Festschrift für Abdoljavad Falaturi. Cologne/Vienna: Böhlau, 1991.
Underhill, Evelyn. *Mysticism. A Study in the Nature and Development of Man's Spiritual Consciousness.* London 1911; repr. New York: E. P. Dutton, 1961.
Vajda, George, 'Les lettres et les sons de la langue arabe d'après Abū Ḥātim Rāzī'. *Arabica* 8 (1961), pp. 11–30.
Vatikiotis, P. J., 'Al-Ḥākim bi-Amrillah, the God-king idea realized'. *IC* 29 (1966), pp. 1–8.
Vaudeville, Charlotte, *Bārahmāsa, les chansons des douze mois dans les littératures indo-aryennes.* Pondichery: Institut d'Indologie, 1965.
Venzlaff, Helga, *Der islamische Rosenkranz.* Wiesbaden: Steiner, 1975.
Vryonis, Speros (ed.), *Islam and Cultural Change.* Wiesbaden: Harrassowitz, 1974.
Waardenburg, J. Jacques, *Classical Approaches to the Study of Religion: Aims, Methods and Theories of Research*, vol. 1. *Introduction and Anthology.* The Hague/Paris: Mouton, 1973.
—— 'Official and popular religion in Islam'. *Social Compass* 25 (1978), 3–4, pp. 315–41.
—— 'Islamforschung aus religionswissenschaftlicher Sicht'. *ZDMG*, supplement C, Ausgewählte Vorträge des XXI. Deutschen Orientalistentages 1980.
—— 'Friedrich Heiler und die Religionsphänomenologie – eine kritische Würdigung'. *Marburger Universitätsreden* 18, Marburg 1992.
Wagtendonk, H., *Fasting in the Koran.* Leiden: Brill, 1968.
Walther, Wiebke, *Die Frau im Islam.* Stuttgart: Kohlhammer, 1980; and reprints.
Watt, William Montgomery, *Free Will and Predestination in Early Islam.* London: Oxford University Press, 1948.
—— *Muhammad, Prophet and Statesman.* Oxford: Oxford University Press, 1961.
—— (ed.), *Der Islam*, 3 vols. Vol. 1 with Alford Welch; vol. 2 with Michael Marmura; vol. 3 ed. by A. Schimmel and others. Stuttgart: Kohlhammer, 1980, 1985, 1990.
Waugh, Earle H., *The Munshidīn of Egypt.* Columbia, SC: University of South Carolina Press, 1988.
Waugh, Earle H., Baha Abu-Laban and Regula B. Quraishi (eds), *The Muslim Community in North America.* Edmonton: University of Alberta Press, 1983.
Weiß, Bernhard, 'Language and law. The linguistic premises of Islamic legal thought', in A. H. Green (ed.) (1984), *In Quest of an Islamic Humanism*, pp. 16–21.

Welch, Stuart Cary, *Imperial Mughal Painting*. New York: The Asia Society, 1979a.
—— *Wonders of the Age. Masterpieces of Safavid Painting, 1501–1576*. Cambridge, MA: Fogg Art Museum, 1979b.
Wellhausen, Julius, *Reste arabischen Heidentums*. Berlin 1897; repr. Berlin 1961.
Wensinck, Arend Jan, *The Muslim Creed*. Cambridge: Cambridge University Press, 1932.
—— *Concordances et indices de la tradition musulmane*. Leiden: Brill, 1936–71.
'What the Shiahs teach their children'. *MW* 6 (1916), pp. 379–98.
Widengren, Geo, *The Ascension to Heaven and the Heavenly Book*. Uppsala: A. B. Lundqvist and Leipzig: Harrassowitz, 1950.
—— *Religionens värld. Religionsfenomenlogiska studier och översikter*, 2nd ed. Stockholm 1953.
Wielandt, Rotraut, *Offenbarung und Geschichte im Denken moderner Muslime*. Wiesbaden: Steiner, 1971.
Williams, John Alden, 'The Khānqāh of Siryāqūṣ: a Mamluk royal religious foundation', in A. H. Green (ed.) (1984), *In Quest of an Islamic Humanism*, pp. 109–19.
Wolff, M., *Mohammadanische Eschatologie, nach den aḥwālu'l-qiyāma, arabisch und deutsch*. Leipzig 1872.
Yeni Yunus Emre [Ismail Emre] *ve Doğuşları*. Istanbul 1951. *Doğuşlar* 2, Adana 1965.
Young, William C., 'The Ka'ba, gender, and the rites of pilgrimage'. International Journal of Middle East Studies 25, (1993), pp. 285–300.
Yunus Emre Divanı, ed. by Abdulbaki Gölpınarlı. Istanbul: Ahmet Halid Kitabevi, 1943.
Zayn al-'Abidin 'Alī ibn al-Ḥusayn, *Al-ṣaḥīfat al-kāmilat as-saǧǧādiyya*. The Psalms of Islam. Translated and introduced by William C. Chittick. London: Muhammadi Trust, 1988.
Zimmer, Heinrich, *Maya*. Zūrich: Rascher, 1957.
Zirker, Hans, 'Er wird nicht befragt ... (Sūra 21:24). Theodizee und Theodizeeabwehr im Koran und Umgebung', in U. Tworuschka (ed.) (1991), *Gottes ist der Orient*, pp. 401–24.
Zwemer, Samuel M., 'The illiterate Prophet'. *MW* 11 (1921), pp. 344–63.
—— 'Hairs of the Prophet', in S. Löwinger and J. de Somogyi (eds), *Ignace Goldziher Memorial*, vol. 1. Budapest 1947, pp. 48–54.

General Index

Index of Koranic Quotations